Broadway Musicals of the 30s

BY

STANLEY GREEN

Introduction by Brooks Atkinson

A DA CAPO PAPERBACK

Acknowledgment is made to the following for permission to reprint copyrighted material:

Chappell & Co., Inc., for lyrics to "Without Love" copyright © 1930 by DeSylva, Brown & Henderson, Inc., copyright renewed, assigned to Chappell & Co., Inc.; "Life Is Just a Bowl of Cherries" copyright © 1931 by DeSylva, Brown & Henderson, Inc., copyright renewed, assigned to Chappell & Co., Inc.; "That's Why Darkies Were Born" copyright © 1931 by DeSylva, Brown & Henderson, Inc., copyright renewed, assigned to Chappell & Co., Inc.; "Home to Harlem" copyright © 1932 by Elar Music Corp., copyright renewed, assigned to Chappell & Co., Inc.; "Johnny's Song" copyright © 1940 by Samuel French, copyright renewed, assigned to Chappell & Co., Inc.; "Men About Town" copyright © 1935 by Chappell & Co., Ltd., copyright renewed; "By Strauss" copyright © 1936 by Chappell & Co., Inc., copyright renewed, assigned to Gershwin Publishing Corp. & New Dawn Music Corp.; "Too Good for the Average Man" copyright © 1936 by Chappell & Co., Inc., copyright renewed; "God's Country" copyright © 1938 by Chappell & Co., Inc., copyright renewed; "Mad About the Boy" copyright © 1932 by Chappell & Co., Ltd., copyright renewed; "Are You Having Any Fun?" copyright © 1939 by DeSylva, Brown & Henderson, Inc., copyright renewed, assigned to Chappell & Co., Inc.; "Ridin' High" copyright © 1936 by Chappell & Co., Inc., copyright renewed; "What Shall I Do?" copyright © 1938 by Chappell & Co., Inc., copyright renewed; "It Ain't Etiquette" copyright © 1965 (unpub.) & 1971 by Chappell & Co., Inc.; "Give Him the Oo-la-la" copyright © 1940, copyright renewed, copyright © 1971 by Chappell & Co., Inc.; "At Long Last Love" copyright © 1937 & 1938 by Chappell & Co., Inc., copyright renewed.

Harold Rome, Florence Music Co., Chappell & Co., Inc., distributor, for lyrics to "Sing Me a Song with Social Significance" copyright © 1937 Mills Music Corp., copyright renewed, assigned to Florence Music Co.; "Doin' the Reactionary" copyright © 1937 Mills Music Corp., copyright renewed, assigned to Florence Music Co.; "One Big Union for Two" copyright © 1937 Mills Music Corp., copyright renewed, assigned to Florence Music Co.; "FDR Jones" copyright © 1938 Chappell & Co., Inc., copyright renewed, assigned to Florence Music Co.; "We Sing America" copyright © Chappell & Co., Inc., copyright renewed, assigned to Florence Music Co.

Irving Berlin Music Corp. for lyrics to "Automat Song" © copyright 1970 Irving Berlin; "Manhattan Madness" © copyright 1931, 1932 Irving Berlin, © copyright renewed 1958, 1959 Irving Berlin; "Man Bites Dog" © copyright 1970 Irving Berlin; "Debts" © copyright 1933 Irving Berlin, © copyright renewed 1960 Irving Berlin; "Lonely Heart" © copyright 1933 Irving Berlin, © copyright renewed 1960 Irving Berlin.

Warner Bros. Music for lyrics to "First Act Finale Strike Up the Band" © 1930 by New World Music Corp., copyright renewed, all rights reserved; "Strike Up the Band" © 1927 by New World Music Corp., copyright renewed, all rights reserved; "Fine and Dandy" © 1930 by Harms, Inc., copyright renewed, all rights reserved; "First Act Finale of Thee I Sing" © 1931 New World Music Corp., copyright renewed, all rights reserved; "Smokin' Reefers" © 1932 by Harms, Inc., copyright renewed, all rights reserved; "Straw Hat in the Rain" © 1934 by M. Witmark & Sons, copyright renewed, all rights reserved; "Yaller" © 1930 by Harms, Inc., copyright renewed, all rights reserved; "Life Could Be So Beautiful" © 1935 by Harms, Inc., copyright renewed, all rights reserved; "Let's Fly Away" © 1930 by Harms, Inc., copyright renewed, all rights reserved; "Eric" © 1935 by Harms, Inc., copyright renewed, all rights reserved; "My Most Intimate Friends" © 1935 by Harms, Inc., copyright renewed, all rights reserved; "Mr. and Mrs. Smith" © 1935 by Harms, Inc., copyright renewed, all rights reserved.

The New York Times for headlines © 1930/32/33/34/35/36/37/39 by the New York Times Company.

The New York Daily News for headlines.

Cover photo (by Vandamm) shows Ethel Merman leading the ensemble in "Blow, Gabriel, Blow," from Anything Goes.

This Da Capo Press paperback edition of Broadway Musicals of the 30s is an unabridged republication of the first edition entitled Ring Bells! Sing Songs! Broadway Musicals of the Thirties. Originally published in 1971 in New Rochelle, N.Y., it is reprinted by arrangement with the author.

Library of Congress Cataloging in Publication Data

Green, Stanley.
  Broadway musicals of the 30s.

  (A Da Capo paperback)
  Reprint. Originally published: Ring bells! Sing songs! New Rochelle, N.Y.: Arlington House, 1971.
  Bibliography: p.
  Includes index.
  1. Musical revue, comedy, etc. — New York (N.Y.). I. Title.
ML1711.8.N3G735 1982   782.81'09747a   81-22127
ISBN 0-306-80165-5 (pbk.)   AACR2

To Kay
For everything

Introduction

When I was preparing some material on the Broadway musical theatre a couple of years ago I was lucky enough to discover a definitive book by Stanley Green—*The World of Musical Comedy*. All the facts I needed were there. But the book also contained something less tangible and more exhilarating. It radiated a sense of enjoyment. Mr. Green had not forgotten that musical comedies are not statistics but expressions of theatre which, in turn, consist of actors and people coming together for a good time.

The bouncy title of Mr. Green's new book, *Ring Bells! Sing Songs!*, proves that he has not altered his point of view. During the decade, 1930 through 1939, covered by this book, only two musical dramas of significant value were produced: the Gershwin *Porgy and Bess*, which has become a world classic, and the Gershwin *Of Thee I Sing*, with a satirical book by George S. Kaufman and Morrie Ryskind—not a classic because it has not survived on the stage, but a memorable and creative work.

But that is academic comment. For Mr. Green's new book is full of the exuberance of a period when great song writers and comedians and stars were filling the evenings with enjoyment. Terrible things were happening outside the theatre—economic disaster and the frightening intimations of another World War. But this book indicates that some other important things were happening simultaneously: Ethel Merman demolishing the poise of an audience by singing the Gershwin "Sam and Delilah" and "I Got Rhythm"; Mary Martin opening a new era of humorous charm by singing Cole Porter's disingenuous "My Heart Belongs to Daddy"; Fanny Brice sardonically miming "Rewolt! Rewolt!" in a *Follies*; Ethel Waters singing Irving Berlin's "Heat Wave" and "Harlem on my Mind"; Beatrice Lillie destroying culture with her venomous "There Are Fairies at the Bottom of My Garden"; Bobby Clark, Ed Wynn, Bert Lahr, Joe Cook, Jimmy Savo, Victor Moore, Jimmy Durante standing the world on its ear with assorted styles of buffoonery; Irving Berlin, Arthur Schwartz, George Gershwin, Cole Porter, Richard Rodgers, Jerome Kern, Harold Rome, Harold Arlen, Kurt Weill—all writing music that has become part of the American vernacular. The world was dreary; but in Mr. Green's considered view, the Broadway musical theatre was brimming over with talent and high spirits.

The next decade was the most creative, I think. *Lady in the Dark, Oklahoma!, South Pacific, Carousel, Guys and Dolls, Brigadoon* represented the musical theatre's final escape from formulas. But Mr. Green points out something very significant about the Thirties: the banality of the traditional musical comedy book began to yield to maturity and reality. The books criticized the political establishment; the song writers recognized the experience of ordinary people in "Brother Can You Spare a Dime," "The Cradle Will Rock" and "Sing Me a Song with Social Significance."

During the Thirties America was losing a bumptious self-confidence that it has never recovered. But Mr. Green's records and comments indicate that the musical theatre was losing nothing but adolescence and insipidity.

BROOKS ATKINSON

Contents

Preface

It was during the Thirties that the modern musical theatre began to take shape. This was a period of experimentation both in form and in content, and there was little doubt that the world beyond Broadway had a profound effect upon what was being presented in this traditionally escapist area of theatrical entertainment. That is why in writing about the musicals of the decade, I have found it essential to deal in some measure with the economic and political developments then affecting everyone's life.

As to the form of the book, I have chosen to cover all productions chronologically, with each chapter devoted to a year rather than to a theatre season. My reason is simple. I know when a year begins and ends but I'm not so sure I know when a season begins and ends. I am aware that most people think of it beginning in September and lasting through May, with June, July and August either a separate summer season or simply in limbo. However, the Pulitzer Prize Committee considers the season from May through April, and the Burns Mantle *Best Plays* yearbooks—at least during the Thirties—covered it from mid-June to mid-June. So for this study, the Broadway decade of the 1930s is clearly marked: from January 1, 1930, through December 31, 1939—or from *Strike Up the Band* to *DuBarry Was a Lady*.

The 175 musicals under discussion include only the more recognizable forms: musical comedy, musical play, revue, operetta, and opera when offered for a regular commercial run. Not included are plays with songs, one-man or one-woman shows, revivals, vaudeville, or foreign productions.

This is not a book of hindsight. I have not attempted to impose the thinking of today on productions that were being offered thirty to forty years ago. The evaluations and receptions reported were the evaluations and receptions at the time of the original presentations. However, I have been selective in pointing out works whose influence has gone beyond their initial duration on Broadway.

Because they offer the most immediate printed reactions to each production and because of their influence in determining a show's acceptance or rejection, critical reviews in daily newspapers have been read thoroughly and quoted extensively. In 1930, the first-string critics of the morning papers were J. Brooks Atkinson (the "J" was dropped two years later) of the *Times*, Percy Hammond of the *Herald Tribune*, Gilbert W. Gabriel of the *American*, Robert Littell of the *World*, Robert Garland of the *Telegram*, Burns Mantle of the *News*, Walter Winchell (alternating with Robert Coleman) of the *Mirror*, and Ed Sullivan of the *Graphic*. Covering the drama scene for the evening papers were John Anderson of the *Journal*, John Mason Brown of the *Post*, Richard Lockridge of the *Sun*, and Charles Darnton of the *Evening World*. The *World*, the *Evening World* and the *Telegram* were merged into the *World-Telegram* in 1931, with Garland as critic (he was succeeded in 1936 by Douglas Gilbert and the following year by Sidney B. Whipple). The *Graphic* ceased publication in 1932. The same year, Bernard Sobel began a three-year stint as drama reviewer for the *Mirror*. In 1936, the *American* and the *Journal* were combined into the *Journal-American*, and John Anderson was retained as critic. Percy Hammond died that year and was succeeded at the *Herald Tribune* by Richard Watts, Jr. Other critics whose opinions have been quoted are Robert Benchley of *The New Yorker*, George Jean Nathan of *Judge*, and Jack Pulaski (Ibee.) and Abel Green (Abel) of *Variety*.

I have been fortunate in receiving firsthand information from many leaders in the field, and I am grateful for their help. They include Irving Berlin, Kitty Carlisle, Howard Dietz, Max Gordon, "Yip" Harburg, Libby Holman, Dennis King, Richard Rodgers, Harold Rome, and Arthur Schwartz. Valuable suggestions regarding the manuscript were offered by Louis Botto, Charles Gaynor and Alfred Simon, and I am particularly indebted to Burt Goldblatt and Phillip Harrington for the many hours they spent copying rare photographs.

Others who have given of their time to assist me have been: John Wharton, trustee, and Florence Leeds, executive secretary, of the Cole Porter Musical and Literary Property Trust; critic-playwright George Oppenheimer; Hilda Schneider, Helmy Kresa and Theodore Jackson of the Irving Berlin Music Corp.; Alice Regensburg, Lino Verdo and Richard Kestler of the Lynn Farnol Group, Inc.; Vivien Friedman and Philip Wattenberg of Chappell Music, Inc.; Irving Brown and Walter Evans of Warner Bros. Music; Dick Clayton of the *Daily News*; definitive Gershwin authority Edward Jablonski; Cole Porter biographer George Eells; and Leon Stein of the ILGWU.

Since so much research had to be done in libraries, I am especially appreciative of the helpfulness of those in charge: curator Paul Myers and assistants Dorothy Swerdlove, Donald Fowle, Dorothy O'Connor, Maxwell Silverman, and Betty Wharton of Lincoln Center's Theatre Collection, New York Public Library, Astor, Lenox and Tilden Foundations; curator Sam Pearce and also Melvin Parks, Maggie Blackmon and Marian Spitzer of the Theatre and Music Collection, Museum of the City of New York; librarian Louis A. Rachow and assistant Carl Willers of the Walter Hamden Memorial Library at The Players, New York; and Robert A. Kimball, curator of the Yale Collection of the Literature of the American Musical Theatre, New Haven. Good people all.

All the advertisements, except those found on *New York Times* theatre pages, first appeared in *The New York Magazine Program,* which in 1934 became known as *The Playbill.* Ethel Merman's recollection of her opening night in *Girl Crazy* was quoted in *Show* magazine for November 14, 1961; Leonard Sillman's description of the opening night of *Who's Who* was written for his autobiography, *Here Lies Leonard Sillman* (Citadel); Mary Martin's comments regarding her first audition were made to Pete Martin for a record album, *Face to Face* (Decca DXD 166); and Marc Blitzstein's remarks about the first public performance of *The Cradle Will Rock* were recorded for the album, *Marc Blitzstein and His Theatre* (Westminster Spoken Arts 717). Permission to reproduce the drawing of *Strike Up the Band* has been graciously granted by its creator, Al Hirschfeld.

Throughout the writing of this book, Susan Green and Rudy David Green offered wise comments and welcome criticisms, and my wife, Kay, made it all much easier than it might have been.

STANLEY GREEN

Prologue

"There are now a great many things to be thought about in our musicals. They no longer permit us to be pleasantly relaxed. They demand us to be jubilantly alert. Our laughter at them is the surest proof that we are thinking. It may be because there is less business than there once was, but our musicals are now produced on the assumption that our business men and women are less tired than they used to be."

John Mason Brown's words were written in 1938. They reflect the remarkable change that had come over the musical theatre during the decade that would soon come to an end. For the Thirties were the years in which the Broadway musical was at last opening its eyes and looking at the world in which it lived. Within the decade, a lean one as far as long-run hits were concerned, could be found a theatre rich in its willingness to dare, to experiment, to reach out and grab an idea because it was fresh and timely and exciting, without worrying too much about the toes being tread upon—or even the financial potential. (Revues and satirical musicals were all ignored by Hollywood and seldom had profitable road tours.)

The spirit of the Thirties musicals broke with the spirit of the Twenties musicals just as decisively as the decade itself broke with the previous decade. The Twenties' greatest achievement had been in introducing the new wave of America's most outstanding theatre composers and lyricists—the Gershwin brothers, Rodgers and Hart, Oscar Hammerstein, 2nd, Cole Porter, Vincent Youmans, DeSylva, Brown and Henderson. Though these men—along with Jerome Kern and Irving Berlin—had been responsible for establishing the preeminence of the American musical theatre, the stories their songs were wedded to, with the possible exception of *Show Boat,* were almost all as giddy and lightheaded as the euphoric age in which they had been spawned.

The Thirties turned everything around. The decade began with the United States suffering from a severe Depression and proceeded inexorably toward the holocaust of World War II. It was a period of soup kitchens and dust storms, bonus marchers and breadlines, the repeal of Prohibition and the profusion of initialed agencies that became synonymous with the New Deal's feverish efforts to cure America's economic ills. The country went through labor pains and labor gains, and nationwide lawlessness on an unprecedented scale. On the more distant stages of the world could be found the rising menace of Hitler, the death of the Spanish Republic, the rape of Ethiopia, Japan's bit-by-bit nibbling away at the continent of Asia, the thefts of Austria and Czechoslovakia, the Nazi-Soviet pact, and the invasion of Poland that exploded into World War II. Everywhere the planet surged and boiled and the fabric of life seemed so thoroughly torn that it looked as if it could never again be sewn together.

The musical theatre—the most opulent, escapist, extravagant, and unabashedly commercial form of theatre—could not hide from what was going on. Of course, it could still provide relief from reality. It could still offer evenings of mirth and song and glamour. But it also showed a growing awareness of its own unique ability to make telling comments on such issues of the day as the folly of war, municipal corruption, political campaigns, the workings of the federal government, the rising labor movement, the dangers of both the far right and the far left, and the struggle between democracy and totalitarianism. It discovered that a song lyric, a tune, a wisecrack, a bit of comic business, a dance routine could say things with even more effectiveness than many a serious-minded drama simply because the appeal was to a far wider spectrum of the theatregoing public.

This is not to say that all musicals of the Thirties were satirical or thought-provoking. Most of them weren't. Most of them were concerned with nothing more than sending audiences out of the theatre smiling and possibly whistling. Nevertheless, during the decade, audiences were seeing less and less of endless showgirls ascending and descending flights of stairs . . . mythical princes in mythical countries serenading mythical milkmaids . . . society life on Long Island and the pressing issue of whether Jerry or Teddy cares more for tennis than for Maisie or Nell . . . the Cinderella tale of the waif who hits the big town and eventually becomes Queen of the *Follies* . . . gold-digging manhunters fleecing wealthy bachelors, or vice versa. The collapse of the nation's economy that had begun in October 1929 virtually dictated the need for fresher, more contemporary themes.

From January 1, 1930, to December 31, 1939, a total of 175 new productions were unveiled that came under the frequently loose term *musical*. (From a high of 32 in 1930, the figure sank to a low of 10 in 1935, and finished with 15 in 1939.) Breaking down the total of 175, we find . . .

68 musical comedies. These were usually fast-paced, loosely constructed, modern in setting, featuring at least one of the more popular buffoons. The most daring examples put the emphasis on political satire, but there was room for such traditional themes as show business, marriage and divorce, gangsters, and college life. And there was plenty of fleet-footed dancing.

32 operettas. They were slower, heavier, with larger casts than those of the musical comedies, and with a far greater dependence upon music in the telling of their customarily florid tales. Vocal skills were a necessity since most of the songs were near operatic in style. The stories were set in exotic locales and were often concerned with aspects of royal romance.

56 revues. Revues could have a theme (around the world; stories in a newspaper) or a point of view (pro-labor; pro-capital), but no sustained story line. Their collection of songs, sketches and dance routines differed from vaudeville because they were conceived as entities, with the component parts, no matter how disparate, made to fit the overall design.

17 all-Negro musical comedies or revues. Except in a few cases, the Negro theatre in the 1930s was considered a separate area. The plots of the musicals were usually almost nonexistent, and both musicals and revues were distinguished by energetic singing and dancing, and a generally self-parodying point of view.

2 operas. The two—*4 Saints in 3 Acts* and *Porgy and Bess*—have been included because they were presented for regular commercial runs in Broadway theatres. Both productions had all-Negro casts, though only *Porgy and Bess* had an indigenous theme.

Considering all categories except the revue, the 1930s offered 111 "book shows"—or musicals with stories. In the matter of original plots versus adaptations, 70 of the 111 (including three imports from London) did not owe their origins directly to previously written works, such as novels, stories, plays, or foreign operettas. Of the 41 adaptations, inspiration was culled from the following sources:

    10 American plays
     6 American novels (of which 2 had also been plays)
     6 Viennese operettas
     3 English operettas
     3 American short stories
     3 German operettas
     2 German musical plays
     2 plays by Shakespeare
     1 German play
     1 Viennese musical comedy
     1 Hungarian operetta
     1 Hungarian play
     1 Yiddish musical play
     1 Spanish novel

Along with the burgeoning satirical musical comedies and revues (*Strike Up the Band, Of Thee I Sing, Face the Music, As Thousands Cheer, Pins and Needles, I'd Rather Be Right, Hooray for What!, Sing Out the News, Leave It to Me!*) and the more serious musical plays (*Johnny Johnson, The Cradle Will Rock, Knickerbocker Holiday*), the Thirties saw a corollary drop in the number of operettas: as many as eight in 1934, not one in 1939. They were, of course, something of an anachronism in the period, with only *The Great Waltz* breaking into the hit class. Jerome Kern, with both *The Cat and the Fiddle* and *Music in the Air*, created a modern form of operetta but the style was his alone and nontransferable.

Revues, however, did keep pace with the book shows, with the emphasis—thanks to the success of *Three's a Crowd* and *The Band Wagon*—veering away from tasteless spectacle toward more closely integrated, artistic concepts. Then along came *Hellzapoppin*.

Of the 17 all-Negro productions, only the rival *Swing Mikado* and *Hot Mikado* were considered praiseworthy.

Revivals of operettas—19 in all—were very much a part of the scene during the early years of the decade, with five offered in 1930 and eight in 1931. Most of these warmed-over extravaganzas were sponsored by either the Shubert brothers or Milton Aborn for limited runs, though one, Ziegfeld's revival of *Show Boat* in 1932, ran a respectable 180 performances.

As for longevity, the Thirties saw only two that ran over the 500 performance mark—and they were both flukes: *Pins and Needles*, a semiprofessional intimate revue produced by the International Ladies Garment Workers Union, which ran 1,108 performances, and Olsen and Johnson's *Hellzapoppin*, a madcap vaudeville-type revue, which lasted 1,404. Other long-run leaders of the Thirties: *Of Thee I Sing* (441 performances), *Anything Goes* (420), *DuBarry Was a Lady* (408), *As Thousands Cheer* (400), *The Cat and the Fiddle* (395), *Flying High* (357), *Music in the Air* (342), *I Married an Angel* (338), and *On Your Toes* (315). The relatively short runs of most musicals were, of course, directly attributable to the Depression and the competition of two less expensive forms of entertainment, radio and the "talkies."

Usually a musical that achieved a run of 200 performances was considered to be in the black. Production costs during the decade were as low as $6,000 for Heywood Broun's *Shoot the Works!* and $8,000 for Max Liebman's *Straw Hat Revue*, and as high as $246,000 for *The Great Waltz*, $300,000 for *White Horse Inn*, and $340,000 for *Jumbo*. Usually, though, the range was between $55,000 and $150,000. The Thirties began with a top ticket price of $5.50, with some attractions getting as much as $6.60. Many blamed the theatre's woes on the high cost of tickets. In an interview in January 1930, producer Florenz Ziegfeld explained the situation in this way: "I've made twenty-one productions of the *Follies* in twenty-one years. I started at $13,000 as the cost of a production and $3,000 a week to run the show. The last *Follies*—in 1927—cost me $300,000 to put on and $33,000 a week. Important stars have cost me more than a thousand dollars a week more than my whole show used to cost in the beginning. At first I got $2.50 for seats and at the latest $6.60. $6.00 really, as sixty cents is for the war tax. My costs have increased more than ten times and my prices two and a half times." The Depression, however, would soon force ticket prices to drop to $4.40, $3.85, $3.30, and lower. Cheapest seats for most musicals were $.55 or $1.10. And there was always Leblang's cut-rate ticket agency.

More than any other period, the Thirties belonged to the clowns. Would you like to poke fun at war and war-makers? Get Bobby Clark to do the poking. Do you want to kid politicians and the government? Send for Victor Moore. How about sticking pins in the upper crust? Bert Lahr's your man. Are you fearful of a nuclear explosion? Let Ed Wynn convey the message. The decade, in fact, offered so many of our very brightest musical-comedy stars that their procession of joint appearances made up a veritable constellatory daisy chain—William Gaxton and Victor Moore and Ethel Merman and Willie Howard and Bob Hope and Jimmy Durante and Lupe Velez and Libby Holman and Clifton Webb and Marilyn Miller and Fred and Adele Astaire and Frank Morgan and Helen

Broderick and Ethel Waters and Beatrice Lillie and Bert Lahr and Ethel Merman and Jimmy Durante and Hope Williams and Frances Williams and Ray Bolger and Bert Lahr and Luella Gear and Bobby Clark and Fanny Brice and Phil Baker and Lou Holtz and Lyda Roberti and Jack Pearl and Gertrude Lawrence and Harry Richman and Ruth Etting and Ed Wynn and . . .

Though we applaud its special knack at pricking balloons and exposing foibles, the musical stage has always been a basically optimistic form of theatrical entertainment. When conditions were at their most severe in the Thirties, it tried to buck up everyone's spirit by telling us that life was just a bowl of cherries. That we should all rise and shine because things looked fine around the corner, and that just around the corner there's a rainbow in the sky. That we should all forget our troubles and c'mon get happy. That life can be so sweet on the sunny side of the street. That everyone would feel better with a shine on his shoes and a melody in his heart. Who cares what banks fail in Yonkers long as you've got a kiss that conquers? So ring bells, sing songs! Blow horns, beat gongs! No more clouds in the sky . . . How'm I ridin'? I'm ridin' highhhhhhhhhhh!

White Studio; Theatre Coll., NY Public Lib.
Clark and McCullough in *Strike Up the Band*.

CHAPTER I

"... OLD MAN TROUBLE, I DON'T MIND HIM ..."

War has been declared. America is mobilizing its might. The armed forces are about to be shipped overseas. But a skeptical newspaperman, Jim Townsend, has been doing some investigating, and he is ready to expose the men responsible for getting his country into the conflict. He has, however, one important advantage over his fellow journalists. Since he is the hero of a Broadway musical comedy, he does not confine his revelations to his newspaper column. He sings them directly to the troops:

> Stop! What is this mischief you're doing?
> Stop! Reflect, consider and pause,
> Can't you see this trouble you're brewing
> Won't be in a worthy cause?

Also because this is a musical comedy, those leaders whom Jim attacks do not simply clap him into jail. They too hurl their accusations in song:

> Be careful of a trick!
> He's just a Bolshevik!

The production in which America's military aggressiveness was turned into an evening of songs, mirth and dances was called *Strike Up the Band*, the year was 1930, and the above musical passages occurred at the beginning of the first act finale. Now the reason Townsend has been so opposed to the war is that it is being masterminded by one Horace P. Fletcher, of the Fletcher Chocolate Company, who had maneuvered the United States into fighting Switzerland as retaliation to that country's opposition to America's tariff on imported chocolate. What has particularly aroused the young man to musical wrath was his discovery that Fletcher, instead of using Grade A milk in his chocolate, has been substituting Grade B.

Now wait a minute. The United States at war over an issue as ridiculous as that? Against a small, weak country? A man branded a Communist for exposing a deceptive business practice? That's pretty strong stuff. So to make everything a bit more palatable, librettist Morrie Ryskind put most of the action in the form of a dream. See, we're only kidding, folks; we know it could never happen.

Notwithstanding the show's general air of festivity and fun, there was no question that *Strike Up the Band* was a distinct departure from standard Broadway fare. It struck up the Thirties with a snicker at self-serving patriots, a laugh at phony heroes, a razzberry at the expense of Babbittry and bungling politicians. What's more, it set the tone for the decade's top musicals—a lighthearted, satirical, yet basically optimistic view of a sorely troubled country and world.

Nothing changes abruptly — or completely. *Strike Up the Band* did not suddenly inspire a steady profusion of muckraking musicals. There was an older, safer tradition that would exist side by side with the decade's sharper, more daring offerings. Nor was *Strike Up the Band*, apart from its official New York opening, strictly speaking a product of the Thirties. Producer Edgar Selwyn had actually first presented it in 1927, with its book then written by George S. Kaufman, but it never made it any closer to Broadway than Broad Street, Philadelphia. Too tough. Too angry. Too close to the real thing, perhaps—remember, the World War had come to an end only eight years before—with the final scene showing the United States preparing to do battle with the Soviet Union (reason: Russia's protest against the American tariff on caviar). And none of it was a dream. But Ryskind's watered-down book—which, among other things, changed watered-down Swiss cheese to watered-down Swiss chocolate—helped make it to Broadway and helped make it a hit. Four other contributions were also important. The show continued to have a brightly satirical score by two of the theatre's outstanding song writers, George and Ira Gershwin, and it now featured the comic presence of two of the theatre's most gifted clowns, Bobby Clark and Paul McCullough.

So the first musical of the decade became the first success of the decade. If audiences could laugh at the idea of the United States becoming embroiled in so ludicrous a conflict, the reason was largely that in January 1930 the country could safely feel that its involvement in another war was equally ludicrous. Didn't the Locarno Pact, signed by all the major European nations, guarantee the existing European frontiers? Didn't fourteen countries, including France, Germany, Great Britain, Italy, Japan, and the United States, just two years before, sign the Kellogg-Briand Pact renouncing war as an instrument of national policy? And wasn't the purpose of the London Naval Disarmament Conference, set to open just one week after the *Strike Up the Band* premiere, to limit and possibly even reduce naval tonnage of the world's five largest naval powers? No, another major conflict was out of the question.

Tariff? Now there was a timely and controversial

issue. Congress, in fact, would shortly begin debate on the severely restrictive Hawley-Smoot Bill, which, when passed, would impose the highest tariff on imported goods in American history. Military warfare may be a thing of the past but economic warfare was becoming a policy of government.

But overriding everything at the time was the concern over the severe business slump. The stock market, which had crashed severely in October 1929, was still not showing any of the predicted signs of picking itself up, despite President Hoover's reassuring statement on January 21 that "business and industry have turned the corner." (By the end of the year, the national income would plummet to $68 billion from its 1929 peak of $81 billion, thus causing unemployment to zoom past the 4.3 million mark.)

But while a theme dealing with the United States doing battle against a small defenseless nation thousands of miles away was not exactly the most contemporary issue to be satirized in a Broadway musical, it was still daring enough to have elicited the following observation from Robert Benchley in *The New Yorker:* "It is about as devastating a satire as has been allowed on the local boards for a long time. I say 'allowed' because only a little over eleven years ago it would have landed Messrs. Ryskind, Gershwin and Selwyn in Leavenworth. Kidding war and war-makers is a sport for which there is an open season and a closed season. The open season is only during those intervals when nobody happens, for the moment, to be wanting to make a war . . . Those who have a right to laugh are only those who laughed (or cried) at the same thing in the days when we were planning a war of our own. . . ."

Unquestionably, despite the alterations in the story, *Strike Up the Band* continued to pack a good deal of zing and sting. There was a poke at Presidential advisors in the character of Col. Holmes (played by Bobby Clark), who was modeled after President Wilson's aide, Col. House. Holmes laid claim to be "The Unofficial Spokesman of the USA" simply because he managed to avoid blunders by keeping his mouth shut. Fletcher, the go-getter, the "Typical Self-Made American," won the musical admiration of his employees because of his firm belief in Motherhood and the Constitution, and his hatred of the Russian Revolution. The dramatic Act One finale was climaxed by the soldiers—of both sexes—singing a jaunty, swinging march that

Drawing by Hirschfeld.
NY *Herald Tribune,* Jan. 12, 1930.

gave the show both its title and, in its verse, a gaily irreverent theme:

> We're in a bigger, better war
> For your patriotic pastime
> We don't know what we're fighting for,
> But we didn't know the last time!
> So load the cannon! Draw the blade!
> Rum ta ta tum tum tum!
> Come on and join the Big Parade!
> Rum ta ta tum,
> Rum ta ta tum,
> Rum ta ta tum tum tum!

The first day of the new decade did not, of course, wipe the slate clean. January was still just another month of the uninterrupted 1929–1930 theatrical season. In fact, there were no less than thirteen musicals held over from the previous year

that playgoers could choose from on January 14, the night *Strike Up the Band* opened. Starting at Times Square, a stroller in search of song-and-dance entertainment could find many pleasurable attractions. On the north side of West 42nd Street, the Lyric Theatre was displaying Cole Porter's first hit, *Fifty Million Frenchmen*, with William Gaxton, Genevieve Tobin and Helen Broderick heading the cast. It would remain there until early in July. Farther west on the same block, a second Porter item, the London import *Wake Up and Dream!*, was on view at the Selwyn featuring Jack Buchanan and Jessie Matthews (whose understudy, Marjorie Robertson, would soon change her name to Anna Neagle). Between the two theatres, the Apollo was showing the tenth edition of *George White's Scandals*, with most of the comedy by Willie and Eugene Howard and most of the songs sung by Frances Williams.

Up two blocks to the north side of 44th Street, the Shubert Theatre's tenant was *The Street Singer*, all about rich George who loves poor flower vendor Suzette and makes her the star of the *Folies Bergère*. Busby Berkeley was responsible for that one. At the Majestic, further west on the same block, there was a new version of Johann Strauss's *Die Fledermaus*

called *A Wonderful Night*, in which a young actor named Archie Leach could be seen. Through Shubert Alley to 45th Street and then walking west, a theatregoer could find the Royale Theatre showing, albeit briefly, something called *Woof Woof*. Across the street, an earlier wartime musical, *Sons o' Guns*, was playing to packed houses at the Imperial. With Jack Donahue starred and Lily Damita featured, it would continue until August. To the right of the Imperial, Broadway's oldest musical attraction, *The Little Show*, with Clifton Webb, Fred Allen and Libby Holman, was winding up its run at the Music Box. Another block north, the 46th Street Theatre was exhibiting *Top Speed*, a bit of fluff about poor boys who woo rich girls. One of the wooed, 18-year-old Ginger Rogers, was receiving more attention than the show.

Further northward, past the Palace vaudeville mecca on 7th Avenue, the Earl Carroll Theatre on 50th Street was featuring undraped girls and unprintable jokes in the *Earl Carroll Sketch Book*. It would have the longest run of the season—400 performances. Over to the south side of 52nd Street, west of Broadway, the Alvin was displaying the latest musical about rum-running and Long Island society called *Heads Up!* Richard Rodgers and

Lorenz Hart had provided the score. Up another block, at Hammerstein's Theatre on the west side of Broadway, *Sweet Adeline* was offering a turn-of-the-century romance that Oscar Hammerstein, 2nd, and Jerome Kern had put together especially for Helen Morgan. Walking one block north, then east to 6th Avenue, a stroller could find the Ziegfeld Theatre attracting customers to Noël Coward's bittersweet *Bitter-Sweet*, starring Evelyn Laye. Those, plus *Strike Up the Band* at the Times Square Theatre, wedged in between the Apollo and the Selwyn on West 42nd, made up the musical comedy fare in the Broadway area through January 1930.

These fourteen productions would seem to offer proof that show business was not yet experiencing the effects of the Depression. But there were signs and portents. The number of new musicals for the year—still an impressive 32—was five less than there had been in 1929. The nonmusical stage was even more noticeably affected, with the total of new productions dropping from 178 to 142. (Among them: *The Last Mile* with Spencer Tracy; Marc Connelly's Negro fantasy, *The Green Pastures*; the George S. Kaufman–Moss Hart Hollywood spoof, *Once in a Lifetime*; Alfred Lunt and Lynn Fontanne in Maxwell Anderson's *Elizabeth the Queen*; and *Grand Hotel* by Vicki Baum.) Most significantly, by the end of the year such formidable impresarios as Florenz Ziegfeld, Charles Dillingham, E. Ray Goetz, Edgar Selwyn, Arthur Hammerstein, and the Messrs. Lee and J. J. Shubert would be in serious financial difficulties.

Nonetheless, there were a number of positive accomplishments during the year. Despite the obvious pitfalls, two enterprising entrepreneurs, Max Gordon and Billy Rose, sponsored their first theatrical productions in 1930. It was also a remarkable period for stellar attractions. If he had the money or the inclination, a musical-comedy buff could, taking in only those musicals that opened during the year, enjoy the performances of such luminaries as Bobby Clark and Paul McCullough, Fred Stone (and his family), Ed Wynn, Gertrude Lawrence, Harry Richman, Jack Pearl, Bert Lahr, Phil Baker, Herb Williams, Jack Benny, Jimmy Savo, Joe Cook, Bill Robinson, Victor Moore, Willie Howard (but minus brother Eugene), Clifton Webb, Fred Allen, Libby Holman, Ethel Waters, James Barton, Fanny Brice, George Jessel, Marilyn Miller, Fred and Adele Astaire, Ann Pennington, Frances Williams, Hope Williams,

ARROW
DRESS SHIRTS
AND COLLARS

Jimmy Durante (plus Clayton and Jackson), and W. C. Fields. There were also some impressive debuts: Ruth Etting in the *Nine-Fifteen Revue*, Natalie and Bettina Hall in *Three Little Girls*, Joe Penner in *The Vanderbilt Revue*, Walter Slezak in *Meet My Sister*. And the most impressive of all: Ethel Merman in *Girl Crazy*.

In spite of the stiff competition, Joe Cook seems to have been the year's favorite funnyman for his performance in *Fine and Dandy*, with *Flying High*'s Bert Lahr, *Strike Up the Band*'s Bobby Clark, and *Three's a Crowd*'s Fred Allen as runners-up. Among composer-lyricist teams, the most celebrated was unquestionably George and Ira Gershwin for both *Strike Up the Band* and *Girl Crazy*. Of the ten revues, the outstanding was *Three's a Crowd*. The longest-running show of 1930 was *Flying High* with 357 performances, followed by *Girl Crazy*, *Three's a Crowd*, *Fine and Dandy*, and the *Earl Carroll Vanities*.

As has been noted, despite its success (though its run stopped short of 200 performances), *Strike Up the Band* sparked no immediate changes in the Broadway output. One month after the musical's premiere, Fred Stone's *Ripples* and Ruth Selwyn's *Nine-Fifteen Revue* competed for critical coverage by opening on the same night. Neither won. The return of veteran trouper Fred Stone (he had been hospitalized for over a year as a result of an airplane accident) couldn't keep *Ripples* going for much more than a month. Nor could the combined efforts of composers Victor Herbert, Rudolf Friml, George Gershwin and Vincent Youmans keep Mrs. Edgar Selwyn's entertainment on the boards for over a week. Actually musical "names" counted for little; the most memorable number, Ruth Etting's rhythmic exhortation, "Forget your troubles c'mon Get Happy," was a contribution of two Broadway neophytes, Harold Arlen and Ted Koehler.

One week after the *Nine-Fifteen Revue* premiere, Ed Wynn opened his grab bag of tricks in *Simple Simon*, produced by Florenz Ziegfeld. It turned out to be a fairly grim fairy tale, combining Mother Goose fantasy with Coney Island foolery, a score by Rodgers and Hart, and, as Robert Benchley put it, "a series of some of the highest-pensioned gags in the GAR." (Straight Man to Wynn: "Business is looking up." Wynn to Straight Man: "It has to, it's flat on its back.") But Ed's childlike innocence, his inexhaustible sight gags, costumes, inventions and puns, all proved as endearing as ever. Who else could have brought down the house with the lisping line, "I love the woodth!"?

Composer Richard Rodgers and lyricist Lorenz Hart never got along well with producer Ziegfeld, whose eye for beauty was far more discerning than his ear. One of Ziegfeld's edicts: the song "Dancing on the Ceiling," which had been in the score during the Boston tryout, would have to be cut (it would reemerge later in the year in the London musical, *Ever Green*). While in Boston, Rodgers wrote a song, "Ten Cents a Dance," that became the best known in the show. At first, though, it didn't look as if there'd be anyone to sing it. Lee Morse, for whom it was intended, was on a binge and could hardly stand, much less sing. Ziegfeld fired her and, with only three days to go before the New York opening, hired Ruth Etting, who had just closed in the *Nine-Fifteen Revue*. So it was, that exactly one week after introducing "Get Happy," the singer was back on Broadway to introduce "Ten Cents a Dance."

Much was expected of Lew Leslie's *International Revue*, a potpourri of songs and sketches tied together in a show-business version of the League of Nations—from London Gertrude Lawrence, from Broadway Harry Richman, from the Lower East

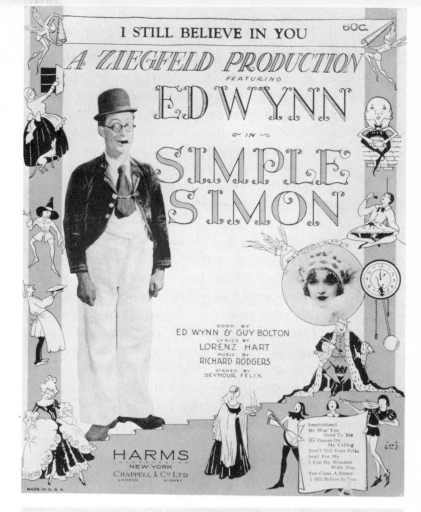

23

Side (but with a German accent) Jack Pearl, and from Spain Argentinita. Argentinita, a matronly, none too agile dancer making her American debut, turned out to be a total disaster. She left after a week with $10,000 as balm to her wounded pride. While the *International Revue* was lavish in production (it cost over $200,000), it was threadbare in material, except for such grand Dorothy Fields–Jimmy McHugh numbers as "On the Sunny Side of the Street" ("If I never had a cent, I'd be rich as Rockefeller") and "Exactly Like You." Jack Pearl managed to extract laughs with his radio character, Baron Munchausen, and his song about "The Margineers," a topic that had already replaced Prohibition as an easy if self-conscious laugh-grabber. The final curtain didn't go down until 12:15 A.M. on opening night, and it stayed down permanently after about three months.

The earthbound woes of early 1930 would indicate that the time was ripe for a musical that took to the air. And so it was. *Flying High*, by Buddy DeSylva, Lew Brown and Ray Henderson, capitalized on the public's fascination with airborne flight. Lindbergh's record solo to Paris in 1927, Amelia Earhart Putnam's solo from Newfoundland to Wales in 1928, and Rear Admiral Byrd's flight over the South Pole in November 1929 were aviation landmarks that caught everyone's imagination.

But timeliness alone does not a hit make. What made *Flying High* take off so spectacularly was the raucous, rowdy antics of a rubber-faced clown named Bert Lahr. His most memorable scene in the show occurred during his preflight medical examination when he filled a vial with Scotch instead of a specimen. (Doctor to Bert: "Nationality?" Bert to Doctor: "Scotch by absorption.") Before doing *Flying High* for producer George White, Lahr had been under contract to producers Alex Aarons and Vinton Freedley, who had planned to feature him in their fall musical, *Girl Crazy*. But after releasing him to White, they discovered that the success of *Flying High* made Lahr unavailable and they substituted Willie Howard. Actually, Aarons and Freedley were not the only ones surprised at the success of *Flying High*. Even as White was assembling a cast and a score, the story remained little more than an outline. It was just as rehearsals were about to begin that the authors suddenly came up with the idea of making Bert a pilot who sets the world's endurance record because he doesn't have the foggiest notion how to

get his plane down. Some fun, eh kid? Gnong! Gnong! Gnong!

Walter Winchell dubbed the show "The Lindbergh of Musical Comedies," a phrase the producer subsequently used on all the posters. Though *Flying High* broke no barriers in musical-comedy construction, it did offer the novelty of leading man Oscar Shaw making his entrance by parachuting from his plane just as leading lady Grace Brinkley finished her opening number, "I'll Know Him." Obviously, it was fate. The musical's hits were "Thank Your Father," which offered evidence that the heroine's birth may not have been legitimate, and "Without Love" ("Life is milk without the cream/ And gone is every scheme you're dreaming of . . .").

Poor Kate Smith. *Flying High* gave her her first stage role, and while some reviewers liked her, others seemed offended by the size of both her girth and her voice. Brooks Atkinson in the *Times* referred to her proportions as "mountainous" and her singing as "lacking the cathedral tone. 'Red Hot Chicago' she bellows in such volume that the

Rusty Krause and Pansy Sparks, better known as Bert Lahr and Kate Smith, in *Flying High*.

orchestra swoons in despair." The show charged the stiff top price of $6.60 for orchestra seats, though most other musicals were scaling their tickets from $5.50, and would soon drop them to $4.40, $3.85, and $3.30.

April ended the 1929–1930 season with two trifles. *Jonica* inauspiciously coupled the names of Dorothy Heyward and Moss Hart as co-librettists, though both disclaimed authorship. Seems that producer William Friedlander, while impressed with the success of Mrs. Heyward's first play, *Porgy* (written with her husband DuBose Heyward), found another of her scripts more to his liking for a musical treatment. So he hired an unknown young playwright named Moss Hart (this was before his first hit, *Once in a Lifetime*) to attempt a transformation of Mrs. Heyward's unproduced play, *Have a Good Time, Jonica*. Hart's work, however, was scrapped and still another writer was assigned to take over. He remained even more unknown than Hart, since he never received billing.

In mid-April, *Three Little Girls*, a Shubert import, was a lavishly mounted operetta that served to introduce Broadway to the Hall sisters, Bettina and Natalie, both formerly of the American Opera Company. The work was a moderately successful example of a once much-used operetta plot involving three generations of lovers, one for each act, with only the final romance ending on a happy grace note.

There were seven musicals presented during the summer months of 1930. The third edition of *The Garrick Gaieties*—some five years after the second —opened early in June at the Guild Theatre. Following in the tradition established by the first two, the revue offered much high-spirited, youthful spoofing, mostly at the expense of the theatre in general and the Theatre Guild in particular. However, it did slightly spread its target area to include the 59th Street crosstown trolley (in the manner of the still-running drama, *The Last Mile*, it had a condemned man making agonizing farewells as the trolley finally reached its destination), and (in a sketch by Carroll Carroll) a Times Square drugstore, where a wide variety of food could be purchased but no bicarbonate of soda. The high point of the entertainment was reached in the first act finale, "They Always Come Back," celebrating the return of New York's dapper former police commissioner Grover Whalen ("the gardenia of the law") to his previous position as president of the John

Wanamaker department store. With Philip Loeb as Whalen, the sketch offered proof of the store's pledge that anything can be returned—in this case, even a police commissioner. As a choral group trills the stirring oratorio of thanksgiving, "Johnny Wanamaker" (by Paul James and Kay Swift), Whalen sets about making some drastic changes—such as traffic lights in the aisles—based on his recent law-enforcing experience. He also indicates, in the Newman Levy–Vernon Duke song, "I'm Grover," that the change in position may have been prompted by Mayor Jimmy Walker's pique at Whalen's hunger for personal publicity:

> I'm back among the drapers
> Because the daily papers
> Hadn't room enough for Jimmy and for me.

Most of the reviewers enjoyed themselves at *The Garrick Gaieties*, and the show had a respectable 158-performance run. It also returned briefly in October, prior to going on tour. This version revived two Rodgers and Hart numbers, "The Three Musketeers" and "Rose of Arizona" (a takeoff on *Rose-Marie*–style operettas), first performed in previous *Gaieties*. And joining such talented performers of the summer edition as Philip Loeb, Sterling Holloway, Albert Carroll, and Imogene Coca, was the former leading lady of Boston's Copley Theatre, Rosalind Russell (she played "Nina Guild" in a *Strange Interlude* burlesque and, in another sketch, was Queen Mary to Albert Carroll's King George).

June also brought in an all-Negro musical, *Change Your Luck* (about an undertaker who becomes a bootlegger), and a Shubert brothers musical, *Artists and Models* ("Paris-Riviera Edition of 1930"). Though the Shubert offering looked and sounded little different from the revue series that had gone through four editions in the Twenties, the show had actually begun life as an adaptation of a British book musical entitled *Dear Love*. But somewhere along the four-week pre-Broadway road tour, what plot there was was all but scrapped in favor of the customary Shubert revue blend calling for a high degree of nudity and a low level of taste. Phil Baker was the chief attraction, but the book and lyric writers fared the best. Neither was identified in the program. The month ended with *Mystery Moon*, whose one-performance run may well have been justified merely by its use of a lyric that

Theatre Coll., NY Public Lib.
High kicking at the far left, Imogene Coca in *The Garrick Gaieties*.

Theatre Coll., NY Public Lib.
Kidding the classic pose from Eugene O'Neill's *Strange Interlude* are four members of the cast of *The Garrick Gaieties'* second edition: James Norris as Ferenc Molnar, Rosalind Russell as Nina Guild, Sterling Holloway as George Bernard Shaw, and Roger Stearns as O'Neill.

went: "A kiss they say will drive the blues away/ So smother me with kisses for it's all O.K."

July 1 ushered in the *Earl Carroll Vanities*, the seventh in the line of annual—or almost annual—revues (for little apparent reason, the previous year's edition had been called the *Earl Carroll Sketch Book*). A witless entertainment for wilted theatregoers, the show proudly claimed to be "Meeting America's Demand for Sophisticated Entertainment," a euphemistic assurance that the girls would be bare and the jokes raw. But Carroll had not misjudged his audience; the show rolled up a successful run of 215 performances. Not long after the opening, however, the police raided it, partly because of the manner in which nude dancer Faith Bacon waved her fans and partly because of a sketch involving Jimmy Savo as a shy window dresser in a department store who is obliged to change the "scanties" of the female dummies. Once the offending scenes were, presumably, altered and the show was permitted to go on, the resultant publicity of course only served as a boon to the boxoffice.

The *Earl Carroll Vanities* of 1930 did achieve two marks of distinction. It was the first (and last) Carroll production to play the prestigious New Amsterdam Theatre, which had formerly been reserved for the attractions of A. L. Erlanger, Florenz Ziegfeld and Charles Dillingham. And it may well have been the first time an elaborate girlie-girlie show ever offered an Act One finale taking an editorial position on a pending piece of legislation.

The "noble experiment" known as Prohibition had been in effect for some ten years. As predicted by opponents of the law, it succeeded primarily in opening up a whole new wave of crime with the widespread traffic in illegal hooch. "Bootleggers" and "speakeasies" became part of the language. During the Twenties, there was much agitation to repeal the law, legalized as the 18th Amendment to the Constitution. "Wets" and "Drys" opposed each other in political contests, the most notable being the Presidential race of 1928 when Wet Al Smith unsuccessfully tried dunking Dry Herbert Hoover.

It was to this issue that Earl Carroll bravely addressed himself. In the show's first act finale, "Let Freedom Ring," Carroll stoutly maintained that Prohibition had been forced upon the American people against their will. In refutation of this wanton disregard of the public weal, he offered patriotic *tableaux vivants* featuring Jack Benny (in

a powdered wig) reading the Declaration of Independence, then, as Abraham Lincoln (without a beard), reading frcm the Gettysburg Address, and, finally, as a stem-winding congressman, enumerating the advantages of legalizing light ryes and gins. Preceding this final peroration, a platoon of doughboys were seen bravely going over the top to the strains of "Over There," while throughout the entire spectacle decorous young ladies, strategically sashed in red and blue satin (the girls provided the white), wearing Swiss Guard plumage, paraded about piping their determined objections to the oppressive law. It was, as Robert Benchley observed, "possibly the means through which Mr. Carroll thought to get himself nominated to the Presidency."

One week following the *Vanities* opening, a cooperative revue came to town made up of unemployed members of the Lambs Club. It was called *Who Cares?* and the answer was few indeed. In August, *Hot Rhythm*, first billed as "A Sepia-Tinted Little Show" and later as "The Little Black Show," made its bow and ran two months. The revue turned out to be the last musical to play the ten-year-old Times Square Theatre, which, in 1933, would be taken over as a movie grind house.

The unofficial theatre season, generally accepted as the period between September and May, began unimpressively with *The Second Little Show*. It was a pale carbon of the sharp, original *Little Show*, first shown in 1929 with Clifton Webb, Fred Allen and Libby Holman. While it was understandable that its producers would shy away from again depending upon the same performers, they were unfortunately unable to secure stars of equal magnetism. Lyricist Howard Dietz and composer Arthur Schwartz, who had begun their partnership writing songs for the first *Little Show*, were also on hand for the second. Still, it was Herman Hupfeld's insinuating "Sing Something Simple" that became the most whistled item in the score. One utopian touch: the first scene of the revue dealt with New York's breaking away from the United States to form a new, independent nation. Among those who auditioned for a role in *The Second Little Show* was a 21-year-old former stenographer from Astoria, Long Island, named Ethel Merman. She lost out to Ruth Tester.

During the Twenties, Broadway's two leading composers of European-derived operetta had been Rudolf Friml (*Rose-Marie*, *The Vagabond King*)

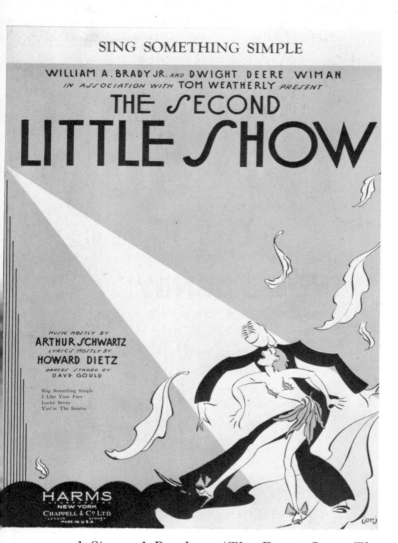

and Sigmund Romberg (*The Desert Song, The New Moon*). In September, each was offering a new work within three days of the other. On the 17th, Friml took a severe drubbing with *Luana*, "A Romance of the South Seas." It was his tenth work produced by veteran operetta-offerer Arthur Hammerstein (uncle of Oscar), and their first joint failure. As reported by Robert Littell in the *World*: "Plentee grass skirtee, plentee girlee swishee grass skirtee. Plenty nood girlee in swimming poolee. Plentee much Viennese waltzee by Rudolf Friml. Sounds mighty strange in middle of Hawaii. *Luana* she old stuffee if you askee. Aloha . . ." (P.S. Sally Rand was one of the nood girlee in swimming poolee.)

Sigmund Romberg's efforts at operetta exotica fared somewhat better. *Nina Rosa*, whose locale was a Peruvian tin mine, won a generally favorable press (Littell called it "solid and meaty") and became the season's first moderate success. Produced by the Shubert brothers—Romberg's 39th score for the Messrs.—it was an elaborately mounted affair with some 150 in the cast and a south-of-the-border

atmosphere that reminded many of the 1927 hit, *Rio Rita*. Sample lyric: "Nina Rosa, I implore/ Be my rose for evermore." Sample joke: Comedian (complaining about flies): "I have insects appeal."

Broadway has never had a more beloved clown than Joe Cook, and it has seldom welcomed a performer or his vehicle with more open-armed affection than it did when *Fine and Dandy* arrived late in September. "Next to Leonardo da Vinci," wrote Brooks Atkinson in the *Times*, "Joe Cook is the most versatile man known to recorded time." In the *Post*, John Mason Brown hailed the show as "one of the best musical comedies New York has seen in a blue moon," a view only slightly topped by Robert Littell's judgment: "One of the best shows I have ever seen." Robert Benchley, playing it safer, merely called it "the funniest musical play in town." Gilbert Gabriel in the *American* found it "pretty nearly everything you've yearned for in the way of 1930 entertainment," a sentiment echoed by Richard Lockridge, who wrote in the *Sun*: "I do not really see what more anyone can want of a musical comedy." And in the *Mirror*, Walter

Winchell dubbed Cook "certainly one of the musical theatre's three geniuses. I can't at the moment think of the other two." All this, plus, as the show's handbill informs us,

75—Perfect Girls, Lustrous and Alluring—75

Fine and Dandy was a pure and simple Cook's tour of maniacal inventions and outlandish gags, both sight and sound, with the story a serviceable enough tale of how foreman Joe Squibb worked his way up to become the head man at the Fordyce Drop Forge and Tool Company—despite his penchant for such conversational non sequiturs as:

Joe: Are you his mother?
Mrs. Fordyce: No.
Joe: His father?
Mrs. Fordyce: No!
Joe: Well, then, how *are* you related to him?
Mrs. Fordyce: I'm not related to him at all.
Joe: Neither am I. Now there's a coincidence.

Demonstrating his Leonardo-like versatility, Cook worked up some of the maddest routines ever performed on any stage. He impersonated four German acrobats, juggled flaming Indian clubs, turned handsprings, juggled cigarettes, hit a golf ball with a shovel, ate lunch from a lunchbox the size of an automobile crate, played the ukulele—and, in his most famous vaudeville routine, offered an hilariously rambling explanation of why he resolutely refused to imitate four Hawaiians. In the first act, he introduced a device for puncturing balloons, cracking walnuts, inflating paper bags, delivering golf clubs through a slot, and punching people in the face with a boxing glove. In the second act, he unveiled a huge dredging machine that was set in motion through the following Rube Goldberg sequence: Joe played the saxophone, which caused a monkey in a tree to drop a cocoanut on the head of a jungle native. The native, not knowing how he had been hit, shot a missionary in the back with a bow and arrow. This somehow gave the signal to an engineer to start the dredger working, eventually causing it to drop flour and crockery all over Dave Chasen, Cook's loyal stooge.

The *Fine and Dandy* score, by Kay Swift and her husband, James P. Warburg (a banker and foreign-policy authority who wrote lyrics under the name of Paul James), attracted much favorable comment,

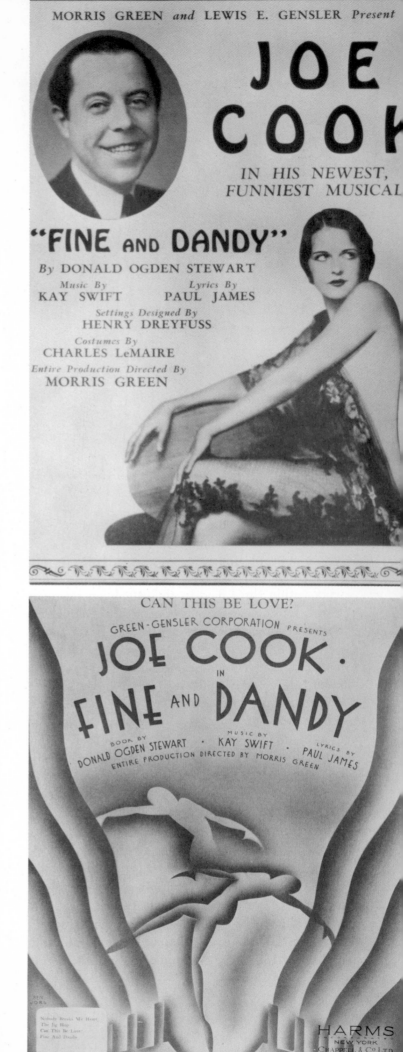

particularly the title song and "Can This Be Love?" "Fine and Dandy" was reprised throughout the show. In a duet, Cook and Alice Boulden added lines dealing with the radio popularity of Amos 'n' Andy, the romance between Napoleon and Josephine, and the Max Schmeling–Jack Sharkey heavyweight title fight of the previous June which had ended with Schmeling winning on a foul. In celebration of the event, the song's third variant concluded with these lines:

> Joe: Just the same
> You be Schmeling.
> Alice: I'll be Schmeling,
> What can I do?
> Joe: Clutch your vitals
> And claim six titles
> And take the boodle home with you!

The unimpressive all-Negro musical *Brown Buddies*, an October entry, was lucky to have Bill Robinson and Adelaide Hall to attract customers for 113 performances. Robinson was hampered during the first few performances because his right arm was in a sling, the result of having been accidentally shot by a policeman in Pittsburgh as he was attempting to foil a robbery.

Neither press nor public was attracted to the charms of *Princess Charming*, a soporific relic of royal romance with a cast including, of all people,

Victor Moore. But if the Graustarkian tale had people nodding, Broadway was wide awake the following night (October 14) when *Girl Crazy* came to town. Had to be, what with Ethel Merman shivering the rafters with "Sam and Delilah" and "I Got Rhythm" . . . Willie Howard as Gieber Goldfarb (the part originally earmarked for Bert Lahr), a New York cabbie who becomes sheriff of Custerville, Arizona (when disguised as an Indian, Howard can make himself understood to a real Indian only by speaking Yiddish) . . . Ginger Rogers gingerly cooing "Embraceable You" and "But Not for Me" . . . The Foursome crooning "I'm Bidin' My Time" (". . . cause that's the kind of guy I'm") . . . Tony and Renée DeMarco gliding silkily across the dance floor . . . the exuberant duet, "Could You Use Me?" ("Go back to flappers and highball lappers") . . . the brisk sound of Red Nichols' pit band that included Benny Goodman, Gene Krupa and Glenn Miller. Who indeed could ask for anything more?

Well, perhaps an original story instead of a hackneyed yarn about an Eastern playboy who finds true love in the rugged West. But with highlights so memorable, there were hardly any complaints. Of all the attractions, however, it was still Ethel Merman who wrapped up the show and made it hers. When producer Vinton Freedley had caught her appearance at the Brooklyn Paramount he became so enthusiastic that he rushed her back

White Studio; Theatre Coll., NY Public Lib.
Postmistress Ginger Rogers and dude Allen Kearns in *Girl Crazy*.

to Manhattan to audition for George and Ira Gershwin at the composer's Riverside Drive apartment. That's all it took; she was promptly signed for the show at $375 per week.

Ethel Merman's first entrance in *Girl Crazy* came toward the end of Act One. As Kate Fotheringill, the local saloonkeeper's wife, she sauntered over the bar, leaned against the oak top, and started singing "Sam and Delilah." It was a moment she has never forgotten: "Nervous? I'd never been nervous in my life. I was just a young punk kid then. I'd done the Palace two a day, like for two weeks and I was over the hump. 'Delilah was a floozie . . . ,' I let go. And the audience went 'Pow!' For a minute I thought I'd lost something I shouldn't. Didn't dare look down. But I hadn't heard anything yet. Believe me. A little while later I plunged into another song, 'I Got Rhythm.' The verse . . . 'Days can be sunny/ With never a sigh;/ Don't need what money can buy.' The chorus . . . 'I got daisies/ In green pastures,/ I got my man/ Who could ask for anything more?' On the second chorus I just held the 'I' . . . one long note . . . while the orchestra played the tune. The audience started clapping after about four bars, clapping, clapping, clapping, and they didn't stop till I'd done I don't know how many encores. It was like electricity."

The following night, with Broadway still reeling from the electric shock, there was more theatrical excitement: the opening of *Three's a Crowd* (also vying for attention that mid-October evening was Bette Davis in a play called *Solid South*). The crowded trio in the new revue turned out to be Clifton Webb, Fred Allen and Libby Holman, the very same stars of the first *Little Show* whom the sponsors had declined to rehire for the second. This temporary unemployment had been all the inspiration fledgling producer Max Gordon needed. If the sponsors of *The Second Little Show* didn't want them, he most certainly did. He not only put them under contract, but also secured the services of Howard Dietz and Arthur Schwartz to write the bulk of the songs (among others to contribute were Vernon Duke and an eighteen-year-old newcomer, Burton Lane). Then Gordon started looking around for the $125,000 he needed to put on the revue. After many sweatful days he managed to raise the capital once the Bank of America made good its promise to lend him $25,000. *Three's a Crowd* went on to chalk up 271 performances, one less than *Girl Crazy*.

Culver Pictures, Inc.
Vocal coach-accompanist Al Siegel and Ethel Merman about to launch into "Sam and Delilah" in *Girl Crazy*. Because of illness, Siegel was replaced as pianist by Roger Edens.

32

Three's a Crowd had not started out smoothly. The main problem—a crucial one in all revues—had to do with slotting the songs and sketches in proper sequence. There was also the matter of Libby Holman's big solo, "Body and Soul," written by Edward Heyman, Robert Sour and Johnny Green. As the singer told the story, "In Philadelphia, I first did 'Body and Soul' on my knees. On a pulley. The stage was totally dark. I sang, 'I'm lost in the dark . . .' Boom! A spot hit my face. I sang the next line, 'Where is the spark for my love? . . .' The pulley jerked forward. They turned on the tiny footlights. I sang the next line. Another jerk! It was awful. The damn thing was making such a racket nobody could hear me. I really got sick over it. They tried putting the song in different places in the show. They got Johnny Green to arrange and conduct it. Nothing worked. I even hung up a sign on my dressing room door, 'TWO'S COMPANY—ONE GOT SICK.'"

The song was finally saved when Howard Dietz, in New York one day, was dashing through Pennsylvania Station on his way to catch a return train to Philadelphia. Suddenly, he spotted Ralph Rainger, the composer-arranger of "Moanin' Low," Libby Holman's great success in the first *Little Show*. Though Rainger was heading in the opposite direction, Dietz spun him around and, despite Rainger's protests, practically shanghaied him onto the train. Rainger worked all night on a new arrangement and that, at last, did it. Overnight, "Body and Soul" was transformed from the weakest to the strongest number in the show.

Also in the *Three's a Crowd* score was "Something to Remember You By," by Dietz and Schwartz. The previous year, under the title "I have No Words" (". . . to say how much I love you"), it had been sung to a snappy tempo as a comic love song in a London musical, and Dietz, still fancying it as a comic number, dreamed up the phrase "I'll give you something to remember me by." And what could that be? A kick in the pants. But, fortunately, both lyricist and composer soon realized that the melody would be better suited to a romantic expression, a change effected merely by reversing the sentiment from a threat to a plea and by slowing down the tempo. As staged in *Three's a Crowd*, Libby Holman sang it to a young French sailor about to board his ship. The matelot was played by 23-year-old Fred MacMurray, a saxophonist with the group known as the California Collegians who also doubled as an actor in the skits. "Yaller," the third emotion-draining piece for Miss Holman, was the anguished plaint of a mulatto who feels shunned by both blacks and whites ("Oh Lord, you can make a sinner a saint/ Why did you start me and then run out of paint?").

An especially radical departure for a revue oc-

Libby Holman sings "Something to Remember You By" in *Three's a Crowd*.
The sailor to whom she pleads? That's right, Fred MacMurray.

curred in the very first scene in *Three's a Crowd*. In it, a husband is seen leaving on a business trip. As soon as he is out of the door, the wife's lover enters. When husband returns unexpectedly for his slippers, lover ducks under the bed. At this moment the sketch is interrupted by Master of Ceremonies Fred Allen with the apology, "Sorry, folks, in this show there ain't gonna be no beds." Whereupon the stagehands promptly cart the bed offstage, and the chorus enters to sing a lusty anthem about the revolutionary edict ("Oh, Lordy, what will we do for blackouts?").

Fred Allen's funniest routine (written by Corey Ford) was his monologue as Rear Admiral Allen, inspired by Rear Admiral Byrd's recent explorations of the Antarctic region. Facing the welcoming throngs in New York, Allen began his speech by explaining the importance of his mission: "In the first place, after a year and a half hard work in the Antarctic region, we discovered and claimed for the United States not fifty, not one hundred, but five hundred thousand square miles of brand new snow . . . The United States now has enough snow to meet any emergency for the next two hundred years. Enough snow to settle the unemployment problem in every city in the country. Four million men are now out of work. It will take seventeen million men thirty-one and a half years to remove all the snow and they won't even make a dent in it." As he proceeded in his talk, Allen showed slides of his airplane, his mess hall, some Eskimos, and the South Pole itself—but all of the photographs turned out blank because of the snow.

Apart from his highly lauded dancing, Clifton Webb appeared in two especially funny skits, "The Private Life of a Roxy Usher," in which he tried separating his wife from her lover in much the same impeccable way he had learned to handle similar situations in the darkened theatre, and "Good Clean Fun," which found Webb, taking a bath in his hotel bathroom, visited by a strange young lady. It is only when he loses the plug and the water drains out that the girl looks over the edge of the tub and recognizes him as an old friend.

Apeda; Max Gordon Coll., The Players
Just returned from the South Pole, Rear Admiral Fred Allen is about to deliver a lecture in *Three's a Crowd*. The stalwart quartet behind him: Harold Moffatt, Fred MacMurray, Alan Jones (not Allan Jones), and Percy Launders.

Almost unanimously, the critics praised the revue for its style, its pace, its decor, its principals, and, yes, its sophistication. "There is no denying it," wrote Robert Benchley in a surge of avuncular praise, "when you Americans put your minds to a thing, you do it up brown. The things you *do* may not be so hot, but you certainly do them right, and I think you're a wonderful, wonderful little people. There, I've said it." Benchley went on to compare American theatre techniques with foreign counterparts. "England (meaning Noël Coward) might produce a revue with as clever skits and as pretty songs as *Three's a Crowd*, but it is doubtful if any English producer would unbelt to the extent that Mr. Max Gordon has in the matter of costumes, scenery, and all the other little Cartier knickknacks which director Hassard Short, because he likes nice things, is accustomed to work with . . . The three stars had a pretty tough spot to come into after the glowing notices they received at the opening of *The Second Little Show* in which they were not . . ."

Producer Lew Leslie had begun his series of *Blackbirds* revues in London in 1926. His first New York edition, in 1928, resulted in the longest-running all-black show ever presented on Broadway. His 1930 sequel—"Glorifying the American Negro," was the subtitle—lasted only two months in spite of the presence of Ethel Waters (in her second musical), Flournoy Miller (temporarily separated from his long-time partner, Aubrey Lyles), and the team of Buck and Bubbles. The show also contained a superior Andy Razaf–Eubie Blake score, including "Memories of You" ("Waking skies at sunrise, ev'ry sunset toooooooo . . ."), "You're Lucky to Me," and the Ethel Waters specialty, "My Handy Man Ain't Handy No More" (he's so shiftless, complained Miss Waters, that "all he does is sit around and let my stove get cold").

Even less fortunate was Lew Fields' *Vanderbilt Revue* (by an odd coincidence it played the Vanderbilt Theatre), which opened early in November. Lulu McConnell won the best notices, but there was a childlike clown in the show named Joe

35

Woodcut by John Held, Jr.

Penner, whose "Wanna buy a duck?" line would soon become a familiar trademark on radio.

An operetta, *The Well of Romance*, followed two nights later. Set in "The Distant Kingdom of Magnesia," the fable included characters with jolly names such as Lt. Schpritzelberger and Baron von Sprudelwasser, but no one could tell if it all was to be taken seriously or not. Surprisingly, Preston Sturges, who had written the successful comedy *Strictly Dishonorable* the previous season, was responsible for libretto and lyrics. The hick outhouse specialist, Charles (Chic) Sale, didn't fare very well either in *Hello, Paris*, which came along soon after. The Shuberts withdrew it after a month.

The second major managerial debut of 1930 occurred on November 17. But unlike Max Gordon's, Billy Rose's was something less than a triumph. Originally, Rose had organized a show self-indulgently titled *Corned Beef and Roses* ("A Helluva High Toned Revue"). It opened in Philadelphia with Fanny Brice (Rose's wife), Hal Skelly and George Jessel, and it received a thorough panning in the press. The score, however, contained such future hits as "Cheerful Little Earful" ("Stocks can go down, Business slow down/ But the milk and honey flow down"), "Overnight," and "You Can't Stop Me from Loving You" (with its tribute to the tallest observation tower in New York: "You can be as aloof as the Chrysler Roof"). Though losing $36,000 of his own money, Rose was undaunted. He reorganized the show, added the humming hymn, "Mm mm mm, Would You Like to Take a Walk?" dropped Skelly in favor of James Barton, and reopened the revue in New York as *Sweet and Low*. Drama critics found it rough and not exactly ready, but it surprised everyone by remaining until the end of April.

Following the Broadway run, Rose again revised

White Studio; Theatre Coll., NY Public Lib.
James Barton, Fanny Brice and George Jessel in *Sweet and Low*.

White Studio; Theatre Coll., NY Public Lib.
The same season Billy Rose brought a revamped *Sweet and Low* back to Broadway and called it Billy Rose's *Crazy Quilt*. Ted Healy and Phil Baker replaced Messrs. Barton and Jessel, but Fanny Brice was still with it.

the show—drastically this time—and came up with a third title: *Billy Rose's Crazy Quilt*. Rose took it on tour in a series of one-night stands and brought it back to New York in May 1931. Phil Baker and Ted Healy had replaced Jessel and Barton, and the show even had a new song hit, an appropriate sentiment of the Depression, "I Found a Million Dollar Baby in the Five and Ten Cent Store" (Fanny Brice sang it wearing top hat and tails). This time the critical thumbs were more up than down, chiefly because everyone liked Phil Baker's sallies at the orchestra ("Play 'Ol' Man River' and throw yourselves in it") and his topical monologues. Cracking at the Bank of United States, which had failed the previous December (three of its officers would later go to prison), Baker remarked, "The bank is going to reopen its doors Monday—to let in four more bank examiners . . . Say, I can remember when *people* robbed *banks*." After about a month and a half, the show packed up again and went off on another tour.

Returning to the fall of 1930, one of the most eagerly awaited theatrical events took place on November 18 with the opening of *Smiles*. The show had practically everything going for it. The story was based on an idea by Noël Coward. It had

White Studio; The Players
Fred Astaire and Marilyn Miller in *Smiles*.

music by Vincent Youmans (including "Time on My Hands"). It starred Marilyn Miller *and* Fred and Adele Astaire. And it was produced by the master showman, Florenz Ziegfeld. And it lasted two months.

Why? Mostly, it was the story—or lack of it. It was not merely slight; it never even had a written script for the second act. The press roasted it. Burns Mantle labeled the show "dull." Atkinson found it "heavy-handed, humorless." To John Mason Brown it was "a cumbersome bore." Benchley called it "dumb." Ziegfeld was in a rage. He had never received such a critical thrashing before. Nor could he accept it without striking back. The night after the show opened, he shot off a telegram to Percy Hammond who, ironically, was the lone daily reviewer to give it a generally favorable notice ("altogether it is to be classed among its impresario's cleanest and most rainbow enterprises"). Apparently, Ziegfeld had Hammond confused with someone else, or his secretary had addressed the telegram to the wrong person. At any rate, the critic was roused out of bed in the early hours of the morning to receive a dispatch from the producer that read, in part:

. . . EVEN THE CREPE HANGERS LAUGHED THE OPENING NIGHT AND I NEVER HAD A SHOW WITH MORE LAUGHS STOP BUT PERHAPS I AM WRONG AGAIN BECAUSE THEY ARE CLEAN LAUGHS NOT LAUGHS THAT WOULD BRING A BLUSH TO YOUR FACE IF YOU HAPPENED TO BE WITH YOUR DAUGHTER OR MOTHER STOP I AM ONE WHO STILL BELIEVES THAT NEW YORK WILL ACCEPT A CLEAN SHOW STOP ALL AUDIENCES DO NOT DEMAND FILTH AND SLIME STOP I BELIEVE THAT THEATERGOERS STILL WANT TO LISTEN TO LILTING MUSIC INSTEAD OF SCREECHING JAZZ AND THAT THEY LOVE YOUTHFUL BEAUTY GLORIFIED AND NOT DEBASED . . .

Within a week, Ziegfeld had calmed down sufficiently to do what he could to rescue the enterprise, including the addition of the popular tune, "You're Driving Me Crazy," for Adele Astaire and Eddie Foy, Jr. But the show was beyond help.

In December, producer E. Ray Goetz took over the Broadway Theatre from the movies, and filled its stage with an adventuresome musical called *The New Yorkers*. Billed as "A Sociological Musical Satire," the show took audiences on a tour of both high and low life, stopping off at Park Avenue ("where bad women walk good dogs"), a speakeasy (in which Frances Williams, Ann Pennington, Clayton, Jackson and Durante, and the Fred Waring Pennsylvanians entertain), a bootleg factory, a street in Harlem, Reuben's Restaurant at Madison Avenue and 59th Street, Sing Sing Prison, and finally a gangland wedding in Miami. The mood of Herbert Fields' libretto was amoral, unsentimental throughout. The socialite heroine (Hope Williams) is attracted to a bootlegger (Charles King) because she is impressed by his coolness in killing people. She is also a heavy drinker; to Jimmy Durante's query, "Are you a wet?" she replies, "I'm so wet if you blow on me I'll ripple." Her father (Richard Carle) is unconcerned about being caught with his mistress (Miss Pennington), and her mother (Marie Cahill) proudly displays her gigolo. Even lovable Jimmy Durante is not above rubbing out his gangland enemies (though, miraculously, they always return to life). There was also a thoroughly cynical view of the law. King, whose murderous proclivities go unimpeded, is sent to Sing Sing for parking his car within six feet of a fire hydrant. (This was almost one year before Al Capone, the nation's most notorious gang lord, whose rackets included bootlegging, gambling, prostitution and extortion, would be sentenced to an eleven-year prison term. His crime? Tax evasion.)

Much of the bitterness in *The New Yorkers* was diluted by the wildly antic behavior of Jimmy Durante in his second Broadway musical. Particularly his riotous first act finale in which he and his partners sang the praises of all the products to be made from wood—and then proceeded to fill up the entire stage with them. Apart from Durante's specialties and a few Fred Waring songs, all the musical numbers came from the pen of Cole Porter, whose string of theatrical successes had recently been launched with *Paris* and *Fifty Million Frenchmen*, both sponsored by Ray Goetz. The more local locale of the current offering provided the composer with the opportunity to write paeans to the city in "Take Me Back to Manhattan" ("That dear old dirty town") and "I Happen to Like New York," the latter offered in counterpoint to the contrasting "Let's Fly Away" ("And find a land that's warm and tropic/ Where Prohibition's not the topic all the live long day"). One song was easily the most talked-about in the show (even if it went unsung and unplayed over the air). As described by Percy Hammond in the *Herald Tribune*: "A frightened vocalist, Kathryn Crawford,

THE NEW YORKERS

Drawing by Peter Arno

sings a threnody entitled 'Love for Sale,' in which she impersonates a lily of the gutters, vending her charms in trembling accents, accompanied by a trio of melancholy crooners. When and if we ever get a censorship I will give odds it will frown upon such an honest thing."

Three days after the opening of *The New Yorkers*, the real New Yorkers were at last jolted into realizing that, despite official pep talks, business conditions were simply not going to get any better, that there were basic wounds in the nation's economy that would take a long time to heal. On December 11, the giant Bank of United States, with 60 branches and over 400,000 depositors (many recently arrived immigrants), was forced to close its doors. Although over 1,300 banks had failed throughout the country since the stock-market crash, this was the one debacle that finally convinced Broadway of the depth and duration of the economic collapse. One by one, managers were compelled to trim production schedules, costs, and prices.

Goetz did what he could. His original plan for *The New Yorkers*, since the theatre seated over

1,700, had been to charge a lower ticket price than usual. Mounting costs, however, had forced him to drop the scheme and he opened the show at the usual $5.50. Then when he did try cutting prices to attract patrons it was too late. Even the voluntary salary cuts taken by the principals couldn't help the show turn a profit, and Goetz was forced to file for bankruptcy.

Producer Arthur Hammerstein was equally hard hit. Within two weeks after the opening of *Bally-hoo* on December 22, he too went bankrupt. W. C. Fields, who starred in the show as Q. Q. Quayle, a promoter of transcontinental foot races, then took over the management himself and ran it as a cooperative venture with the rest of the cast. But the libretto was so dull and routine, according to most critics, that even Fields was unable to keep the musical running longer than two months. It was to be the comedian's final appearance on Broadway.

The Messrs. Shubert finished up the year with another German importation, *Meet My Sister*. Seems that brother Lee, having seen the original Berlin production, dispatched brother J. J. to acquire the American rights and sign up the leading actor. J. J., however, failed to see the desired actor, Oscar Karlweiss, because he was on vacation, but he did see—and sign—his understudy, Walter Slezak.

White Studio; Theatre Coll., NY Public Lib.
Bettina Hall and Walter Slezak in *Meet My Sister*.

When Lee Shubert met the well-proportioned Slezak in New York, he was dumbfounded. This wasn't the slight, mousy actor he had expected. Not quite knowing how to put it to Slezak, the producer mumbled something about remembering him looking shorter and thinner. "Oh," replied the quick-witted actor, "you must have seen my understudy."

Meet My Sister, which featured Bettina Hall in her second Shubert operetta of the year, was a more modern variation on the customary continental goo, allowing no chorus (though this was dictated more by economics than art) and a theme dealing with the patching up of a divorcing couple. The musical highspot: Slezak's linguistic display as he sang "She Is My Ideal" in English, French and German.

The musical lasted a respectable 167 performances. But in the 1930–1931 season that wasn't good enough. Although the Shubert productions for the year totaled five new musicals, four operetta revivals and thirteen new plays, the mighty producing and theatre-owning empire would register a net loss for 1930. The year before, it had reported a profit of over a million.

CHAPTER II

"... WHO CARES IF BANKS FAIL IN YONKERS?..."

The times get grimmer. Breadlines and soup kitchens and apple sellers become visible symbols of an economically and spiritually defeated country. Five out of every six who look for work cannot find jobs. The nation's number of unemployed—almost ten million by the end of 1931—is more than double that of the year before. Over twenty-eight thousand businesses and almost twenty-three hundred banks report failures. Gold hoarding becomes common. For the first time in its history, the United States finds more people leaving its shores than coming to them to settle. By the fall of the year, ten percent wage reductions go into effect in all major companies—first U.S. Steel, followed by General Motors, U.S. Rubber, then the railroads. Ford cuts wages even more than ten percent.

Every area of American life is affected. Movie attendance is off 40 percent; theatres offer double bills, bank nights, free dishes, anything to lure audiences away from Amos 'n' Andy on the radio. On Broadway, acting jobs become scarcer as more and more legitimate theatres go dark, even though the number of new plays produced—137—is only five less than in 1930. (Among the nonmusical attractions: Noël Coward and Gertrude Lawrence in Coward's *Private Lives*; Katharine Cornell in *The Barretts of Wimpole Street*; Eugene O'Neill's *Mourning Becomes Electra*; the Lunts in *Reunion in Vienna*, by Robert E. Sherwood; Paul Muni in the Elmer Rice drama, *Counsellor-at-Law*.) Musicals, however, decline much more sharply, down to 24 from the previous year's 32.

Still, patience is rewarded. Toward the very end of the year—just one day after Christmas—a musical satire called *Of Thee I Sing* opens. It has songs by the Gershwin brothers and a story by George S. Kaufman and Morrie Ryskind. Politics, touched upon in *Strike Up the Band*, now becomes the direct target, and the musical relationship is more firmly structured in the story than in any previous musical comedy. And when the votes are tallied the following May, *Of Thee I Sing* becomes the first song-and-dance show to win the Pulitzer Prize as the best play—not just the best musical—of the season. With its 441 performances, it would also become the longest-running book musical of the decade. (Other boxoffice hits of 1931: *The Cat and the Fiddle*, with almost 400 performances, and the *Earl Carroll Vanities*, *The Band Wagon*, *The Laugh Parade*, and *George White's Scandals*, all registering over 200.)

Apart from *Of Thee I Sing*, quality was not a hallmark of the year's book shows, though Jerome Kern's score for *The Cat and the Fiddle* deserved its many champions. As for revues, *The Band Wagon* dominated in a field of eight, with *George White's Scandals* a respectable runner-up. Among performers, Victor Moore in *Of Thee I Sing*, Ed Wynn in *The Laugh Parade*, and Fred and Adele Astaire in *The Band Wagon* won the year's heaviest applause.

Nineteen thirty-one was the last year in which the three most famous revue series—the *Follies*, the *Scandals*, and the *Vanities*—all competed against

LEGIT ACTORS WORK LITTLE

Looks Like Shubert-Hued M. P. A. Folding—Appeal to Meet $8,000 Debt

The Managers' Protective Association, a group of Shubert affiliate managers, may dissolve within a week and along with it the Basic Minimum Agreement with Equity. M.P.A. has no money in the treasury and the manager-members do not appear inclined to pay assessments necessary to take care of obligations. At least one of the group is broke.

This condition came to light last when Lawrence Weber, letter to er, in tive

L. A. DRAMA CRITIC SAW SOMETHING NOT THERE

Los Angeles, June 21.

Scared of the cops, "Bad Girl" was introduced here by Lou C. Wiswell at the downtown Biltmore sans its third act obstetrical scene. Although completely eliminated Monroe Lathrop, dramatic editor of the "Evening Express" devoted a third to this non-ex-

NO EQUITY CASH AID IF IN NEED

One-Third of Equity's Paid-Up Members Did Not Work at All Last Season —Another Third Dropped Off Rolls — Same with Chorus Equity

ONLY NON-RELIEF UNION

Par's Legit Subsid, Ray-Minor, Stops Lining Up Plays—Summer's Cuts

STOCK HOUSE TURNED OVER TO ACTORS

Winnipeg, Can., June 22.

C. L. Lutes, whose lease on the house is not up until next fall, shortingly told the the Democratic he

Retrenchment of its legit branch has been decreed by Paramount, with Ray-Minor, its legit subsid, dropped to only its two principals for the summer. Dayton Stoddard left Saturday (20) and Walter Hart goes to the coast to direct pictures. With Arthur Lubin having several weeks and the company of only Walter Hart and M.

"Elmer has more sense than I gave him credit for."

"What do you mean?"

"Why, he's finally changed to Kelly Springfield tires."

each other. And it was the first year on Broadway for three distinctive entertainers: Lyda Roberti, Hal LeRoy and the nation's radio heartthrob, Rudy Vallee. Architecturally, the major event was the unveiling of the stunning new Earl Carroll Theatre, at 50th Street and 7th Avenue.

Lyda Roberti got the year off to an effusive start on January 19th. She arrived in an inconsequential "musicollegiate" romp called *You Said It*, which, to quote Robert Littell, "is not the show for you if you like your fun clean or your dirt funny." But the singing of the Polish-born, platinum-haired comedienne of a rhythmic ditty called "Sweet and Hot" (the "h" in "hot" pronounced with a guttural "ch") was so charged with good-natured, sexy magnetism that the show was soon billing itself "The Sweet and Hot Musical." That song, as well as all the others, was composed by Harold Arlen who, in partnership with lyricist (and co-producer) Jack Yellen, was making his debut as the creator of a complete Broadway score. Comic Lou Holtz (the other producer) was good for chuckles, though, at 31, he seemed more like a superannuated intruder than an undergraduate.

The motion-picture sound revolution had begun in October 1927 with the release of Al Jolson in *The Jazz Singer*. The "talkies" ended careers, spawned new ones, created legends, and, because the screen now could take full advantage of music, lured many song writers from their customary New York Alleys. Including Richard Rodgers and Lorenz Hart. The writers, who had had their first stage success with *The Garrick Gaieties* back in 1925, had gone west five years later to write songs for a film called *The Hot Heiress*. Their experience in the land of sunkist entertainment convinced them of one thing: their next show would be a satire on the movie industry. The result, *America's Sweetheart*, opened in February under the aegis of Laurence Schwab and Frank Mandel.

Librettist Herbert Fields, writing his seventh musical in collaboration with Rodgers and Hart, made sure his barbs took every opportunity to make the cinema capital seem to be populated entirely by idiots. He had a character in *America's Sweetheart* describe a Hollywood conference room as the place where good plays are turned into bad pictures. His film tycoon makes his secretary wire New York to put Gilbert and Sullivan under contract. *Camille* is made into a movie called *Lovey Dovey*. The general manager of Premier Pictures expresses deep

THE MUSICOLLEGIATE COMEDY HIT!

"YOU SAID IT"

NEW YORK'S FASTEST, PEPPIEST, FUNNIEST MUSICAL SHOW
WITH

MARY LAWLOR LOU HOLTZ STANLEY SMITH

AND BROADWAY'S PREFERRED POLISH BLONDE
LYDA ROBERTI

•

NOW PLAYING

CHANIN'S 46th STREET THEATRE

EVES. (Exc. Sat.)	WED. MAT.	SAT. MAT.
$1.00 to $400	$1.00 to $2.50	$1.00 to $3.00

Phone LAckawanna 4-1219

admiration for the works of the Bird of Avon. The comic highlight, though, had nothing to do with the written script. It was the filmed sequence in which the aural accompaniment turns it into a nightmare of uncoordinated sound effects.

The story of *America's Sweetheart* was the durable saga of two innocents in Hollywood: the girl becomes a star in the waning days of silent films and the boy is ignored; come the talkies and the situation is reversed. The leading roles were played by Jack Whiting and Harriette Lake, whom *Time* described as "a lovely synthesis, one part Ginger Rogers, one part Ethel Merman." The synthesis would later go to Hollywood herself and blossom out with a personality all her own as Ann Sothern. Among the Rodgers and Hart offerings was a Depression-inspired catalogue of material possessions called "I've Got Five Dollars" ("Debts beyond endurance/ On my life insurance"). The musical lasted on Broadway until June, nobly aided by the ticket brokers who overloaded their racks to help keep it going.

The familiar theme of bootleggers trying to rub out other bootleggers turned up again in *The Gang's All Here*. The critical verdict: not quite all there. Ted Healy starred in it, and it lasted three weeks.

Apeda; courtesy Lynn Farnol Group
Movie star Jeanne Aubert surrounded by the boys, in *America's Sweetheart*,
including Lee Dixon.

Five nights after the opening brought a curiosity called *The Venetian Glass Nephew*. In the fantasy, an 18th-century cardinal, anxious to have a nephew, simply has one made out of glass. Glass nephew falls in love with cardinal's flesh-and-blood niece and they marry. They live happily ever after once she has been baked into porcelain. Theatregoers found the fable so fragile they were afraid to touch.

Al Jolson, who had dominated the musical stage during the Twenties, made entertainment history by becoming the first actor to sing in a talkie. Following his 1927 screen debut in *The Jazz Singer*, he remained in Hollywood, but after a few years was anxious to reestablish himself on Broadway. To welcome him back in *The Wonder Bar*, the surprisingly open-handed Shubert brothers had the Nora Bayes rooftop theatre rebuilt to simulate the interior of a Continental cabaret. The stage jutted right out into the audience, with members of the cast, as nightclub patrons, seated at tables surrounding the rim. When the real audience filed in, they found the curtain already up and couples dancing on the stage.

The Wonder Bar, which opened in March after having been a hit in Berlin and London, told a none too distracting story concerned with stolen jewels, the stock-market crash, and the preparation of the cabaret revue. Jolson, sans blackface for the first time, had little difficulty adjusting to his mammy's new locale as he sang of his *mère* and his *père* who live down south in France on the Rivier' and how he hoped to hop on a *chemin de fer* and be right there. Lee Shubert blamed the disappointing two-and-a-half-month run on the reluctance of people to part with $5.50 to see Jolson in the flesh when they could see him on the screen for only a quarter.

Indomitable Lew Leslie tried varying his *Blackbirds* formula in May by offering *Rhapsody in Black*. Variously described as "a Harlem oratorio" (Gilbert Gabriel), "a sing-song of spirituals and Negro chanteys" (Richard Lockridge), "a sort of Harlem *Chauve-Souris*" (Howard Barnes), and "a sort of concert vaudeville" (Burns Mantle), the entertainment featured Ethel Waters and others in a program of song unrelieved by sketches, comic routines, or scenery. The repertory ranged from "St. Louis

44

Blues" to "Rhapsody in Blue" to the Hebrew chant, "Eli Eli." *Rhapsody in Black* had a fair run and was the final musical presentation of the 1930–1931 season.

Fully matching Leslie's indomitability were producers Dwight Deere Wiman and Tom Weatherly. Undismayed by the failure of their *Second Little Show*, they brought in a *Third Little Show* on June 1. This time they went a long way toward

justifying the show's claim as "The Aristocrat of All Revues" by spotlighting two authentic stars, Beatrice Lillie and Ernest Truex. The general critical verdict: better than the Second, still not up to the First. Miss Lillie, however, maintained her position as Broadway's favorite British madcap. Her best musical number found her seated in a rickshaw in a tropical locale, surrounded by tourists and natives, expressing her utter disdain that "Mad Dogs and Englishmen go out in the midday sun." (Noël Coward had dreamed up the song the previous year while motoring in Indo-China from Hanoï to Saigon.) Her best sketch was "On the Western Plain," a burlesque of monologuist Ruth Draper ("In this little sketch," confided Miss Lillie, "I want you to imagine far too much").

White Studio; Culver Pictures, Inc.
Patsy Kelly and Al Jolson
in *Wonder Bar*.

Whatever favor *The Third Little Show* was enjoying was suddenly eclipsed the night after the opening by the arrival of *The Band Wagon*. Here, at last, was a revue that for color, pace, beauty, and style, surpassed practically everything that had ever gone before. Seldom had audiences found sketches so adroit or uproarious, settings more striking or inventive, performances more skillful, or a score of such uniform excellence.

Plans for *The Band Wagon* had begun shortly after the opening of *Three's a Crowd* the previous October, when producer Max Gordon sounded out Howard Dietz and Arthur Schwartz about the possibilities of doing a new revue. Fine, they told him, but first they had a few conditions. Because they felt strongly that a revue should have the same homogeneity of style as a book musical, they proposed that only George S. Kaufman and Dietz be allowed to contribute sketches and that all the songs in the score be the creation of Dietz and Schwartz. Once these conditions had been met, they tossed in a few more: Fred and Adele Astaire would have to star in it and, oh yes, no other theatre than the New Amsterdam would possibly do.

Drawing by John Held, Jr.

Gordon, as usual, was short of money, but he was able to raise most of the necessary $100,000 from ticket brokers in exchange for choice seat locations. In addition to the Astaires, the producer signed comedians Helen Broderick and Frank Morgan and ballet dancer Tilly Losch (who bore a striking resemblance to Adele Astaire), plus two holdovers from *Three's a Crowd*: director Hassard Short and designer Albert Johnson. Johnson's double revolving stage was a particularly effective device, not merely as a means for changing scenery, but as an integral part of the sketches and musical numbers. For the first time, too, footlights were eliminated, with all the lighting emanating from the front of the balcony.

The combination of the revolving stages and the musical numbers was particularly effective in three sequences. In "The Beggar Waltz," Fred Astaire first appears as a beggar on the steps of the Viennese Opera House, enamored of the star ballerina. He falls asleep and, as he dreams, the set turns round to reveal the stage of the theatre. There, in his dream, Fred and his beloved (Tilly Losch) perform an appropriately ecstatic dance. As it ends, the set once more revolves to show the beggar on the steps awakening just in time to see the ballerina leave the theatre. Their eyes meet and, in a final gesture of sympathy, she tosses him her purse. In the joyous "Hoops" number, Fred and Adele play two *enfants terribles* cavorting through Paris's Parc Monceau, gossiping about their parents and, with the stage going round and round, wreaking havoc on everyone and everything in sight. "I Love Louisa" offers an irresistible oompah beat to the first act finale as the cast spins gaily about on a festively bedecked Bavarian merry-go-round.

Other musical highlights? The opening number of the show with the company in formal garb appearing on stage as if they were members of the audience taking their seats while chorusing the skeptical refrain: "It better be good/ It better be good and funny/ It better be good/ It better be worth the money" . . . the Astaires, with a menacing wolf at the door, bucking up their spirits with the "Sweet Music" Fred plays on his music box . . . Fred in white tie and tails preening before a mirror while exultantly singing "New Sun in the Sky" . . . Helen Broderick in a braided blonde wig fluttering from window to window pining "Where Can He Be?" while surrounded by the boys in the chorus . . . the compelling "Dancing in the Dark" scene,

Vandamm; courtesy Howard Dietz
Tilly Losch is the ballerina and Fred Astaire the beggar in the opening scene of the "Beggar Waltz" number in *The Band Wagon.*

with John Barker serenading Tilly Losch as she dances on a slanted, mirrored floor illuminated by constantly changing lights . . . Fred and Adele, in matching stylized evening dress, slithering about to the propulsive beat of "White Heat."

Among the sketches, "Pour le Bain," in which various plumbing fixtures were exhibited as works of art, was considered by some to be in questionable taste. But there was nothing but praise for the other skits, particularly "The Pride of the Claghornes." In this one, Col. Jefferson Claghorne (Frank Morgan), a patriarch of the Old South, toasts his mint julep to the health of his daughter, Breeze (Adele Astaire), and her fiancé, Carter Simpson (Fred Astaire). The colonel's bliss is interrupted by the arrival of Carter's parents, who announce that they have forbidden their son to go through with the wedding. Why? "There's talk in town that Breeze is a virgin!" Horrors! Claghorne is shattered. His wife Sarah (Helen Broderick) is indignant ("Well, if it's true then it's your boy's fault, that's all I can say"). Claghorne, of course, must do what he must do. "From this day forth I have no daughter," he says, choking back the tears, as he sends her from the old plantation. Alone with his wife, the shattered old man sadly shakes his head as he mutters, "I just can't understand this modern generation."

Even during the Philadelphia tryout, the word quickly spread that *The Band Wagon* would be a certain hit. By the time it opened in New York on June 3, its unanimously enthusiastic critical reception was almost a foregone conclusion. In the words of Brooks Atkinson: "Mr. Schwartz's lively melodies, the gay dancing of the Astaires, and the colorful merriment of the background and staging begin a new era in the artistry of the American revue. When revue writers discover light humors of that sort in the phantasmagoria of American life, the stock market will start to rise spontaneously, the racketeers will all be retired or dead, and the perfect state will be here."

Though the run of 260 performances was less than might have been anticipated, it was enough to leave Max Gordon with a $90,000 profit. But there was one major loss—following the run, Adele Astaire retired permanently from the stage to marry Lord Charles Cavendish.

Vandamm; courtesy Howard Dietz
The "Hoops" players: Adele and Fred Astaire in *The Band Wagon.*

Vandamm; courtesy Howard Dietz
"The Pride of the Claghornes" sketch in *The Band Wagon.* Helen Broderick as Sarah Claghorne, Adele Astaire as Breeze Claghorne, Frank Morgan as Col. Claghorne, and Fred Astaire as Simpson Carter.

A revue of more accustomed type was Mr. Ziegfeld's *Follies of 1931*, the first in four years and the twenty-second in the series. Critics attending the July 1 premiere found the quality uneven. Eye-filling and earfilling yes, but hardly in a class with *The Band Wagon* in matters of wit or originality. It did, however, contain its share of pleasures, provided by a stellar cast led by Master of Ceremonies Harry Richman, two torchbearing ladies, Ruth Etting and Helen Morgan (with little to do), and dialect comedian Jack Pearl. Still, it was a young tap dancer named Hal LeRoy who won the loudest applause and stole all the notices.

The most ambitious section of the *Ziegfeld Follies* depicted New York night life as it once had been and as it now was in 1931. After a theme song, "Broadway Reverie" ("That grand old street is on the blink/ It looks like Coney Isle/ It's not the place it used to be/ For romance, life and style . . ."), the first of two scenes showed the elegant gold and red plush interior of Rector's early in the century. Such dazzling figures as Lillian Russell and Diamond Jim Brady are on hand to applaud Nora Bayes (Ruth Etting) singing "Shine on Harvest Moon," Al Jolson (Harry Richman) dramatically confessing, "You Made Me Love You," and Sam Bernard (Jack Pearl) doing the comic number, "Rip Van Winkle." Then a quick change and the scene is updated to the present. Rector's is now a speakeasy presided over by an effeminate M. C. Hal LeRoy displays his agile footwork and Ruth Etting,

Painting by Alberto Vargas.

White Studio; Theatre Coll., NY Public Lib.
The stars of Ziegfeld's last *Follies*: Ruth Etting, Jack Pearl, Helen Morgan, and Harry Richman.

as a cigarette girl, bemoans her lot in "Cigarettes, Cigars," a gin-soaked relative to "Ten Cents a Dance" ("I work in a speak that's dull and dingy/ Where spenders are pretenders, cheap and stingy"). The speakeasy is seething with racketeers, and it soon erupts into a shootout between two rival gangs. LeRoy is shot and, as the curtains close, dies in the cigarette girl's arms.

The mood of the rest of the *Follies* was considerably more optimistic. As a Depression antidote, Harry Richman prescribed one and all to "Help Yourself to Happiness" ("There's plenty of sunshine for you and your neighbors"), and the first act finale was built around one of the few things New Yorkers could take pride in, the newly erected Empire State Building. The edifice, which had been built in record time, opened just two months before the show's premiere and now dominated the city's skyline as the tallest structure in the world. Standing 1,472 feet high, with 102 floors, it had quickly taken its place as the number-one tourist attraction in the city—even if, because of the Depression, entire floors would remain unoccupied for many months to come. In the *Follies*, the building provided the backdrop for a suitably upbeat, up-to-date finale, with Harry Richman and the entire company, in a surge of Gotham pride, urging everyone to "Do the New York" ("Get the sound, the crash and pound/ Of the subway underground . . ."). Balloons, streamers, and confetti filled the vast Ziegfeld stage as the curtain went down.

Far from the sleekness and the professionalism of such entertainments as *The Band Wagon* and the *Ziegfeld Follies* was a haphazardly thrown together revue called *Shoot the Works!* It also opened in July. The story behind the show was actually more interesting than the show itself. It was conceived by columnist Heywood Broun as a cooperative venture with the sole aim being to give work to unemployed actors, singers, dancers, and technicians. It cost $6,000 to open and no one who contributed expected any returns on his investment; only the performers and crew would get paid so long as the revue kept running. Another unique touch: not only did Broun appear in the production as master of ceremonies, but he also came back after the show was over to offer his own critical appraisal of what had gone on. To Percy Hammond, *Shoot the Works!* may have been "as full of fun as a Socialist picnic," but it did succeed in giving jobs

to over one hundred people for eleven weeks. Including Imogene Coca and a singing hoofer named George Murphy who introduced, among other things, Irving Berlin's romantic variation on the theme of mendicity, "Begging for Love."

When the *Earl Carroll Vanities* opened late in August, audiences were treated not only to the seventh revue of the year but, according to the program, to "America's Greatest Revue." Nonetheless, the show itself was almost a secondary attraction. What primarily brought the customers flocking to the Earl Carroll Theatre was the Earl Carroll Theatre, a spanking, sparkling new citadel built on the exact site—the southeast corner of 7th Avenue and 50th Street—where the original Earl Carroll Theatre had been built nine years before.

It was unquestionably something to see. It had 3,000 seats—each equipped with a reading light—and claimed to be the largest legitimate theatre in the world. It had black velvet walls, chromium fixtures, and carpets in three shades of green. The orchestra pit could be raised or lowered. There were 5,000 acoustical discs concealed in the auditorium walls. Ticket sellers, in tuxedos with gardenias in their lapels, sat behind a long counter rather than in a grilled boxoffice cage. The check room was free. There was also no charge for soft drinks that were served during intermission from specially built wagons pushed up and down the aisles. Four-color light circuits were in the auditorium as well as on the stage—and no fixtures were visible to the audience. A cooling system dispensed filtered and reconditioned air. Cast

Architect George Keister's drawing of the Earl Carroll Theatre.

principals, chorus girls, stagehands and musicians all had their own separate recreation rooms. Every usher was over six feet tall and garbed in a resplendent military uniform. One thing, however, was retained from the old theatre: over the stagedoor was the legend, "THROUGH THESE PORTALS PASS THE MOST BEAUTIFUL GIRLS IN THE WORLD." The total cost to open both showplace and show came to $4,500,000. The total cost to the theatregoer was $3.30 for the best seat in the house.

Which may well have been worth it, so far as the theatre itself was concerned. But the goings-on on the stage revealed once again Mr. Carroll's rather innocent proclivity for vapid spectacle, interspersed with anatomical humor and display. To quote John Mason Brown's description of the ladies of the ensemble: "As they loll on a sliding platform to show their linguistic prowess while droning out the very cosmopolitan verses of their introductory number; as they shake their concentrated supply of feathers to the insinuating rhythms of Ravel's 'Bolero'; as they strut nonchalantly hither and yon twirling parasols as Eugenie, Sans Gene, Creole and DuBarry; or as they languidly propel a 'Prehistoric Curtain' on its endless course across the stage representing such unrelated allegorical figures as 'Primordial,' 'Dawn,' 'Awakening,' 'Fetish,' 'Flesh,' 'Monster,' and 'Peace,' it is undeniably true that every mother's daughter of them is beautiful. But just as surely as each and every one of Mr. Carroll's sylphs, olympias and figurines is beautiful, so almost the whole of his new *Vanities* is dumb."

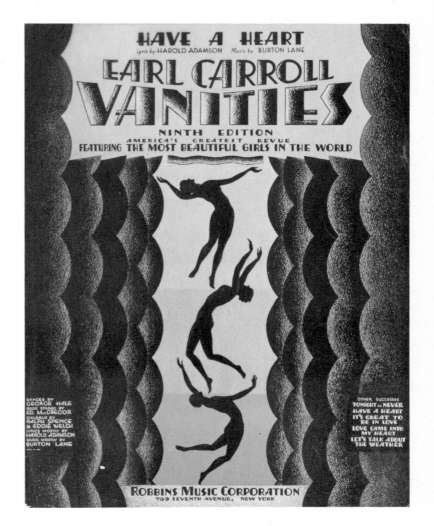

51

Such numbing dumbness appalled the usually even-tempered Robert Benchley, who fumed at the first act finale as "that monstrosity of bad taste and bad coloring which, to the rather faulty accompaniment of dozens of tom-toms, is supposed in some way to be related to Ravel's 'Bolero'

. . . My jaded senses refuse to thrill to three stages full of assorted loincloths and scimitars, with rising platforms disgorging dozens more at every beat of the drums, and a strange, unaccountable set-piece of some sort, studded with naked ladies who do not fit into any picture except that of a *carte postale*, moving slowly up and down and up and down against the backdrop." Benchley concluded, "Mr. Carroll is offering a frightening example of how *not* to spend money at a time when any money at all is hard enough to get. Revolutions have been started with less provocation."

The *Vanities* may have enjoyed a 278-performance run, but the cost of maintaining the theatre and the show (particularly at the lowest ticket scale of any Broadway musical since the world war) proved too much for Mr. Carroll. Within only five months after his gala opening, he was forced out of his own theatre and had to continue his revue at the 44th Street Theatre. Florenz Ziegfeld, Carroll's long-time rival, then leased the showplace, changed its name to the Casino, and carefully obliterated every chiseled or painted reference to its former owner. However, Ziegfeld was able to use the Casino for only one production, a revival of the 1927 classic, *Show Boat*, which reopened the theatre in May. Two months later the producer was dead.

The unofficial 1931–1932 Broadway season began on September 8 with *Free for All*, a Laurence Schwab–Frank Mandel production starring Jack Haley. Not only did it do without the customary chorus line (*Meet My Sister* had done that already), but it had a highly original plot concerned with a communistic movement at Leland Stanford College and poked most of its fun at such modern targets as psychoanalysis, what was then called the Russian Experiment, and free love. But the story struck reviewers—save for its lone champion, Robert Benchley—as labored and dull, straining so hard to be satirical that, as George Jean Nathan wrote, "it quickly ruptures itself." The show also marked the disappearance of the proud name of Hammerstein from a New York theatre marquee. When Schwab and Mandel took over Hammerstein's Theatre at 53rd and Broadway, they changed the name to the Manhattan.

The journey from Manhattan's Lower East Side to West 42nd Street proved too perilous for *The Singing Rabbi*, a translated Yiddish musical that lasted one night. Its demise also hastened the doom of the Selwyn as a legitimate theatre. The following year the 14-year-old playhouse would become a movie grind house.

By mid-September things were back to normal with another splashy revue. Now it was George White's turn. The eleventh edition of his *Scandals* (he had skipped the previous year) was, by all accounts, one of the best he had ever offered, easily eclipsing—in quality at least—the rival *Follies* and *Vanities*. The show boasted a lively and melodic collection of Lew Brown–Ray Henderson songs (no fewer than five of them would become hits), a first-rate company, an energetic, attractive chorus, and a fleet-footed production. Unscheduled, however, was the brief scuffle in the lobby of the Apollo Theatre opening night between the pugnacious Brown and the equally quick-tempered White.

But that was hardly anything to keep the other first-nighters from enjoying the evening. Just as the *Follies* had done, the *Scandals* included a scene celebrating the opening of the Empire State Building, with Ray Bolger impersonating the building's president, former governor Alfred Smith (it provided set designer Joseph Urban with a special challenge since he had also been the *Follies* designer). Ethel Merman, who had joined the revue during its tryout in Newark, blasted the foundations and lifted the spirits with her gaily fatalistic anthem, "Life Is Just a Bowl of Cherries" ("The sweet things in life to you were just loaned/ So how can you lose what you've never owned?"). Willie and Eugene Howard did their "Pay the Two Dollars" skit, in which Willie's fine for a minor spitting offense almost leads to the electric chair because of the stubbornness of his lawyer, brother Eugene. Rudy Vallee, in his first musical, made his entrance in cutaway and striped trousers to croon the nuptial introduction, "This Is the Missus" (with Vallee's future protégé, Alice Faye, among the bridesmaids).

One of the biggest laughs of the show occurred when tiny Willie Howard, as a big-game hunter just back from Africa, answered an interviewer's question about his skill at shooting a lion by explaining, "I bagged him and I bagged him—but he wouldn't go away!" The Rudy Vallee–Ethel Merman duet, "My Song," taking its references to Schubert and Irving Berlin as a cue, originally had Everett Marshall as Schubert interpolate the "Serenade" and Willie Howard, as Berlin, sing "Always."

White Studio; Theatre Coll., NY Public Lib.
Rudy Vallee and Ethel Merman in *George White's Scandals*. The song? "My Song."

The Berlin impersonation, however, was dropped by the time the show reached New York.

The first act finale of the *Scandals* offered a novel theme for a 1931 Broadway revue: a compassionate look at Negro fortitude in the face of injustice. Accompanied by a host of angels bearing scant relevance to the message, Everett Marshall, in blackface, boomed the philosophical acceptance of racial submission:

> Someone had to laugh at trouble
> 'Though he was tired and worn
> Had to be contented with any old thing
> That's why darkies were born.

Following the quickly shuttered Negro revue, *Fast and Furious*, which had opened the night following the *Scandals* premiere, Broadway was presented with an offbeat item called *Nikki*. Nikki had been around. First she had been the heroine of a series of short stories by James Monk Saunders, then of a novel and eventually of a movie, all of them dealing with the Hemingwayesque adventures of a group of post–World War I aviators. In the musical version, these drifters of the lost generation spend their time boozing, loving and fighting as they meander from café to café on their aimless way from Paris to Lisbon. In the end, one is killed in a bullring, one kills another accidentally and is killed in return, and another disappears after committing a murder. All this and songs, too. Fay Wray played Nikki, Douglass Montgomery her lover, and Archie Leach the one she is left with after everyone else has either died or disappeared. Leach, whose role was that of Cary Lockwood, would soon take off for Hollywood, keeping his stage character's first name but adopting Grant as his last name.

October—and the Shubert brothers—favored New York with *Everybody's Welcome*, an adaptation of a recent comedy hit, *Up Pops the Devil*. All about the ups and downs of married life in Greenwich Village and memorable chiefly as the production in which Herman Hupfeld's song, "As Time Goes By," was first sung. Frances Williams introduced it. In the romantic lead, Oscar Shaw and Harriette Lake (Ann Sothern) also had a song. It was called "All Wrapped Up in You," and went, in part, "I don't have to button my overcoat because I'm all wrapped up in you." The highlight of the production was a sample stage and screen

offering at Roxy's (here called Proxy's), then the largest movie palace in the world. Although the reviews were unanimously negative, *Everybody's Welcome* was able to keep the doormat out for four and a half months, thanks mostly to the sale of cut-rate tickets.

White Studio; Theatre Coll., NY Public Lib.
Oscar Shaw, Harriette Lake (Ann Sothern) and Ann Pennington in a scene from *Everybody's Welcome*.

The show was the only relatively bright spot for Lee and J. J. Shubert that month. On the 21st of October, their vast, powerful business structure went into receivership, a polite way of saying bankruptcy. In time, however, they would recover.

Max Gordon's second offering of the year, *The Cat and the Fiddle*, was his first book show and his third straight hit. A bit old-fashioned as to dialogue, a bit soggy as to plot, this "Musical Love Story" was nevertheless a brave and generally successful attempt to put the dated florid operetta form into a contemporary setting and give it a strictly modern treatment. In so doing, librettist Harbach purposely did away with choruses, spectacle, dragged-in comic routines or any other of the expected irrelevancies. Set in the Brussels of 1931, it told of a dour Roumanian composer of opera (Georges Metaxa) and his romance with a vivacious American composer who has a penchant for jazz (Bettina Hall). Most important, it carefully set about making all the musical pieces pertinent to the story. For composer Jerome Kern was concerned here with creating what amounted to an almost continuous flow of melody; not only were the songs brought in as logical outgrowths of the situations, but even the most casual conversations were underscored by musical passages.

And the critics were highly receptive. At least as far as the Kern contributions were concerned. Percy Hammond wrote, "At the risk of detouring playgoers from attending, it must be reported that it contains no bathroom scenes, no jokes about plumbing, but is just a slightly wicked, smart, cleanly and tuneful fable." Other appraisers, however, were less defensive, particularly when it came to a score containing such gems as "The Night Was Made for Love," "I Watch the Love Parade," "Try to Forget," "She Didn't Say 'Yes'" ("She didn't say, 'No'"), and "A New Love Is Old." John Mason Brown held it to be "the loveliest, most ambitious score that Mr. Kern has yet written," and Robert Garland hailed it as "a score as fine as anything Mr. Kern has ever done. Finer really." But Gilbert Gabriel, not content merely to compare Kern with Kern, stoutly insisted, "Broadway has not heard lovelier music in all its life."

Messrs. Schwab and Mandel, having failed with their perhaps too advanced *Free for All* the previous month, now, at the end of October, reverted to the more familiar terrain of grand operetta in *East Wind*. Set mostly in and around Saigon, of

White Studio; Max Gordon Coll., The Players
The final scene of *The Cat and the Fiddle* at the al fresco café, La Petite Maison. Welcoming Natalie Hall is José Ruben, and behind her, wearing hat, is George Meader. Eddie Foy, Jr., has his head turned in the foreground, and the couple at the right are Odette Myrtil and Lawrence Grossmith.

all exotic places, the work was the creation of Oscar Hammerstein, 2nd, and Sigmund Romberg, who had, in the Twenties, provided Schwab and Mandel with such heroic romances a *The Desert Song* and *The New Moon*. Unfortunately, their new work was greeted by a critical chorus of negative reactions including "dull," "dreary," "tedious," "dumb," "old-fashioned," "flat," and "fudgy." The failure terminated the producing partnership but it did help launch the radio career of the quacking comic, Joe Penner.

Ed Wynn opened in a revue called *The Laugh Parade* early in November. It was his biggest success of the decade. It also indicated the power of the new entertainment medium called radio. During most of the show's run the Tuesday evening performance had to be canceled so that Wynn could make his weekly "Fire Chief" broadcasts for Texaco. Before signing the comic, however, the company made sure it was taking no chances on his appeal as a strictly aural entertainer. They sent their chief advertising man to the show four times —but had him sit in a box with his back to the stage to determine if Wynn would be equally as funny as an unseen voice as he was in person. Apparently he passed the test.

Ed was all over the place in *The Laugh Parade*, his costumes never more outlandish, his inventions never more bizarre, his gags never more foolishly hilarious. He introduced a brown derby with a removable brim so that the wearer could tip his hat in the winter and not catch cold. About to practice his skills at tossing three balls in the air, he advised the orchestra leader, "Just play something in a jugular vein." He told the story of the man who had an apartment on the 99th floor of the Empire State Building but who also had a place on the 4th floor where he could stay when he didn't want to go home nights. He displayed a miniature bed for trapping bedbugs. He explained the elaborate scenario of a film called *You're My Everything* just to set up a duet for the expansively romantic title song. He boasted of his parrot's pedigree: "It's one of the Parrots of Wimpole Street." In addition, he operated a one-man Punch and Judy show, rode a two-man camel, played a piano on wheels, led the orchestra, and became hopelessly entangled with an acrobatic act. Wynn was, quite simply, as John Mason Brown pointed out, "the only master of his own special brand of nonsense, a comic law unto himself."

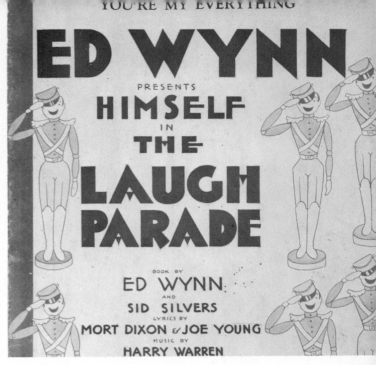

With Clark and McCullough starring, with cartoonist Peter Arno writing and producing, and with Johnny Green and Edward Heyman (the "Body and Soul" team) doing the score, *Here Goes the Bride* gave indications of being one of the year's happiest attractions. It folded in a week. On Christmas Day, Flournoy Miller and Aubrey Lyles, reunited after their temporary break, appeared in *Sugar Hill*, "An Epoch of Negro Life in Harlem." It lasted four days longer.

But the best was saved for last. *Of Thee I Sing*, the final musical of the year was unquestionably the finest musical of the year. An extension and broadening of the *Strike Up the Band* format, it was a sharp, witty, satirical thrust at the institutions of government as seen through the mocking eyes of George S. Kaufman and Morrie Ryskind and George and Ira Gershwin. Heading the cast were William Gaxton and Victor Moore, united for the first time in their winning ticket of John P. Wintergreen and Alexander Throttlebottom, candidates for President and Vice President of the United States.

In its depiction of the follies and foibles of politics, *Of Thee I Sing* deliberately shied away from either personal attacks or comments on the pressing issues of the day. It aimed its barbs instead at institutions and establishments; the themes it found for its cutting edge were no more pertinent in 1931 than they would have been in an earlier or a later period—campaign slogans, political issues and rallies, backroom doubledealing and hypocrisy, marriage, the Supreme Court, diplomacy, the role of the Vice President, congressional debate, and motherhood. Few actual individuals of the day were

To get the spoofing spirit across to the audience right away, *Of Thee I Sing* opened to the blaring beat of "Wintergreen for President" (with its entire lyric consisting of two lines: "He's the man the people choose/ Loves the Irish and the Jews"), as a stageful of political enthusiasts parade about with banners containing such slogans as "VOTE FOR PROSPERITY AND SEE WHAT YOU GET" . . . "TURN THE REFORMERS OUT" . . . "HE KEPT US OUT OF JAIL." In the smoke-filled room following the convention, no one can remember the name of the Vice Presidential candidate, nor can anyone recognize him when he shows up. Upon arriving at the meeting, the Presidential candidate's opening crack is, "So here I am, gentlemen—nominated by the people, absolutely my own master, and ready to do any dirty work the committee suggests." The Madison Square Garden campaign rally is interrupted by a wrestling match, and the scene is climaxed by the candidate's proposing marriage through his campaign song, "Of Thee I Sing, Baby." The institution of marriage gets its share of lumps as the candidate is first willing to marry the winner of a bathing-beauty contest and then declares his preference for another simply because he likes the way she makes corn muffins.

specifically mentioned, the sole political figure being former President Calvin Coolidge. Perhaps that is why the mere mention of his name always evoked one of the biggest laughs in the show. In the smoke-filled room scene, once it's been decided that the campaign theme would be the single word "Love," a powerful newspaper publisher, Matthew Arnold Fulton, telephones his chief editor, barks out a series of orders and finishes with: "And call up Coolidge and tell him I want a thousand words on love tomorrow morning." (Even here they had to abandon the reference to Coolidge following his death in January 1933.)

Despite the purposely nonspecific nature of the satire, there was little doubt that Gaxton, particularly in his campaign stump style, was deliberately mimicking the voice and gestures of New York's Mayor James J. Walker, an interpretation at odds with the spirit of the enterprise. The Depression, now over a year old, received only glancing references—an offhand comment by Wintergreen's beloved Mary Turner (played by Lois Moran) that she could bake corn muffins for the unemployed, a line in the song "Who Cares?" about banks failing in Yonkers, a pun on Hoover's assurance, "Prosperity is just around the corner," in the song title "Posterity Is Just Around the Corner."

With his beloved Mary Turner (Lois Moran) beside him, Presidential candidate John P. Wintergreen (William Gaxton) stirs up the crowd at the Madison Square Garden rally in *Of Thee I Sing*.

The President and Vice President of the United States: John P. Wintergreen (William Gaxton) and Alexander Throttlebottom (Victor Moore) in *Of Thee I Sing*.

When President Wintergreen is sworn into office, he is also married at the same time. As for poor Throttlebottom, now the Vice President, the only chance he gets to visit the White House is on a guided tour. He hasn't the foggiest idea of what his duties are until the guide tells him he presides over the Senate. He's just in time too; there's a vote going on to impeach Wintergreen for his refusal to marry the contest winner, Diana Devereaux, who just happens to be "the illegitimate daughter of an illegitimate son of an illegitimate nephew of Napoleon." When Wintergreen discovers he is about to become a father, he is saved from impeachment because, by God, the United States has never impeached an expectant President. So Throttlebottom, as a loyal Vice President, now assumes the President's duties and marries Diana Devereaux.

Apart from sticking pins into more or less sacred institutions, *Of Thee I Sing* marked a definite advance in musical-comedy form. Like the recently opened operetta, *The Cat and the Fiddle*, music was used almost continuously, either as individual songs or as underscoring, or simply to take over an entire scene, dialogue and all. Consider the bathing-beauty contest in which the winner's prize is to be candidate Wintergreen himself. From the moment of publisher Fulton's entrance to reveal the winner ("As the chairman of the committee,/ I announce we've made our choice . . ."), the entire climax of the scene is told through music and lyrics: the choice of Diana Devereaux as the winner; the thrilled reaction of the crowd; the committee's explanation of how it had arrived at the decision; Fulton's order to invite the newspapermen in; Wintergreen's explosive, staccato interruption ("Stop! No!/ Tho' this may be a blow/ I simply cannot marry/ Diana Devereaux!"); the angry reaction of the crowd and the jilted Diana; the committee's insistence on an explanation; Wintergreen's admission of his love for Mary Turner; the committee's consternation ("What shall we do now?/ What is our cue now?"); Diana's threat of legal action and her demand to know Wintergreen's reason for preferring Mary; his explanation ("My Mary can bake corn muffins"); and, once tasting them, the committee's complete agreement with Wintergreen!

Thus, the entire Finaletto of the scene proceeds with a logic both musical and dramatic through a variety of solos, choruses and even one contrapuntal touch (in which, as Wintergreen sings the lyrical

"Some girls can bake a pie . . . ," the judges sing an obligato, and Diana and the girls sing a counter-melody beginning, "Don't surrender! Don't be tender!").

The same kind of broadening of the musical-comedy form was also apparent in the impeachment scene and the roll call of senators. Even the "commercial" songs—principally "Of Thee I Sing, Baby," "Who Cares?" and "Love Is Sweeping the Country" ("Waves are hugging the shore")—conveyed an attitude completely consonant with the playful slant of the musical.

The leading contender for the Pulitzer Prize for the season 1931–1932 was Eugene O'Neill's *Mourning Becomes Electra*. But to universal amazement, the committee, for the first time, honored a musical as the best play of the season. (Of no little influence on the judges, one suspects, is the fact that O'Neill had already won three Pulitzers.) All the creators of *Of Thee I Sing* were cited for their contributions —except George Gershwin, who was ruled out on the technicality that, since the award was for dramatic literature, music did not qualify in this category. How ironic. Without George Gershwin's music, there simply would have been no *Of Thee I Sing*—and Eugene O'Neill would have taken home his fourth Pulitzer.

CHAPTER III

"... JUST AROUND THE CORNER ..."

The Honorable James John Walker was mayor of the city of New York from 1926 through most of 1932. His charm, his cockiness, his brazen flaunting of his extramarital romance with musical-comedy actress Betty Compton somehow made him the personification of the hedonistic, holiday spirit of the big city during the booming Twenties. After a determined start to give New York a responsible administration, Walker proved too weak to stem the tide of corruption engulfing almost every area of municipal government—police, judicial, administrative, and legal. Although he swamped Congressman Fiorello LaGuardia in his reelection bid, Walker soon became trapped by revelations of "gifts" that had been uncovered by the state investigation begun by Judge Samuel Seabury in March 1931. While removal proceedings were in progress under the personal direction of Governor Franklin D. Roosevelt, Walker resigned as mayor in September 1932, and took off for France.

Because of his flair and his jaunty style, Jimmy Walker was a ready target for mimicry in musical revues. As already mentioned, William Gaxton had done an unmistakable takeoff on his platform manner in *Of Thee I Sing*. But the most scathing satire of all on Walker and his regime was a musical in which Hizzoner was neither impersonated nor even mentioned. It was called *Face the Music*, and it opened at the New Amsterdam Theatre on February 9, 1932.

In contrast to *Of Thee I Sing*, which it followed by little less than two months, *Face the Music* actually faced the music. Instead of swatting at the impersonal and the general, it went after the personal and the specific. Instead of avoiding any reference to actual political figures, it named names, though it was careful not to implicate Walker directly. Instead of dealing with national institutions, it aimed its darts at purely local conditions, as it extracted all the humor possible out of living in a corrupt city in the midst of a depression.

Despite their differences in approach, *Of Thee I Sing* and *Face the Music* did possess a similarity in satirical outlook. This was only natural. Sam H. Harris was the producer of both, and the book of *Face the Music* was directed by *Of Thee I Sing*'s

Vandamm; courtesy Irving Berlin
While the social register dines at the Automat, Katherine Carrington and J. Harold
Murray listen as producer Andrew Tombes describes his new musical in *Face the Music*.

co-author and director, George S. Kaufman. Writing his first Broadway musical (not counting *Jonica*) was Kaufman's quondam collaborator, Moss Hart, and supplying the songs was Irving Berlin, returning to Broadway after a four-and-a-half-year absence.

Face the Music found many ready targets. Act One opened in an Automat where, because of the Depression, the Whitneys, Goulds and Vanderbilts have now been forced to dine. And where a rubbernecking chorus serves as guide:

> Come along and you will see
> Mrs. Astor with a grin
> And a dab of ketchup on her chin.
> With pearls around her neck
> Mrs. Woolworth eats her mutton,
> And then she splits the check
> With her girl friend, Mrs. Hutton.

The Palace Theatre, we are advised, now is presenting a bill consisting of Ethel Barrymore, Professor Albert Einstein and Tony the Talking Horse, plus lunch—all for a nickel. For a dime, Roxy Theatre patrons are being offered four feature attractions and a room and bath. So it's not surprising that hard-luck producer Hal Reisman (played by Andrew Tombes) cannot raise the money for a new show because Woolworth won't advance him credit. Into the Automat flounces Mrs. Martin Van Buren Meshbesher (Mary Boland), aglow with diamonds and awarm in furs ("On a clear day you can see me from Yonkers"), who grandly lets it be known that she and her husband are simply "lousy with money." And who is Mrs. Meshbesher's husband? He's a police sergeant. And how did he get all that money? Well . . . The point is, the new state in-

White Studio; courtesy Irving Berlin
Andrew Tombes, Mary Boland and Hugh O'Connell in *Face the Music*.

vestigation committee is putting the heat on all the boys in blue, and they must find some way of ridding themselves of the loot they've stashed away. What better way than to invest their money in a Broadway musical, particularly one produced by so flop-prone an impresario as Mr. Reisman? So they all become angels and the show is, predictably, a disaster. But then someone gets the bright idea of dirtying it up and *The Rhinestones of 1932* (actually a takeoff on a typical Ziegfeld extravaganza) becomes a smash hit. Seabury conducts his investigation into police corruption (Mrs. Meshbesher shows up for the hearings atop a papier-maché elephant), but since this is still musical comedy, the boys manage to get off and there are smiles on all the faces at the final curtain.

In comparing *Face the Music* with *Of Thee I Sing*, critics pointed out that while Gershwin's songs had been sharp-edged, satirical, staccato in rhythm, the musical approach in the new show, equally effective, was just the reverse. Here Hart's abrasive libretto was strikingly balanced by Berlin's basically optimistic and romantic melodies and lyrics. A jaunty jingle of the Depression, "Let's Have Another Cup o' Coffee," struck a hopeful note even though it was actually a satirical compilation of chins-up clichés—assurances that just around the corner there's a rainbow in the sky, that trouble's just a bubble, and that John D. Rockefeller is looking for the silver lining and Herbert Hoover is urging everyone to buy. Berlin also kidded the times by maintaining that the only way young lovers could find happiness was to thumb their noses at the real world ("I say It's Spinach and the hell with it!"). Or to be swept up in a dream world of "Soft Lights and Sweet Music." Or by imagining "A Roof in Manhattan" turning into a Castle in Spain. A more realistic view of the island, "Manhattan Madness," was a driving paean to the city's cacophonous magnetism ("Newsies that shout sensational headlines/ Peddlers with things to sell/ Noisy cafés and whispering breadlines/ Children that scream and yell").

As Robert Garland summed it all up: "Everything is spoofed, nothing is spared. And by everything, I mean policemen with little tin boxes, Miss Mae West and the clean show crusaders, automatic restaurants and torch songs, the bills at the Palace and the penthouses on Park Avenue, the 18th Amendment and the hotels where missing judges stay, the nouveaux riches and the dear old Crinoline Days, Police Commissioner Mulrooney and Judge

Seabury, the speakeasies Mr. Urban designed on 58th Street and the Casino Mr. Solomon manages in Central Park, the drama critics and the Empire State Building, the Depression and the Messrs. Shubert . . . I wouldn't be surprised if *Face the Music* were still running when Mr. Hoover is again popular, the Empire State Building is filled with tenants, and the mere mention of Goldman-Sachs by Mr. Eddie Cantor fails to produce a laugh."

Garland's enthusiasm was shared by all the reviewers but his prediction proved way off the mark. *Face the Music* continued for only a little under five months. Perhaps the barbs were aimed too accurately and the situations were too current and too close. And then again perhaps it was just the depressed condition of the country's economy.

For 1932 was the nadir of the Depression years. Everything was hitting bottom. The Dow Jones averages, 381.17 in 1929, were now 41.22. General Motors, listed on the New York Stock Exchange at 73 in 1929, was down to 8; U.S. Steel went from 262 to 22; American Telephone and Telegraph from 304 to 70. Dividends were off 56.6 percent from their 1929 peak. Industrial production was down 50 percent. Average salaries dropped 40 percent, and average family income was less than $1,600 for the year, with only one family in five with $3,000 to spend. More than 500 millionaires had filed income-tax returns for 1929; by 1932 the figure was 20. Unemployment reached over 12 million, or roughly one out of every seven adults.

Nations abroad were all affected, in one way or another, by America's financial plight. Germany had six and a half million men without jobs. The situation became so critical that aging President Paul von Hindenburg was forced to deal with the ambitious Adolf Hitler who, backed by his strong-arm Nazi party, was threatening to take over the government. Hindenburg did, however, beat Hitler in the race for the Presidency in March, and was able to block him from assuming the post of Chancellor—at least for a year. French Premier Pierre Laval was ousted early in February, and three months later President Paul Doumer was fatally shot by a crazed Russian assassin. In the same bloody month, rioting militarists in Japan murdered Premier Ki Inukai, whom they accused of being too moderate. To the rest of the world, however, the motivation may have been puzzling since the Japanese had already violated the Kellogg-Briand Pact by invading Manchuria; in February they had renamed the country Manchukuo and installed puppet emperor Henry Pu Yi as ruler.

In the United States, the summer months were marked by violence in the nation's capital. Late in May, the bonus marchers—20,000 strong at one point—encamped outside Washington in a vain attempt to pressure Congress into authorizing their war bonus payments. In July, the last of the scraggly army was routed from their shacks at Anacostia Flats by federal troops led by Chief of Staff Douglas MacArthur riding on a white horse.

At the Democratic Convention that summer the party did not pick Wintergreen and Throttlebottom as its standardbearers against Republicans Hoover and Curtis. It picked Roosevelt and Garner, and their theme was not "Love" but, as FDR pledged in his acceptance speech, "A New Deal for the

American people." Swept into office by the stark economic ills of the country and by his own campaigning skills, Roosevelt bested Hoover by a smashing seven million votes. And on the same day, November 8, New York had a new mayor. He was John P. O'Brien, and his greatest contribution to the office was his answer when asked by reporters for the name of a new appointee. "I don't know," he said. "I haven't been told yet." Worthy of a Throttlebottom.

Apart from *Face the Music*, none of the book musicals of 1932 dealt with the world of 1932. Though most of the offerings were cut pretty much to formula, there was one—the Jerome Kern–Oscar Hammerstein *Music in the Air*—that did make notable strides in achieving a close fusion of music and story. It also proved that the adventurous often pays off: with 342 performances, it was far and away the year's biggest hit. (The more conventional *Gay Divorce* and *Take a Chance* were the only other two to run over 200 performances.) Of the year's ten revues, the most impressive was *Flying Colors*, and its star comedian, Charles Butterworth, seems to have been the most favored male actor of the year (though some held out for Bert Lahr in *Hot-Cha!*). Among the ladies, Ethel Merman scored resoundingly in *Take a Chance*, Beatrice Lillie triumphed in *Walk a Little Faster*, and Mary Boland shone as brightly as her diamonds in *Face the Music*. The total number of new musicals produced during 1932 was 22, dramas and comedies a surprisingly high 147 (among them: Katharine Hepburn in *The Warrior's Husband*; George S. Kaufman's and Edna Ferber's *Dinner at Eight*; *The Late Christopher Bean* by Sidney Howard; Ina Claire in S. N. Behrman's *Biography*; and the Ben Hecht–Charles MacArthur *Twentieth Century*).

Neither one of the first two musicals of 1932—both produced in January—found a particularly friendly welcome. *A Little Racketeer* featured Queenie Smith as a tomboy who yearns to become a public enemy. It was withdrawn in a month and a half. *Through the Years*, a sentimental Vincent Youmans romance based on the play, *Smilin' Through*, didn't even last a month. Particularly surprising was the generally negative critical reception accorded the score, which included such superior pieces as "Through the Years," "Drums in My Heart," and "You're Everywhere." Edward Heyman was the lyricist.

"You're certainly lucky, Betty. You never seem to have any trouble with this car."

"It isn't luck, Jane. All our Chevrolets have been like that."

NEW
CHEVROLET
SIX

Following *Face the Music*, March brought in *Marching By*, which paraded for less than two weeks. The tale, which involved Austrians and Russians during the World War, was the Shubert brothers' first attempt of the year to revive operetta's fading appeal.

Florenz Ziegfeld also reverted to a more innocent era with *Hot-Cha!*, a cut-to-pattern musical farce that, depending upon one's viewpoint, either wasted Bert Lahr's time, or, being sufficiently loose-jointed, gave the comedian ample opportunity for uninhibited clowning. Recalling Ziegfeld's pride in the cleanliness of *Smiles*, it distressed many that he would ally himself with an entertainment that had originally been titled *Laid in Mexico*, and that would continue to retain the phrase as a subtitle. Ziegfeld had actually come into the picture because of the strained relationship between lyricist Lew Brown and producer George White that had resulted in their throwing punches at each other at the premiere of the 1931 *Scandals*. What better way for Brown to get back at White than for him and partner Ray Henderson to take their next show to White's oldest and bitterest rival?

The plot of *Hot-Cha!* returned to the well-worn theme of gangsters on the lam, with Bert ending up a bullfighting hero. The show was so proudly old-fashioned it even took a swipe at the more modern satirical musicals by referring in a song to "Park Avenue librettos by children of the ghettos," an obvious crack at the humble origins of the creators of *Of Thee I Sing* and *Face the Music.*

Hot-Cha! was the last original musical to be produced by Florenz Ziegfeld (although in May he revived the 1927 classic, *Show Boat,* at the Casino Theatre, formerly the Earl Carroll). Nearly in a coma opening night, Ziegfeld died four months later at the age of 64. But neither ill health nor Depression could inhibit the producer's lavish hand. He gave Lahr the biggest salary of his career, $2,250 per week, plus a bonus of $250. Nor did he ever lose his optimism. When, during the Washington tryout of *Hot-Cha!,* a reporter asked him his views of the nation's economy, Ziegfeld replied, "I look upon the Depression primarily as a lack of confidence. One of the songs in *Hot-Cha!* deals with this. In 'It's Great to Be Alive,' we have the line, 'There's just as many flowers, just as many trees.' It's all in the people's minds to a great extent."

An attempted rival to the all-black *Blackbirds* revues (none too successful themselves) was the all-black *Blackberries.* That was the lone musical entry in April. The next month brought two more mistakes. Hyman Adler's *There You Are* was dismissed by Robert Benchley as "a revival without ever having been produced before. It is a revival of practically everything that we never wanted to see again." Its eight-performance run was halved by the second offering, the Negro revue, *Yeah Man.* Mantan Moreland, late of the *Blackberries,* found equally brief employment in this one. And that was that for the 1931–1932 season.

A modest revue, *Hey Nonny Nonny,* starring Frank Morgan, was the single new musical attraction offered on Broadway during the summer months. It arrived early in June and lasted through the month. Although reviewers were in no mood to carp, boxoffice queues could scarcely have been expected from such adjectives as "affable," "unexciting," "satisfactory," and "good natured." E. B. White, Frank Sullivan and Ogden Nash were among those contributing sketches.

The unofficial opening of the 1932–1933 season began two days early—on August 30—with the return of the Stone family, Fred, daughter Dorothy and her husband Charles Collins. Stone had toured his show, *Smiling Faces,* for many months prior to bringing it to Broadway (though with Dorothy's

JUNE MacCLOY
MARJORIE WHITE
LUPE VELEZ
BERT LAHR
JUNE KNIGHT

HOT-CHA!

ZIEGFELD THEATRE

6th AVENUE AND 54th STREET

65

sister, Paula, in the lead), and it turned out to be nothing more than another excursion into the doings of the Long Island social set. Out of date and out of touch was the general verdict.

The season's first revue, *Ballyhoo of 1932*, opened one week later. Inspired by the humor magazine *Ballyhoo*, the show was co-produced and written by its editor, Norman Anthony. Anthony did much to keep the stage version a reasonable facsimile of the slightly risqué, lampooning periodical that, at the time of the musical's presentation, could boast a circulation of over one million. Best exemplifying the show's point of view was the first act finale, "Ballyhujah," which ridiculed huckstering by offering Willie Howard in blackface as a Southern preacher exhorting his flock that ballyhoo was the one sure way to end the Depression ("Sing and shout and let the bunk roll out"). "While pandemonium reigns on various stage levels," wrote Wilella Waldorf in the *Post*, "topped by two white brewery horses galloping furiously on a treadmill drawing a wagon full of beer kegs, half a hundred people, on stage and off, seem to be trying to sell something at the top of their voices." No one knew what, but it was one wow of a finale.

Drawing by Russell Patterson

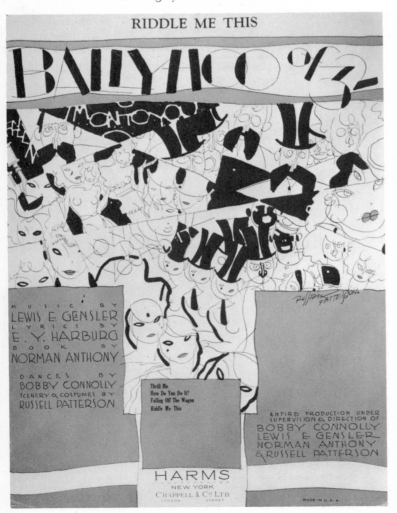

Otherwise, the show offered Bob Hope (his first time on Broadway out of a chorus line) as a glib master of ceremonies, Mr. Howard on a soapbox in Columbus Circle screaming "Rewolt! Rewolt!" and Jeanne Aubert, as "Margreta Garbitch," getting into the proper mood to be the screen's most seductive vamp. It was also in *Ballyhoo* that Willie and Eugene Howard first offered their classic *Rigoletto* Quartet routine. Flanking two buxom female singers, the brothers nightly brought down the house with their sly glances at the ladies' heaving décolletage every time they went after the high notes.

The Yip Harburg–Lewis Gensler songs were singled out by the first-night reviewers for special praise. Among them, "Falling Off the Wagon" suggested love as a cure for still illegal demon rum by maintaining "John Barleycorn can't compare with you." There was also a torchy number, "Thrill Me," which ended in an anything-for-a-laugh manner by having the gigolo to whom Miss Aubert sang it, flash a "TRY EX-LAX" sign from the front of his formal dinner jacket.

On the night of September 15, the audience at the premiere of Max Gordon's newest revue, *Flying Colors*, was startled to hear, as the opening number, a rousing tribute that went, in part:

> In the hardest year for getting dough
> At a time when everything had hit the lowest low
> When Morgan, Schwab and Astor
> Were fighting off disaster,
> Max Gordon raised the money,
> The money for another revue!

It hadn't been easy. Broadway well knew of Gordon's heavy indebtedness and his previous struggles, but eventually the producer did manage to raise the required $125,000. And in those days it was something to sing about.

Money, however, was only part of Gordon's woes. Rehearsals had gone poorly. The Philadelphia tryout opening had been a near disaster. Gordon was so overcome at the prospect of impending doom that he suffered a nervous breakdown and even tried to commit suicide.

One of the biggest problems concerned the number, "Smokin' Reefers." (As the program explained, "A reefer is a narcotic cigarette made from the marihuana weed, frequently smoked in the tropics and recently popular in Harlem.") Originally, Agnes de Mille, who was to have made her choreographic

MAX GORDON presents
Clifton WEBB
Charles BUTTERWORTH
Tamara GEVA Patsy KELLY
in the new HOWARD DIETZ revue

FLYING COLORS

DESIGNED AND LIGHTED BY NORMAN BEL-GEDDES
DANCES BY AGNES DE MILLE AND WARREN LEONARD
COSTUMES BY CONSTANCE RIPLEY
ORCHESTRA CONDUCTED BY AL GOODMAN

Alone Together
A Shine On Your Shoes
Smokin' Reefers
Louisiana Hayride

WORDS AND MUSIC BY
Howard Dietz AND Arthur Schwartz

Note that cover was designed before Agnes de Mille was replaced by Albertina Rasch.

debut with the revue, had engaged a dozen Negro dancers for the number, a daring enough innovation in itself. But the major conflict was with set designer Norman Bel Geddes. To convey the feeling of getting high on the weed, the designer's scheme was to put the dancers on a series of platforms some twelve feet above the stage, but the choreographer strongly opposed the idea because of the danger. Though she was finally forced to agree to it, the whole idea had to be thrown out anyway because the platform collapsed. Miss de Mille quickly came up with something new—and, as she later admitted, totally inappropriate. Now she had the dancers interpret a voodoo ritual, which hardly made sense illustrating a lyric dealing with the effects of marihuana ("Smokin' reefers, you hear the angels sing away/ Helping you fling away/ Your worry and trouble and care"). When, during the tryout, Miss de Mille was told she would have to dream up five new dances in five days, she quit and was replaced by Albertina Rasch.

Another problem had to do with lineage. *Flying Colors* was the son of *The Band Wagon* just as *The Band Wagon* had been the son of *Three's a Crowd* and *Three's a Crowd* had been the son of the first *Little Show*. Apart from *The Little Show*, Max

Gordon had produced all of them. Howard Dietz and Arthur Schwartz had supplied the songs for all four (*Flying Colors* was being billed as "The Howard Dietz Revue," since he was director, lyricist, and sketch writer). Albertina Rasch had been the choreographer of the last three. Clifton Webb, an alumnus of *The Little Show* and *Three's a Crowd*, was now starring in *Flying Colors*, along with another *Three's a Crowd* performer, Tamara Geva.

The familial heritage that had been passed on was one of style, smartness and sophistication. Apart from tone, it was also easy to spot certain specific resemblances, particularly between *Flying Colors* and its most immediate progenitor, *The Band Wagon*. Instead of the dark, moody "Dancing in the Dark," the new revue offered the dark, moody "Alone Together." Instead of "Sweet Music" as an antidote to hard times, it offered "A Shine on Your Shoes." Instead of the lively Teutonic "I Love Louisa," it offered the lively Teutonic "Meine Kleine Akrobat." In his *Sunday Times* piece titled "Flying the Band Wagon Colors," Brooks Atkinson acknowledged the legitimacy of the lineage, but added, "Now that the freshness of style has worn off in the fourth generation the aristocracy of musical entertainment needs new blood." But other critics, to the surprise of everyone concerned with the disaster-plagued revue, were almost all in a hat-tossing mood. As, for example, John Anderson, who termed it "smart with the wry humors of the town's merriest wags; exotic with Harlem's smouldering sex and sin singers; moody when it pleased to be; bright, swift and full of sweet sounds."

There were three particular musical highlights in *Flying Colors*. In "A Shine on Your Shoes" (whose verse proposes a shoeshine to help the shiftless gain employment), dancers Vilma and Buddy Ebsen, singer Monette Moore and harmonica wizard Larry Adler all cavorted merrily around a shoeshine stand. In "Alone Together," as Jean Sargent intoned the sentiment, Miss Geva and Mr. Webb danced a sinuous illustration of how two people can, eventually, become as one. In the jubilant first act finale, "Louisiana Hayride," as Gilbert Gabriel described it, "over the thronged passengers and the horses' ears, the backdrop suddenly dissolves into a leafy country road of motion picture texture, so cool, so shady, so almost smelling of pine and fern that the hot audience stopped fanning itself for once and waved its programs overhead."

White Studio; Theatre Coll., NY Public Lib.
Clifton Webb and Tamara Geva "Alone Together" in *Flying Colors*.

One of the funniest sketches was "The American Plan," in which Charles Butterworth registers at a hotel run by Clifton Webb and Patsy Kelly for the benefit of suicidally inclined Depression victims. Webb and Kelly are most methodical and solicitous; they carefully check off the names of the jumpers as they fall, and are happy to provide a room on the 24th floor for a dollar extra. But the truly inspired bit was Howard Dietz's monologue for Charles Butterworth, "Harvey Woofter's Five Point Plan," which found Butterworth the epitome of glazed-eyed befuddlement, bumbling his way through a soapbox speech at Columbus Circle: ". . . I was a sand sculptor by trade but I went all to pieces . . . I'm against the full dinner pail. I want a bigger pail so the food need be filled only half full and won't drip over the sides . . . My first point: less work and more of it . . . I come out flatly for shorter hours for the working man, or for the working man who is not working. The present hour is now 60 minutes. I propose we make it 40 minutes. Everything would be reduced in proportion. The minute would be 40 seconds, a second would go by in a jiffy, and the jiffy would hardly be worth mentioning . . . I think if we changed the name of the dollar it would bring back more confidence. Over in Europe they have the right idea. They name the money after people, like Frank or Mark. Now suppose we do the same thing and rename the dollar. Call it Harvey or Clarence . . . The other day I saw a girl with an awful bulge in her stocking. I went right over to her as she was walking down the street and said, 'You're hoarding.' She slapped my face . . ."

Originally playing to a top ticket price of $4.40, *Flying Colors* was forced to cut the price in half three and a half months after the opening: a $2.20 top for evenings and a $1.65 top for matinees. It helped for a while, but the revue barely eked out a half-year run.

If *Flying Colors* could be faulted for hewing too closely to the little crowded band-wagon formula, the *Earl Carroll Vanities*—the tenth in the line—adhered to an even older tradition. "America's Greatest Revue, Featuring, as Usual, the Most Beautiful Girls in the World," having been dispossessed from the sumptuous confines of the Earl Carroll Theatre during the run of only one edition, opened at the ample Broadway Theatre late in September. There were other changes, too, primarily concerned with trimming some of the fatty extravagance of previous years. But there were still many visual delights—presided over by 19-year-old Vincente Minnelli, here designing his first Broadway show. Among those delights was a particularly striking number that found the girls parading about with glass tubes on a darkened stage, then exposing them to an electromagnetic field that lighted them up in all kinds of colors and designs.

With regard to the songs, reviewers favored such pieces as "My Darling" and "Along Came Love" to the Ted Koehler–Harold Arlen "I Gotta Right to

White Studio; Max Gordon Coll., The Players
"A Shine on Your Shoes" in *Flying Colors*. The participants: Buddy Ebsen, Monette Moore, Vilma Ebsen, and Larry Adler.

Sing the Blues." And with regard to the performers (Milton Berle, Helen Broderick, Will Fyffe), they preferred the girls. As Percy Hammond gushed, "There are many shapely females—white, slim, rounded, dimpled and unashamed. They cluster, as is their habit, in sensuous tableaux, representing now a garden of gardenias, then a luminous maypole, then a railroad locomotive, lit up by the more or less magic of the electricians. They sing, in a manner of speaking, and wave their pretty legs in the vague gestures of the ballet." Nevertheless, despite such customarily crowd-fetching pleasures, the show ran only 87 performances to become the shortest-running edition in the history of the *Vanities*.

New Americana, particularly when compared to recent revue entries, stood out in its daring and originality. The third in the line of J. P. McEvoy's *Americana* revues, it was a pioneering effort in the use of modern dance choreography in the commercial musical theatre. Charles Weidman and his company (including Letitia Ide and José Limon) and Doris Humphrey's group contributed strikingly individual work, most notably in a highly stylized prizefight and in a rousing, gyrating Shaker meeting. Among other attractions were the Sue Hastings Marionettes, which offered the sight of John D. Rockefeller trying to remove a lady's dog from the last tree in New York, and also a skit that physically pitted Al Smith against Herbert Hoover.

The most unforgettable sequence in the *New Americana* revue depicted a breadline (the idea was based on the current breadline rivalry between competing newspaper publishers William Randolph Hearst and Mrs. Ogden Reid) from which Rex Weber stepped to deliver the Yip Harburg–Jay Gorney plea, "Brother, Can You Spare a Dime?" As Harburg explains it, "This man isn't bitter. He's bewildered. Here is a man who had built his faith and hope in this country. He was able to take advantages of its opportunities and make his fortune. Then came the crash. Now he can't accept the fact that the bubble has burst. He still believes. He still has his faith. He just doesn't understand what could have happened to make everything go so wrong." The song became something of the theme of the Depression years—according to historian Mark Sullivan, "as characteristic and as familiar as bank-closings, money-hoarding, and seedy-genteel men selling apples on street corners." In a lighter topical vein, "Let Me Match My Private Life with Yours" allowed Albert Carroll to do the Jimmy Walker bit as he commented cynically on the double standards of his detractors. (The song's title was a paraphrase on the ex-mayor's snappish retort when queried about his romantic proclivities: "I can match my private life with any man's.")

Tell Her the Truth, the second October entry, had the odd distinction of being the second musical to be derived from a single source. Just five years

NEW YORK'S LEADING THEATRES and ATTRACTION

"AS THOUSANDS CHEER"
MUSIC BOX, 45th St., W. of Broadway
A Musical Revue
By Irving Berlin and Moss Hart.
MARILYN MILLER, CLIFTON WEBB, HELEN BRODERICK, ETHEL WATERS.
Matinees: Thursday and Saturday.

"BIRTHRIGHT"
49th STREET THEATRE, 49th St., W. of Broadway
A new play of life in Germany under the Nazi Regime. By Richard Maibaum.
Matinees Wednesday and Saturday.

"CHAMPAGNE, SEC"
44th STREET THEATRE, 44th St., W. of Broadway
Johann Strauss' Famous Viennese Operetta.
Starring PEGGY WOOD, HELEN FORD, GEORGE MEADER.
Matinees: Wednesday and Saturday.

"DOUBLE DOOR"
RITZ THEATRE, 48th St., W. of Broadway
A Melodrama by Elizabeth McFadden.
Matinees: Wednesday and Saturday.

"GROWING PAINS"
AMBASSADOR THEATRE, 49th St., W. of Broadway
A comedy by Aurania Rouverol with JUNIOR DURKIN.
Opening November 23rd.
Matinees Wednesday and Saturday.

"HAYWIRE"
BIJOU THEATRE, 45th St., W. of Broadway
A comedy by Kennon Jewett, with TOM POWERS.
Opening Thanksgiving Night.

"HER MASTER'S VOICE"
PLYMOUTH THEATRE, 45th St., W. of Broadway
A comedy by Clare Kummer.
ROLAND YOUNG and LAURA HOPE CREWS starred.
Matinees: Thursday and Saturday.

"HOLD YOUR HORSES"
WINTER GARDEN, Broadway at 50th St.
JOE COOK in
A Musical Runaway in 24 Scenes.
HARRIET HOCTOR and Cast of 100
Matinees: Thursday and Saturday.

"I WAS WAITING FOR YOU"
BOOTH THEATRE, 45th St., W. of Broadway
Matinees Wednesday and Saturday.

"LET EM EAT CAKE"
IMPERIAL THEATRE, 45th St., W. of Broadway
A Musical Comedy sequel to "Of Thee I Sing."
Book by Geo. S. Kaufman and Morrie Ryskind. Music and lyrics by George and Ira Gershwin.
With WILLIAM GAXTON, LOIS MORAN and VICTOR MOORE.
Matinees: Wednesday and Saturday.

"MEN IN WHITE"
BROADHURST THEATRE, 44th St., W. of Broadway
A Drama
By Sidney Kingsley.
With the Group Theatre Acting Company
Matinees: Wednesday and Saturday.

"SHE LOVES ME NOT"
46th STREET THEATRE, 46th St., W. of Broadway
A new comedy in 19 Scenes.
Matinees Wednesday and Saturday.

"THE DARK TOWER"
MOROSCO THEATRE, 45th St., W. of Broadway
Opens Saturday, Nov. 25th.
Matinees Wednesday and Saturday.

"THE DRUMS BEGIN"
SHUBERT THEATRE, 44th St., W. of Broadway
Opening Friday, Nov. 24
Matinees Wednesday and Saturday

"THE FIRST APPLE"
CONRAD NAGEL in a comedy by Lynn Starling, with IRENE PURCELL.
Coming soon.

"THE GREEN BAY TREE"
CORT THEATRE, 48th St., E. of Broadway
By Mordaunt Sharp.
Matinees: Wednesday and Saturday.

"TEN MINUTE ALIBI"
ETHEL BARRYMORE THEATRE, 47th St., W. of B'way
By Anthony Armstrong.
Matinees: Wednesday and Saturday.

"THREE AND ONE"
LONGACRE THEATRE, 48th St., W. of Broadway
By Denys Amiel. Adapted by Lewis Galantiere and John Houseman.
Matinees Wednesday and Saturday.

"THUNDER ON THE LEFT"
ELLIOTT THEATRE, 39th E. of Broadway
A dramatization by Jean Ferguson Black of the Christopher Morley novel of the same name.
Matinees Wednesday and Saturday.

Famous Sunday Night Concerts at the Winter Garden Every Sunday at 8.30. Brightest Spot on Broadway.

earlier, *Yes, Yes, Yvette*, based on the novel, *Nothing but the Truth*, had its brief affirmative fling on Broadway. Then four Englishmen tried their hands at musicalizing the same story and they called it *Tell Her the Truth*. Results: a hit in London, a miss in New York.

On election night in November, in addition to Franklin D. Roosevelt as President and John P. O'Brien as New York's mayor, there were two other major winners: Jerome Kern as composer and Oscar Hammerstein, 2nd, as librettist-lyricist. Their *Music in the Air*, the most resounding success of the year, was a highly attractive combination of rich, ripe melodies and an engaging tale of warmth, humor and bucolic charm. It also, as Hammerstein readily admitted, "owed a great deal to its predecessor, *The Cat and the Fiddle*. It too was a play not depending on a large chorus but achieving a kind of intimate reality that the audience found refreshing." There were other points of similarity. Both musicals had scores by Jerome Kern, though the former had book and lyrics by Otto Harbach. Both used music as an indispensable adjunct to their stories. Both plots were concerned with the creation of musical productions. And both were set in modern Europe (the former in Brussels, the latter in Bavaria), though both scrupulously avoided any political overtones.

As far as the story went, *Music in the Air* was little more than a variation on a familiar backstage theme: two innocents from the country (Katherine Carrington and Walter Slezak) travel to the big city (in this case, Munich), where they become involved with an operetta star (Natalie Hall) and a librettist (Tullio Carminati); eventually disillusioned, they return to their less complicated roots. There was, however, one notable departure from traditional form. When the naive ingenue gets the opportunity to star in the librettist's new operetta, *Tingle Tangle*, she muffs it because, essentially, she lacks the dedication and training to be anything more than a talented amateur. The scene in which the librettist upholds the value of professionalism in the theatre provided a backbone of reality to the basically soft and sentimental fable.

But what attracted the customers to *Music in the* Air was the music itself and the way it was presented in the story. "At last, the musical drama has been emancipated," proclaimed Brooks Atkinson in his review. "What *The Cat and the Fiddle* gallantly began last year, Mr. Kern and Mr. Hammerstein have now completed by composing a fable that flows naturally out of a full-brimming score . . . No precision dancing troupes; no knockabout comics; no flamboyant song numbers; no grandiose scenic play—none of the hackneyed trumperies.

Vandamm; courtesy Lynn Farnol Group
In *Music in the Air*, Katherine Carrington and Walter Slezak tarry with Reinald Werrenrath at Stony Brook on their way to Munich.

Having a music box filled with tunes in all his most alluring genres, Mr. Kern has found a way to sing them spontaneously and Mr. Hammerstein has spun him a sentimental adventure that warms the vocal chords . . . The innocence of 'I've Told Ev'ry Little Star,' the nostalgic sentiment of 'In Egern by the Tegern See,' and the sweet rapture of 'When the Spring Is in the Air,' represent Mr. Kern in his freshest vein." But it was Alexander Woollcott, writing in his "Shouts and Murmurs" column in *The New Yorker*, who was by all odds the most effusive appraiser. Hailing the production as "that endearing refuge, that gracious shelter from a troubled world," Woollcott ended his notice with the ringing statement: "Once again, as so often before, Jerome Kern has deserved well of the Republic."

During the Thirties, many an ailing theatrical exhibit owed the prolongation of its life to the ministrations of Joe and Tillie Leblang, who operated a theatre ticket agency in Gray's Drug Store, located on the southeast corner of Broadway and 43rd Street. There, an hour before curtaintime, unsold tickets would be rushed from boxoffices to be offered at half price. But Tillie wanted to do more than merely sell tickets to other people's shows. She wanted to sell them to her own. Her unsuccessful—and unbilled—managerial debut had taken place in *Tell Her the Truth*, and less than a month later, on November 22, she joined producer Morris Green to sponsor another import, *The DuBarry*, starring Grace Moore. Miss Moore, who had begun her Broadway career in Irving Berlin's *Music Box Revue of 1923* and had gone on to become a Metropolitan Opera diva, now had but one ambition: she wanted to be a star on the silver screen and she considered the French operetta the perfect means for bringing her to the attention of the hierarchs of Hollywood. *The DuBarry* was a lavish and costly affair (Vincente Minnelli had designed both sets and costumes) and Miss Moore was sufficiently impressive—particularly in her singing of "I Give My Heart" in a rowdy bordello scene—that she won the desired movie contract. As for the operetta itself, though reviews were mostly favorable, even Tillie Leblang's ticket agency couldn't keep it going longer than three months.

On the same evening *The DuBarry* was being unveiled in New York, George White was also showing off a new production. Feeling the economic pinch, he offered a vaudeville-type revue, the *Music Hall Varieties*, and charged $2.50 for the best seat in the huge Casino Theatre. Willie and Eugene Howard again did their "Pay the Two Dollars" routine (held over from the previous year's *Scandals*), and Harry Richman sang up a brassy storm with his "I Love a Parade" first act finale. It was in the *Varieties* that Bert Lahr first attempted toning down his accustomed raucous clowning. One of his best routines found him doing a takeoff of Clifton Webb (called "Clifton Duckfeet"), in which he perfectly caught the essence of Webb's clipped, precise personality.

There have not been many phoenixes in the musical theatre. Once dead on the road, a show usually remains dead, immune to any efforts to make it rise from the ashes. But there have been exceptions: *Strike Up the Band*, for one. In 1932 there was another. On September 12, a musical called *Humpty Dumpty* opened in Pittsburgh. It was all about a rich theatrical angel (Lou Holtz) who, with his mother (Lisa Silbert), brother (Sid Silvers), and sister (Doris Groday), had put up $75,000 to finance a revue which they viewed from a box in the theatre. The show itself was a series of sketches and songs kidding incidents in American history, including the courtship of Miles Standish and the Boston Tea Party, and it depicted such historical figures as Washington, Betsy Ross and Lincoln. Ethel Merman and Eddie Foy, Jr., were on hand to take care of most of the songs and the comedy in the show within the show. But the framework didn't work; it just never added up to a full evening's entertainment, and *Humpty Dumpty* fell after five days. Total disaster.

But not quite. The authors—Buddy DeSylva and Laurence Schwab, who also happened to be the producers—simply refused to give up. Within three weeks they were ready with an entirely new concept. It was still about putting on a revue called *Humpty Dumpty*, but the sketches were pared down to three, and instead of having a dialect comic as the leading backer of the show, they transformed the angel into a handsome leading man (Jack Whiting) involved with the leading lady (June Knight). Then they sought out composer Vincent Youmans to beef up the score by Richard A. Whiting and Nacio Herb Brown (unaccountably known as Herb Brown Nacio for this one occasion), made some cast changes (Miss Merman was still in it, but Mitzi Mayfair was substituted for Miss Groday and Jack Haley for Mr. Foy), and tied up the package with a new—and more personally meaningful—title, *Take a Chance*. It was well worth the taking.

Take a Chance, which opened on Broadway late in November, was a good old-fashioned knockabout musical comedy with an outstanding cast, some memorable songs, some hilariously funny situations, and a pace that never flagged. And the critics and the public ate it up.

Not everything that had been in *Humpty Dumpty* was thrown away; in fact, the biggest show-stopper, "Eadie Was a Lady," turned out to be one of the happiest salvage operations of the Thirties. Originally, Buddy DeSylva had the idea of writing a turn-of-the-century-type ballad for Walter O'Keefe in much the same style as the O'Keefe specialty, "The Man on the Flying Trapeze." DeSylva dreamed up the "Eadie" lyric, Whiting composed an appropriate musical setting, but the song was dropped when O'Keefe decided against appearing in the show. During rehearsals, one of Ethel Merman's numbers had been "Poppy Smoke," but this too had to be scratched once the writers caught a showing of *Flying Colors* and discovered that "Poppy Smoke" had a theme almost identical to that of "Smokin' Reefers." What should take its place? "Well," said DeSylva, "we still have that number about Eadie. Ethel could do it and we could build a whole scene around it." So they did. As presented in *Take a Chance*, it was sung in a saloon setting at the time of the Spanish-American War, with Miss Merman regaling audiences with chorus after chorus about the deceased bordello madam who had class with a capital "K."

The Vincent Youmans interpolations were of great help, too. Among them were two stirringly revivalistic pieces for Ethel Merman: "I've Got Religion" and the Depression-inspired trumpet call to "Rise 'n' Shine" ("Don't be a mourner/ Things look fine around the corner"). These would be the last songs Youmans ever wrote for the theatre.

Once sister Adele had forsaken show business for British nobility, Fred Astaire was faced with the problem of finding a suitable leading lady. His first solo outing, *Gay Divorce* (about a mixup of co-respondents set in an English resort), was hardly the sturdy vehicle he and his sister had had in, say, *The Band Wagon*, but it proved conclusively that Fred could carry both a weak show and a new dancing partner. On this one occasion she was Claire Luce who acquitted herself well, as did the trio of comedians, Luella Gear, Erik Rhodes and

White Studio; Theatre Coll., NY Public Lib.
Ethel Merman sings the sad tale of "Eadie Was a Lady" in *Take a Chance*.

73

Eric Blore. The reviews were only so-so, with Gilbert Gabriel writing, "When Fred Astaire and Claire Luce do their dances, *Gay Divorce* is terrapin to the carriage trade. But when they aren't doing ditto, it is just about pfui to the cut rates." Apart from Astaire, the show did possess one other singular advantage: a Cole Porter song called "Night and Day."

Porter once claimed that the lyrical inspiration for the ballad sprang from an evening while dining with Mrs. Vincent Astor. Irritated by the sound of a broken eaves spout, she spluttered, "That drip drip drip is driving me mad!" Melodically, Porter had been influenced by the chanting of a Mohammedan priest he had heard in Morocco. The vast popularity of "Night and Day" helped draw the audiences, though it also had the effect of eclipsing most of the other numbers. The possibility of the Prince of Wales marrying was considered momentous enough for a song sung by Eric Blore, "What Will Become of Our England?" ("When the Prince of Wales finds a wife?"), and Luella Gear's unflagging devotion to her native land was proudly asserted in "I Still Love the Red, White and Blue":

> In spite of cyclones and prairie fires,
>   Earthquakes and floods,
> Luckies, Chesterfields,
>   Camels and Spuds,
> Grifters and grafters, con men and gun men,
> And men I've been married to,
> I still love the red, white and blue.*

With 248 performances (achieved, as Gilbert Gabriel predicted, through discount tickets), *Gay Divorce* became the second longest-running musical of 1932. It was also Fred Astaire's final appearance in a Broadway musical.

After the death of Abraham Lincoln Erlanger in 1930 and the subsequent fall of his theatrical empire, Erlanger's Theatre on West 44th Street was renamed the St. James by landlord Vincent Astor. The first tenant for the retitled showplace was the revue, *Walk a Little Faster*, which opened on December 7. Though hoping to emulate the success of the Gordon-Dietz-Schwartz revues, the new attraction unfortunately contained little that was original or inspired, despite the pairing of Beatrice Lillie with Bobby Clark and Paul McCullough. One of the highlights was the Lillie-Clark

White Studio; Theatre Coll., NY Public Lib.
The final scene from *Gay Divorce*, involving Roland Bottomley, Erik Rhodes, Claire Luce, and Fred Astaire.

spoof of the Geva-Webb "Alone Together" dance in *Flying Colors* (thus making Mr. Webb the butt of both Bert Lahr and Bobby Clark in two concurrently running revues). It was also in the new revue that Beatrice Lillie first tried one of her wackiest bits of business. Appearing in a formal gown, she introduced one of the sketches in her most regal manner—and then hiked up her skirt and roller-skated off the stage. S. J. Perelman was responsible for two sketches in the revue: one for Miss Lillie in which she played the part of Penelope Goldfarb, a 1906 scamp of the campus, and one for Clark in which he imitated Soviet dictator Joseph Stalin. Song writers Yip Harburg and Vernon Duke could offer hardheaded practicality in "Speaking of Love" ("Give me a frank account/ How is your bank account?"), but they could still weave romantic dreams such as "April in Paris," inspired by a chance remark once made by director Monty Woolley. Its introduction in *Walk a Little Faster*, however, caused scarcely a ripple since Evelyn Hoey, who sang it, had laryngitis opening night.

White Studio; Theatre Coll., NY Public Lib.
Bobby Clark, Paul McCullough, and Beatrice Lillie in *Walk a Little Faster*.

Walk a Little Faster was followed by *Shuffle Along of 1933*, whose pace turned out to be so deliberate that it barely made it to the year of its designation. The initial all-Negro *Shuffle Along*, which had opened in 1921, reached 504 performances; its long-delayed successor closed after 17. Mantan Moreland was in this one, too, along with veterans of the original, Flournoy Miller, Noble Sissle and Eubie Blake.

But that still wasn't the final stage musical of the year. The evening after *Shuffle Along* opened, December 27, Ray Bolger, Doc Rockwell, Titto Ruffo, Martha Graham, Harald Kreutzberg, the Sisters of the Skillet, Patricia Bowman, the Flying Wallendas, the Tuskegee Choir, DeWolf Hopper, Weber and Fields, and Jimmy McHugh and Dorothy Fields all appeared on the largest stage in the world, the Radio City Music Hall, as the inaugural bill of the Showplace of the Nation. Though acts have changed, and motion pictures soon became an important part of the attraction, the symphony orchestra, the Rockettes, the Corps de Ballet, and the Glee Club have all continued to provide what has, in effect, become the longest-running stage musical of all time.

CHAPTER IV

"... THE NEW DAY IS HERE ..."

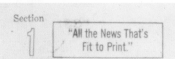

The New York Times.

Section 1 | "All the News That's Fit to Print." | LATE CITY EDITION | Section 1

VOL. LXXXII...No. 27,434.   NEW YORK, SUNDAY, MARCH 5, 1933.   TEN CENTS

ROOSEVELT INAUGURATED, ACTS TO END THE NATIONAL BANKING CRISIS QUICKLY; WILL ASK WAR-TIME POWERS IF NEEDED

PLAN TO USE SCRIP HERE

Bankers Ready to Issue Clearing House Paper at End of Holiday.

WILL MEET WOODIN TODAY

Eastern Financiers to Join Parley at Capital on Plans to Permit Reopenings.

STOCK EXCHANGES CLOSED

Drain on the Gold Reserve Is Halted — Cash Being Set to Meet Payroll

VICTORY FOR HITLER

Checks Still Accepted Here For Federal Income Taxes

READY TO CALL CONGRESS

President Probably Will Summon Extra Session for Wednesday.

WORKS ON LEGISLATION

Cabinet Ordered to Meet With Him Today to Draft Banking Reform Measures.

AID LIKELY IN A WEEK

Steps Considered Include Deposit Guarantee, Use of Scrip and Tax on Hoarded Gold.

THE NEW PRESIDENT TAKING THE OATH OF OFFICE.

100,000 AT INAUGURATION

President, Grim, Tersely Pledges 'Adequate but Sound Currency.'

SCORES 'MONEY-CHANGERS'

In Fighting Speech He Demands Supervision of Credit and Investments.

STICKS TO CONSTITUTION

Ro'-se-velt is President!
Ro'-se-velt is President!

March 4, 1933. In the afternoon, the inauguration of the 32nd President of the United States ("Let me assert my firm belief that the only thing we have to fear is fear itself"). In the evening, the premiere of a splashy Broadway revue, *Strike Me Pink*, which commenced its revels with the chorus chirping the borrowed tune of "Wintergreen for President" in toothy celebration of the day's major event.

The country, reeling from the worsening Depression, particularly the frightening number of bank failures during February, took heart in the determination and dedication of the new President. Within the famous "Hundred Days" of his administration, FDR almost singlehandedly gave the country a renewed spirit. He made ten speeches, sent fifteen

messages to Congress, held two press conferences weekly, and pushed through a dizzying succession of important New Deal edicts and reforms—the national bank holiday (March 6); the Emergency Banking Act to reopen the banks (March 9); the Beer and Wine Revenue Act to legalize 3.2 percent beer (March 22); the creation of the Civilian Conservation Corps (CCC) (March 31); the abandonment of the gold standard (April 19); the Federal Emergency Relief Act (FERA) for immediate aid to the poor and unemployed (May 12); the Agricultural Adjusting Act (AAA) to stabilize farm prices (May 12); the Tennessee Valley Authority (TVA) to maintain and operate a power plant at Muscle Shoals (May 18); the National Industrial Recovery Act to set up codes for business to comply with governmental price and wage controls (June

NY *Herald Tribune*, June 17, 1933.

16); and the Public Works Administration (PWA) (June 16).

On March 12, Roosevelt gave his first Fireside Chat over radio ("It is safer to keep your money in a reopened bank than under the mattress"). On March 16, he sent a message to the fifty-four nations meeting at the Geneva Conference urging them to sign a nonaggression pact. In August, the Blue Eagle ("We Do Our Part") was to be seen everywhere signifying compliance with the NRA codes, and in the same month the National Labor Relations Board was created to enforce the right of collective bargaining. Toward the end of the year, the Civil Works Administration (CWA) was created under the FERA to provide emergency jobs for four million unemployed over the winter months.

The activities of the federal government in 1933 were staggering. The theatre too was staggering— but not from activity. Half the theatres were dark. More than half the actors were without work. In an attempt to compensate for the dearth of new plays, there was a record number of revivals, usually offered at a top price of $1.50 or $1.00. Broadway chronicler Burns Mantle flatly stated in his *Best Plays* volume for the 1933–1934 season, "The day of the $3, $4, $5, and $6 theatre is about over."

The number of all new stage productions for 1933 was 132, down 42 from 1930. Among the leading dramatic offerings were the Lunts and Noël Coward in Coward's *Design for Living*; Maxwell Anderson's Pulitzer Prize winner of 1932–1933, *Both Your Houses*; Sidney Kingsley's *Men in White*, which won the Pulitzer the following season; George M. Cohan in *Ah, Wilderness!*, Eugene O'Neill's only comedy; Maxwell Anderson's *Mary of Scotland*, with Helen Hayes; and the play that would set the longevity record for Broadway, Jack Kirkland's *Tobacco Road*.

Of the 132 productions, musicals accounted for 14, less than half the total of three years before. And of these, except for *As Thousands Cheer*, there was little that was cheerful. One after another the giants fell. *Pardon My English* was the worst disaster to overtake George and Ira Gershwin. Sigmund Romberg fared only slightly better with *Melody. Strike Me Pink*, despite the attractions of a cast headed by Jimmy Durante, Lupe Velez and Hope Williams, could only attain slightly more than 100 performances. Kurt Weill's *Threepenny Opera*, already a classic in Europe, lasted less than two weeks. *Roberta*, though a hit, had to survive a rough press. So did Earl Carroll's *Murder at the Vanities*. Even the usually adored Joe Cook could do little to attract patrons to *Hold Your Horses*. *Let 'Em Eat Cake* offered hardly any nourishment, even though it had been assembled by the same people responsible for *Of Thee I Sing*. Nor could Bill Robinson keep *Blackbirds* flying more than three weeks.

MY COUSIN IN MILWAUKEE

Alex. A. Aarons & Vinton Freedley
Present
the new musical comedy
PARDON MY ENGLISH
with
Jack Pearl
Book By
Herbert Fields
Lyrics By
IRA GERSHWIN
Music By
GEORGE GERSHWIN
Musical numbers staged By
Georgie Hale

So What?
Isn't It A Pity?
My Cousin In Milwaukee
Lorelei
Luckiest Man In The World
I've Got To Be There
Where You Go I Go

NEW WORLD MUSIC
CORPORATION
HARMS
NEW YORK
MADE IN U.S.A.

star of the show, England's musical-comedy idol, Jack Buchanan, became so dissatisfied with his role after it had been hacked to bits that he quit before the New York opening and was replaced by George Givot. Freedley himself tried his hand at directing the musical but gave up and called in John Mc-Gowan to try to rescue what was left. Very little, as it turned out. By the time of the official January 20 Broadway premiere, it was a confused and confusing tale, relying for all its limited life on the appeal of dialect comic Jack Pearl, as the police chief of Dresden, the effusive personality of Lyda Roberti, and some dandy Gershwin songs (such as "Isn't It a Pity?" "Lorelei," and "My Cousin in Milwaukee").

The first-night reviewers were brutal except for kindly Percy Hammond, who admitted enjoying himself because "Mr. Pearl's comic sorceries changed the pasty book into what seemed to be gems of humorous bon mots and badinage" (presumably they included Pearl's opening crack upon being told by a lieutenant that the coast was clear: "What the hell do I care about the weather in California?"). The failure of *Pardon My English* was so crushing that Freedley was forced to flee the country to avoid creditors.

As Thousands Cheer was the outstanding production of the year, artistically, musically (the score was by Irving Berlin), and commercially, with its 400-performance run making it the third longest running revue of the decade. (The other two musicals of 1933 to run over 200 performances: *Roberta* and *Murder at the Vanities*.) Jimmy Durante was the clown of the year in *Strike Me Pink*, and Ethel Waters gave the leading female performance in *As Thousands Cheer*. Among the debuts were Kitty Carlisle, who scored impressively in *Champagne, Sec,* and choreographer Robert Alton, who began his Broadway career with *Hold Your Horses*.

Pardon My English started the year off on a justifiably apologetic note. Alex Aarons was to have produced the show independent of his usual partner, Vinton Freedley, but the cost—in the neighborhood of $90,000—sent him scurrying to Freedley for financial help. From then on, Freedley took over. Almost from the very beginning the enterprise suffered one setback after another. Six play doctors were summoned for surgical consultation during Philadelphia-Boston-Brooklyn trial run. The

NEW YORK'S LEADING THEATRES AND ATTRACTIONS

AMERICANA
SHUBERT THEATRE, 44th St., W. of Broadway
Most novel revue ever staged.
PHIL BAKER and a cast of 100.
Eves. at 8:30. Mats. Wed. and Sat. at 2:30.

ANOTHER LANGUAGE
BOOTH THEATRE, 45th St., W. of Broadway
Arthur J. Beckhard presents the much talked-about success by Rose Franken, with GLENN ANDERS, DOROTHY STICKNEY, MARGARET WYCHERLY, JOHN BEAL, MAUDE ALLAN, WYRLEY BIRCH.
Eves. at 8:50. Mats. Wed. & Sat. at 2:40.

AUTUMN CROCUS
MOROSCO THEATRE, 45th St., W. of Broadway
A new play by C. L. Anthony. Presented by Lee Shubert in association with Basil Dean featuring FRANCIS LEDERER and PATRICIA COLLINGE.
Eves. at 8:30. Mats. Wed. and Sat. at 2:30.

BALLYHOO OF 1932
44th STREET THEATRE, 44th St., W. of Broadway
The Lewis Gensler, Bobby Connolly, Russell Patterson, Norman Anthony Revue with WILLIE and EUGENE HOWARD, JEANNE AUBERT, LULU McCONNELL, BOB HOPE, VERA MARSHE and a chorus of beautiful girls.
Eves. at 8:30. Mats. Wed. & Sat. at 2:30.

COUNSELLOR-AT-LAW
PLYMOUTH THEATRE, 45th St., W. of Broadway
PAUL MUNI in the Elmer Rice success—now in its 46th week.
Eves. at 8:30. Mats. Thurs. & Sat. at 2:30.

DINNER AT EIGHT
MUSIC BOX THEATRE, 45th St., W. of Broadway
Sam H. Harris presents a new play by George S. Kaufman and Edna Ferber. The cast includes CONSTANCE COLLIER, CONWAY TEARLE, MARJORIE CHURCHILL, ANN ANDREWS, MALCOLM DUNCAN, MARGARET DALE, PAUL HARVEY and many others.
Eves. at 8:30. Mats. Thurs. & Sat. at 2:30.

EARL CARROLL VANITIES
EARL CARROLL'S BROADWAY THEATRE.
Broadway at 53rd St.
10th and most stupendous edition, with a cast of over 200 leading European and American stars.
Eves. at 8:30. Mats. Wed. and Sat. at 2:30.

FLYING COLORS
IMPERIAL THEATRE, 45th St., W. of Broadway
Max Gordon presents the new Howard Dietz revue starring CLIFTON WEBB, CHARLES BUTTERWORTH, TAMARA GEVA and PATSY KELLY. Words and music by Howard Dietz and Arthur Schwartz.
Eves. at 8:30. Mats. Thurs. & Sat. at 2:30.

OF THEE I SING
46th ST. THEATRE, 46th St., W. of Broadway
Sam H. Harris presents a new musical comedy with WILLIAM GAXTON, LOIS MORAN and VICTOR MOORE.
The Pulitzer Prize Winner 1931-32.
Eves. at 8:30. Mats. Thurs. & Sat. at 2:30.

SUCCESS STORY
MAXINE ELLIOTT'S THEATRE, 39th St., E. of B'way
The Group Theatre presents a new play by John Howard Lawson.
Eves. at 8:40. Mats. Wed. and Sat. at 2:40.

THE PERFECT MARRIAGE
BIJOU THEATRE, 45th St., W. of Broadway
A new play by Robert Goodrich, starring FAY BAINTER and EDITH BARRETT.
Eves. at 8:40. Mats. Wed. and Sat. at 2:40.

THE SILENT HOUSE
AMBASSADOR THEATRE, 49th St., W. of Broadway
Carl Hunt's Stock Company presents a mystery thriller by John G. Brandon and George Pickett.
Eves. at 8:30. Mats. Wed. and Sat. at 2:30.

Certainly of no boxoffice help was the musical's German setting. Adolf Hitler, whom President Von Hindenburg had vainly tried to keep from assuming power, had finally succeeded to the post of Chancellor early in January. And on February 27— the night *Pardon My English* closed—the Reichstag in Berlin was mysteriously set ablaze. Without investigation, Hitler branded the fire the work of Communists, and used it as an excuse for a wave of repressive decrees to combat "subversion."

While traditional *Mitteleuropa* was changing at a frightening rate, traditional *Mitteleuropean* operetta seemed serenely impervious to any change whatever. As, for example, the three-generation romance. *Melody*, the sole musical entry for February, was cast in exactly the same mold as *Three Little Girls*, which the Shuberts had imported less than three years before. In the new operetta, whose score was written by Sigmund Romberg and Irving Caesar, the lovers separate in 1881 in Paris because the heroine is forced to marry a vicomte, their children

have an equally teary time of it in 1906, but their grandchildren make out just fine in 1933.

The operetta was originally to have served as the means through which producer Arthur Hammerstein would make a comeback. Once he bowed out, Ziegfeld showed interest in sponsoring it, but he died before any agreement could be reached. It was then that George White picked it up and presented it as *George White's Melody* (did he really want everyone to think he had dreamed up that creaky plot all by himself?). As it was, though, the reviews were fairly sympathetic. Brooks Atkinson said it had "all the virtues of the breed save inspiration," while Robert Benchley took a more philosophical attitude. "The more confused and complicated our daily lives become," he wrote in *The New Yorker*, "the simpler seem to be the agencies of entertainment. Just to sit back and look at *Melody* is a warming experience in these days of denim and seersucker."

Melody had a difficult time filling the 3,000-seat Casino Theatre—the rental was $7,000 a week— and White closed it after 79 performances. It was the last "legitimate" attraction to play the theatre. Following a vaudeville show, *Casino Varieties*, in 1934, it reopened as the French Casino, a theatre-restaurant, and later as Billy Rose's Casa Manana. Then it was torn down and replaced by a Woolworth's.

The lone March entry, *Strike Me Pink*, struck everyone as little more than a showcase for the exuberant—or, to use his own term, "exibulant"— antics of Jimmy Durante. Originally, however, it had been producer Lew Brown's intention to offer a revue, called *Forward March*, that would parade the talents of a cast of relatively unknown performers. Brown was joined in the venture by bootlegger Waxey Gordon, whose greatest ambition was to be a theatre impresario. When *Forward March* looked as if it would be halted even before the New York opening, Gordon began pouring more money into the show. First Lou Holtz was added. Then the producers tried unsuccessfully to get Beatrice Lillie and Fred Allen. Ted Healy also turned them down. Smith and Dale added their Dr. Kronkeit humor during the Washington engagement, and Stoopnagle and Budd were all set to join the cast when the revue folded. Still Gordon wouldn't give in. He had the show retitled, rewritten, restaged, and recast with such boxoffice attractions as Jimmy Durante (at a salary of $3,000 per week), Lupe Velez

79

Theatre Coll., NY Public Lib.
Jimmy Durante and Lupe Velez in *Strike Me Pink*. One
night Jimmy put a monkey wrench in his pocket.

and Hope Williams. By the time *Strike Me Pink*
finally made it to Broadway, it had cost the underworld leader over $150,000.

Strike Me Pink may have been a generally loose-
jointed frolic, but on one occasion it seems to have
carried spontaneity to excess. In a scene calling for
a hip-bumping routine between Lupe Velez and
Jimmy Durante, Jimmy decided to have some fun
by putting a monkey wrench in his overalls pocket.
After being subjected to the pounding a few times,
Lupe realized what was wrong and reached into
Jimmy's pocket. She then chased him up and down
the aisles brandishing the tool, and finally caught
him. Following a brief tussle, Durante tossed the
fiery Mexican into the orchestra pit.

"Not often do our troubadours throw together
so festive a jubilee as the new Lew Brown–Ray
Henderson skylark," enthused Percy Hammond
about *Strike Me Pink*. "It has speed, good looks,
tickling tunes, laughs of the essential Broadway
improprieties, and a genial air of celebration." Most
of the other aisle-sitters found it lavish in everything
save taste and inspiration. And it also struck many
as having a genial air less of celebration than of a
George White's Scandals.

A perfectly understandable reaction since *Strike
Me Pink* did have songs by two veterans of the

series as well as the brisk high-stepping pace so
identified with impresario White. The title tune
quickly became popular, and the score also contained the essential optimistic hymn, though this
one, "It's Great to Be Alive," turned out to be a
holdover from the previous year's *Hot-Cha!* Two
numbers, however, did try to face reality, if only
through the optical distortions of a Broadway revue.
The first act finale, "Restless," a commentary on
the shallowness of contemporary life, was described
thusly by John Platt in *Stage* magazine: "Here are
a dozen girls shaking flat on the floor in their satin
gowns to a song that weeps over the skelter life of
moderns. The lights shutter from light to dark.
Chorus girls shudder their way to the front, and it
finishes with visions of a glowering Atlas, as high
as the flies of the stage, with a weary world on his
shoulders. Twenty girls climb the rigging to his
whiskers. Silver confetti floats down. The orchestra
bangs a wild crescendo." Curtain!

In the other contemporary number, "Home to
Harlem," Brown and Henderson reverted to the
social consciousness of the last *Scandals*' "That's
Why Darkies Were Born." The mood, though, was
no longer one of a Negro's philosophical acceptance
of life's injustices but that of his aggressive determination to find freedom among his own people. Be-

fore a cyclorama (designed by Henry Dreyfuss) showing a Florida chain gang, a cabin in the cotton, a winding road, the New York skyline, and Connie's Inn in Harlem, singer George Dewey Washington, as a chain gang prisoner, expressed his yearning for the promised land:

> I need music I need lights,
> Tired of slaving for these whites;
> They feels bigger
> I'm plain nigger
> But up in Harlem
> I'se got rights . . .

Failure is a great leveler. Both *Hummin' Sam* and *The Threepenny Opera* opened in April. The first, an all-Negro musical, lasted one performance. The second lasted 12. Both received thrashings in the public print. But *The Threepenny Opera*, with a score by Kurt Weill, had come to Broadway with the reputation of its unparalleled triumphs throughout Europe following its Berlin opening in 1928. Not an importation for the Shubert brothers, perhaps, but one whose Bertolt Brecht text, based on the 200-year-old British musical, *The Beggar's Opera*, was generally regarded as just about the bravest, most penetrating depiction of the moral decay then so symptomatic of German life. The American adaptation by Gifford Cochran and Jerrold Krimsky and the style of the production, which utilized the original Caspar Neher designs,

tried to be faithful to its source. But the critics roasted it. Percy Hammond said it was "a mummy grinning on a dung hill." John Mason Brown found it "the most appallingly stupid book with which any production that benefits from music has been cursed with in recent years." To Gilbert Gabriel, it was "a dreary enigma." Richard Lockridge called it "sugar-coated communism."

But there were those who saw in its sordid depiction of thieves, cutthroats and beggars and the relationship between the underworld and the police, a universality that had much to say to the world of the Thirties. Hiram Motherwell, in *Stage*, condemned the "wilful blindness" of the daily reviewers, Lewis Nichols in the *Times* found it "worth the seeing," and Robert Garland felt it "might have been a first rate triumph if it were more professional." And, to a man, the critics were impressed with the Kurt Weill music.

Nineteen thirty-three recorded the hottest New York summer on record. Neither of the two summertime musicals offered much in the way of entertainment relief. June brought *Tattle Tales* all the way from Los Angeles where it had originally been assembled by Frank Fay. For New York, his wife, Barbara Stanwyck, made a brief appearance principally to plug her latest movie. The second hot-weather item, temptingly called *Shady Lady*, turned up in July. Boop-boop-a-doop girl Helen Kane was featured in it, but she didn't even boop once. The show was gone in a month.

Vandamm
The final scene in *The Threepenny Opera*. Macheath (Robert Chisholm) is about to be hanged when Sheriff Brown (Rex Evans) rides in with the pardon. Looking on at the left are Lucy Brown (Josephine Huston), Mrs. Peacham (Evelyn Beresford), Jonathan Peacham (Rex Weber), and Polly Peacham (Steffi Duna). At the far right can be seen Filch (Herbert Rudley) and Walter (Harry Bellaver).

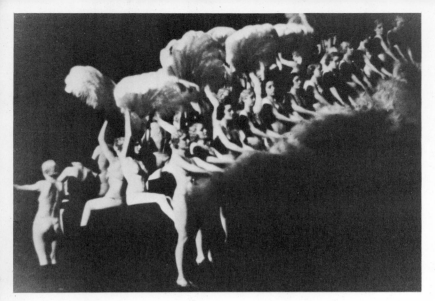

Theatre Coll., NY Public Lib.
Fan dancers in *Murder at the Vanities*.

Drawing by Sam Berman

The 1933–1934 theatrical season began early in September with a contribution from Earl Carroll. Concerned that the public may have wearied of the revue format—his last *Vanities* had lasted only 87 performances—he sought to vary the entertainment by putting on a revue within the framework of a backstage story. Since it was about a murder at the *Vanities*, he called it *Murder at the Vanities*. The critics found it pretty much of a botch, with Burns Mantle observing, "The girls offer a song boasting their virginal wrappers of cellophane and go quite nude in a fan number that introduces adhesive tape as a support for the last remaining girdle . . . I know who did the murder. So far as I'm concerned his name is Carroll." Despite reviews such as this—or because of them—Leblang's did a brisk sale of cut-rate tickets and the show managed to last through the season.

Judging by his previous outings, Joe Cook could do no wrong. With *Hold Your Horses*, he finally succeeded. Originally under the helm of John Shubert, J. J.'s son, the musical had a disastrous tryout tour, going through one director after another. J. J., who had allowed his son a free hand, now scurried up to Boston to try to patch things up. He added girls, specialty numbers and songs (including "If I Love Again," which won out over his original anachronistic choice, "The Last Roundup"). Although the Shuberts were in firm control, their name did not appear as sponsor when this "Musical Runaway in Two Acts and Twenty Scenes" opened at the Winter Garden late in September. Joe Cook played the part of a hackie in the Gay Nineties who became mayor of New York, and Cook's inventive lunacy saw to it that his hansom cab was equipped with bath, kitchenette, Frigidaire, and elevator. But the book was too much. Or too little.

By the fall of 1933, there were a few signs that the theatre was finally picking itself up. Although renewed activity along Broadway was not really to become apparent until the following year, October brought an especially luminous portent. It was called *As Thousands Cheer.*

As Thousands Cheer reunited the masterminds of *Face the Music*—producer Sam H. Harris, author Moss Hart, song writer Irving Berlin, director Hassard Short, and designer Albert Johnson. Like the previous musical, this too was a satire on the current state of the world though the new attraction, being a revue rather than a book show, had even greater latitude. The show was designed in the form of a daily newspaper, with national news, international news, social news, theatre news, a lonely-hearts column, a comic section, a rotogravure section, even a weather report. It cost about $100,000 to put on, attracted customers for almost a year, and grossed $1,200,000.

At a top ticket price of $4.40, audiences were treated to a bright and brazen look at the people whose exploits inspired the headlines of the day, depicted either in sketch or in musical number. And in the following order:

PROLOGUE

In the dining room of a wealthy Park Avenue couple (Helen Broderick and Leslie Adams), the master of the house is growing increasingly irritated at his wife's excessive concern over her pet Pekingese. When Fido bites him, he is unable to control

himself any longer and bites the dog back. Blackout. At the city room of a local newspaper, editor Jerome Cowan is screaming orders. When a dog bites a man it's no news, but when a man bites a dog it's a hold-the-presses story. As soon as the paper hits the stands, the news so excites the boys and girls of the chorus that they break out into joyous song and dance all over Columbus Circle:

Not a great big manly he-dog—a little she-dog, a bitch,
Which gives us a headline off the beaten track:
"A Bitch Bit a Man and the Man Bit the Bitch Right Back"

ACT I

Headline: FRANKLIN D. ROOSEVELT INAUGURATED TOMORROW

Roosevelt had defeated Hoover in a landslide the previous November. On their final day in the White House, Lou Hoover (Helen Broderick) and husband Herbert (Leslie Adams) are busily packing. Lou is bitter that Herbert had ever run for the Presidency. "What did you want to be President for?" she asks him. "You had a good job. Four years in the White House and what did we get out of it?" Hoover replies dryly, "What did anyone get out of it?" Looking around the room, Lou decides to take one of the paintings. Herbert: "You can't take that. It's government property." Lou:

Courtesy Irving Berlin
Hassard Short directs the "Man Bites Dog" number in *As Thousands Cheer*.

Vandamm; Culver Pictures, Inc.
The opening scene in Act One of *As Thousands Cheer*: President and Mrs. Hoover (Leslie Adams and Helen Broderick) packing up during their last day in the White House.

"Why can't I? The White House is lousy with paintings of George Washington." Then she gets a bright idea. Why not call up the Cabinet members and tell them exactly what he thinks of them? Hoover begins by gleefully telephoning his Secretary of State, Henry Stimson—and gives him the Bronx cheer.

Headline: BARBARA HUTTON TO WED PRINCE MDIVANI

Woolworth heiress Barbara Hutton (Marilyn Miller), the world's richest woman, is surrounded by assorted titled beaux. But only Georgian Prince Alexis Mdivani (Clifton Webb) is smart enough to woo her to the romantic strains of "How's Chances?"

Headline: HEAT WAVE HITS NEW YORK

The highly animated weather reporter (Ethel Waters) explains how the city's record hot spell had come from Martinique via a certain young lady who "started the heat wave by making her seat wave." Letitia Ide, José Limon and the Charles Weidman dancers help stir up a few breezes.

Headline: JOAN CRAWFORD TO DIVORCE DOUGLAS FAIRBANKS, JR.

The four-year marriage of screen stars Joan Crawford (Marilyn Miller) and Douglas Fairbanks, Jr. (Clifton Webb) is breaking up. But all that concerns them is which one will get the publicity rights to the divorce. Their problems are even more compounded when they receive word that there will be far less publicity than they had expected—Mary Pickford and Doug Sr. have just announced *their* separation.

Courtesy Irving Berlin
Ethel Waters creating her own "Heat Wave" in *As Thousands Cheer*.

Joan Crawford (Marilyn Miller) and Douglas Fairbanks, Jr. (Clifton Webb) discuss their coming divorce with movie czar Will Hays (Leslie Adams) in *As Thousands Cheer.*

Headline: *MAJESTIC SAILS AT MIDNIGHT*

Among the passengers are the representatives of England, Italy, Germany, and France (Leslie Adams, Hal Forde, Harry Stockwell, and Jerome Cowan) who have been in Washington discussing their countries' war debts. Now that the United States is off the gold standard, they sing that they are happy to pay their debts in silver—and, in the future, possibly zinc, tin, or wood. Helen Broderick, as the Statue of Liberty, cannot remember the words to "The Star-Spangled Banner," but she lustily sings:

> Let the pound go up—
> The franc go up—
> The mark go up as well,
> Uncle Sam will be in Heaven
> When the dollar goes to Hell!

Headline: LONELY-HEART COLUMN

Harry Stockwell pens his lonely appeal ("Miss Lonelyheart, what will I do?/ I am a lonely heart writing to you"), while his unrequited condition is illustrated by dancers Letitia Ide, José Limon and the ensemble.

Headline: WORLD'S WEALTHIEST MAN CELEBRATES 94th BIRTHDAY

At his birthday party, withered John D. Rockefeller (Clifton Webb) is being feted by the John D. Rockefeller, Jrs. (Leslie Adams and Helen Broderick). The climax comes when Junior wheels in a huge birthday cake shaped in the form of Rockefeller Center, and informs his father that his birthday present will be Radio City. The old man snorts: "This isn't a birthday present, it's a dirty joke." With mouth firm and eyes blazing, he picks up the cake knife and brandishes it in the air as he totters after his son croaking, "You sell it right back to the feller who sold it to you."

John D. Rockefeller (Clifton Webb) celebrates his 94th birthday with his son and daughter-in-law (Leslie Adams and Helen Broderick) in *As Thousands Cheer.*

Vandamm; courtesy Irving Berlin
Marilyn Miller in *As Thousands Cheer* with some of her favorites in "The Funnies":
Boob McNutt, Barney Google, the Katzenjammer Kids, Skippy, and Mickey Mouse.

Headline: THE FUNNIES

A little girl (Marilyn Miller) delights in the characters found on her favorite page in the paper. They obligingly come to life and dance with her.

Headline: "GREEN PASTURES" STARTS THIRD ROAD SEASON

In "To Be or Not to Be," Ethel Waters expresses irritation at the thespian aspirations of husband Hamtree Harrington, who can never get over the fact that he once had a line to read in *The Green Pastures*.

Headline: ROTOGRAVURE SECTION

An old-fashioned look, in browns and tans, of the Easter Parade of 1883. The scene opens with the strollers frozen behind a scrim, who then come to melodic life with Marilyn Miller and Clifton Webb leading the grand parade.

ACT II

Headline: METROPOLITAN OPERA OPENS IN OLD-TIME SPLENDOR

Not quite. The opera is now being broadcast over radio and the commercials are continually interrupting Verdi's *Rigoletto*.

Headline: UNKNOWN NEGRO LYNCHED BY FRENZIED MOB.

During 1933, there were 42 known lynchings in the South. The railroading of the nine "Scottsboro Boys" on the charge of raping a white woman was further cause for racial concern. It was against this background that Ethel Waters, in a dilapidated Southern shack, tries to set the dinner table for her two children. Suddenly she stops and in the searing lament, "Supper Time," pours out her anguish that "that man o' mine ain't comin' home no more."

Headline: GANDHI GOES ON HUNGER STRIKE

Because of his long-time opposition to British rule in India, Hindu leader Mahatma Gandhi had been imprisoned many times during his career. In May 1933, while still in jail, he had undergone a three-week fast to protest his country's treatment of the Untouchables. Also during the year, Aimee Semple MacPherson, the American evangelist, had continued to attract thousands to her Angelus Temple in Los Angeles to hear her fiery sermons preached from a floodlit pulpit. In this scene, Moss Hart devised a meeting of the two spiritual leaders. The skeletal Gandhi (Clifton Webb), who insists that the press take photographs of him as he fasts in a restaurant, is visited by Sister Aimee (Helen

Vandamm; Culver Pictures, Inc.
Mahatma Gandhi (Clifton Webb) and Aimee Semple MacPherson (Helen Broderick) in *As Thousands Cheer*.

Broderick). Because they are both experts at grabbing headlines, she suggests they form a team to sell religion. At the end they bound off the stage doing a soft-shoe dance.

Headline: REVOLT IN CUBA

The uprising against Cuban dictator Gerardo Machado had begun in April; by September, the "revolt of the sergeants" had led to Top Sergeant Fulgencio Batista assuming power as Chief of Staff. In an expressionist dance, revolutionaries Letitia Ide and José Limon reveal the seeds of their discontent.

Headline: NOËL COWARD, NOTED PLAYWRIGHT, RETURNS TO ENGLAND

All those working in the New York hotel where Noël Coward has stayed have come under his influence. Chambermaid Marilyn Miller, scrubwoman Ethel Waters and waiter Clifton Webb now affect clipped accents and spout attempted epigrams. Miss Miller even turns into Lynn Fontanne. Housekeeper Helen Broderick's deadpan reaction: "Well, I'll be goddamned!"

Vandamm; courtesy Irving Berlin
In *As Thousands Cheer*, scrubwoman Ethel Waters, maid Marilyn Miller, housekeeper Helen Broderick, and waiter Clifton Webb are all under the influence of Noël Coward.

Headline: SOCIETY WEDDING OF THE YEAR

Before a backdrop representing New York's fashionable St. Thomas' Church on Fifth Avenue, the assembled bridesmaids and ushers sing of the impending nuptials while awaiting the arrival of the bride and groom. When the curtains part, they reveal the young couple (Marilyn Miller and Clifton Webb) just awakening in bed together. Though they must hurry to the church, they still find time to sing their tender duet, "Our Wedding Day."

Headline: PRINCE OF WALES RUMORED ENGAGED

Royal consternation. Britain's Queen Mary (Helen Broderick), King George (Leslie Adams) and Prime Minister Ramsay MacDonald (Hal Forde) read about the Prince's recent Brazilian fling in Walter Winchell's column. So the Queen ("George, you stay out of this") summons her son (Thomas Hamilton) to get the lowdown. By this time, the real Prince of Wales, then 39, had already met Mrs. Wallis Warfield Spencer Simpson of Baltimore, the lady he would later marry.

Headline: JOSEPHINE BAKER STILL THE RAGE OF PARIS

St. Louis-born Josephine Baker has been a headliner at the Folies Bergère and the Casino de Paris ever since 1925. Here, *La Bahkair* (Ethel Waters), bored with her luxurious surroundings, admits in "Harlem on My Mind" that she secretly longs to return to her former hi-de-ho haunts.

Headline: SUPREME COURT HANDS DOWN IMPORTANT DECISION

And what could that be? That musicals are forbidden to end with reprises of their most popular numbers. One by one the principals try to conform to the time-honored tradition, and one by one they are silenced by the nine Supreme Court justices. The solution? A new song, of course: "Not for All the Rice in China," sung by Marilyn Miller and Clifton Webb.

Though the success of *As Thousands Cheer* was overwhelming, the revue had had its share of crises before reaching New York. Particularly involving two songs. As Irving Berlin remembers it: "I was

Vandamm; courtesy Irving Berlin
King George and Queen Mary (Leslie Adams and Helen Broderick), in *As Thousands Cheer*, want to know all about the escapades of their son, the Prince of Wales (Thomas Hamilton).

old-fashioned melody. Except that now, of course, I made the words apply to an Easter Parade.

"Then there was the problem of 'Supper Time.' Ethel Waters once said that if one song could tell the whole tragic story of her people, that was the song. And here it was in the middle of a big light-hearted revue! When we opened in New Haven, the number got very little applause. It was a real shock. People told me I was crazy to put in a dirge like that. They said it would kill the show. But I was equally convinced that a musical dealing with headline news needed at least one serious piece, and I knew that Ethel Waters had the quality to sing something really dramatic. After we got to Phila-delphia, we found that the show was shy about ten minutes in the music department. So I wrote a new opening, a new closing, and four new songs. One of them, 'Harlem on My Mind,' was also for Ethel Waters."

The opening-night critics comprised a solid cheer-ing section. But no one outdid the enthusiasm of John Mason Brown, who wrote: "I tremble to think of the fate that would await Miss Waters, Miss Miller, Miss Broderick, Mr. Webb, Mr. Ber-lin, Mr. Hart, and Mr. Harris if they had ventured to win laughs of the kind they won so freely Satur-day night while living in the shadow of the Kremlin, in Mussolini's Italy, in Hitler's Germany, in Doll-fuss's Austria, or even in the liberal England of George and Mary. Siberia, a firing squad, exile, or the darkest dungeon in the Tower would have been the mean thanks their exceptional talents would have received. Fortunately, America is more hospi-table to such monkeyshines. It relishes irreverence; delights in holding its headlines in check by means of good-natured laughter, and does not hesitate to stand up in meeting and mock them by their proper names. Its satire is as daring as it is convulsing, and proves conclusively in its own gay way that in spite of the many jibes and much evidence to the con-trary, America is still the land of the free, at least as far as entertainment is concerned, and that the Music Box continues to be the home of the brave."

By the time *Champagne, Sec* arrived on Broadway in October, New York had already seen two previ-ous English-language versions of Johann Strauss's *Die Fledermaus—The Merry Countess* in 1912 and *A Wonderful Night* as recently as 1929. The new Dwight Deere Wiman production, adapted by Lawrence Langner under the *nom de drame* of Alan

stuck for a song for the Rotogravure Section. I'd written a couple of old-fashioned-type songs but they were lousy. So I reached back to something I'd written in 1917. It went, 'Smile and show your dimple, you'll find it's very simple . . .' It was a poor imitation of the cheer-up kind of songs of the day, like 'Pack Up Your Troubles in Your Old Kit Bag.' But I'd always liked the main four-bar theme. So for *As Thousands Cheer*, instead of trying to write a new old-fashioned melody I simply used a real

White Studio; Theatre Coll., NY Public Lib.
Helen Ford as Adele and Kitty Carlisle as Prince Orlovsky in *Champagne, Sec*, a new version of Strauss's *Die Fledermaus*.

Child, was generally well received, with the loudest applause reserved for Kitty Carlisle making her New York bow in the male role of Prince Orlovsky. While the production contained much that sparkled and bubbled, it unfortunately recalled a Vienna all too far removed from the city as it was in 1933. For ever since coming to power the previous March, German Chancellor Hitler had made it clear that he aimed to gain control of the country of his birth. He had, in fact, been stirring up so much agitation within Austria that Chancellor Engelbert Dollfuss had been forced to dissolve the local Nazi party. And on the very day *Champagne, Sec* opened, Hitler ordered the German delegation to walk out of the League of Nations' Disarmament Conference.

It was brave of producer Sam Harris and all the others involved with *Of Thee I Sing* to attempt a sequel. But inviting comparisons was only one of the problems that plagued the follow-up production, *Let 'Em Eat Cake*. The mood was excessively sour, the plotting contrived, and much of the satire had an uncertain point of view.

The new musical took up the fortunes of President John P. Wintergreen and Vice President Alexander Throttlebottom (William Gaxton and Victor Moore again) after their defeat for reelection. Fol-

lowing an unsuccessful business venture manufacturing blue shirts (this, like corn muffins, was another Mary Turner Wintergreen speciality), Wintergreen leads a blue-shirted army (recalling the Nazis' brown shirts and the Fascists' black shirts) in a bloodless overthrow of the government. He sets up a "Dictatorship of the Proletariat" and faces such adversaries as the Supreme Court, foreign countries who renege on their war debts, and a counterrevolution. All this might have been accepted as a timely warning except that Wintergreen was supposed to be the hero! The authors further expected audiences to be amused when, on the basis of his having made an unpopular decision as umpire of a baseball game between the Supreme Court and the nine debt-owing nations, poor Throttlebottom must pay for his sins by being guillotined along with deposed dictator Wintergreen. They were both saved, of course, by loyal Mary Wintergreen (played by loyal Lois Moran) who stirred up the women of America to counter the counterrevolutionaries' ban on all but blue dresses.

White Studio; Theatre Coll., NY Public Lib.
Mary Wintergreen (Lois Moran), in *Let 'Em Eat Cake*, pleads to the women of America to save the life of deposed Vice Dictator Throttlebottom (Victor Moore). Deposed Dictator Wintergreen (William Gaxton), wearing his striped prison pants, awaits his turn at the guillotine.

The satire rang truest in the George and Ira Gershwin score. There was good fun at the expense of Union Square radicals ("Happiness will fill our cup/ When it's down with everything that's up"). There were well-placed digs at the Union League Club ("Cloistered from the noisy city/ Standing pat and sitting pretty"), whose moribund members agree to back the revolution once Throttlebottom spreads the alarm that the British are marching on Bunker Hill. And there was a jaunty routine by the foreign diplomats who, whenever summoned to discuss the war debt, can only respond musically with "It's very very funny/ But each time you mention money/ No comprenez, no capish, no versteh." The show also had a title song, in which Wintergreen, proclaiming "The New Day is here!" offers the downtrodden masses not only bread but cake.

Among the reviewers, only Percy Hammond ("as keen, wholesome and lovely a show as it seems possible for the powers to fabricate") favored it over *Of Thee I Sing*. Other notices, while admiring the show's daring, were quick to point out its shortcomings. Brooks Atkinson's verdict: "More like a rowdy improvisation in one bitter, hysterical mood than a stage entertainment."

Few musicals that have since been anointed as classics were ever received by so divided a press as was *Roberta*, the lone November entry. Out of the nine daily critics only two (Anderson and Gabriel) thought highly of it, two (Atkinson and Hammond) liked it but had reservations, two (Mantle and Bernard Sobel of the *Mirror*) were more negative than positive, and three (Lockridge, Brown and Garland) said forget it. To Robert Benchley, "its bad points are so distracting that it turns out to be one of those praiseworthy musicals during which one is constantly looking at one's program to see how much more of it there is going to be."

Of course, Max Gordon gave it a tastefully elegant production (cost: $92,000); complete with eye-dazzling sets and costumes (it was, after all, about a couturiere's establishment). Of course, its Jerome Kern melodies had the proper ear-clinging qualities. And of course it had its share of talented performers (including Lyda Roberti, Tamara, Bob Hope, Ray Middleton, Fay Templeton, Sydney Greenstreet, and George Murphy). But what was most distressing was that the close weaving of music and story that had so distinguished *The Cat and the Fiddle* and *Music in the Air* had all but disappeared

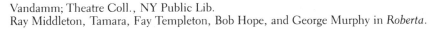

Vandamm; Theatre Coll., NY Public Lib.
Ray Middleton, Tamara, Fay Templeton, Bob Hope, and George Murphy in *Roberta*.

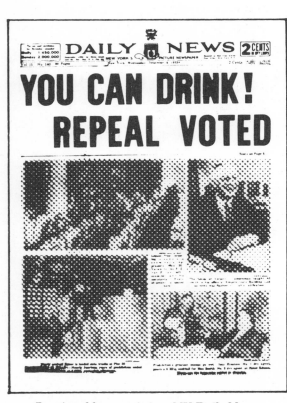

Reprinted by permission, *NY Daily News*.

in an ill-fitting formula show (even the approving John Anderson said "the book and music have nothing in common except a cast").

There were jokes. He: "Underneath she has a heart that's gold." She: "Did you say 'gold' or 'cold'?" Or, "Long dresses don't bother me. I have a good memory." There were lyrics. "When I think of who you are/ What a gem true blue you are" in "You're Devastating." Or, "Joyous free and flaming life forsooth was mine" in "Yesterdays." Or, "So I chaffed them and I gaily laughed" in "Smoke Gets in Your Eyes." And there was a story about an American college halfback who inherits his aunt's dress salon in Paris and falls in love with a Russian princess. It was, according to John Mason Brown, "as eventful as a ride on the shuttle."

But *Roberta* did have those Jerome Kern songs going for it. Especially "Smoke Gets in Your Eyes,"

which Tamara sang while seated on a bare stage wearing a peasant costume and stroking a guitar.

Partly because of the widespread popularity of this song, the musical, after a few shaky weeks, found its audience and became the second longest running production of the year.

All December offered was the indefatigable Lew Leslie and his third *Blackbirds* revue. Even Bill Robinson couldn't keep it winging past the New Year, and it closed in three weeks.

Christmas and New Year's Eve, however, turned out to be particularly festive occasions in 1933. On December 5, Utah became the 36th—and deciding —state to ratify the 21st Amendment to the Constitution, thereby repealing the 18th. For the first time in almost fourteen years, liquor was being guzzled legally all over the country.

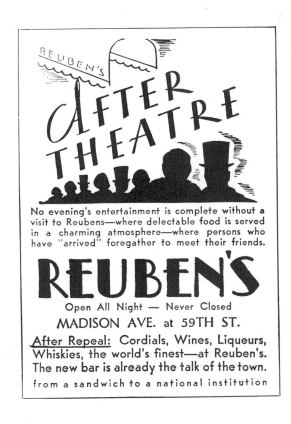

Culver Pictures, Inc.
Times Square, New York.

CHAPTER V

"...DREAMERS WITH EMPTY HANDS..."

During 1934 the spirally decline of the nation's economy was at last showing some signs of being checked, if not actually reversed. The rush rush rush of experimention and innovation was beginning to slow down even though the year did introduce three new major initialed federal agencies—the Securities and Exchange Commission (SEC), the Federal Housing Administration (FHA), and the Federal Communications Commission (FCC). But opposition to the New Deal and its bureaucratic regulations was beginning to be heard—and from all sides. Radicals attacked Roosevelt for moving too slowly; conservatives damned him as a dictator. The NRA found itself constantly embroiled in dissention and was obviously losing momentum and effectiveness. In the fall of the year, its chief, Hugh Johnson, would bow to mounting pressures and resign. The grim fact was that despite all the government's efforts, unemployment was still a serious problem, with almost five million families on relief. The encouraging fact was that the number of jobholders rose during 1934 by almost 2,300,000.

Musical shows somehow found this a time to try new ways to tell old tales. The year saw the *Ziegfeld Follies* brought back by Ziegfeld's old rivals, the Shubert brothers. It also found Max Gordon, whose name had become synonomous with modern, innovative musicals, choosing to revive the waltzes of the two Johann Strausses in *The Great Waltz*, and hiring the bright and brittle Moss Hart to write its libretto. The equally bright and brittle Noël Coward restored the elegance of the Regency period in *Conversation Piece*, while Howard Dietz and Arthur Schwartz, those purveyors of the sleek and the smart, dug up an ancient Spanish fable as

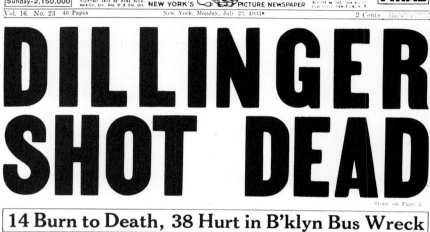

Reprinted by permission, *NY Daily News*

inspiration for their *Revenge with Music*. Even Balfe's *Bohemian Girl* was resurrected as *Gypsy Blonde*. And as indicated by its title, *Anything Goes*, the year's top attraction, was a prime example of spit-and-glue musical comedy at its protean best. Perhaps the clearest indication of all about the mood of the musical theatre in 1934 was that—by a ratio of 8 to 3—there were more costume operettas produced on Broadway than there were contemporary book musicals.

Not that the year was totally without progress. A surrealistic opera, *4 Saints in 3 Acts*, found itself in a Broadway theatre. The Shuberts' *Life Begins at 8:40*, the best of seven revues presented during the year, was notable for its contemporary style, decor and satirical wit. And New Face Leonard Sillman brought in the first of his sporadic series of tyro talent shows.

The year also found room to display some of the theatre's prize funnymen and funnywomen, with Victor Moore (*Anything Goes*) and Bert Lahr (*Life Begins at 8:40*) taking honors for the men, and Fanny Brice (*Ziegfeld Follies*) and Ethel Merman (*Anything Goes*) winning the palms for the ladies. In the crowded operetta field, Yvonne Printemps was reason enough to visit *Conversation Piece*. Among music men, Cole Porter surely gave the best account with his hit-filled score for *Anything Goes*. Notable newcomers? Brice Hutchins (who would soon become known under his real name, Robert Cummings) and Eve Arden (who had just changed her name from Eunice Quedens) both in the *Follies*; Henry Fonda and Charles Walters in *New Faces*; Judy Canova, Martha Raye and Ella Logan in *Calling All Stars*. Of the 20 musicals presented during the year, *Anything Goes*, *The Great Waltz* and *Life Begins at 8:40* had showings that went over the 200-performance mark.

If the artistic trend of most of the year's musicals found them looking backward, the economic trend of the theatre in general was definitely moving upward: the average weekly gross, for both musicals and nonmusicals, rose from $228,000 in 1933 to $381,000 in 1934. There was even a slight boost in the overall number of new productions, from 132 to 152. Among the most highly regarded dramas and comedies were two by Sidney Howard, *Dodsworth* and *Yellow Jack*; Kaufman and Hart's *Merrily We Roll Along*; Henry Fonda in *The Farmer Takes a Wife*; *The Children's Hour* by Lillian Hellman; and Samson Raphaelson's *Accent on Youth*.

Far from Broadway, however, the year had its share of tragedies. Principally the dust storms that blew some 300 million tons of topsoil from Texas, Oklahoma, Kansas, and Colorado clear across the country. As a result, Okies and Arkies, some 350,000 farmers in all, began their spirit-breaking trek to California. The S.S. *Morro Castle* went down in flames with a loss of 125 lives. The arrest of Bruno Richard Hauptmann for the death of the Lindbergh baby was a chilling reminder of the two-and-a-half-year-old crime. Deaths of the year included Bonnie Parker and Clyde Barrow, Public Enemy Number One John Dillinger, and foreign leaders Chancellor Dollfuss of Austria (assassinated by Nazis) and President Paul von Hindenburg of Germany. But the year also brought five notable births: the Dionne Quintuplets.

At first the Broadway musical-comedy year looked almost too normal. Another *Ziegfeld Follies*. Here we go again with Fanny Brice in her sixth edition plus veteran comics Willie and Eugene Howard. More of the good old days. But not exactly. For one thing, it was a Ziegfeldless *Follies*, with the Messrs. Shubert taking over the reins at the request of Ziegfeld's debt-ridden widow, Billie Burke. For another, the experienced hand of director Bobby Connolly had let things slip so badly during the out-of-town tryouts that John Murray Anderson had to be rushed in to take charge. As composer Vernon Duke once recalled, "After weeks of quarrels, tantrums, firings, hirings, Connolly's disappearances, Lee Shubert's dreaded entrances, money and tears flowing, stagehands fleeing, we got off to an unpromising start in Boston." And the show, which cost $110,000 to bring in, would remain unpromising almost until the January 4th premiere at the Winter Garden.

Ben Pinchot
Willie Howard and Fanny Brice in the *Ziegfeld Follies* takeoff on the play, *Sailor Beware*.

Alfredo Valente
Judith Barron and Brice Hutchins (Robert Cummings)
sing "I Like the Likes of You" in the *Ziegfeld Follies*.

"Only God can make a knee—and that's where we come in," chimed the fifty chorus girls reassuringly in the opening number. But the accent of the show was less on leg joints than on comedy. Particularly Fanny Brice comedy. As "Soul-Saving Sadie," a "reformed substitute," she did a takeoff on Aimee Semple MacPherson ("I'm Soul-Saving Sadie from Avenue A/ Vending salvation and making it pay"). As "Sunshine Sarah," she did a spoof on "noodists." As "Countess Dubinsky," without her kolinsky, who right down to her skinsky is working for Minsky, she was a leering, ogling fan dancer. As Baby Snooks, she appeared as a bratty, lying kid, completely unimpressed by the story of George Washington and the cherry tree. Willie Howard, somewhat overshadowed by Miss Brice, had his moments too, especially in a sketch dealing with the frequency with which dictators take over in Cuba. After appearing as the outgoing El Presidente, Willie reappeared in the same sombrero and scraggly mustachio as the incoming El Presidente, proclaiming the New Raw Deal, and sporting a bull's-eye on his back as the one sure protection against being shot by his fellow countrymen. And both Fanny and Willie, as Stonewall Annie and Dyna-

mite Moe, had themselves a wildly bawdy time kidding the current Broadway smash, *Sailor Beware*.

Two melancholy melodies by Billy Hill, "Wagon Wheels" (sung by Everett Marshall in blackface) and "The Last Roundup" (sung by Don Ross in chaps and spurs, and reprised by Willie Howard with a Yiddish accent) became the popular hits. However, two Yip Harburg–Vernon Duke pieces, "I Like the Likes of You" and "What Is There to Say?" were more in keeping with the stylish flavor of the revue.

One daringly somber note was struck in the *Follies* with "To the Beat of the Heart," an impassioned indictment of—no less—both war and the League of Nations. The League, which had been launched with such high hopes following the World War, had first shown its impotence in 1931 when it was unable to force Japan to withdraw from Manchuria. Instead, Japan withdrew from the League. Hitler's accession as Germany's Fuehrer following president von Hindenburg's death had further pointed up the League's weaknesses when it was powerless to prevent Germany from rearming. Germany, too, stalked out of the League in 1933. To lyricist Harburg and composer Samuel Pokrass, it was obvious

that something more personal was needed to maintain world peace. In the *Follies*, the curtains part to reveal a beautifully landscaped terrace on the League of Nations grounds in Geneva. Uniformed officers of various countries gaily waltz with their ladies. Suddenly, there is a drum roll, the dancing stops and the men snap to attention. Before a backdrop of specters with death scythes in their hands, soldiers slog through no-man's-land until they drop, while Everett Marshall sets the theme:

> From the shores of death they come
> Without a bugle or a drum
> It's the tramp, tramp, tramp
>   of the unknown men.
> Glorified hosts
> Of marching ghosts
> Crying, "Why why why
> Did we die die die
>   in vain?
> Why were we slain?"

The chorus that followed was an impassioned plea that men allow themselves to be led not by the beat of a drum but by the beat of the heart. However, the mood of indifference returns after the song as, once again, the officers are twirling their ladies round and round the terrace. Unfortunately, only Boston saw the number staged that way. By the time the revue got to Broadway, though the song still remained, it was presented much more simply with the emphasis on showing off the girls in a variety of military drills.

January ended in *Zenda* fashion with an operetta, *All the King's Horses* (king becomes movie star; movie star becomes king). The reviews were divided, with "enjoyable," "ingratiating" and "pleasant" vying with "lumbering," "old-fashioned" and "musty." The public sided—more or less—with the affirmative verdicts and the operetta lasted a surprising 120 performances.

Opera—or as the program redundantly explained, "An opera to be sung"—made its way to Broadway with *4 Saints in 3 Acts*. It opened February 20 under the sponsorship of Harry Moses, "by special arrangement with the Friends and Enemies of Modern Music." Immediately the work became the town's most controversial theatrical entertainment. The Gertrude Stein text and the Maurice Grosser scenario were far out, surrealistic, completely unrelated to the worlds of either musical theatre or opera. It was, quite possibly, the most beautifully scored, sung and staged non sequitur of all times.

To begin with, of the four saints of the title, one, St. Theresa, has an alter ego to allow her to talk to herself. And she—was played by a man. Also, the work was presented in four acts, not three. Recalling the origins of the opera, composer Virgil Thomson once wrote: "In 1927 I asked Gertrude Stein if she would like to write me an opera libretto. She said yes she would and she did. *4 Saints* is about saints in Spain, chiefly St. Theresa of Avila and St. Ignatius Loyola. Gertrude was very attached to Spain which she had often visited. And I was

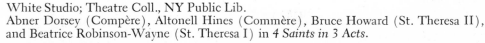

White Studio; Theatre Coll., NY Public Lib.
Abner Dorsey (Compère), Altonell Hines (Commère), Bruce Howard (St. Theresa II), and Beatrice Robinson-Wayne (St. Theresa I) in *4 Saints in 3 Acts*.

attached to religious music because I had spent my youth as a church organist in Missouri. So she made a libretto for me which showed saints moving about in Spain doing all the things that saints do, such as praying, singing hymns, seeing visions, performing miracles, traveling and organizing . . . In the first act St. Theresa is posed in a series of living pictures on the steps of the cathedral at Avila—a sort of Sunday school entertainment showing scenes from her saintly life. The second act is an outdoor party. The third act takes place in a monastery garden with St. Ignatius seeing the Holy Ghost ('Pigeons on the grass alas'), and drilling his Jesuit disciples in military discipline. In an epilogue called Act Four all the saints hold communion in heaven while the choir chants 'When this you see remember me.' "

The verses devised by Miss Stein deliberately used words less for literal meaning than to evoke something of the childlike gaiety and mysticism of the leading characters. In general, critics praised the all-Negro cast (that had been Thomson's idea), the stirring music, and Florine Stettheimer's cellophane settings, but had themselves a ball kidding Miss Stein's all too vulnerable libretto. Wrote Lawrence Gilman in the *Herald Tribune*: "Virgil Thomson is a composer is a rose is a rose is a rosemary for remembrance is Alice B. Toklas Toklas Toklas Tok is last but not least is Gertrude Saint Gertrude in three or four or fifty acts is good clean fun clean fun clean fun—which is a fact."

Newness of a more corporeal nature distinguished *New Faces*, which Leonard Sillman shepherded to Broadway in mid-March. Sillman had first produced the revue the previous May in Pasadena as *Low and Behold*, and, encouraged by Lee Shubert's offer to produce it, brought it east under the doting eyes of patronesses Elsie Janis and Mary Pickford. But Shubert kept stalling so long that Miss Janis eventually had to persuade the ailing Charles Dillingham to come out of retirement to be its nominal sponsor. Fact was that Dillingham, once one of the most successful Broadway producers, was then near poverty and was grateful to accept the offer of a salary in exchange for the use of his name. Once so prominent a man of the theatre became associated with the enterprise, the way was paved for the necessary $15,000 it cost to open the show. Even so, 137 auditions were needed to raise the money before they could raise the curtain.

Elfin Imogene Coca in *New Faces*.

New Faces had a cast of twenty-four, including Imogene Coca (the only not quite new face whose Broadway career had begun in 1925 in *When You Smile*), composer-singer James Shelton, dancer Charles Walters, actor Henry Fonda (he had just left a job as Humphrey Bogart's understudy in *I Loved You Wednesday*), singer Louise "Teddy" Lynch, and writer-actress Nancy Hamilton (she had recently been Katharine Hepburn's understudy in *The Warrior's Husband*, so, fittingly, she did a Hepburn imitation in the revue). There was one actor whom everyone had wanted but who posed a problem because of his physical similarity to his good friend, Henry Fonda. After his audition they tossed a coin to see which one would be signed. Henry Fonda won, James Stewart lost.

The reviewers who attended *New Faces* were impressed by its dewy, high-spirited and somewhat precocious manner—and also its inescapable re-

Alfredo Valente
Henry Fonda in *New Faces*.

semblance to *The Garrick Gaieties*. Among its comic highlights was Imogene Coca, wearing Chuck Walters' buttoned-up polo coat, walking casually across the stage carrying a single ostrich feather. Grinning impishly, she held it aloft and announced to the audience: "Fan Dance." There was also much praise for a sketch in which Walt Disney's Three Little Pigs enacted their tale in the manner of three different recent plays—*Ah, Wilderness!*, *The Green Bay Tree*, and *Tobacco Road* ("I ain't et anything, pappy, since we et mammy last week"). Musical highlights included James Shelton singing his own "Gutter Song" ("She's resting in the gutter and she lovvvvvvves it!") and "Lamplight" (soon to become a Hal Kemp favorite), and also Billie Heywood doing "My Last Affair."

The summer months, usually reserved for—if anything—lighthearted revues, were ushered in by two operettas in June: *Caviar* (American prima donna marries Russian prince for publicity) and *Gypsy Blonde* (Balfe's *Bohemian Girl* in the marble halls of Westchester). *Keep Moving*, the August entry, reverted to the more expected type. It was a revue featuring Tom Howard and the Singer Midgets, and it moved out after 20 performances.

The 1934–1935 season began a bit early with the Shubert revue, *Life Begins at 8:40*, opening late in August. Building on what Lee minus J. J. had accomplished the previous year with the *New Americana*, the revue was a smart, artistic, imaginative entertainment bearing relationship to both *The Band Wagon* (in its style) and *As Thousands Cheer* (in its topicality). Primarily responsible for the chicness and sheen were two *Ziegfeld Follies* hold-overs, director John Murray Anderson and designer Albert Johnson, who were now given a far freer hand. Gone were the accustomed secondhand look, the gauze curtains, and the gaudy display of half-naked showgirls that had long distinguished Shubert revues. As Anderson explained at the time, "There are no drapes, no drops, no hanging scenery of any sort. All the sets are built either in full size or in miniature, but they are all constructed sets. Our revolving stage also includes an inner and an outer rim so that two groups of dancers, interpreting, say, sentimental and satirical themes, can be poised against each other for contrasting effect. Sort of a contrapuntal ballet." The opening scene in the revue made particularly imaginative use of this device, with a charmingly ornate mechanical clock revolving center stage while masked performers, mounted on wooden discs on the outer rim, circled past in the opposite direction. Each time the clock would turn around the performers would strike poses depicting the typical ingredients of a revue: the comic, the crooner, the hoofer, the husband-lover-wife sketch, etc., with the chorus chiming appropriate musical commentary introduced by the recurrent lines, "At exactly eight-forty or thereabout, this little play world—not of the day world—comes to life."

Life Begins at 8:40 (the title had been inspired by Walter Pitkin's bestseller, *Life Begins at Forty*) was, in fact if not in name, the successor to the previous season's *Ziegfeld Follies*. In it Bert Lahr was seen at the height of his technique, displaying a control and subtlety that made his burlesquing all the more hilarious. His highborn Frenchman contemplating suicide, his stage Englishman with a frozen upper lip, and his Wall Street investor about to be clipped again by his broker were all major additions to Lahr's gallery of inspired lunacy. Ray Bolger was at his best in the skit, "The Window Dresser Goes to Bed," in which he arranged his clothes as if he were still on the job, and his dance interpretation of the recent Max Baer–Primo Carnera heavyweight championship fight (Baer won).

The contributions of Ira Gershwin, Yip Harburg and Harold Arlen were especially well received. In a jaunty mood were "You're a Builder-Upper" (". . . a breaker-downer, a holder-outer, but I'm a giver-inner") and the itinerary of delayed adventure, "Let's Take a Walk Around the Block." "What Can You Say in a Love Song?" (". . . that hasn't been said before") spoofed the love song itself in scenes depicting excessively ardent couples in 1780, 1880 and 1934.

But the greatest acclaim was saved for the special material. At a ladies garden party, Bert Lahr did an uproarious takeoff on a stuffy concert singer spluttering about the "utter utter utter loveliness of things" (the scene ended with a sweet old lady throwing a pie in his face). In a disillusioned mood, Luella Gear revealed that even after trying such aids to romance as Fleischmann's Yeast, Kellogg's Bran and Coty's Sunburn Tan, "I Couldn't Hold My Man" ("I even bought the Five Foot Shelf/ But I'm still sleeping by myself"). There was a "Quartet Erotica," with Lahr as Balzac, Bolger as Boccaccio, Brian Donlevy (yes, Brian Donlevy) as de Maupassant, and James MacColl as Rabelais lamenting their fall from favor as creators of popular pornography. "We thought that our erotica was very very hotica," they chorused, but today found, "A volume like *Ulysses* makes us look like four big sissies."

The revue's finale, "Life Begins at City Hall," was a freewheeling burlesque of life under New York's recently elected reform mayor, the peppery Fiorello LaGuardia ("a fellow who never curries favor nor favors Curry," went one of the lines in

White Studio; Culver Pictures, Inc.
Ray Bolger and Dixie Dunbar dance to "You're a Builder-Upper" in *Life Begins at 8:40.*

reference to his opposition to Tammany Hall's iron-fisted boss). As part of LaGuardia's campaign to beautify the city, the mayor (Lahr) is about to launch a gondola to Staten Island, with Mr. and Mrs. Jimmy Walker (Ray Bolger and Frances Williams) as stowaways and four Grover Whalens in attendance. Rushing in to help officiate at the ceremony is the nation's peripatetic First Lady, Eleanor Roosevelt (Miss Gear), who breathlessly reveals her day's activities:

At seven o'clock this morning in Poughkeepsie
I spoke at the opening of a bridle path
Had breakfast in Savannah and flew to Indiana
To dedicate a ladies Turkish bath.
I christened a ferris wheel in Chattanooga
And then I unveiled a western barbecue;
A Warner Brothers palace I opened next in Dallas
And here I am to launch a gondola for you.

The night after *Life Begins* began, *Saluta* came to town and received less than enthusiastic greetings

LET'S TAKE A WALK AROUND THE BLOCK

MESSRS SHUBERT PRESENT

LIFE BEGINS AT 8:40

A MUSICAL REVUE
WITH
BERT LAHR
RAY BOLGER
LUELLA GEAR &
FRANCES WILLIAMS

LYRICS BY
IRA GERSHWIN
& E. Y. HARBURG
MUSIC BY
HAROLD ARLEN

SHOEIN' THE MARE
FUN TO BE FOOLED
YOU'RE A BUILDER UPPER
WHAT CAN YOU SAY IN A LOVE SONG?
LET'S TAKE A WALK AROUND THE BLOCK

A
JOHN MURRAY ANDERSON
PRODUCTION

HARMS
NEW YORK
CHAPPELL & C° LTD
LONDON SYDNEY
MADE IN U.S.A.

THE CENTER THEATRE

PROGRAM PUBLISHED BY THE NEW YORK THEATRE PROGRAM CORPOR.

BEGINNING
MONDAY EVENING,
DECEMBER 17, 1934

NRA

MATINEES
WEDNESDAY A
SATURDAY

MAX GORDON

Presents

A New Musical Play

Production Conceived and Directed by

HASSARD SHORT

THE GREAT WALTZ

Book by MOSS HART

Lyrics by DESMOND CARTER

Music by

JOHANN STRAUSS

(Father and Son)

Dances and Ballet by ALBERTINA RASCH

Settings by ALBERT JOHNSON . . . . Costumes by DORIS ZINKEISEN
Additional Costume Designs including Bridesmaids and Ballet by Irene Sharaff
Orchestra under the direction of FRANK TOURS
Book based on the libretto by Dr. A. M. Willmer, Heinz Reichert, Ernst Marischka, Caswell Garth, Desmond Carter

Lighting, Staging, Scenic and Mechanical Effects
Created by
HASSARD SHORT

(Burns Mantle gave it a Bronx saluta). Milton Berle, of the nightclub and vaudeville circuits, not only was the featured comedian but also shared lyric-writing credit. The show desperately tried for topicality: it was all about a gang of Italian mobsters who force Berle to go to Italy to stage an opera in competition with Mussolini's state-owned company. The Italian dictator was even depicted on stage, coming in at the end to smash the underworld ring and save our hero's life. John Anderson found it "so feeble as to be practically bed-ridden," and it soon folded after a loss of over $60,000 for its producer, wealthy Wall Street broker, Arthur Lipper, Jr. (whose identity was hidden under the pseudonym, R. A. Reppil).

If the brothers Shubert could switch artistic signals with *Life Begins at 8:40*, so surely could Max Gordon with *The Great Waltz*. And he could best them at their own operetta game. Hassard Short, having staged the Viennese *Waltzes from Vienna* in London, prevailed upon Gordon to produce a local version of the story of the bickering Johann Strausses, *Vater und Sohn*. But the producer didn't want to do just another slushy operetta. No, he would get Moss Hart, then best known for his satiric *As Thousands Cheer*, to do the adaptation, and he would house his production in the

mammoth Center Theatre at Rockefeller Center, which was then being used for movies. And when Gordon got all finished with it, what did he have? Another slushy operetta, only on a more opulent scale than anything that had ever been attempted before.

Apart from the Strauss music, the attraction of *The Great Waltz* (as it was called in New York) was the theatre it was housed in and the wonders therein that could be wrought. The Center seated 3,822 people, with an orchestra capacity greater than the entire New Amsterdam Theatre. The stage was a marvel of electronic magic, with cantilevered and revolving platforms to shift and move scenery in full view of the audience, and an orchestra pit that could rise and travel wherever anyone wanted it to go.

When *The Great Waltz* opened on September 22, the sheer statistics dwarfed anything else then on view. There were 42 principals and assorted feature players, 100 singers in the chorus, 40 Albertina Rasch dancers, 53 musicians in the pit, and a backstage crew of 91. Over 500 costumes were needed, including replicas of all the dress-parade uniforms of the entire Austrian army. And it cost the staggering sum of $246,000. (Cole Porter was to celebrate the fund raising later in the year in a

Vandamm; Theatre Coll., NY Public Lib.
"The Blue Danube" sequence in *The Great Waltz*. That's Papa Strauss (H. Reeves-Smith) interrupting the proceedings as son Schani (Guy Robertson) leads the orchestra.

line in the title song of *Anything Goes*: "When Rockefeller still can hoard en-ough money to let Max Gordon produce his shows, Anything Goes!")

The Great Waltz could certainly lay claim to having the most spectacular theatrical climax of the decade. The scene was Dommayer's Gardens in Vienna. First a brass band parades across the stage and there is a fireworks display. Everyone is awaiting the arrival of the Waltz King, Johann Strauss, Sr., who is to conduct. But a Russian countess has made sure he will not be there, and she convinces the restaurant owner that Strauss's son, Schani, would be the perfect replacement. Young Strauss strides to the podium in the orchestra pit and strikes up the shimmering strains of "The Blue Danube." As the musicians play, they are lifted bodily to the level of the stage, moved slowly back to the rear, and are elevated again to a balcony. All the while, the setting itself is falling into place—eight blazing chandeliers, each illuminated by sixty light bulbs, float down from above, and ten columns, each aglow with thirty candles, are wheeled in from left and right. Thus the scene is transformed from a simple garden into a glittering, eye-boggling sight of musicians sawing and trumpeting away, thirty couples waltzing gaily across the stage rimmed by twenty-four military dancers in white-plumed shakos. Throughout everything, the theatre's amplifiers are raising the decibel count with the hypnotic melody created by the new Waltz King being crowned this night. Even Papa Strauss eventually shows up to give his blessing.

Which is more than most critics did. Although Burns Mantle awarded the musical his seldom-awarded "****" and Percy Hammond termed it a "refined and lovely mammoth," other appraisers seemed determined to outdo each other with the waspishness of their comments. "More of a great waste than a Great Waltz," harrumphed Gilbert Gabriel. "The mouse labored and brought forth a *papier maché* mountain," snorted George Jean Nathan. "The town's most brilliant parade going. I suspect, nowhere," snooted John Anderson. "A great big beautiful bore that chases itself around in circles," hooted Robert Garland. But the customers, over a million of them, kept oohing and ahhing, and the waltzers kept whirling and twirling for 298 performances. At a $3.30 top price, the show even made a little money.

Another nosegay of a gayer past, the London import *Conversation Piece* was Noël Coward's elegant return to Regency England. It had charm, great globs of it, the brilliant, scintillating Yvonne Printemps (for whom it had been written), period flavor, brittle humor, tender romance, and no audience. How indeed could anyone be expected to beat a path to its doors when even the favorable reviewers—and the press was decidedly divided—used such terms as Robert Garland's "mannered and immaterial" and John Anderson's "lace handkerchief theater." Unfortunately, while Mlle. Printemps won deserved praise, few seemed to appreciate the beauties of the score, though Percy Hammond did allow that " 'I'll Follow My Secret Heart' is worthy of Harry Akst [*sic*], Sigmund Romberg, or Irving Berlin." Mr. Coward's own summation of his work: "The play itself has, I think, a certain amount of charm. The lyrics are good and the music excellent."

Conversation Piece was, admittedly, perhaps too special for mass New York appeal. Two weeks after it opened, on November 8, a musical comedy appeared that was, by all accounts, cut to everyone's taste. *Say When* featured a popular nightclub entertainer in Harry Richman, a bright young comic in Bob Hope, a slight but funny story about a couple of vaudevillians who break into both radio and Long Island society, and a melodic score (by Ted Koehler and Ray Henderson) by turns breezy ("When Love Comes Swinging Along") and tender ("Say when—so my heart may beat,/ So our lips may meet . . ."). Almost to a man the critics greeted the show with what Broadway calls "money" notices: "A lively show, made to order for the itinerant trade of the Great White Way"—Atkinson . . . "A good, lively, lusty show"—Gabriel . . . "A daffy and hilarious show"—Anderson . . . "Above par Broadway musical comedy"—Hammond . . . "Amusing, fast-moving, merry and tuneful"—Brown . . . "Should run indefinitely with everybody's blessing"—Lockridge . . . "Crackles with wisecracks and rumbles with melodies that are the lifeblood of Broadway"—Mantle . . . "More laughs than your ticket calls for"—Garland . . . "A real musical comedy"—Benchley . . . "Merriest laugh, song and girl show in town"—Winchell. No mannered, immaterial, lace-handkerchief theatre

104

White Studio; Theatre Coll., NY Public Lib.
Pierre Fresnay and Yvonne Printemps in *Conversation Piece.*

Vandamm
Harry Richman and Bob Hope, as a couple of vaudevillians, in *Say When.*

this. So *Say When* settled down for a long and prosperous run, right? No it didn't. It didn't even last three months. The producers knew when to say when but nobody could really say why.

Well, maybe there was a partial reason. Maybe it had to do with the competition that loomed over Broadway just two weeks following the *Say When* opening. *Anything Goes* had everything. It was the quintessential musical comedy of the mid-Thirties, and audiences flocked to it in such numbers that it became not only the biggest hit of the year but the fourth longest running musical of the decade. And it was conceived in disaster.

Remember *Pardon My English* back in 1931? That lulu that caused producer Vinton Freedley to skip the country? While safely if temporarily free from creditors, Freedley spent most of his time in a boat fishing off the Pearl Islands in the Pacific Ocean. As he fished he dreamed of a comeback. It would be with a musical comedy, of course, but not just another musical comedy. It would be a super musical comedy. Freedley would hire the theatre's outstanding comedy team, William Gaxton and Victor Moore. His female lead would be his own discovery, Ethel Merman. For the story,

he'd get the theatre's wittiest librettists, P. G. Wodehouse and Guy Bolton (Bolton had already co-authored Aarons' and Freedley's *Girl Crazy*). As for the score, since the Gershwin brothers were tied up with an opera, of all things, it didn't take much more dreaming to come up with the logical replacement: Cole Porter.

Once his debts were paid off, the producer began rounding up his people. He made a hurried trip to France, where Wodehouse was living, and outlined to him and Bolton (who had come over from England) a rough idea of what he wanted: something to do with a group of oddball characters on board a pleasure ship and the way they react to a shipwreck. Freedley returned, signed his stars and song writer, and received the script in mid-August. Somehow it wasn't exactly what he had in mind, but with everyone set to go he put the show into rehearsal under Howard Lindsay's direction. Then a tragedy occurred that made the entire concept impossible. On September 8, the S.S. *Morro Castle*, returning to New York from a seven-day cruise to Havana, was swept by fire as it was nearing Asbury Park, New Jersey. It went down with the loss of 125 lives.

Since the sinking was the worst maritime disaster of the Thirties, obviously there could no longer be any thought of a fun-filled musical comedy about a shipwreck. With Wodehouse in France and Bolton in England, Freedley was in a panic. Where could he find a new plot? In desperation he turned to Lindsay, who had just authored a successful play called *She Loves Me Not*. Would Lindsay be willing to write the new book as well as direct the show? Yes, said the director, but only on the condition that the producer get him a collaborator. But whom to get and where to get? Magazine illustrator Neysa McMein, a close friend of all concerned, happened to have lunch with Porter the following day and he told her of the dilemma. That night she had a dream about another friend in the theatre, Russel "Buck" Crouse, a Theatre Guild press agent, who had collaborated on Joe Cook's last vehicle, *Hold Your Horses*. At eight in the morning, she telephoned Porter and told him about her dream. Since it was as good an omen as any, Porter relayed the message to Freedley who then spent the entire day searching for Crouse. Late in the afternoon, the producer happened to look out of his office window in the Alvin Theatre and noticed someone leaning out of a window at the Theatre Guild office across the street. There was Russel Crouse. Within an hour an agreement was signed at Lindsay's apartment and the Lindsay-Crouse partnership was officially born.

Hectic days followed. They went into rehearsals with only two-thirds of the first act completed and no second act at all. In an attempt to cover up for the blank pages, Lindsay, in reading the story to the cast, simply mumbled something to the effect that "we're working on some very funny stuff here but we just haven't found time to put it down on paper." Actually, the script wasn't completed until just before the out-of-town opening in Boston—and even then no one had a clear idea how to end the show. Designer Donald Oenslager pleaded for some clue so that he could get the scenery for the finale built in time for the premiere. Freedley's solution: "Give us an exterior set with an interior feeling."

The new plot still kept the action on board an ocean liner, but there was nary a hint of disaster in the tale about a Wall Street executive (Gaxton), an Aimee Semple MacPherson–type evangelist-turned-nightclub singer (Merman), and Public Enemy Number 13 (Moore) who, disguised as a clergyman, walked around with a machine gun (his little pal, Putt Putt Putt) concealed in a saxophone case. As if to herald the chaotic nature of the undertaking, the musical, which had been first known as *Hard to Get* and later *Bon Voyage*, was officially christened *Anything Goes*.

Because, in the story, Gaxton had to stow away on ship to be near the society belle he adores (Bettina Hall), he too was compelled to don a number of disguises. For one scene, the authors

Vandamm; Theatre Coll., NY Public Lib.
William Gaxton, Ethel Merman and Victor Moore in *Anything Goes*.

had Merman snatch a pair of clippers from the ship's barbershop and, while Moore was distracting a lady passenger, pick up her Pomeranian dog and carry it behind the scene where Gaxton was waiting. When the supposedly same dog was returned it was completely shorn and Gaxton emerged from the wings sporting the dog's hair on his face as a beard. One of the biggest laughs in the show came when, to the lady's question, "You're Spanish, aren't you?," Gaxton replied, "No, ma'am, I'm Pomeranian."

At least three of the songs from *Anything Goes* became almost instant classics. However, radio stations refused to play "I Get a Kick Out of You" because of the line "Some get a kick from cocaine." Porter changed it to "Some like the perfume from Spain," possibly the only tribute ever accorded Iberian perfume. But the show-stopping number was unquestionably the catalogue—or "laundry list"—song, "You're the Top," with its superlatively rhymed collection of superlatives: Colosseum and Louvre Museum, symphony by Strauss and Mickey Mouse, Bendel bonnet and Shakespeare sonnet, Tower of Pisa and Mona Lisa, Mahatma Gandhi and Napoleon Brandy, night in Spain and cellophane, National Gallery and Garbo's salary, turkey dinner and Derby winner, Ritz hot toddy and Brewster body, Zuyder Zee and broccoli, Nathan panning and Bishop Manning, night at Coney and Irene Bordoni, Arrow collar and Coolidge dollar, Fred Astaire and Camembert, O'Neill drama and Whistler's mama, *Inferno's* Dante and Great Durante, Waldorf salad and Berlin ballad, old Dutch master and Mrs. Astor, steppes of Russia and Roxy usher, Tower of Babel and Whitney stable, stein of beer and stratosphere, dress from Saks's and last year's taxes, Drumstick Lipstick and the Irish Svipstick. Merman and Gaxton could have gone on all night.

But Porter didn't stop there. In his title song, he gave the topsy-turvey world of the mid-Thirties a theme song as he itemized such symptoms of moral decay as the shortened length of women's skirts, authors who use only four-letter words, grandmothers who go out with gigolos, and nudist parties, plus such odd alliances as those of Sam Goldwyn teaching Anna Sten diction and Mrs. Roosevelt doing a radio series for the Simmons Mattress Company. The world was going mad all right—but to a far more horrifying degree than Cole Porter, or anyone else for that matter, could possibly imagine.

Note that cover designed before Lindsay and Crouse revised book.

An all-Negro musical, *Africana*, opened five days after *Anything Goes* at the former Al Jolson's Theatre, renamed the Venice. Donald Heywood's ambitious "Congo operetta" had, apparently, only one distinction. During the first of its three performances, an irate spectator in evening clothes dashed down the aisle, grabbed an empty chair in the orchestra pit and swung it at the composer while he was conducting. Later, at the police station, the man gave as his reason the fact that Heywood had plagiarized his idea. He should have waited to see the reviews.

Also in November, Howard Dietz and Arthur Schwartz made their joint debuts as creators of a book musical. Their choice of story was an ancient Spanish tale of cuckolds and cuckolders, Pedro de Alarcón's *El Sombrero de Tres Picos* (*The Three-Cornered Hat*), which they renamed *Revenge with Music*. It had no less than four directors on the road, cost $120,000, earned back $45,000, and remained at the New Amsterdam until the end of March. The plot wasn't too strong, but the score was one of the most impressive achievements of the year. Songs like "If There Is Someone Lovelier than You" ("... then I am blind/ A man without a mind"), "You and the Night and the Music"

("... fill me with flaming desire"), and "When You Love Only One" captured all the color and passion so essential in musicalizing the hot-blooded tale. (Actually, "You and the Night and the Music" proved too passionate. The fact that anyone could be so filled with flaming desire that his or her being is set on fire was deemed so incendiary that for a while the song was banned from the air.)

It was in *Revenge with Music* that Libby Holman, absent from the stage since *Three's a Crowd*, made her return to Broadway. Georges Metaxa and Charles Winninger were her co-stars.

Four musicals opened in December. At the Hollywood Theatre (its first time out as a legitimate theatre after years as a movie showplace), Lew Brown produced, directed and wrote sketches and lyrics for *Calling All Stars*, which turned out to be less of a prideful announcement than a cry for help. The show was around for only a little over a month despite its cast of popular performers such as Lou Holtz (bellowing his celebrated "Maharajah" story), Phil Baker, Gertrude Niesen, Everett Marshall, and, in lesser roles, Martha Raye, Judy Canova and Ella Logan. Marshall, who had delivered the plea for peace, "To the Beat of The Heart," in the *Ziegfeld Follies* earlier in the year, here offered an-

other socially significant first act finale, "Straw Hat in the Rain." Though the economy of the nation had been stimulated by the multiple measures of the New Deal, there were still five million families on relief, a fact that stirred Lew Brown and composer Harry Akst to come up with a metaphorical appeal to the "haves" to help the "have nots":

Hey there, High Hat,
You're a high and dry hat,
Won't you do a little something
For the straw hat in the rain?

Apparently, the appeal went unheeded. Act One ended with everyone getting drenched.

Fools Rush In, Leonard Sillman's second revue of the year, rushed in on Christmas night and rushed out two weeks later. Marilyn Miller had contributed $25,000 to assure employment for her husband, dance director Chet O'Brien, and so became the unbilled co-sponsor with William A. Brady. On opening night, the revue had to compete for critical attention with three other productions: Walter Hamden in *Hamlet*, *Piper Paid* with Spring Bying-

ton, and Samson Raphaelson's *Accent on Youth* with Constance Cummings. Sketches included a meeting between Mrs. Hoover and Mrs. Roosevelt and a scene depicting the birth of the Dionne Quintuplets (with Mr. Sillman, Richard Whorf and Charles Walters as three of them).

Two musicals, an operetta, *The O'Flynn*, and a revue, *Thumbs Up!*, were both unveiled on December 27. *The O'Flynn*, despite a mostly favorable press and a tuneful $75,000 contributed by the Standard Oil Company, called it quits after only 11 performances. Somehow New York audiences just couldn't whip up much concern over a plot that dealt with the aborted effort to put James II back on the throne of England.

Thumbs Up! generally rated them. It was a lavish, comic-filled, *Follies*-type revue, sponsored by Eddie Dowling and imaginatively staged by John Murray Anderson. Ray Dooley (Mrs. Dowling),

who romped away with most of the plaudits, was seen scrambling to the top of a pyramid formed by a troupe of acrobatic Arabs, and as Sonya in a *Merry Widow* travesty, scurrying over the bowed backs of her guardsmen. Bobby Clark, who played her prince in that one, was at his funniest in the "Aired in Court" sketch as a microphone-hogging judge in a murder trial that was being broadcast over radio. The opening "Skating in Central Park" number evoked both Currier and Ives and the "Easter Parade" sequence in *As Thousands Cheer*. The show even had two song hits: "Zing! Went the Strings of My Heart!" (by James F. Hanley), sung and danced by Hal LeRoy and Eunice Healey, and Vernon Duke's "Autumn in New York," sung by J. Harold Murray before two photomural views of the Manhattan skyline. Business, however, was not as brisk as might have been expected, and *Thumbs Up!* gave up after 156 performances.

The year ended with an operetta, *Music Hath Charms*, Rudolf Friml's final work for the Broadway theatre. Here was a switch on the familiar three-generation romance so dear to the hearts of operetta fashioners. This time a modern girl is affected not by her grandmother's love affair but by her great-grandmother's. Under the title *Annina*, Maria Jeritza and Allan Jones had toured in it during the winter. With a revised script and Natalie Hall and Robert Halliday as the lovers in the New York version, it expired in less than a month. "Dull" was the word that cropped up most frequently in the reviews.

The same day the opening-night audience was being beguiled by the charms Mr. Friml's music hath, Japan took the occasion to renounce both the Washington Naval Treaty of 1920 and the London Naval Disarmament Treaty of 1930. Henceforth, it declared, it would pursue a course dictated only by its own national interests.

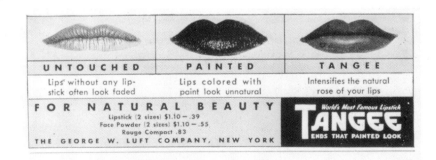

"...OH, WHAT A WONDERFUL WORLD..."

In 1935, the Interstate Commerce Commission (ICC) was strengthened, the Social Security Act was enacted, the Federal Reserve Board received new powers, the Rural Electrification Administration (REA) was established, the Wagner Labor Labor Relations Act became law, and the Works Progress Administration (WPA) was created— and still the year saw few indications of actual economic recovery.

Certainly none could be found along Broadway. The appalling fact was that no more than ten musicals were offered during the year—exactly half the number of 1934. For the record, they were three book shows, six revues, and one opera. And of the ten, there wasn't one boxoffice success. Artistic successes, yes. Three of the productions were, in fact, major events of the Thirties. No presentation was brighter or more sophisticated than *Jubilee*, yet it lasted a mere 169 performances. *Porgy and Bess*, surely a landmark in the development of American opera, remained at the Alvin for only 124. Even the longest-running musical of the year, *Jumbo*, with the biggest press buildup and some of the decade's most enthusiastic notices, closed after 233 showings—and lost money (as, in fact, did the two other musicals to make it over the 200-performance mark, *May Wine* and the *Earl Carroll Sketch Book*).

Although there was high praise for the operatic contributions of Anne Brown and Todd Duncan in *Porgy and Bess*, the comics dominated the rather constricted scene, with Jimmy Durante in *Jumbo*, Mary Boland in *Jubilee*, and Beatrice Lillie in *At Home Abroad* (easily the year's outstanding revue) winning the greatest accolades. Rodgers and Hart's musical efforts for *Jumbo* won top honors of the year, even though Cole Porter's for *Jubilee* and

George Gershwin's for *Porgy and Bess* had their champions (as well as detractors). The year's most notable neophytes all turned out to be directors: George Abbott for *Jumbo*, Vincente Minnelli for *At Home Abroad*, and Rouben Mamoulian for *Porgy and Bess*.

Among the 111 nonmusical offerings of 1935—off twenty from the previous year—were Robert E. Sherwood's *The Petrified Forest*, with Leslie Howard and Humphrey Bogart; the Pulitzer Prize winner of the 1934–1935 season, *The Old Maid*, by Zoë Akins; the John Cecil Holm–George Abbott farce, *Three Men on a Horse*; the Clifford Odets dramas, *Awake and Sing* and *Waiting for Lefty*; Maxwell Anderson's *Winterset*, inspired by the

Sacco-Vanzetti trial; the Lunts in *The Taming of the Shrew*; *Dead End* by Sidney Kingsley; Bella and Samuel Spewack's *Boy Meets Girl*; and Helen Hayes in *Victoria Regina*.

No less than 53 plays had been unveiled on Broadway before the year's first musical, *Parade*, put in its appearance. The date was May 20—just in time to close the 1934–1935 season. The revue had prestigious backing (the Theatre Guild), a popular clown (Jimmy Savo), and the most unrelentingly far-left point of view of any commercial musical up to that time.

Parade's first sponsor was to have been the proletariat-leaning Theatre Union. Then it was to arrive under the aegis of the Group Theatre. Finally, the Theatre Guild agreed to take it under its presumably left wing. While much had been diluted since the show's original concept, primarily the work of Paul Peters and George Sklar, the results were still firmly pro-mass and anti-class. Well-dressed first-nighters could be seen huffily leaving the theatre during the performance, but even the workers, despite courtesy discounts, wouldn't come. *Parade* lasted no longer than a month and lost $100,000.

Right from the start, the show made no bones about its sympathies. The first scene was in a police station. A sergeant and a desk officer are playing tic-tac-toe. Constant radio reports of murders and holdups are completely ignored. Nothing disturbs their total concentration until they hear that the starving poor are parading down Fifth Avenue. That does it! They promptly swing into action, issue a riot call, and the scene dissolves into the first musical number, "On Parade," with the cast grimly proclaiming its mission.

If little else, the revue did have a consistency of slant. There was a song-and-dance trio consisting of Father Coughlin (an early FDR supporter who now opposed him as a tool of international bankers), Huey Long (Jimmy Savo played the Louisiana "Kingfish"), and General Hugh Johnson (the irascible NRA boss who had quit the previous fall). In the song. "You Ain't So Hot," singer Avis Andrews, as a put-upon domestic, expressed her contempt for her wealthy mistress. "The Tabloid Reds," sung before a background of doom-filled headlines, belittled the idea that there was a Red menace through the odd device of beginning with a bomb explosion and then allowing three supposed figments of

Vandamm; Theatre Coll., NY Public Lib.
Jimmy Savo, Charles D. Brown and Eve Arden live like 100 percent Americans in the *Parade* sketch, "Home of the Brave."

Hearstian imagination to revel in the newspaper accounts of their incendiary deeds ("Here it says that Cousin Kate/ Set fire to the Empire State"). This was the first act finale.

Eve Arden, fresh from the more affluent surroundings of the *Ziegfeld Follies*, was on hand to "Call Out the Militia," ridiculing those who are quick to send for the troops to settle some minor disturbance. In the sketch, "Home of the Brave," everyone was shown wanting to live like Indians because the Fascists in control had decreed that only 100 percent Americans are permitted to live freely. There were gibes at the failures of the AAA, businessmen who think they can run their businesses without their striking workers (Savo got all entangled in machinery in this one), and flabby liberals unwilling to take sides on major issues ("Let us have calm debate and never be uncouth/ Let ev'ry person state his version of the truth"). The overall theme of *Parade* was summed up in these lines:

> Life could be so beautiful
> Life could be so grand for all
> If just a few didn't own everything
> And most of us nothing at all.

The press took delight in skewering the production, with three critics using almost identical epithets: "neither fish, fowl, red herring" (Atkinson); "neither fish nor fowl nor even good red Goering [*sic*]" (Gabriel); and "neither fact, fancy, nor good red propaganda" (Garland). Percy Hammond, though, seemed to be the most aggrieved: "Although the librettists seem dervish in their devotion to peace, I, who never won a wager, will bet that all of them are eager to melt their pens into tomahawks, and to scalp and overthrow in battle the boneheads who are mismanaging us. The United States, one gathers, is the land of the heel and the home of the knave."

From *Parade* it was quite a jump to the *Earl Carroll Sketch Book*, in which Carroll ventured with his own summertime musical lampoon. In his book, *Musicals of the 1930s*, Melvin Parks commented that Carroll's idea of topicality "ran to such items as President McKinley emerging to remark that he had long been fond of Hawaiian music, whereupon the stage erupted with the 'Most Beautiful' dancing in moonlight and mirrors to 'Silhouettes Under the Stars' accompanied by Bert Lynn on the Vibrolynn ('a new musical instrument

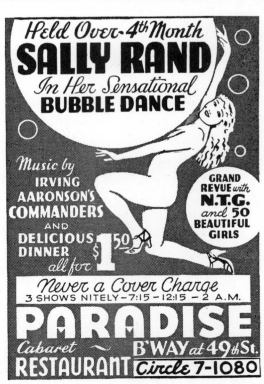

introduced for the first time')." Anyway, this "Hysterical Historical Revue," as it was billed, purported to be a chorus girl's view of American history, with the ladies inaugurating the academic revels by chirping: "Now bear us out and you will see/ Our little book of history." Thence it proceeded to hit most of the highlights from 1776 through the Louisiana Purchase, Indian uprisings, pioneer days, the Civil War, and on up to the present, pausing only briefly from such educational matters to offer Mlle. Nirska and her Butterfly Dance as the first act finale. The ladies of the chorus, though, were still the major attraction, and John Anderson appraised them thusly: "The girls stand behind curtains and then come out in front of them; or vice versa. They wear feathers and they don't wear feathers. They put on costumes and take them off, sit on the edge of the stage, and throw their garters at the audience. The girls can sit, stand, dance, lie down, and move their arms and legs. And they can do it all with or without mirrors. They probably can say 'mama' and 'papa.' "

Apart from an unfortunate "Musical Laugh Tour" yclept *Smile at Me*, nothing new was offered during the summer of 1935 to provide amusement for theatregoers who enjoy music with their entertainment. The 1935–1936 season, however, began encouragingly on September 19 with *At Home Abroad*, billed as "A Musical Holiday." Once again

the brothers Shubert showed their adaptability by sponsoring another adult, tasteful, melodic, and visually stunning revue. For the first time, Vincente Minnelli was put in complete charge as director as well as designer (and to prove it, the show was officially designated "A Vincente Minnelli Production"). To assure first-rate talent in every department, Minnelli engaged such stellar players as Beatrice Lillie, Ethel Waters, Eleanor Powell, Herb Williams, Paul Haakon, Reginald Gardiner (his American debut), and Eddie Foy, Jr. And back to revue went lyricist Howard Dietz and composer Arthur Schwartz.

Like *As Thousands Cheer*, *At Home Abroad* was a revue with a theme. This time it was a world cruise, with Otis and Henrietta Hatrick (Herb Williams and Vera Allen) taking in all the sights and sounds. In England, the couple learn of British sportsmanship at Eton with top-hatted Eleanor Powell tapping out "That's Not Cricket," and, at a London department store, they find out the difficulties encountered by Mrs. Blogden-Blagg (Beatrice Lillie) in ordering a dozen double damask dinner napkins. In the African Congo, they discover the Empress Jones (Ethel Waters), a "Hottentot Potentate" who has brought Harlem civilization to her subjects ("Cartier rings they're wearin' in their noses now"). In Monte Carlo, they observe the tantrums of a tough-toed Russian ballerina

113

A scene from *At Home Abroad*: James MacColl, Reginald Gardiner and Eddie Foy, Jr., try to assist Beatrice Lillie (as Mrs. Blogden-Blagg) in the "Dozen Double Damask Dinner Napkins" sketch.

(Miss Lillie) who cannot "face the mujik." In Paris, they hear the charms of the city described by the enraptured Miss Lillie perched halfway up the backdrop. In the Swiss Alps, they take part in the yodeling ("O Leo") first act finale. In Vienna, they come across madcap Mitzi (Miss Lillie), who gaily proclaims, "I'm the toast of Vienna and most of Vienna/ Can boast they've been host of the toast of Vienna." In the British West Indies, they fall under the spell of Ethel Waters as she describes the cargo of the good ship Panama Lady in "Loadin' Time." In Spain, they view a choreographed bull-fight with Paul Haakon as matador. In Tokyo, they accept Miss Lillie's helpful advice, "Get Yourself a Geisha" ("When you enter her house you take your shoes off . . . It's better with your shoes off"). In the words of the revue's finale, "Oh, what a wonderful world! What a thrill and a glow!"

Most critics, while feeling that the sketches could have been a bit stronger, seemed to agree with John Mason Brown's assessment that it was "as pleasant and profitable a world cruise as any stay-at-home could possibly invest in." And why not? The world of *At Home Abroad* was infinitely gayer than the world as it actually was during the show's half-year run; though tourists may not have noticed, it is doubtful that a voyage anywhere in the fall of 1935 and the winter of 1936 could have touched many countries unaffected by the darkening international situation.

Three weeks before the musical opened, Congress, at the peak of its isolationism, had passed the first Neutrality Act, prohibiting sales of munitions to belligerent powers and also travel by Americans on ships under the flags of belligerent powers. Just four days before the revue's premiere, Hitler's Nuremberg Laws had rescinded the citizenship of all German Jews, thereby unleashing the systematic waves of anti-Semitism that were being carried out in all parts of that country. *At Home Abroad* carefully skirted any German ports of call, though there was hardly a place it visited or people it saw that were not undergoing some form of crisis during the show's stay on Broadway. In England, following the collapse of Ramsay MacDonald's coalition government, Prime Minister Stanley Baldwin led his Conservative Party to victory in the October election on a platform of rearmament; in December, the unproductive second London Naval Conference took place; in January, King George V died and was succeeded by Edward VIII, the former Prince of Wales. In Africa, not far from the Hottentot Potentate's Congo domain, the ruthless Italian invasion of Ethiopia began in October; nine days later the League of Nations voted sanctions against the aggressor but they had little effect.

In Russia, the Moscow purge trials, which began in February, would result in the execution of dozens of leading Communists for plotting to overthrow party boss Joseph Stalin. In Paris, Premier Pierre Laval, in office since July, was forced to resign in January over his secret policy of appeasing Mussolini by granting Italy large chunks of Ethiopian land. In Vienna, Chancellor Kurt von Schuschnigg was desperately attempting to strengthen Austria's defensive might in order to prevent Hitler's forces from seizing his country. In Spain, death in the afternoon did not occur exclusively in the bullring; at the same time El Presidente Niceto Alcala Zamora was clamping down martial law and press censorship, the threats from the far right were becoming so ominous that he was forced to postpone elections from November to February. In Tokyo, ultranationalists were embarking on a campaign to exterminate moderate political and business leaders; an attempt on the life of Premier Keisuke Okada in February forced his resignation and strengthened the power of the military in its program to repress "dangerous thoughts." On March 7, 1936, the day *At Home Abroad* closed, German troops, in violation of the Locarno Treaty, began occupying the demilitarized Rhineland. Ohhhhh, what a wonderful world!

The march of the modern musical during the decade was marked by a vague though generally prescribed course. Satirical, sure. Topical, of course. Meaningful, hopefully. But whether it was a musical comedy or a revue, the accent was on a light, bright look at a world that never was nor ever could be, with smiling girls, "catchy" music, beautiful decor,

NY Times, Oct. 3, 1935.

and madcap clowning. Thus whatever "significance" there was could be accepted and digested so much easier. Revues occasionally broke away to offer something somberly thought-provoking, but on the whole an evening of the stark and the grim found little room on Broadway; anything that wasn't expected to make the customers laugh or whistle was derided and could expect little in the way of an audience.

That's why it seemed so strange that George Gershwin, the cigar-smoking man about Manhattan parties, the composer of *Girl Crazy* and *Of Thee I Sing*, was spending all of his time composing an opera. In fact, so singleminded was his dedication to the task that, following *Pardon My English* in January 1933, he refused every opportunity to write a musical-comedy score, and—except for winning his bread as a radio host—was burying himself in his work. And what was the topic of his preoccupation? The wretched, poverty-ridden existence of

WHAT A WONDERFUL WORLD

MESSRS SHUBERT PRESENT AT HOME ABROAD A MUSICAL HOLIDAY WITH WORDS AND MUSIC BY HOWARD DIETZ AND ARTHUR SCHWARTZ

PRICE 75c

• LOVE IS A DANCING THING
• GOT A BRAN' NEW SUIT
• O LEO
• THIEF IN THE NIGHT
• FAREWELL, MY LOVELY
• WHAT A WONDERFUL WORLD

CHAPPELL

A VINCENTE MINNELLI PRODUCTION WITH BEATRICE LILLIE ETHEL WATERS HERB WILLIAMS ELEANOR POWELL

the Negroes of Charleston, South Carolina, a theme totally foreign to Gershwin's own background and experience.

Even the method of collaboration on the new work was unusual. Gershwin's inspiration, DuBose Heyward's novel, *Porgy*, had already been dramatized by the author and his wife in 1927. It took a good deal of persuading to convince Heyward that an opera could also be made from the story of the crippled beggar in the goat cart, and both author and composer set about the task early in 1933. Gershwin still continued his music studies. He did research on Negro life. He soaked up atmosphere by visiting Charleston's Cabbage Row, the Negro ghetto that was to become Catfish Row in the opera. During the summer of 1934 he was at Folly Island off Charleston, where he heard—and took part in—the "shouting" of the Gullah Negroes at their church services. Most of the collaboration, however, was done by mail; Gershwin tied to New York by a radio contract, Heyward preferring to work in his Charleston home. Soon after the postal collaboration had begun, Ira Gershwin made it a triangular partnership by joining the venture as co-lyricist.

The Theatre Guild produced *Porgy and Bess* at a cost of $70,000. Rouben Mamoulian, who had directed the play, *Porgy*, was signed to stage the musical version. Alexander Smallens, the conductor of *4 Saints in 3 Acts*, became music director (there were 42 in the orchestra). Gershwin himself wrote all the orchestrations. Todd Duncan, a Howard University tutor, was cast as Porgy, and Anne Brown, a Juilliard alumna, became his Bess.

Porgy and Bess made a conscientious effort to depict Negro life as realistically as possible. Gone was the energetic hoofing and the self-parodying that had long characterized the Negro musical (in which, traditionally, black men blackened their faces and exaggerated their features). Heyward wrote at the time: "Now at the dawn of an artistic emancipation, the Negro may reach back across the years, forgetting for the time the well-worn mask of laughter, and speak seriously of his own themes, his hopes and aspirations." Moreover, it was not lost on anyone that *Porgy and Bess* offered Negro singers the opportunity to appear in a work that demanded voices of operatic quality utilized in a story dealing directly with Negro life.

The combinations of opera and musical theatre,

Gershwin Archives
Ruby Elzy, as Serena, sings "My Man's Gone Now" in *Porgy and Bess*. Georgette Harvey (Maria) is at left.

Gershwin Archives
The Hurricane scene in *Porgy and Bess*.

Gershwin Archives
John Bubbles (Sportin' Life), Todd Duncan (Porgy), and Anne Brown (Bess) in
Porgy and Bess.

Broadway's Gershwin and Charleston's Heyward, Catfish Row and Shubert Alley, had a tough time cracking through the shell of those who felt uncomfortable at works not easily catalogued. The daily press—at least those papers with large enough staffs—played it safe by dispatching not only the drama critics to the Alvin on October 10 but the music critics as well. Notices were divided. Drama critics, for the most part, appreciated the work more than did the music critics, whose general tone was somewhat disdainful of the aspirations of the composer. Olin Downes wrote in the *Times*: "The result has much to commend it from the musical standpoint, even though it does not utilize all the resources of the operatic composer, or pierce very often to the depths of the simple and pathetic drama. . . . What had become of the simplicity and poignancy of the drama of *Porgy*? Let Mr. Atkinson answer . . ." Mr. Atkinson did—but he disagreed completely with Mr. Downes. In an adjoining column, he wrote: "Mr. Gershwin has contributed something glorious to the spirit of the Heyward's community legend. If memory serves, it always lacked a glow of personal feeling. . . . The fear and pain go deeper in *Porgy and Bess* than they did in penny plain *Porgy*."

Porgy and Bess would have had difficulties even had it won unanimous raves; with a divided press, despite its being both a musical and a theatrical event, it could last only four months on Broadway before embarking on a brief tour. The work was Gershwin's final creation for the Broadway theatre; soon after it opened he would depart for Hollywood, where he died of a brain tumor less than two years later.

Just two nights following the *Porgy and Bess* opening, a second heralded theatrical even occurred. It was the premiere of *Jubilee* at the Imperial Theatre, and it was quite a change. Not only was it a more conventional musical undertaking; it was the essence of bright, brittle, luxuriant Broadway entertainment. At the time Cole Porter was Gershwin's only real rival in the musical theatre (Kern and Berlin were in Hollywood, Youmans had retired, and Rodgers was yet to receive the acclaim that would soon be his). While Gershwin had sweated over his *Porgy and Bess* score in New York, Porter and librettist Moss Hart went on a four-and-a-half-month, 34,000-mile cruise aboard the S.S. *Franconia* to write the show that would emerge as *Jubilee*. While the Gershwin production was peo-

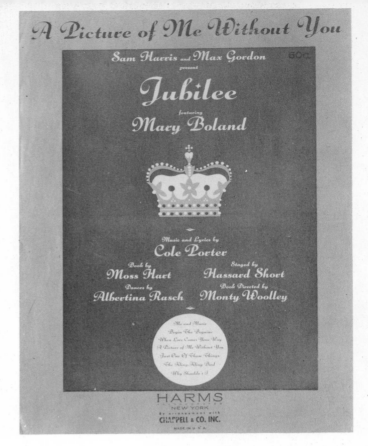

pled with conservatory-trained Negro singers, the Porter musical favored Broadway and Hollywood performers, headed by Mary Boland, Melville Cooper and June Knight. The Heyward text for *Porgy and Bess* was earthy and tragic; the Hart text was an airy concoction dealing with the escapades of a mythical royal family, rather loosely inspired by the recent Silver Jubilee of England's King George V. And if the Gershwin offering had difficulty in finding its audience partly because of the distance of the locale and characters to the theatregoing public of New York, the Porter musical was equally far removed at the other end of the social scale. Porter himself realized this. As he once told columnist Lucius Beebe, "You can't serve dramatic fare that is the stage equivalent of truffled foie gras and quail in aspic and hope for a wide appeal. Polished, urbane and adult playwrighting, in the musical field anyway, is strictly a creative luxury."

The reviewers certainly should have had the customers queuing up. Brooks Atkinson called it "the aristocrat of American festivals to music." To Percy Hammond, it was "the most satisfying fete of its kind that this pleasure-seeker has seen in what might be called ever so long." Gilbert Gabriel was even more overcome: "It is an extravaganza extraordinary, raised by its lovely scenery and clothes, and by its gay staging, to realms almost fabulous."

Vandamm

The King and Queen (Melville Cooper and Mary Boland) of *Jubilee*, while at Feather-more Castle, make their plans to become plain "Mr. and Mrs. Smith." Encouraging their escapade are Prince James (Charles Walters), singer Karen O'Kane (June Knight), movie star Charles Rausmiller (Mark Plant), party-giver Eve Standing (May Boley), playwright Eric Dare (Derek Williams), and Princess Diana (Margaret Adams).

Vandamm

The finale of *Jubilee*. King Melville Cooper bestows honors on Derek Williams, in a ceremony witnessed by June Knight, Jackie Kelk and Montgomery Clift (as two princes), Margaret Adams, Charles Walters, and Queen Mary Boland.

What nay-saying there was, curiously, seemed to be directed at Cole Porter's score. Four reviewers (Atkinson, Lockridge, Brown, and Anderson), while admiring the songs, still admitted preferring the ones for *Anything Goes*, and one (Garland) turned thumbs completely down ("There is no whistling-as-you-walk-out melody ripe for one's pucker up endeavors"). Among the musical numbers, "Begin the Beguine" was easily the most appreciated, prompting such encomia as "exotic originality" (Atkinson), "alluring" (Hammond), "a honey" (Gabriel), "insinuating" (Brown), "ranks with Porter's best" (Anderson), and "standout number" (Jack Pulaski, *Variety*). Another superior, though never popular item, "The Kling-Kling Bird on the Divi-Divi Tree," was almost equally admired (Porter had actually seen both bird and tree in Jamaica). There was also favorable press mention of "A Picture of Me Without You" (which, in the "You're the Top" laundry-list vein, catalogued the great inseparables) and "Me and Marie," an old-fashioned music-hall turn for Miss Boland and Mr. Cooper. Almost totally ignored: "Why Shouldn't I?" and "Just One of Those Things."

In his review of *Anything Goes*, Robert Benchley had referred to Porter's lyrics as being "devised with an eye to pleasing perhaps eighteen people." There were also many examples in *Jubilee*. For the entrance of his Noël Cowardish character, Eric Dare, Porter put down both himself and his contemporaries with:

When he wasn't here to write new tunes
We were stuck in the muck Bing Crosby croons.

When the Elsa Maxwellian party-giver describes her forthcoming bash, she takes a dig at George Gershwin's propensity for hogging the piano at parties:

'Twill be new in ev'ry way,
Gershwin's promised not to play.

And in "A Picture of Me Without You," Porter took after the theatre's most domineering stage mother:

Picture brother Cain without his Abel
Picture Clifton Webb minus mother Mabel.*

The composer's rather glossy view of the world came through even in the song in which the king and queen, dreaming of being just plain "Mr. and Mrs. Smith," contemplate life in the United States:

For months and months I've waited
To know just how it felt
To be NRA-diated
By Mr. Roosevelt.
And now that I can have my way
I want to do my best
To see the unemployed at play
And the government at rest.

After only a little more than four months, Mary Boland decided she'd had enough and went back to California. Her replacement, Laura Hope Crews, couldn't attract the customers and the show began to lose money. It finished with only 45 more performances than *Porgy and Bess*.

A modest trifle, *Provincetown Follies*, opened off-Broadway early in November and, surprisingly, stayed two months. But the year's third musical comedy event, *Jumbo*, easily dwarfed everything else.

Literally. The Hippodrome on 43rd Street and 6th Avenue had been a theatrical showplace ever since 1902. Once the home of Charles Dillingham spectacles (girls marching into a tank of water was a classic bit), it had not been in use for five years when impresario Billy Rose decided it was just the place for his musical comedy-circus-vaudeville-revue-spectacle-menagerie called *Jumbo*. Not content with merely hiring a hall, Rose had it completely rebuilt by designer Albert Johnson. The auditorium was gutted and refitted to resemble an actual circus arena, with the audience seated in a grandstand sloping up from a circular revolving stage. To direct the enterprise, Rose called in John Murray Anderson, with George Abbott making his musical-comedy debut staging the book. To write the songs, he signed Rodgers and Hart, who had recently returned from Hollywood, and for his story the playwrighting team of Ben Hecht and Charles MacArthur. For stars, Rose teamed Jimmy Durante, an elephant named Big Rosie, and Paul Whiteman seated on a white horse. That was only for starters.

Billy Rose would later boast that there was only one ring to watch at the Hippodrome. Keeping tabs on the rehearsals, however, was like watching the most mammoth three-ring circus of all time. Twenty-one principals rehearsed in a church on

48th Street; the chorus (consisting of nine show-girls, sixteen dancers, seventeen aerial performers, and thirty-two male singers) and the thirty-one circus acts (including 75-year-old bareback rider Josie DeMotte, the iron-jawed slide-for-life girl, Tiny Klein, and A. Robins and his bananas) were all at the Manhattan Opera House; and the animals —they claimed over a thousand of them but the actual figure was closer to five hundred—were being put through their paces at a riding academy near Prospect Park in Brooklyn.

All this was going on before Rose had officially leased the Hippodrome—or had any substantial backing. He had put up his own $35,000 to get things started, but only one audition was necessary to pry most of the needed $280,000 from millionaire John Hay "Jock" Whitney. (By the time the show opened the figure would rise to an unprecedented $340,000, with Herbert Bayard Swope and Bernard Baruch included among the angels.)

Rehearsals began in June with the opening night set for Labor Day. In August, Actors Equity ruled that the show was a circus not a musical, thus relieving Rose of any obligation to pay its members a salary before the official premiere. Once the Hippodrome was in usable condition, the producer put up a huge sign on the side of the building reading, "SH-H-H-H! 'JUMBO' IS REHEARSING!" Labor Day came and went. *Jumbo* was still rehearsing. During September, Ella Logan was replaced by Gloria Grafton in the leading feminine role. In mid-October, to help keep interest alive, Rose ran an ad in the newspapers seeking a "modern Diamond Jim Brady" to attend "an advance showing IN SOLITUDE. $10,000 for ONE SEAT —and the Hipprodrome and *Jumbo* is yours alone FOR A NIGHT—from Durante to Whiteman, from Mabel to Millicent, from aardvark to zebra." There were no serious takers. Anyway, it was common knowledge that people could simply drop in to watch a dress rehearsal anytime they wanted. Finally, eleven weeks late—and after a total of six postponements—Rose signed a sworn affidavit that *Jumbo* would officially open on the night of November 16. And it did.

People could hardly believe it. "Well, they finally got *Jumbo* into the Hippodrome," commented *The New Yorker*. "Now all that remains is to complete the Triborough Bridge [they did] and enforce the sanctions against Italy [they didn't]." The premiere was a plushy, pushy affair. Tickets were nine times

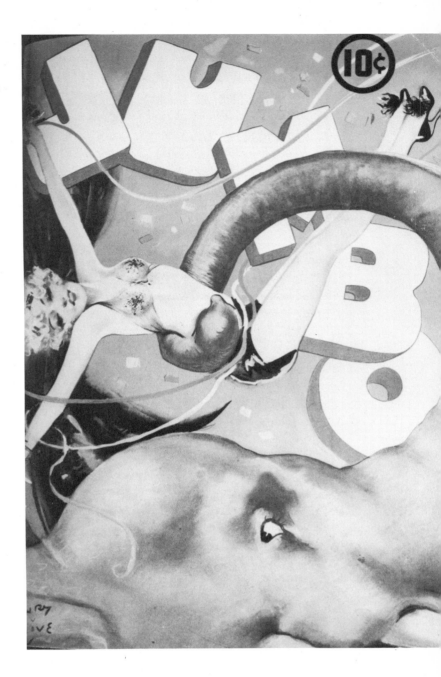

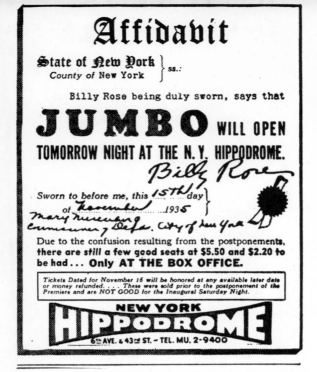

Vandamm; courtesy Lynn Farnol Group
Jimmy Durante and Jumbo (played by Big Rosie) in *Jumbo*.

new wrinkles. For one thing it had no chorus (all right, so that had been done before). For another, its slightly clotted story was about that up-to-the-minute subject, psychoanalysis. Some of the reviewers applauded its attempts at streamlining the musty theatrical form, though to others it was still the same stale Viennese pastry. Robert Benchley wrote, "While it is very pleasant it can hardly be called red meat for us lions to toss about in the cage . . . One can go to it and sit back and listen to Romberg's music with no more mental effort than is involved in murmuring 'Wien, Wien, nur du allein,' and sobbing softly into one's Schnurrbart." Far more scathing was George Jean Nathan who dismissed the whole thing as "a musical mothball laid scenically in Vienna and critically in Cain's."

But apparently there were enough customers who found *May Wine* to their liking: its 213-perform-ance run was only ten shy of *Jumbo's*.

George White's Scandals, the master's Christmas present for 1935, stuck tenaciously to the familiar George White Way that had been inaugurated some fifteen years before. Not counting *George White's Music Hall Varieties* in 1932, a full four years had elapsed since the last *Scandals*—but it looked as if it had never been away. Ray Henderson was back for the fifth time to compose the music, though he did bring along a new lyric-writing partner, Jack Yellen. Three headliners from the celebrated 1931 edition, Rudy Vallee and Willie and Eugene Howard were back, along with Bert Lahr, who had appeared in the *Varieties*. Sketch writer Billy K. Wells was on hand for his sixth assignment for White. Loyalty, however, was only partially rewarding.

What raves were bestowed by the critics turned out to be for the dance team of Sam, Ted and Ray, which did a highly spirited routine as Ethiopia's Emperor Haile Selassie and two of his generals (Willie Howard got into that one as Mussolini singing, "The people of my land must have room to expand, and that's why darkies were born"). Otherwise, Willie continued to wow the faithful with his hilarious *Rigoletto* routine and his imitation of a French professor. Bert Lahr also stepped into the

123

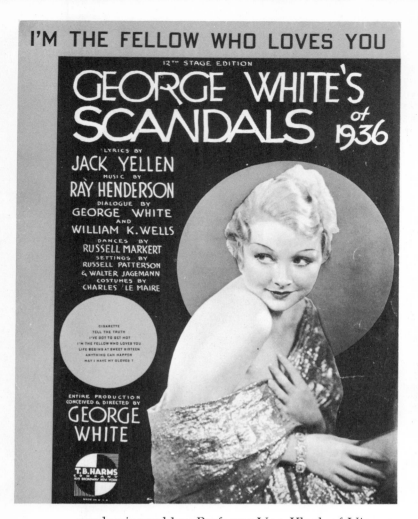

academic world as Professor Von Kluck of Vienna, a visiting gastronomical authority who demonstrated the proper ingredients to mix into his patent soup—including his toupee. Rudy Vallee's material, while not up to the songs he had had in the 1931 *Scandals,* still offered pleasures in the unexpected social self-consciousness of "I'm the Fellow who Loves You" ("Your folks have been pillars of society . . . My folks are the everyday variety"), and "The Pied Piper of Harlem," which found him in blackface for the Act One finale. Singer Gracie Barrie went from the teenage innocence of "Life Begins at Sweet Sixteen" to the disillusionment of "I've Got to Get Hot," a nightclub singer's lament that she must abandon Verdi and Puccini to pay the rent. The newspaper judges turned in a split verdict, although Percy Hammond was practically gurgling at the sight of so many female "knees, elbows, buzzums, knuckles, shanks, ankles and abdomens mixed in a pot-pourri with buffoons, acrobatic dancers and the music of the better alleys."

Vandamm; Theatre Coll., NY Public Lib.
Willie Howard as Prof. Pierre Ginsberg in *George White's Scandals of 1936.*

124

CHAPTER VII

"... SEE THE PRETTY APPLE ..."

Ever since 1866, when someone got the inspired idea of adding a stranded French ballet troupe to a floundering melodrama called *The Black Crook*, many a dull stretch in a musical comedy has been saved by the resounding cry, "Bring on the girls!"

What to do with them once they were brought on was, of course, another matter. Revues were relatively simple. Display a hundred or so girls wearing ostrich feathers and little else and have them strut up and down a flight of stairs as the nations of the world or the sirens of history. Or put the dancing girls through some rudimentary military drills or such jazzier turns as the tap or the Charleston. Or go arty with an underwater or a butterfly ballet, always a good excuse for undraping the ladies in the name of Artistic Freedom. It was much the same with book shows, though here there was usually some relevance—no matter how tenuous—to the plot. Often this was achieved by the simple device of presenting a show within the show, or putting the dance in the form of a dream (*anything* can happen in a dream). But no matter

how it was inserted, the dance routine was not so much to advance the plot as to stop it—to make the customers so overwhelmed by the sheer brilliance of the spectacle that the production would literally be halted in its tracks by prolonged hand-clapping and huzzahs.

By the Thirties, despite efforts to achieve a closer fusion of music and story, the dance routines continued to be little more than, hopefully, applause-catching appendages. In fact, the earliest efforts to free the dance from its accustomed mold were not in book shows at all, but in revues such as *The Band Wagon* and the *New Americana*.

In 1936, though, a musical, *On Your Toes*, and a choreographer, George Balanchine, got together and for the first time demonstrated that the dance could be utilized as an integral part of a story. Of course, since the subject dealt with a ballet company, Balanchine was given a framework within which classical dances were expected to be performed. But the former choreographer of Diaghilev's Ballet Russe de Monte Carlo did more than

White Studio; Theatre Coll., NY Public Lib.

create new ballets. In the first of his two major works, "La Princesse Zenobia," the Act One finale, Balanchine was able to kid the excesses of the traditional form so well that, during the first week of the show's run, the Playbill carried an ad for Col. de Basil's Ballet Russe, then at the Metropolitan Opera House, proclaiming "Only the Great Deserve the Darts of Satire." The sequence also provided one especially hilarious bit of business. The musical's hero, Junior Dolan (Ray Bolger), having been pressed into service as a last minute substitute for a dancer playing a Nubian slave, absentmindedly forgot to blacken his body below the neck. Once he discovered his mistake, Bolger turned his embarrassment into one of musical comedy's most side-splitting scenes.

The chief reason On Your Toes has been accepted as something of a musical theatre landmark was the final scene. Here at last a dance sequence, "Slaughter on Tenth Avenue," was actually conceived both as a separate dance and as an integral part of the story line itself. The play's denouement, something to do with gangsters mistaking the hero for another dancer who had welshed on a bet, simply could not have been played without it. The ballet was performed as a daringly modern work introduced by a classical ballet company, with Ray Bolger as the Hoofer, Tamara Geva the Stripper, and George Church the part of Big Boss. Here, in outline, is both the dance and its development within the musical's plot:

The scene is a seedy nightclub, expressionist in design. A small stage is at stage right. Tables crowded with shady-looking characters are around the room, leaving the center clear for dancing. At opening, Hoofer is seated on a high stool at the bar. While the bodies of the people sway, Stripper dances on the small stage, removing each piece of clothing until, down to the last shred, she exits. One of the men jumps on the stage to kiss her. Big Boss comes over, grabs him, throws him down and shoots him. Two bartenders come from back of bar with push brooms. They sweep the body over to the bar and throw it out of sight.

Stripper returns to small stage. Hoofer hands a wad of bills to Big Boss who lifts Stripper down to the floor. She and Hoofer perform *pas de deux*. At the high point of the dance, Big Boss, now jealous, separates them roughly and holds their necks as they sink to floor. Three Cops come down stairs, there is general confusion, and everyone scatters.

After Cops leave, Stripper sits alone at bar. Hoofer returns, throws chair on floor, runs over to bar, and pours whisky for Stripper and himself. They resume dance. Big Boss enters on small stage pointing gun. Stripper rushes to him but he pushes her aside. As she shields Hoofer, Stripper is shot and drops to floor. Hoofer makes leap for Big Boss, hits him on chin, grabs gun, and shoots Big Boss who falls dead center stage.

Hoofer carries Stripper over to small stage, and suddenly realizes that both she and Big Boss are dead. He now begins dancing crazily around body of Big Boss. At the climax of the dance, the plot of On Your Toes takes over. A distraught Frankie (Junior's girl) rushes onstage from the left and hands Junior a note. He reads as he dances, then, frightened, looks out at the audience to see two killers aiming their guns at him from box right. Though the orchestra finishes the number, Junior keeps dancing to avoid being a target and motions

White Studio; courtesy Lynn Farnol Group
Ray Bolger, George Church and Tamara Geva in the "Slaughter on Tenth Avenue" ballet sequence in *On Your Toes*.

to the leader to resume playing. This business is repeated three times. At the end of the third time, with Junior so exhausted he cannot dance another step, police appear in the theatre box and grab the would-be killers. Junior looks up and with a sigh of relief, collapses on top of Big Boss's body.

On Your Toes, which arrived at the Imperial Theatre April 11, had a book written by Rodgers and Hart and George Abbott. (Abbott, because of numerous postponements, was forced to exit as director. He did, however, return to help out during the show's Boston run.) Rodgers and Hart had first dreamed up the story in Hollywood as a possible vehicle for Fred Astaire. Fred turned it down because it didn't give him the chance to wear top hat, white tie and tails.

One of Lorenz Hart's most adroit lyrics was inspired by a 1934 FDR Fireside Chat in which the President had firmly allied himself with the aspirations of "the average man." In the song, Hart switched the idea around by having two moneyed characters (played by Luella Gear and Monty Woolley as a ballet company impresario) self-kiddingly enumerate all the "finer things" that were "Too Good for the Average Man." Things like

Courtesy Lynn Farnol Group
Ray Bolger and Doris Carson dance to "It's Got to Be Love" in *On Your Toes*.

127

2nd Year
BOY MEETS GIRL
CORT THEATRE, 48th St., E. of B'way
A George Abbot production.
By Bella and Samuel Spewack.

Messrs. Shubert present

Dennis KING   Helen GLEASON   Ernest TRUEX
in
Franz Lehar's New Operetta
"FREDERIKA"
Staged and Directed by
HASSARD SHORT
Opens at the 46th Street Theatre, February 4th

HOWDY STRANGER
LONGACRE THEATRE, 48th St., W. of B'way
A new comedy by Robert Sloane and Louis Pelletier, Jr., starring FRANK PARKER.

The Theatre Guild presents
IDIOT'S DELIGHT
SHUBERT THEATRE, 44th St., W. of B'way
A play by Robert E. Sherwood with ALFRED LUNT & LYNN FONTANNE

SAM H. HARRIS presents
STAGE DOOR
MUSIC BOX THEATRE, 45th St., W. of B'way
A new play by GEORGE S. KAUFMAN and EDNA FERBER with MARGARET SULLAVAN
"Charged with laughter."—Lockridge-Sun.

THE HOLMESES OF BAKER STREET
MASQUE THEATRE, 45th St., W. of B'way
Basil Mitchell's comedy. Adapted for the American stage by William Jourdan Rapp and Leonardo Bercovici.
With HELEN CHANDLER, CYRIL SCOTT and CECILIA LOFTUS.

Messrs. Shubert present

Beatrice Lillie   Bert Lahr
in Vincente Minnelli's New Musical
The Show Is On
Reginald Gardiner   Mitzi Mayfair   Paul Haakon
Winter Garden, Broadway and 50th Street
Mats.: Thursday and Saturday
"The season's most sidesplitting, opulent and genuinely satisfying musical."—John Mason Brown, Post.

MAX GORDON presents
THE WOMEN
BARRYMORE THEATRE, 47th St., W. of B'way
A new comedy by Clare Boothe.
Cast of 40—All Women.

Gilbert Miller presents
TOVARICH
PLYMOUTH THEATRE, 45th St., W. of B'way
A new comedy by Jacques Deval—English Text by Robert E. Sherwood, featuring MARTA ABBA and JOHN HALLIDAY.
"The season's first hit."—N. Y. Times.

Gilbert Miller presents
VICTORIA REGINA
BROADHURST THEATRE, 44th St., W. of B'way
A play by Laurence Housman starring HELEN HAYES.

SAM H. HARRIS presents
YOU CAN'T TAKE IT WITH YOU
BOOTH THEATRE, 45th St., W. of B'way
A farcical comedy by MOSS HART and GEORGE S. KAUFMAN.
"The best comedy these successful authors have ever written."—Atkinson—Times.

caviar, smoky supper clubs, adultery, alcoholism, plastic surgery, fancy foods, neurasthenia, anti-Communism, birth control, and psychoanalysis. (The last line: "Psychoanalysts are all the whirl,/ Rich men pay them all they can;/ Waking up to find that he's a girl/ Is too good for the average man.") Still, the musical hit of the show was the sentimental ode to the attractions of a simple, quiet, small hotel in the country.

On Your Toes was easily the premier attraction of 1936. And Ray Bolger's performance elevated him to the rare company of such luminaries of the year as Ethel Merman and Jimmy Durante in *Red, Hot and Blue!*, Beatrice Lillie and Bert Lahr in *The Show Is On* (the year's best revue), and Fanny Brice in the *Ziegfeld Follies*. As for the score, the Rodgers and Hart collection for *On Your Toes* clearly outdistanced the field. The year was also marked by three notable debuts in various capacities: Monty Woolley (his role had originally been intended for Gregory Ratoff) in *On Your Toes*; choreographer Balanchine, of course, with both the *Follies* and *On Your Toes*; and German refugee composer Kurt Weill with his first American score, *Johnny Johnson*. Regarding the number of musical

productions, if Noël Coward's *Tonight at 8:30* is included, the year was one up on 1935's all-time low of ten. The productions, however, were more successful: *On Your Toes* ran over 300 performances, and showings of over 200 were racked up by *The Show Is On*, the *Ziegfeld Follies* (if we combine the two editions), and *White Horse Inn*.

Nonmusical productions, however, resumed their numerical decline. Of the 98 dramas and comedies, the year offered such pleasures as Raymond Massey in *Ethan Frome* by Owen and Donald Davis; Katharine Cornell in Shaw's *Antony and Cleopatra*; Robert E. Sherwood's antiwar play, *Idiot's Delight*, with the Lunts, which won the Pulitzer Prize for the season 1935–1936; John Gielgud in *Hamlet*; Sherwood's translation of Jacques Deval's comedy, *Tovarich*; *Stage Door* by George S. Kaufman and Edna Ferber; the 1936–1937 Pulitzer Prize winner, *You Can't Take It With You*, by Kaufman and Moss Hart; George Abbott's production of *Brother Rat*; and Clare Boothe Luce's all-women *The Women*.

George Balanchine's initial choreographic contributions on Broadway were first viewed the night of January 30, when the second Shubert-sponsored *Ziegfeld Follies* had its premiere. (The first musical of the year had been *The Illustrators' Show*, which marked Frank Loesser's unheralded stage debut as a lyricist. The revue lasted five performances.) At the unusually steep top price of $5.50, the new *Follies* seemed to be a new version of the last *Follies*, featuring such alumni of the 1934 edition as Fanny Brice, Cherry and June Preisser, Eve Arden, composer Vernon Duke, lyricist Ira Gershwin, directors John Murray Anderson and Edward Clark Lilley, and Balanchine's fellow choreographer, Robert Alton. It was generally conceded to be an even better *Follies* than the last one, although the much-touted appearance of Josephine Baker, the St. Louis–born flame of Paris, provoked so even-tempered a critic as Brooks Atkinson to fume, "Her singing is only a squeak in the dark and her dancing is only the pain of an artist."

But that seems to have been the only cause for complaint. Fanny Brice, in "He Hasn't a Thing Except Me," kidded her own "My Man" trademark by beginning the scene leaning against a lamppost; once she began to sing, however, even the lamppost withdrew its support and walked offstage. Her biggest laughs, though, were saved for her saga about her Red-tinged husband, "Modernistic Moe," whom

THAT MOMENT OF MOMENTS

MRS. FLORENZ ZIEGFELD PRESENTS

ZIEGFELD FOLLIES OF 1936

PRICE 75c

LYRICS BY
IRA GERSHWIN
MUSIC BY
VERNON DUKE
DEVISED AND STAGED BY
JOHN MURRAY ANDERSON

ISLAND IN THE WEST INDIES
WORDS WITHOUT MUSIC
THAT MOMENT OF MOMENTS
I CAN'T GET STARTED
MY RED LETTER DAY

CHAPPELL

she must please by performing impressionistic dances ("Rewolt! Rewolt!"), and another bit as Baby Snooks, this time raising hell on a Hollywood set (Bob Hope played the director). The show also offered exotic color in "Island in the West Indies" ("Away from Reuben's and from Lindy's"), intoned by Gertrude Niesen's foghorn and danced by Josephine Baker, and political satire in "Of Thee I Spend," with Bob Hope impersonating FDR braintruster Rexford Tugwell.

In one scene, Bob Hope and Eve Arden, both in evening attire, are seen on a street corner. Obviously immune to Bob's charms, Eve tries vainly to get a taxi. But Bob won't give up easily, and in "I Can't Get Started," blithely enumerates his accomplishments: flying around the world in a plane, settling Spanish revolutions, charting the North Pole, scoring under par in golf, receiving offers to star in the movies, serving as a consultant to Roosevelt, winning the role of God in *The Green Pastures*. Still no response from Eve. Then, impulsively, he kisses her a good, solid smack. Wow! She's all his! But now it's Bob's turn to play it cool and he departs with a jaunty, "That's all I wanted to know. Well, good night."

The first act finale of the *Ziegfeld Follies* kidded the current crop of screen musicals, while also predicting the future shape of Hollywood epics. In a trailer for the extravaganza, *The Gazooka* (named for the exciting dance successor to "The Continental" and "The Carioca"), the film is advertised as being "In Techniquecolor on the Wide Screen," with interminable credits flashing on the screen. Snippets from the epic involve Ruby Blondell (Fanny Brice), Bing Powell (Bob Hope), and Dolores Del Morgan (Gertrude Niesen).

Forced to close in May because of Miss Brice's illness, the *Follies* reopened in September with Fanny back again but with Bobby Clark taking over most of Bob Hope's part, Jane Pickens subbing for Gertrude Niesen, and Gypsy Rose Lee doing whatever Eve Arden did—and a little bit more. This version lasted almost the same number of performances as the original.

Bligh-Colbert; Culver Pictures, Inc.
Bob Hope and Fanny Brice, the main attractions in the *Ziegfeld Follies of 1936*, go veddy British in the skit, "Fancy Fancy."

129

The 1935–1936 Broadway season ended with a third Leonard Sillman revue, *New Faces of 1936*, opening late in May. As usual, the producer had his problems finding money; it had taken him over a year to raise $15,000. Faithful New Face Imogene Coca had one of her best numbers in "Cinderella's Night Out," in which a burlesque fairy godmother, Marian Martin, grants the slavey's request to be a stripper—in a polo coat. Helen Craig appeared as "Lottie of the Literati" ("No matter who said it/ Dorothy Parker gets the credit"), with Van Johnson playing Sinclair Lewis and Ralph Blane as George Jean Nathan. The Hearst press was in a special dither over the monologue, "Marion Never Looker Lovelier," with Elizabeth Wilde as Hearst columnist Louella Parsons gushing over Hearst concubine Marion Davies. All the critical Hearstlings (except for Walter Winchell) belittled the show, which somehow never received a line of publicity in the columns of the *Mirror*, the *American*, or the *Journal* throughout its run.

The chief backer of *New Faces* was Martin Jones, owner of the Vanderbilt Theatre in which the revue appeared, who took over artistic control of the production within three months after the opening. In the fall, to hypo business, Jones incongruously added the well-worn faces of the Duncan Sisters to repeat their "Topsy and Eva" bit, first performed on Broadway in 1924. The reviews? No raves, but full of adjectives such as "cheerful," "amiable," "unpretentious," and "intermittently amusing."

The entertainment during the summer of 1936 was left entirely to the politicians. Alf Landon was nominated for the Presidency by the Republicans in June, and shortly thereafter Roosevelt was renominated by the Democrats. Abroad, things were mostly quiet. In June, Léon Blum became the first Socialist premier of France and helped bring about

a temporary spur in the French economy. In July, Germany and Austria signed a treaty guaranteeing Austria's frontier. The Italian conquest of Ethiopia had ended in May, so, at least, the bombing of civilians had stopped. In China, Japanese forces were mostly digging in, trying to consolidate their gains.

But just as things were looking calm in most major trouble spots of the world, violence suddenly erupted in a new area. In Morocco, in July, a military rebellion, led by General Francisco Franco, touched off the Spanish Civil War. It quickly spread to the mainland, and on October 1, Franco was officially installed as head of the Insurgent government.

On the same day, the Broadway musical theatre season of 1936–1937 began with a sumptuous Rockefeller Center's Theatre presentation, *White Horse Inn*. The Erik Charell spectacular, which had been a great European success ever since its 1930 premiere in Berlin, was initially to have cost $150,000 (Warner Brothers was then the chief backer), but by the time the curtain went up, the amount had soared to $300,000 (mostly supplied by the Rockefeller family). Little wonder. The entire theatre was transformed into an Alpine village, with the main lobby becoming the main street in the town and local atmosphere enhanced by putting Tyrolean costumes on all the ushers. In the auditorium, scenic mountains rose on all sides to a star-studded ceiling. On the stage, there were such tourist-fetching novelties as a steamboat sailing across the stage bearing fifty chorus girls, a rainstorm using 1,000 gallons of water,

Lucas-Pritchard; Theatre Coll., NY Public Lib.
The entrance of Emperor Franz Josef (Arnold Korff) in *White Horse Inn* is an occasion
for the cast to spill out into the auditorium of the Center Theatre.

a rotating merry-go-round (on one of three revolving stages), real goats, real pigeons, a real pony, four mechanical cows, one sight-seeing bus, and one Austro-Hungarian emperor. In short, a full evening of super-duper Radio City Music Hall stage shows—all for $3.85. William Gaxton (in a role originally intended for Jimmy Savo) played the headwaiter in Kitty Carlisle's larger-than-life Bavarian hostelry. The run, while hardly as awesome as the show, was still a satisfying 223 performances.

Since Cole Porter, Howard Lindsay, Russel Crouse, Vinton Freedley, Ethel Merman and William Gaxton had clicked so well with *Anything Goes*, it seemed logical for them to team up again for another musical. And so they did, except that by the time it had gone into production, Mr. Gaxton had been succeeded by Bob Hope. One other major change: for the chief clown, instead of the meek Victor Moore, they now had the explosive Jimmy Durante. The musical, which had first been known as ——*but Millions!* and later *Wait for Baby*, opened as *Red, Hot and Blue!* at the Alvin on October 29.

Well aware of the rumors regarding the musical's political slant, co-author Russel Crouse, in a magazine article, kiddingly sought to explain the show's deeper significance and hidden meaning. "The whole thing, of course," he wrote, "is done in symbols. Even the orchestra is composed entirely of symbol players. For instance, Ethel Merman, you will find, is playing a wealthy young widow. But if you look behind Miss Merman—I mean, if you look behind Miss Merman's characterization—you will find that she represents much more than wealth and youth and widowhood. She is really in the play as a symbol of the class struggle between freshmen and sophomores. The same applies to Jimmy Durante. When Mr. Durante says 'Hot-cha-cha!' he doesn't mean 'Hot-cha-cha!' at all, but something much more intangible, something that reaches to the very core of industrial life today, something fine and good and true, something you can put away and forget about."

The story of *Red, Hot and Blue!* was a wild idea about a national lottery to discover a girl who had sat on a waffle iron at the age of four. Some observers noted a superficial resemblance to *Of Thee I Sing*, with the show's use of a contest to pick the wife of the leading man and his firm opposition to the winner once she's been chosen. They'd even planned the wedding to take place on the White House lawn. Actually, whatever few satirical thrusts could be found were aimed at such mild targets as luxurious prisons (that had already been done in *The New Yorkers*), the poverty of the government (three senators enter the contest to win money to help replenish the treasury), and the Supreme Court (they vote, by a six-to-three decision, that the lottery is unconstitutional on the grounds that it might benefit the American people).

131

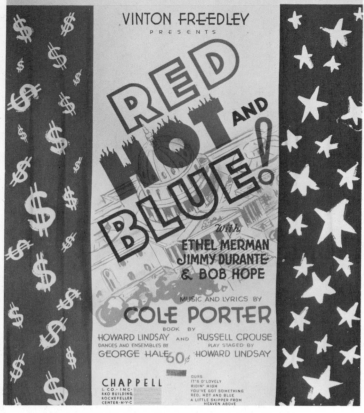

A LITTLE SKIPPER FROM HEAVEN ABOVE

Note that name of Russel Crouse is misspelled.

But the plot was easily overlooked (its connecting links, according to Brooks Atkinson, consisted of "Oh, hello, Bob's" and "I was looking for you's"), when audiences could enjoy Ethel Merman and Jimmy Durante having themselves such a footloose time. Miss Merman, of course, had all the rousers in the Porter collection, including "Ridin' High," with its clarion proclamation of ecstatic bliss once

true love has been found. (This condition further prompts the lady to reveal, in two patter sections, her lack of envy of Olympic swimming champ Eleanor Holm Jarrett's aquatic surroundings, Dorothy Parker's wit, Mrs. FDR's writing fees, Tallulah Bankhead's jewelry, Mae West's curves, society leader Mrs. Harrison Williams' clothes, Woolworth heiress Barbara Hutton's automobiles, Wallis Simpson's king, Katharine Hepburn's nose, and Marlene Dietrich's legs.) In the propulsive title song, Miss Merman, disdaining the classics, trumpeted her love for melodies that are "red, hot and blue." In a bitter mood, she confessed, despite her elegant surroundings, "I'm deserted and depressed/ In my regal eagle nest/ Down in the depths on the 90th floor." And in the perky "It's De-Lovely," she and Bob Hope traced their romance from a walk at night and the first kiss, right through to a wedding, a honeymoon and the arrival of the first baby.

Durante as the captain of the polo team of Lark's Nest Prison had one song, "A Little Skipper from Heaven Above," in which he admitted that he was really a woman about to be a mother. Schnozzola, apparently, was able to put it across. And, of course, with Merman and Durante on stage together, it wasn't hard to bring the house down with an exchange such as:

Durante: Don't cry. Please don't cry. Don't be lugubrious.
Merman: What's lugubrious mean?
Durante: Go ahead and cry.

Courtesy Louis Botto
Jimmy Durante, Ethel Merman and Bob Hope in *Red, Hot and Blue!*

"All the News That's Fit to Print."

The New York Times.

FINAL EXTRA
Rain and much colder today. To-morrow fair, with little change in temperature.
Temperatures Yesterday—Max., 52; Min., 48

Copyright, 1936, by The New York Times Company.

LXXXVI.....No. 28,774.

Entered as Second-Class Matter, Postoffice, New York, N. Y.

NEW YORK, WEDNESDAY, NOVEMBER 4, 1936.

TWO CENTS in New York City. | THREE CENTS Within 200 Miles. | FOUR CENTS Elsewhere Except in 7th and 8th Postal Zones.

ROOSEVELT SWEEPS THE NATION;
HIS ELECTORAL VOTE EXCEEDS 500;
LEHMAN WINS; CHARTER ADOPTED

HOUSE SHIFTS | Landon Congratulates President, Who Replies | BIG CHARTER VOTE | Smith Plans Comment On the ... ion Today | LEHMAN VOTE CUT | ... | ... SETS RECORD

Next to the escapades of the Prince of Wales, the early madcap life of King Carol of Roumania made for good newspaper copy during the Twenties. An affair of his youth with a diplomat's wife was the odd inspiration for a Sigmund Romberg–Otto Harbach operetta, *Forbidden Melody*, which arrived on Broadway early in November. It proved a none too auspicious debut for Danish leading man Carl Brisson as it won a unanimously negative verdict from the critics (Richard Lockridge found it "chiefly remarkable for the fact that the verb 'twit' appears openly for the first time in several decades"). *Forbidden Melody* was the final musical to play the New Amsterdam Theatre, which, since its opening in 1903, had been one of the major Broadway showplaces. Its years as a movie grind house would begin in 1937.

On the night following the opening of *Forbidden Melody*, Franklin D. Roosevelt was reelected by a whopping eleven-million-vote plurality over Alf Landon, and an electoral vote of 523 to 8 (for Maine and Vermont). At the time, few governments in the world were undergoing internal warfare so peacefully, or had won over the people so decisively. In Ethiopia, the Italian invaders were finding it increasingly difficult to suppress the raiding bands of natives. In France, with the franc devalued and inflation rampant, Premier Léon Blum was having a stormy time presiding over the shaky left-wing alliance known as the *Front Populaire*. In England, the people were deeply troubled over the decision of their new king, Edward VIII, to renounce the throne to wed the twice-divorced Wallis Simpson. In Spain, Franco's forces had begun the siege of Madrid. In Asia, leaders of the

Reprinted by permission, NY *Daily News*

Chinese republic were attempting some sort of agreement with the Communists in a desperate effort to turn back the Japanese forces. Germany, however, continued to be the most serious threat to world peace. With its armies already fortifying the demilitarized Rhineland, it had just joined with Italy in a military alliance known as the Rome-Berlin Axis.

One of the victims of Hitler's repressive policies was to become one of the most significant composers in the American musical theatre. He was Kurt Weill, the composer of *The Threepenny Opera*, which had had such a disappointing run on Broadway in 1933. Weill arrived in New York two years later to create the score for the Max Reinhardt biblical pageant, *The Eternal Road*. When financial problems forced Reinhardt to delay the production, Weill began searching for a new theme and a new librettist. Despite his treatment by the Nazis, the composer was convinced that another war against Germany would be a catastrophe from which the world could never recover, and he was anxious to become involved in a production that would express that feeling. Through Lee Strasberg of the Group Theatre, Weill met playwright Paul Green and together they created a stinging, farcical antiwar musical, *Johnny Johnson*.

Johnny Johnson, which opened November 19, did not receive an altogether favorable press. Critics were reminded of Charlie Chaplin's *Shoulder Arms*, Alban Berg's opera *Wozzeck*, and the Polish classic, *The Good Soldier Schweik*, and most of the comments emphasized the conglomerate nature of the work. To Richard Watts, Jr. (the *Herald Tribune's* new first-string critic following the death of Percy Hammond), it was "a disturbing and often hilarious medley of caricature, satire, musical comedy, melodrama, farce, social polemic, and parable," but to Robert Landry of *Variety* it was "a hodgepodge of whimsy, farce, social propaganda, stark realism, and fantasy." Words such as "bungling," "fumbling," "confused," "disconnected" and "amateurish" cropped up in reviews much to the exasperation of Robert Benchley. "My God," he exclaimed, "if we don't grab onto something really big when it comes along, even if it does have flaws, the theatre may go right on as it started this year . . . This is the first antiwar play to use laughing gas in its attack on the stupidity of mankind, and to my mind the most effective of all satires in its class." Anyway, despite their carping, the drama critics surprisingly voted *Johnny Johnson* the runner-up to Maxwell Anderson's *High Tor* as the best play of the 1936–1937 season.

Curiously, *Johnny Johnson* was never considered a musical; the printed text referred to it as "A Fable of Ancient and Modern Times," and most of the reviewers treated the songs—which they admired—as something auxiliary to the drama. The story traces the adventures of Johnny Johnson, a simple stonecutter, who joins the army in the world war because he is convinced that it will be the war to end wars. Although army examiners consider Johnny crazy, they ship him off to France anyway. At the front he is hit in the seat of his pants, is sent to a hospital, but escapes with a canister of laughing gas. He makes his way to the Allied High

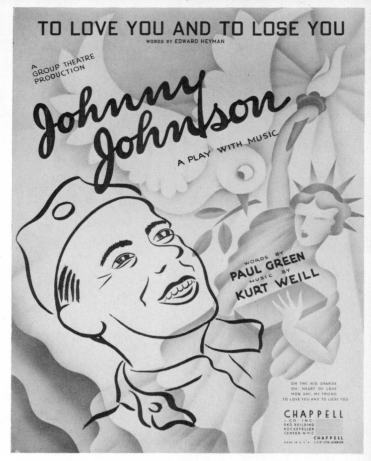

Command, tells the generals that the German soldiers are rebelling, and pleads with them not to launch their planned attack. When they refuse, he sprays them with the gas, causing the military leaders to break out into wild hysterics. Pershing makes Johnny a general and the first thing he does is to order a halt to the war. The Americans and the Germans embrace, but the Allied leaders, now fully recovered, order the offensive to begin and Johnny is arrested.

Back home, he is placed in an asylum. Still there ten years later, Johnny—who by now resembles Woodrow Wilson—chairs a meeting of the inmates, all of whom look like Senators Henry Cabot Lodge, William Borah and Hiram Johnson, Wilson's Vice President Thomas Marshall, and former President Theodore Roosevelt. They debate the merits of a League of World Republics. Johnny argues against the concept that building a stockpile of arms is a deterrent to aggression. Eventually, though some reluctantly, all vote to establish the League. When Johnny is last seen, he has been let out of the asylum and is on a street corner selling toys (but no toy soldiers) while everyone in town is whooping it up for war. But Johnny hasn't despaired and he reaffirms his optimism in his refrain, "We'll never lose our faith and hope and trust in all mankind;/ We'll work and strive while

enly cavorted through "Has Anybody Seen Our Ship?" and then, as two rather seedy dandies, did a light, polite and slightly pathetic soft shoe ("As we stroll down Picc-Piccadilly/ All the girls say, 'Who's here?/ Put your hat straight, my dear,/ For it's Marmaduke and Percy Vere de Vere'"). The propulsive beat of "Play, Orchestra, Play" and the airy "You Were There," both sung in *Shadow Play*, were also full of typical Noël Coward sparkle. *Family Album* gave the author the opportunity to return to the England of 1860, with songs full of ideals about dying for the Empire and doing one's best for the nation. There were also a tender tune from the music box and one piece actually called "Hearts and Flowers."

Vandamm
"Red Peppers" Noël Coward and Gertrude Lawrence sing "Has Anybody Seen Our Ship?" in *Tonight at 8:30*.

Bligh-Colbert; Theatre Coll., NY Public Lib.
Russell Collins, in the title role in *Johnny Johnson*, sells his toys and sings his song in the final scene of the production.

we're alive/ The better way to find . . ." As he disappears down the long street, he whistles the song a bit more bravely—as the curtain falls.

Five nights after the *Johnny Johnson* opening, it was time again for pure froth. Noël Coward's *Tonight at 8:30*, in which he appeared opposite Gertrude Lawrence, was a collection of nine one-act plays, presented in rotating groups of three, of which one was always a musical. The three this volume is concerned with: *Red Peppers*, described by Mr. Coward as "a vaudeville sketch sandwiched in between parodies of music-hall songs"; *Shadow Play*, "a pleasant theatrical device which gave Gertie and me a chance to sing as romantically as we could, dance in the moonlight, and, we hoped, convince the audience that we were very fascinating indeed"; and *Family Album*, "a sly satire on Victorian hypocrisy adorned with an unobtrusive but agreeable musical score."

Those music-hall parodies in *Red Peppers* turned out to be irresistible show-stoppers as Coward and Lawrence, first in sailor suits and red wigs, drunk-

Composer Donald Heywood, who had been hit over the head at the first showing of his *Africana* two years before, fearlessly came back to Broadway in December. This time two stench bombs exploded during the opening-night performance of his all-black musical, *Black Rhythm*. The show fizzled out in less than a week.

The year's Christmas present, though, was a genuine dazzler, *The Show Is On*. Under the auspices of the Messrs. Shubert, Vincente Minnelli was back in stylish form to create a gay, smart, elegant revue, with much of the same flavor—and people—as his *At Home Abroad*. Joining Minnelli again were Beatrice Lillie, Reginald Gardiner, Paul Haakon, and Vera Allen, plus a new co-star, Bert Lahr. However, instead of being the product of one song-writing team, as *At Home Abroad* had been, the new revue enlisted the services of a whole passel of composers and lyricists, including Vernon Duke and Ted Fetter ("Now"), the Gershwin brothers ("By Strauss"), Rodgers and Hart ("Rhythm"), Stanley Adams and Hoagy Carmichael ("Little Old Lady," the hit of the show), and Yip Harburg, Norman Zeno and Will Irwin ("Long as You've Got Your Health"). *The Show Is On*, as befitting a successor to *At Home Abroad*, also had a theme: around the world of show business.

In Minnelli's perusal of a variety of theatrical exhibits, there were few areas that did not come in for a sketch or a song (except, possibly, jazz, though Bunny Berigan was to have been featured in a jam session that was cut before New York). The show went on, fittingly, with a Howard Dietz–Arthur Schwartz Shakespearean takeoff (Reginald Gardiner played the Bard), in which characters from Shakespeare's plays were presented as they might have been had he written them for Broadway (as Juliet sang it to Romeo, "I'm not the kind of a girl for a boy like you/ I am a Capulet, You're a Montague"). In a sketch, Bert Lahr played film star Ronald Traylor (complete with a widow's peak extending almost to his eyebrows) whose assignment was to woo a certain Baltimore divorcée so that she would return with him to Hollywood and let the King of Titania remain on his throne. In "Rhythm," Beatrice Lillie, wearing a huge spray of bobbing orchids, was the rhythm singer to end all rhythm singers as she extolled her calling amidst interpolated bars from such diverse tunes as "On Your Toes" and "The Star-Spangled Banner" ("Up everybody!"). Even the piano collapsed. "By Strauss" was the Gershwin brothers unexpected homage to the pleasures of the waltz and its progenitor:

Drawing by Gard

Lucas-Pritchard; Theatre Coll., NY Public Lib.
"The Reading of the Play" sketch in *The Show Is On*. Beatrice Lillie and Reginald Gardiner are at opposite sides of the table.

Away with your music of Broadway
Be off with your Irving Berlin
Oh, I give no quarter
To Kern or Cole Porter
And Gershwin keeps pounding on tin!

The operatic, Chaliapin-type baritone got his lumps in "Song of the Woodman," cataloguing (as had Jimmy Durante six years before in *The New Yorkers*) all the varied wonders to be made from wood ("Seats all shapes and classes/ For little lads and little lasses"). In an old-fashioned setting, "The Reading of the Play" developed into a series of tart comments by Miss Lillie as a *grand dame* of the theatre ("The play," says the producer, "is about a man and a woman." "Too much plot!" snaps Miss Lillie). Depicting a music-hall temptress, the British comedienne was seen perched precariously on a migratory half moon that swung out over the first few rows of the orchestra. As she sang "Buy Yourself a Balloon," she coquettishly bestowed her ready supply of garters on favored bald heads in the audience. In the sketch, "Tovarisch," a parody on the recently opened play about exiled Russian nobility, a Republican couple working as servants in a household of Democrats secretly worship at

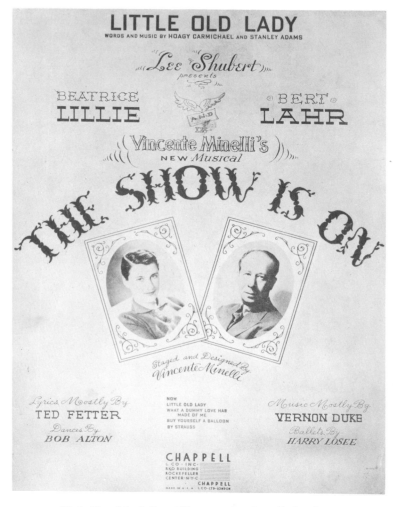

Note that Mr. Minnelli's name is misspelled twice.

the shrine of Little Father Herbert Hoover (his likeness is hidden beneath a portrait of Thomas Jefferson). The big production numbers featured a Tom Show cakewalking parade with Bert Lahr as Uncle Tom and Beatrice Lillie as Little Eva, and a burlesque of burlesque, with Bert as a red-nosed comic and Bea as the featured stripper.

Perhaps the most celebrated skit was the Moss Hart inspiration, "Mr. Gielgud Passes By." New York at that time was playing host to two simultaneously running productions of *Hamlet*, John Gielgud's and Leslie Howard's. In the revue, the Winter Garden stage permitted audiences to see Gielgud (Reginald Gardiner) on stage in his theatre as well as the audience in the first three rows of the orchestra. As the play progresses, along comes Mrs. Slemp (Beatrice Lillie) totally impervious to the sign forbidding seating during the first scene, as she noisily makes her way to her seat (to anyone who shushes her, she hisses "Communist!"). Because of her incessant chatter, Mrs. Slemp forces Gielgud to speak louder and louder to make himself heard—which only succeeds in the lady complaining that he's trying to drown her out. Finally, the actor, completely distraught, stops in the middle of a soliloquy, leans over the stage apron, and offers Mrs. Slemp a ticket to Leslie Howard's production. "Oh, I couldn't take it," she trills sweetly. "Mr. Howard gave me the ticket to come here." Blackout.

"Radiant high jinks," "luminous work of art," "gaily infectious," and "bright, beautiful and gay," were some of the critical praises heaped upon this welcome yuletide present. And it turned out to be one gift that would continue to offer pleasure throughout the entire theatre season.

"... SING ME OF WARS AND SING ME OF BREADLINES ..."

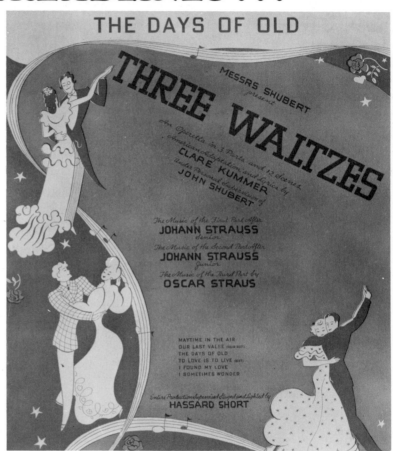

As far as the musical theatre was concerned, 1937 was the decade's battlefield. More sharply than did any other year, it pitted the old versus the new, the traditional versus the experimental, escape versus involvement. And when the twelve months had ended, it was clear that, on balance, the world of musical comedy had elected to become part of the real world.

At first, this seemed hardly likely. It was a year that gave us two turn-of-the-century musical melodramas, *Naughty-Naught ('00)* and *The Fireman's Flame*, with which the brothers Krimsky filled their American Music Hall. It found the family Rockefeller going even further back in time with their elaborate tale of colonial days called *Virginia*. And while it may have heard in Rodgers and Hart's *Babes in Arms* a battle cry of youth, the musical was concerned with nothing more militant than a bunch of kids putting on a show. Perhaps the dichotomy of the year's output was most apparent in the four productions offered by the brothers Shubert. Two of them, *Frederika* and *Three Waltzes*, moved to the more leisurely bygone beat of Lehár and the Strausses. One, *Between the Devil*, was saddled by an outdated story but had a very sleek and modern score. And one, *Hooray for What!* took on the very pressing theme of war and war-makers.

Despite the variety of output, there was no question that the major productions of 1937 were inspired by the headlines of 1937. In addition to *Hooray for What!* the year spotlighted three daringly topical musicals. June brought *The Cradle Will Rock,* an uncompromising parable on the

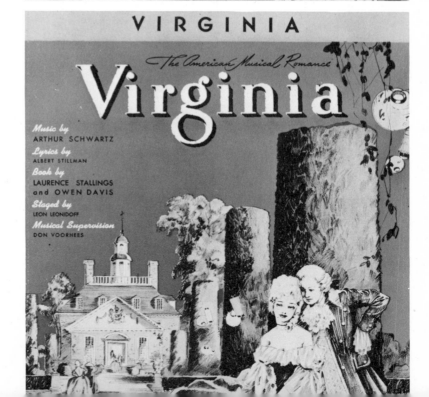

evils of capitalism and the virtues of labor. *Pins and Needles*, which arrived in the fall, touched on many topics of concern to members of the International Ladies Garment Workers Union. The theatrical event of the year and possibly of the decade was *I'd Rather Be Right*, which became the first book musical ever to deal directly with a living President of the United States and his administration.

George M. Cohan's portrayal of Franklin D. Roosevelt won the acting honors of the year (runner up: Ed Wynn in *Hooray for What!*), but the best musical-comedy production would seem to have been *Babes in Arms*. That show also made Rodgers and Hart the year's top song writers, with the most impressive newcomer to the field Harold J. Rome for *Pins and Needles*, the year's lone revue. Other major debuts: Marc Blitzstein, the composer-lyricist-librettist-pianist of *The Cradle Will Rock*, and actor Howard DaSilva in the same show; also Mitzi Green, Ray Heatherton, and Wynn Murray in *Babes in Arms*. There were, in all, 15 musicals presented in 1937, with those running over 200 performances being *Pins and Needles* (it would eventually set the record as the longest-running musical in Broadway history), *Babes in Arms*, *I'd Rather Be Right*, *The Fireman's Flame*, and *Hooray for What!*

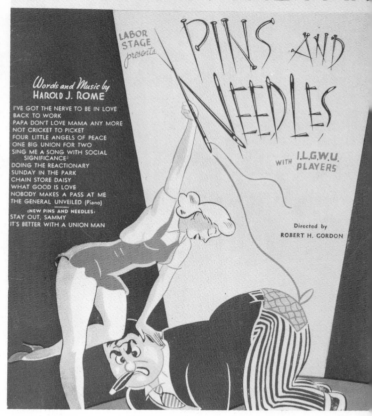

The year's number of nonmusical plays and comedies was down again—to only 82. But among them, playgoers could enjoy Maxwell Anderson's *High Tor* with Burgess Meredith; Maurice Evans' revival of Shakespeare's *Richard II*; George Abbott's production of *Room Service*; a second Anderson play, *The Star Wagon*, also with Burgess Meredith; Gertrude Lawrence in Rachel Crothers' *Susan and God*; Alfred Lunt and Lynn Fontanne in *Amphitryon 38*; Clifford Odets' play, *Golden Boy*, sponsored by the Group Theatre; Orson Welles' modern dress *Julius Caesar*; and *Of Mice and Men*, by John Steinbeck.

On January 23, just three nights after President Roosevelt was inaugurated for his second term, *Naughty-Naught* ('00) became the first Broadway musical of the year. Only it wasn't even near Broadway. John and Jerrold Krimsky had taken over an old movie house on East 55th Street and had it remodeled to resemble a turn-of-the-century beer hall. Drinks were served during the show as an appropriate adjunct to the unpretentious, cornball melodrama concocted by Jerrold Krimsky (under the alias of John Van Antwerp), lyricist Ted Fetter, and composer Richard Lewine. The critics, hardly knowing how to appraise so purposely outlandish a musical (how do you hiss something in print after being invited to hiss during the performance?), simply sat back and enjoyed themselves. The production, which dealt with undergraduate doings of the Yale class of Naughty-Naught, proved so successful that it led to a series of similar ventures under the same sponsorship and authorship. The second item, *The Fireman's Flame*, opened in October and had an even slightly longer run. Ben Cutler headed the cast as the leader of the Blue Bird Hose Boys, volunteer firefighters and rivals

Vandamm; Theatre Coll., NY Public Lib.
Hero Bartlett Robinson squares off with tough Howard Sullivan in *Naughty-Naught*. Harry Meehan is the bartender and Gloria Worthing is the girl.

of the more socially prominent Red Heart Hose Boys. The third in the series, *The Girl from Wyoming*, came along in October 1938. By then, however, the form had begun to lose its novelty.

The youthful Johann Wolfgang von Goethe, no less, was the hero of *Frederika*, an operetta that opened early in February. Named for the poet's first great love, the bittersweet tale was unfolded amid an elaborate Shubert production staged by Hassard Short. Dennis King and Helen Gleason, as the socially mismatched couple, sang most of the lush Franz Lehár score. The operetta had first been presented in Berlin almost nine years before, where it had caused something of a storm because it dared show Germany's canonized literary hero singing on the musical stage. In New York, most daily reviewers found it reasonably entertaining (Atkinson said it "made a virtue of avoiding originality"), but it was too stodgy to attract customers longer than three months.

A more up-to-date theme of youth was found in the wide-awake, apple-cheek charm of *Babes in Arms*, the lone April entry. Rodgers and Hart's slight Depression-inspired story told of a group of youngsters and their struggle to put on an original musical revue in order to avoid being sent to a work farm (their parents, all vaudevillians, had gone off to earn meager salaries working for the Federal Theatre Project). At a $3.85 top price, the musical became the first solid hit of the year, and turned a greater profit (total gross: $474,700) than most shows with longer runs. Reason: it had cost producer Dwight Deere Wiman a mere $55,000 to put on. What kept costs down was, primarily, the cast of relative unknowns and the modest settings and costumes. No one could care less. The

critics were all sufficiently enchanted to come up with such happily paired adjectives as "genial and buoyant" (Atkinson), "fresh and likeable" (Watts), "gay and sprightly" (Lockridge), "joyous and delectable" (Brown), and "dewy and precocious" (*Time*).

No other score by Rodgers and Hart ever contained so many durable numbers. They included "Where or When," the psychological phenomenon of strangers believing they had met before; the splenetic catalogue of domestic irritations, "I Wish I Were in Love Again"; the tenderly insulting "My Funny Valentine" (that was the boy's name); the spirited saga of the vocal freak, "Johnny One Note," performed by Wynn Murray in a makeshift Egyptian setting (towels and clothes hooks for headdresses, and scrub mops for wigs made up most of the costumes); and the saga of the lady whose normal behavior and attitudes (such as dining early, arriving at the theatre on time, staying awake at the opera, refusing to go slumming in Harlem, and disliking California) have branded her a tramp.

Lucas-Pritchard; courtesy Lynn Farnol Group
Mitzi Green, Ray Heartherton and Duke McHale in *Babes in Arms*.

The show also spotlighted a George Balanchine ballet, "Peter's Dream," in which young Peter (Duke McHale) imagines himself a rich prince and goes on a fantasy trip to Hollywood, Radio City, Europe, Africa, and finally back to reality.

The title tune, a ringing, evangelical chorale in which the kids proclaim themselves no longer babes in arms but babes in armor, could very well apply to the emergence of the young members of the cast. Among them: 16-year-old Mitzi Green, who'd been a child actress in Hollywood; 25-year-old Ray Heatherton, a radio singer; 16-year-old Wynn Murray, who'd never sung professionally before; Fayard and Harold Nicholas, primarily known as nightclub hoofers; 17-year-old Rolly Pickert, whose

specialty was dancing on stilts; 19-year-old Duke McHale, the leading ballet dancer; 22-year-old Alfred Drake who sang "Babes in Arms"; and 18-year-old chorus boy Dan Dailey.

No one preferred *Orchids Preferred*, the first of two openings in May, despite a spicy item called "I'm Leaving the Bad Girls for Good." It lasted a week. *Sea Legs*, the second opening of the month, starred Dorothey Stone and husband Charles Collins, and folded in two weeks. Thus endeth the 1936–1937 season, as far as musicals were concerned.

June, however, contrary to all recent form, produced not only a musical but one of the most highly controversial musicals of the decade: *The Cradle Will Rock*.

A major addition to the initialed bureaucracy of Washington had begun in 1935 with the establishment of the Works Progress Administration (WPA). Headed by Harry Hopkins, the agency in its seven-year existence spent nearly $20 billion on such projects as reforestation, flood control, rural electrification, school construction, slum clearance, and student scholarship. Its main purpose, of course, was to take people off the dole and put them back to work in, hopefully, worthwhile projects.

One of the most controversial features of the WPA was the area employing artists, musicians,

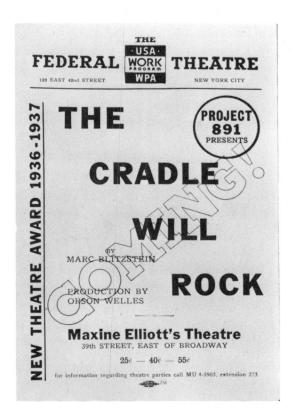

Alfredo Valente
Marc Blitzstein, creator of *The Cradle Will Rock*, onstage during a performance.

writers, and actors. When the Federal Theatre Project was set up under the direction of Hallie Flanagan, some 5,000 actors in New York City alone were jobless; throughout the country, almost 30,000 people connected in some way with show business were on relief. To help correct this situation, the FTP, during its four-year life, employed over 12,000 men and women at an average wage of $23.86 per week.

Almost as soon as it had begun, the FTP was the center of controversy. Congressional committees branded it a haven for Communist influence and referred derisively to it as a boondoggle. Notwithstanding the constant sniping, the project did manage to offer a rich but inexpensive fare of Shakespeare, children's plays, experimental dramas, "Living Theater" documentaries, and plays with all-Negro casts. In the summer of 1937, it was about to offer its first musical.

Marc Blitzstein, a classically trained composer-lyricist, had dashed off *The Cradle Will Rock* in five weeks in 1936. But his efforts to interest Broadway producers made little headway. And for a good reason. The play was about the struggle for union recognition in a steel town—called Steeltown—and the producers felt, with justification, that no matter the musical's quality, the strong anticapitalistic tone would make it an extremely risky venture. The real-life background of the struggle had begun in August 1936 when John L. Lewis, the head of the United Mineworkers Union, led a walkout of industrial-type unions from the craft union-dominated American Federation of Labor. The rebellious

eight unions, under the collective name of Committee for Industrial Organization (CIO), then set their sights on organizing workers in such industries as coal, automobile, garment, rubber, and steel. Steel was the first major target. Headed by Philip Murray, the Steel Workers Organizing Committee achieved an initial victory in March 1937 when U.S. Steel bowed to its demands. The next target—five companies banded together under the combine known as "Little Steel"—offered stiffer opposition both on the picket line and in the courts. (After a two-year struggle, it too would capitulate.)

Despite the understandable chariness of producers to tackle anything so militantly anti-big business as *The Cradle Will Rock*, one producer and one director were determined to put it on. They were John Houseman, who headed Federal Theatre Project 891, and a 21-year-old director named Orson Welles. The scheduled opening was to be June 16, at the Maxine Elliott Theatre, on 39th Street east of Broadway. Tickets were priced at 25¢, 40¢, and 55¢.

As the opening date neared, there were rumblings that the FTP would never permit the show to go on. Mrs. Flanagan, by then under almost daily attack for waste and mismanagement, had been forced to cut New York activities by 30 percent. As a result, she issued a directive that no new production would be permitted to open before July 1. So it was that on the night of June 16, the Maxine Elliott Theatre was barred to actors, crew and audience. But the audience, unaware of the ban, had begun gathering outside the theatre. Welles was defiant. He was determined to go through with the production. But where? And under what conditions? Actors Equity had told him the company could not perform the play on any other stage

Alfredo Valente
Union organizer Howard DaSilva registers his feelings about capitalism in *The Cradle Will Rock*. Olive Stanton is the laughing prostitute.

under any other auspices. The Musicians Union had told him the musicians could move but that they would have to be paid according to Broadway scale. So that was out. And still Welles refused to admit defeat. Calling the cast together, he outlined his plan: "There is nothing to prevent you from buying your way into whatever theatre we find. Then, why not get up from your seats, and speak your piece when your cue comes. And since we cannot afford to pay musicians, why not have Marc appear alone on the stage at the piano?" With a cheer, the plan was enthusiastically agreed on. But by now it was past eight o'clock and they were still unable to find an empty theatre that would take them in. Then, according to Blitzstein's account, a stranger who had been listening to Welles piped up with an offer to let them use his theatre, the Venice, up on 59th Street and 7th Avenue.

As Blitzstein described the scene: "The new theatre's address was then announced to the audience waiting in front of the Maxine Elliott. And now commenced a parade up Broadway with taxis containing Welles, Houseman, Abe Feder, our lighting man, myself, and reporters, all followed by an entire audience on foot marching to see a show. By the time we reached the Venice, our original audience of 1,000 had doubled as the word spread."

Everyone who could squeeze into the Venice that night was conscious that he was present at an historic event. Alone on the bare stage was Blitzstein in shirtsleeves, his piano gutted to give it greater tone, illuminated by Feder's single spotlight. The first song, "I'm Checkin' Home Now," was sung by Olive Stanton (as the prostitute) from a right loge, with Feder swinging his spot around to catch her. Then another actor, seated in midorchestra, spoke his piece. And so it went. Actors rising from all parts of the house when their cues came, with Feder frantically switching his spot to pick up as many as he could. At the end of the performance pandemonium broke out as the entire audience rose to its feet.

The Cradle Will Rock continued at the Venice for 19 performances. Later in the year, on December 5, Houseman and Welles, who by then had quit the Federal Theatre to organize the Mercury Theatre, offered it for a series of Sunday night performances during the run of their modern dress version of Shakespeare's *Julius Caesar*. At last, on January 3, 1938, theatre owner Sam Grisman sponsored it for a regular Broadway run at his Windsor Theatre

(top price: $1.65). It remained there for 108 performances.

All of the productions were staged simply, without scenery and with the composer at the piano. This, however, was far from the original Wellesian concept. As initially planned—and as it was actually performed at its single dress rehearsal at the Maxine Elliott on June 15—the actors stood on glass wagons, lit from beneath, which, for the cradle-rocking finale, rocked back and forth as blinding lights shot up from below. While everyone was singing the surging title song ("That's thunder, that's lightning!/ And it's going to surround you! . . ."), the trumpets, fifes and drums of the steelworkers' parade blared out of loudspeakers from all over the auditorium.

Obviously, no matter how it was presented, this "Play in Music," as it was billed, was not everyone's idea of what a musical should be. The story (described by Irving Kolodin as "a modern immorality play") was little more than an animated political cartoon set to music. Mr. and Mrs. Mister, who own Steeltown, are the embodiment of power, greed and corruption, and their children, Junior Mister (why not Master Mister?) and Sister Mister, are vacuous birdbrains. Only the striving workers, led by incorruptible Larry Foreman, are pure of heart and noble of spirit. Not only was the story concerned with the blessings of industrial unionism; it was equally concerned with prostitution, both the obvious kind as personified by the sympathetic streetwalker, and the more devious type, "the sellout," as Blitzstein has written, "of one's profession, one's talents, one's dignity and integrity at the hands of big business or the powers that be." This form of prostitution was also personified: the Arts by Dauber the painter and Yasha the composer, the Press by Editor Daily, Education by President Prexy, Religion by Reverend Salvation, and Medicine by Dr. Specialist.

The reviewers didn't get around to see *The Cradle Will Rock* until its Broadway premiere in January (at which performance, it was duly noted in the press, four elegantly groomed first-nighters in the second row remained but fifteen minutes and then, to a scattering of boos, rose and strode out of the theatre). These critics, while accepting the fact that the work was an obvious piece of propaganda, expressed general admiration for the skill with which it had been put together and its uncompromising "savagery" and "bitterness"—the two most frequently used descriptive nouns.

Much of this was in the music and lyrics. In Editor Daily's credo, "The Freedom of the Press" means, "We must be free to say whatever's on our chest . . . For whichever side will pay the best." When Dauber and Yasha, those sycophantic spongers, sing "Art for Art's Sake," they urge, to a staccato beat:

> Be blind for Art's sake,
> And deaf for Art's sake,
> And dumb for Art's sake,
> Until for Art's sake,
> They kill for Art's sake
> All the Art for Art's sake!

In a scene in the college president's office, after Mr. Mister has asked for a speaker to enlist the students for military training, Professor Trixie fills the bill with a rah-rah cheer ("Army training— Port in a storm!/ There's nuttin' like a uniform!"). In his more sincerely felt pieces, Blitzstein penned a mournful dirge about the power of money in "Nickel Under the Foot," and a roaring, blazing title song as warning to all those who would oppose the will of the people.

With the Federal Theatre permitting, July brought a second WPA musical to town. *Swing It*, a product of the Negro unit, had a score by Eubie

Blake and Cecil Mack that included Mr. Mack's celebrated number, "Shine." Though the musical was thoroughly harmless (it dealt, rather loosely, with organizing a showboat on the Harlem River), the FTP was by then sufficiently cowed to insert the following note in the program: "The viewpoint of this play is not necessarily that of the WPA or any other agency of the government." The press was divided and the entertainment stayed two months. (The third Federal Theatre–sponsored musical of the year, *A Hero Is Born*, opened early in October. The book was by Theresa Helburn [one of the co-founders of the Theatre Guild], the score by Agnes Morgan and Lehman Engel, and it lasted 50 performances.)

What next to fill the Center Theatre? That was still the problem—at least for the Rockefellers. Now they had a new idea: since they'd already recreated *Alt Wien* for *The Great Waltz* and the Tyrolean Alps for *White Horse Inn*, why not give the public something closer to home, something celebrating a page in American history? And what could be more fitting than a story about colonial Williamsburg, in Virginia, particularly since the Rockefellers had recently financed its restoration at a cost of $13 million? So they hired a major dramatist, Laurence Stallings (*What Price Glory?*) to devise an original libretto, which turned out to be something about the first theatrical troupe in America and the efforts of its leader to smuggle a letter to General Washington from sympathizers in England. When more help was needed, they called in another well-known playwright, Owen Davis (co-author of the previous year's *Ethan Frome*). Arthur Schwartz was signed to write the music, with words supplied by Music Hall staff lyricist Al Stillman and, upon occasion, Mr. Stallings. Titled *Virginia*, the production opened September 2, thus inaugurating the 1937–1938 musical theatre season.

Despite the commendable efforts to extoll America's beginnings in spectacular fashion, and despite a score of unquestionable distinction (including "An Old Flame Never Dies" and "Goodbye, Jonah"), the results were greeted by a near unanimity of critical opinion that it was all pretty stuffy and overblown (as Richard Watts, Jr. put it, "It was so much like an endless succession of prologues from the nearby Music Hall that I found myself waiting for the Astaire-Rogers picture to begin"). A month after the premiere, Harry Wagstaff Gribble came in to tighten the story line and restage the production. All in vain. After two months *Virginia* gave up, $250,000 in the red.

In November 1937 there were, incredibly, only two musicals to be seen in the environs of Broadway. And both of them, equally incredibly, had music and lyrics by Richard Rodgers and Lorenz Hart. They were *Babes in Arms*, which had been on the boards since April, and the most eagerly awaited musical-comedy event of the year, *I'd Rather Be Right*.

Two main reasons accounted for this anticipation. One was sentimental: it marked the return to the musical stage of George M. Cohan who, though he had been in *Ah, Wilderness* in 1933, had not been seen in a musical since his own production, *The Merry Malones*, ten years before. The other reason had to do with the new show's boldness: its central character was the President of the United States. Not just a fictitious President of the United States, mind you, but the real thing, Franklin Delano Roosevelt himself. Never before had a play dared depict the head of the government during his lifetime not only by name but as a figure of fun and the butt of jokes. What feelings Germans may have had about their beloved Goethe being portrayed in *Frederika* could scarcely compare to the amazement that greeted the news that FDR would be singing and prancing on a Broadway stage.

The book of *I'd Rather Be Right* was devised by George S. Kaufman and Moss Hart, and the producer was Cohan's old partner, Sam H. Harris. *Of Thee I Sing* may have kidded some of America's most sacred institutions, *Face the Music* may have faced up to up-to-date municipal scandal, but the distinction of *I'd Rather Be Right* was that—except for wife Eleanor—almost everyone of importance connected with Roosevelt and his administration was up there on the stage getting his lumps in the genial ribbing. Lest anyone take offense, however, Kaufman and Hart went back to the old *Strike Up the Band* ploy of putting most of the action in a dream.

The locale of *I'd Rather Be Right* is New York's Central Park. The date is the Fourth of July. Peggy and Phil, in the park to hear a band concert, are troubled because they can't get married until President Roosevelt balances the budget. Phil falls asleep and dreams that they actually meet the President strolling in the park. Touched by their problem, Roosevelt promises to do what he can—and right away. He summons his Cabinet, whose leading

Drawing by Don Freeman

members all sing verses appropriate to their positions (Secretary of the Treasury Morgenthau: "I have achieved, you must admit, the biggest goddamned deficit"). First order of business, however, is politics, which FDR discusses with his chief patronage dispenser, Postmaster General James A. Farley.

> Farley: This fellow is Chairman of the Fourth Assembly District in Seattle. He wants to be Collector of the Port of New York.
> Roosevelt: But we've *got* a Collector of the Port of New York.
> Farley: Not in Seattle.

Roosevelt appeals to his Cabinet for suggestions about balancing the budget so that Peggy and Phil can get married. Hundred-dollar postage stamps? Tax government property? Government agents as pickpockets so that the people won't know their money is being taken? That's it! But the Supreme Court, which FDR had vainly sought to "pack" with added members the previous January, dashes out of the bushes to stop the President almost as soon as Roosevelt commands his Attorney General, "Cummings, take a law." In a Fireside Chat, Roosevelt next appeals to the women of America to give up wearing cosmetics for a year and to donate the money they save—$3 billion—to the government. He gets nowhere.

A Federal Theatre unit enters (it must give a performance whenever three or more people are

147

seen together) and does an ersatz Viennese number. Roosevelt decides that the only way to keep the Supreme Court from constantly opposing him is to get chummy with the justices. They, however, are still smarting over his referring to them as old fogeys; to disprove the allegation, they bring on their girls ("We're the girls they never say 'no' to"). FDR introduces Peggy and Phil to his proud mother ("What do you think of my son being President of the United States? . . . Twice, too."), but their conversation is interrupted by the Cabinet, which bursts in with a new idea: take the gold out of Fort Knox and use it to balance the budget. Great! But the news quickly leaks out and the stock market tumbles.

Phil introduces Roosevelt to a group of former business tycoons who now earn $23.86 per week ("Let the market crash, we collect our cash") in the PWA, and who couldn't be happier because the government can't take a cent of it. In an effort to settle a labor dispute that takes place in the park, Roosevelt asks to see the Wagner Act, which turns out to be a couple of acrobats (Hans and Fritz Wagner, Federal Theatre Project 34268). In desperation, the President asks the advice of the White House butler—who happens to be Alf Landon. But the defeated GOP Presidential candidate replies icily: "It's true I didn't photograph well nor did I have that smile. And I will frankly admit that I was lousy on the radio. But Mr. Roosevelt, I balanced my budget. So as we say in Kansas, Mr. Roosevelt—try that on your ukulele!"

Ignoring such rebuffs, FDR admits, in his "Off the Record" comments, that he still likes being President, despite and because of his problems with Congress, his avoidance of Vice President Garner, his sons' wealthy wives, his recent squabble with labor leader John L. Lewis (over differences involving the CIO's problems with Little Steel), the current stock-market decline, and wife Eleanor's prolonged absences. And then to prove how happy he is, Roosevelt does a hopping, bobbing and weaving dance just like George M. Cohan. FDR, in fact, wants to keep his job and reveals to his Cabinet that he is planning to seek a third term. He goes on the air with a variety program to sell the country on the idea, but the Supreme Court says its unconstitutional. It even declares the Constitution unconstitutional.

In a Fourth of July speech, the President admits that the country faces many problems but he bids the people take heart: "It seems that there is something in this country—a sort of spirit that holds us all together—that always sees us through. And we mustn't ever lose that. Just remember, folks, that even though things are a little wrong right now, we've got a chance to make 'em right, because at least this is a country where you can come and *talk* about what's wrong. And there aren't many left like that nowadays." Vowing to keep trying to balance the budget, Roosevelt advises Peggy and Phil to get married anyway. And that's exactly what they plan to do when Phil wakes up from his dream.

The top price for tickets to *I'd Rather Be Right* was $4.40, but on opening night, November 2 (the same day New York's Mayor LaGuardia was elected to his second term), tickets went for as high as $150 a pair. Thousands were in the street in front of the Alvin Theatre and two squadrons of mounted police lined 52nd Street. It was, according to George Jean Nathan, "the biggest opening since the Grand Canyon." The next day's reviews practically elected Cohan to the Presidency, but almost all contained reservations about the rather sketchy plot and most of them compared it unfavorably with *Of Thee I Sing*. Nevertheless, they all had words of praise for the political climate that enabled such a work to flourish. As John Mason Brown wrote: "It should swell our pride in the freedom we enjoy and in the gift for laughter which must be counted among our national assets. The more good humored liberties Mr. Kaufman and Mr. Hart's satire takes, the more liberty its mere performance bespeaks."

The same month that *I'd Rather Be Right* made its gala bow on Broadway (it would run 290 performances), a modest semiamateur revue called *Pins and Needles* opened at a tiny theatre on 39th Street and 6th Avenue. By the time its run was over, however, it would establish the longevity record for a musical production with a total of 1,108 performances. (As far as actual paying customers are concerned, the figure is somewhat misleading. The Labor Stage, née the Princess Theatre, where *Pins and Needles* played more than a year and a half of its run, seated 447; the Alvin, the home of *I'd Rather Be Right*, seated 1,334.)

Pins and Needles took everyone by surprise. Here was a labor show, even sponsored by a labor union, the ILGWU, but instead of militantly proclaiming the blessings of the trade union movement —as had *The Cradle Will Rock*—it was a light-

Vandamm
The President (George M. Cohan) introduces Peggy (Joy Hodges) and Phil (Austin Marshall) to his mother (Marie Louise Dana) in *I'd Rather Be Right*. The grim-faced butler carrying the cake is Alf Landon (Joseph Allen).

Vandamm; courtesy Lynn Farnol Group
President George M. Cohan needs little encouragement to break out into dance in *I'd Rather Be Right*.

Rea Irvin, *Stage* magazine

hearted revue, jabbing its pins and needles into itself as well as into its capitalistic adversaries. Primarily responsible for the revue's flavor and flair was a 29-year-old composer-lyricist, Harold J. Rome, making his Broadway—or near Broadway—debut.

As Rome remembers it: *"Pins and Needles* got started a couple of years before it was actually shown in the theatre. Louis Schaffer, who headed the theatrical activities of the ILGWU, had heard about some topical songs I had written at a summer resort called Green Mansions. I auditioned for him and he accepted my songs. Even gave me a job as rehearsal pianist. Our first problem came when we found that none of the union members wanted to do our show. They wanted something more serious. So Schaffer got the notion of hiring a professional company to put on the revue just for the union members to show them how effective it would be. That was in June 1936. Earl Robinson and I played the two pianos. The owner of the Belmont Theatre happened to be there that night and he wanted to put on the show, just as it was, in his theatre. But by now the garment workers were all for doing it, and Schaffer dashed our hopes by insisting that it could be done only by the ILGWU.

"With Charles Friedman directing, we rehearsed *Pins and Needles* for a year and a half, three nights a week. Remember, these were untrained kids for the most part and at times it was pretty slow going. When we finally opened I was still playing one of the pianos and Baldwin Bergersen came in to play the other. At first the show was scheduled only for weekends, Fridays and Saturdays, and no one thought much about it. Then word began trickling, and before we knew it it seemed as if the whole town had to see our little revue. What's more, our cast of dressmakers, cutters, embroiderers, and the like, were now full-fledged professionals, with Equity cards to prove it."

The spirit of the enterprise was set early in the show as the chorus burst out with their tongue-in-cheek demand, "Sing Me a Song with Social Significance," a takeoff on the conventional boy-girl duet, with such lines as "Sing me of wars and sing me of breadlines/ Tell me of front page news." The liberal's attitude toward reactionaries became a lively dance step: "Close your eyes to where you're bound/ And you'll be found/ Doin' the Reactionary." In a more plaintive mood, "One Big Union for Two," the lovers cooed such sentiments as "No court's injunctions can make us stop/ Until your love is all closed shop" and "We'll have no lockouts to make us frown/ No scabbing when I'm out of town." Ruth Rubinstein (Local 32, Underwear) sang of the plight of the Vassar girl reduced to selling ladies underwear at Macy's ("I used to be on the daisy chain,/ But now I'm a chain store daisy"), and Millie Weitz (Local 22, Dressmakers)

Courtesy ILGWU
The original program cover.

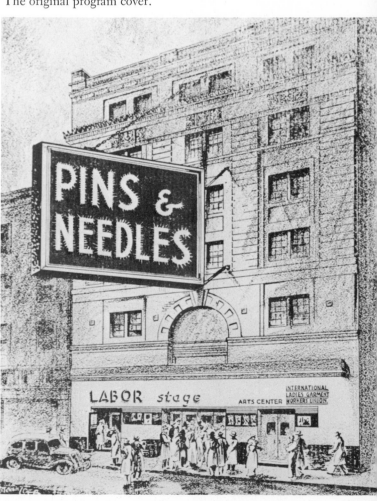

revealed the sad tale of the girl who has tried all the beauty products advertised on the radio but still cries, "Oh dear, what can the matter be?/ Nobody Makes a Pass at Me." The show even had a Hit Parade hit, "Sunday in the Park," sung by a variety of characters in the first act finale reveling in the bucolic charms of Central Park, "our fash'-nable resort until it's dark." At the end of the scene, a rainstorm ruins the one day in which the workers can relax.

Every sketch and dance routine made its point with equal effectiveness. "The Little Red School-house" satirized proletariat dramas, especially Bert Brecht's play, *Mother*. "We'd Rather Be Right" took the 100 percent Americans to task for condemning any change as being un-American. Marc Blitzstein, still smarting over his treatment by the Federal Theatre because of *The Cradle Will Rock*, tilted at government censorship in "FTP Plowed Under" (an FTP-sponsored play about the AAA had been called *Triple-A Plowed Under*). In a ballet sequence, a woman's club unveils a statue of a general on the anniversary of his birth. In the midst of a pantomime address by Mr. Warmonger (played by Irwin Corey during part of the run), the general comes to life and stirs everyone up to fighting with each other. When the general returns to his pedestal, the group becomes somberly aware of how easily it had been led.

The problem of any contemporary revue is, of course, to keep abreast of the headlines. Because *Pins and Needles* ran longer than any other such revue, it was subject to constant changes in lyrics and sketches. In December 1938, as a result of Great Britain's capitulation to Germany's demands at Munich, a sketch called "Britannia Waives the Rules" (by John Latouche and Arnold Horwitt) was added. When World War II broke out nine months later, it had to be removed. (One casualty: Prime Minister Chamberlain's celebrated tagline, "If at first you don't concede, fly, fly again.") "Papa Lewis, Mama Green," added in April 1939, was an animated political cartoon depicting the warring heads of the rival CIO and AFL organizations, with Harry Clark (Local 102, Truckdrivers) and Berni Gould (Local 117, Cloakmakers) as the quarreling parents. In May 1939, a new number, "The Red Mikado," used the rivalry of the concurrently running *Hot Mikado* and *Swing Mikado* to score satirical points at the expense of the far right. In this abbreviated comic opera, "Three Little Maids" became members of the Daughters of the American Revolution ("Three little DAR's are we/ Full to the brim with bigotry"), a slap at the patriotic group that had recently barred Negro contralto Marian Anderson from singing in its Constitution Hall in Washington. The Lord High Executioner (Harry Clark) had a "little list" of society offenders

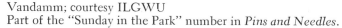

Vandamm; courtesy ILGWU
Part of the "Sunday in the Park" number in *Pins and Needles*.

"The General Is Unveiled" ballet in *Pins and Needles*: Irwin Corey as Mr. Warmonger, Harry Kadison as the General's Statue, and dancer Hilda Rubens.

The Three Little Maids (Nina Harary, Alma Charmat and Ida Mandel) in the *Pins and Needles* variation, "The Red Mikado."

that included American Nazi Fritz Kuhn, bigots, reactionaries, former President Hoover, Neville Chamberlain, Fascists, and, of course, the DAR (when executed, they leave blue blood on the ceremonial sword).

At about the same time, the revue added "Mene Mene Tekel," equating the biblical warning addressed to Belshazzar with a modern warning to all dictators. Despite its anti-Fascist, anti-Nazi, anti-Communist convictions, *Pins and Needles*, during almost all of its run, never veered from its staunch antimilitaristic stand and its opposition to involvement in the European conflict. After World War II had begun, Harold Rome added "Stay Out, Sammy," a musical parable in which a Negro mother, Dorothy Harrison (Local 38, 5th Avenue Dressmakers), warns her son, Talley Beatty (Shipping Clerks, Chicago), against getting mixed up in other kids' fights. (It would be withdrawn in June 1940, when the fate of the world seemed increasingly dependent upon American assistance to the British and French.)

The number that went through the greatest mutations caused by the international situation started life in November 1937 as "Four Little Angels of Peace." Originally, the angelic quartet consisted of British Foreign Secretary Anthony Eden to sing of his country's atrocities against the Boers, the Irish and the Indians; and unspecified Japanese (apparently neither Hirohito nor Tojo was considered well enough known at the time) to offer excuses for Japan's invasion of China; Mussolini to rationalize Italy's takeover of Ethiopia; and Hitler, while plotting Germany's Anschluss with Austria, to deny any ambitions greater than conquering the whole world. No matter how foul the deed, each Angel protested that what he had been doing was "just for peace, peace, peace." In its original

Alfredo Valente; Theatre Coll., NY Public Lib.
At the end of "The Red Mikado" sequence in *Pins and Needles*, the Three Little Maids have been decapitated by the Lord High Executioner (Harry Clark). At extreme left and right are the picketing shades of W. S. Gilbert (Al Eben) and Arthur Sullivan (Paul Seymour).

Theatre Coll., NY Public Lib.
The original "Four Little Angels of Peace" in *Pins and Needles*: Anthony Eden (Hy Gardner), Mussolini (Al Eben), a Japanese (Murray Modick), and Hitler (Paul Seymour).

version, the song didn't last longer than four months. By March 1938, Germany's bloodless annexation of Austria made it necessary to alter a few lines in Hitler's verses. Two months later, with the resignation of Anthony Eden, Prime Minister Neville Chamberlain, the umbrella-carrying symbol of Britain's muddle-through policies, replaced him in the quartet. In September 1938, following the Munich Pact, Hitler's lyrics were changed again, and Chamberlain now began his refrain, "Though we sold out the Czechs to protect our own necks . . ."

One year later, with Great Britain at war with Germany and Italy, it was considered prudent to eliminate Chamberlain and reduce the Angels to three. The following month, the song was dropped altogether and was replaced by a trio sung by three of America's most strident voices of the far right, Father Charles Coughlin, Senator Robert Reynolds of Virginia, and Nazi bund leader Fritz Kuhn, who team up to form a vaudeville act known as "The Harmony Boys from Demagogue Lane." But by November, the Angels had returned, only this time there were five with the reinstatement of Chamberlain and the addition of Soviet dictator Joseph Stalin (he now qualified because of the USSR's pact with Germany that had resulted in the Russian invasion of eastern Poland). Chamberlain, however, was permanently out in May 1940, when the real Chamberlain was replaced as British Prime Minister by Winston Churchill, and the group was once again a quartet.

By the time Broadway critics straggled over to see *Pins and Needles*, they found, much to their surprise, that it was fresh, impudent fun. John Mason Brown wrote: "By turning its propaganda into good entertainment its message is doubly insured, and doubly telling as propaganda." In an obvious slap at *The Cradle Will Rock*, George Jean Nathan found that it was "welcome evidence that Labor can not only laugh at itself now and then but that it doesn't always regard a piano as a musical soapbox." And from Heywood Broun, writing in *Pic*: "Although the raillery is sharp and pointed, the wounds inflicted are not painful since the weapons are anaesthetized with humor . . . The piece is not revolutionary in its temper, and while stout ladies in ermine must realize that they are being kidded, few if any have rushed screaming into the night."

During its two-and-a-half-year run, *Pins and Needles* underwent changes in songs, sketches, personnel, location, even its name. In May 1938 the original cast went on tour and a fresh company took over at the Labor Stage. Soon after the first company's return in April, a new edition, *Pins and Needles 1939*, with both old and new material, was put on view. The show was relocated in June at the Windsor Theatre, an 849-seat Broadway house, where the top price was $1.65. In September 1939 the title was altered to *Pins and Needles 1940*, and in November it became *New Pins and Needles*. A fresh, stirringly affirmative note was struck in this last edition with a chorale, "We Sing America," proclaiming, in part:

> We sing to a man's dignity and his place
> With no thought of creed or race
> We sing a land that is too free and great
> To sow the seeds of hate.

Just four nights after the opening of that very first *Pins and Needles* in 1937, a new Shubert musical, *Hooray for What!*, had its premiere on December 1. Despite the fact that it starred "The Perfect Fool," Ed Wynn, it became the fourth song-and-dance show of the year to voice concern about a serious, contemporary issue. Disarmament was both the theme and the cause of *Hooray for What!* as it traced the fanciful adventures of Chuckles (Mr. Wynn), a horticulturalist who invents a gas to kill worms in his apple orchard (dancing worms, you know, because they love to go into the big apple), but then discovers it is also capable of killing humans.

Culver Pictures, Inc.
Ed Wynn tries to save his secret formula from spy Leo Chalzel in *Hooray for What!*

MOANIN' IN THE MORNIN'

MESSRS SHUBERT PRESENT

ED WYNN

in the new musical comedy

HOORAY for WHAT

with JACK WHITNG · JUNE CLYDE · PAUL HAAKON

lyrics by
E.Y. Harburg
music by
Harold Arlen
conceived by
E.Y. HARBURG
book by
LINDSAY · CROUSE · HARBURG
production staged and directed by
VINCENTE MINELLI

IN THE SHADE OF THE NEW APPLE TREE
GOD'S COUNTRY
LIFE'S A DANCE
DOWN WITH LOVE
MOANIN' IN THE MORNIN'
I'VE GONE ROMANTIC ON YOU
BUON WON'T BUD

CHAPPELL

Note misspelling in Jack Whiting's and Vincente Minnelli's names.

This discovery sparks an arms race among the war-eager powers of Europe and they all try to steal Chuckles' formula. At the Grand Hotel de l'Espionage in Geneva (where even the oil paintings conceal spies), a lady spy does manage to see the formula but, since she must copy it with the aid of her hand mirror, takes the whole thing down backwards—thus turning it into a laughing gas causing not death but brotherly love.

A musical exposing the folly of world warfare was especially timely in December 1937, since some form of warfare was either a fact or a threat in almost every part of the globe. In August, Japan had captured the Chinese capital of Peiping and had followed it up by landing marines in Shanghai. Two months later, FDR had made his provocative "quarantine" speech in Chicago, pledging the United States and other peace-loving nations to take whatever steps were necessary to quarantine aggressors. In November, Italy had joined Germany and Japan in an anti-Comintern pact. The same month, Franco's Insurgents proclaimed that they had successfully blockaded every Loyalist port in Spain. During the half-year run of *Hooray for What!*, Italy formally withdrew from the League of Nations; the U.S. gunboat *Panay* was sunk by Japanese bombers while in Chinese waters; the

Spanish Insurgents began their daily bombardment of Barcelona; and Hitler at last found himself strong enough and brazen enough to reach out and scoop up Austria. As Chuckles lisped in *Hooray for What!*: "The trouble with the world ith that Italy'th in Ethiopia, Japan ith in China, and Germany ith in Authtria. Nobody thtayth home."

Although its concern for peace was genuine and it did include Paul Haakon in Agnes de Mille's stark, cynical "Hero Ballet," the musical was hardly the bitter indictment of, say, *Johnny Johnson* (which had also made use of laughing gas as a military deterrent). How could it be with Ed Wynn in the chief role, cavorting with teams of tumblers and trained dogs and making smoke come out of his ears? And, of course, there were jokes. Such as Ed Wynn on politics: "Thith gath will revive the dead. I've got a big offer from the Republican Party." Or Ed on diplomacy: "Generally thpeaking, diplomatth are generally thpeaking." Or Ed talking to the delegates in Geneva about the war debt: "Don't you fellowth know that if you mith two more paymentth, America will own the latht war outright?"

Most of the newspaper critics found *Hooray for What!* much to shout about, and few could resist the temptation of the show's title to describe both the musical and its star. Brooks Atkinson: "Hooray principally for Ed Wynn." Sidney Whipple (the new first-string reviewer for the *World-Telegram*): "Ed Wynn is the answer to 'Hooray for What?'" Robert Coleman: "Hooray for Ed Wynn and Hooray for What!" John Mason Brown: "Deserves to be known as 'Hooray for Ed Wynn and a Darn Good Show.'" Richard Lockridge: "Hooray for what? Hooray for Ed Wynn!"

The music and lyrics of Harold Arlen and Yip Harburg, in their first collaboration on a book musical, caught the breezy topicality of the story. "God's Country," in particular, blithely reflected a renewed feeling of national pride—even though the event that had inspired it was the erection of a munitions plant. For this was a time when Americans had only to listen to radio news programs or read the daily dispatches from all over the world to appreciate fully the singular freedom to be enjoyed in their country. And just as Broadway's song writers had dreamt up optimistic numbers to help the nation's sagging morale during the Depression, they were now happy to do a little flagwaving. "Hi there, chappie, look over the seas be happy," was the theme of "God's Country," which contained such self-assuring, self-kidding lines as:

> We've got no Mussolini
> Got no Mosley
> We've got Popeye
> And Gypsy Rose Lee.

With such productions as *The Cradle Will Rock, I'd Rather Be Right, Pins and Needles,* and *Hooray for What!* 1937 was assuredly the most socially conscious musical-comedy year of them all. But, as is usually the case, safer, more traditional forms always exist side by side with the more daring undertakings. No better examples could be found than the final offerings of the year, *Between the Devil* and *Three Waltzes,* two relics of earlier forms of popular musical theatre conventions.

Wrote Richard Watts, Jr., about *Between the Devil*: "Somehow, amid the mood of brittle gaiety, there is a certain wistful suggestion of the day before yesterday when all the songs didn't have social significance, all the comedy wasn't political satire, plots had something or other to do with sex, and all of us were young." Watts enjoyed the musical, which is more that could be said for most other reviewers. According to Brooks Atkinson, "It was saddled with one of those musical stage imbecilities that were risqué in 1917, piquant in 1927, and only a pain in the first and second acts today . . . If it weren't for the book, it would probably look and sound as frisky as it pretends to be. But oh, these bigamists! Oh, these wicked Parisian chanteuses! Oh, these improper situations! Oh!"

The Howard Dietz–Arthur Schwartz score, led by "I See Your Face Before Me," "By Myself," and the tongue-twisting "Triplets," was, by contrast, a bright collection of very modern Broadway show tunes. And the cast was headed by a particularly attractive *menage à trois,* Jack Buchanan, Evelyn Laye and Adele Dixon. The tale concerned itself with a married Englishman (Mr. Buchanan) who, masquerading as a Frenchman, is also married to a French girl (Miss Dixon). It all ended rather inconclusively with the chorus coming out to admit that no one could think of a satisfactory solution to the dilemma, and so they simply left the conclusion up to the audience. Such a theme, of course, afforded the principals the opportunity to get off many jokes about matrimonial pluralism. Including one that resulted when Miss Laye, as

the English spouse, responded with shock to her husband's revelation of his foreign entanglement.

> Laye: You admit you're a bigamist. Why, you might even have three wives!
> Buchanan: Oh, no! That would be trigonometry!

Three Waltzes, which lasted about a month longer than *Between the Devil,* was the Shuberts' third offering of December, and also their somewhat warmed-over Christmas present. For here they were again with the familiar three-generations operetta plot. In the first act (1865), nobleman (played by Michael Bartlett) loves poor girl (Kitty Carlisle), but she gives him up. In 1900, the second act finds nobleman's son (Michael Bartlett) in love with poor girl's daughter (Kitty Carlisle), but that romance also must end. The last act brings us up to 1937 when nobleman's grandson (Michael Bartlett) meets poor girl's granddaughter (Kitty Carlisle), and it finally looks as if the kids are going to make it. As George Jean Nathan wrote: "Certainly, the three-generation love story has already served enough time to be paroled."

The oft-told tale, however, did serve a valid musical and theatrical gimmick. Oscar Straus, Vienna's leading composer of operetta, had been commissioned to fashion the score by adapting the music of Johann Strauss, Sr., for the first act, Johann Strauss, Jr., for the second, and by writing his own

DeMirjian; Theatre Coll., NY Public Lib.
Michael Bartlett and Kitty Carlisle in *Three Waltzes*.

new music for the third. As *Drei Walzer*, the operetta was first presented in 1935 in Zurich, Switzerland, a locale dictated by the mounting political tensions then building up in Vienna. Its success prompted an even greater success in Paris, with Yvonne Printemps and Pierre Fresnay in the leads.

Straus felt let down by the New York production. First of all, co-adapters Clare Kummer and Rowland Leigh, not without reason, changed the names of the first pair of lovers from Fanny Pichler and Count Rudolf Schwarzenegg to Marie Hiller and Count Rudolph von Hohenbrunn. More important, though, there was a general coarsening of the operetta's tone, as well as one particularly serious casting problem. With just three days to go before the Broadway premiere, Kitty Carlisle was rushed to Philadelphia to take over the leading role from London star Margaret Bannerman (in a rare gesture of graciousness, Miss Bannerman sent Miss Carlisle flowers on opening night). Also, not content to let the action remain in Vienna throughout the entire production, the authors switched the second act to Paris and the third to London.

In December 1937 such geographical alterations were perfectly understandable. In a way they were even symbolic. By the end of the year, Hitler was leaving no doubt that Austria itself would soon be removed from the map.

Bob Golby; Theatre Coll., NY Public Lib.
The Can-Can number in the second act of *Three Waltzes*.

Culver Pictures, Inc.
Times Square, 1938.

Brown Bros.
Times Square, 1938.

CHAPTER IX

"...IS IT GRANADA I SEE OR ONLY ASBURY PARK?..."

Unpredictability is, of course, a built-in element of any new theatrical enterprise. But for musical-comedy surprises, no year of the decade could match 1938. Consider . . .

A virtually unknown Berlin-born Norwegian ballerina named Vera Zorina, making her Broadway bow in *I Married an Angel*, was hailed as the year's outstanding female performer.

Mary Martin, a 24-year-old singer from Weatherford, Texas, with absolutely no theatrical experience, came to town in *Leave It to Me!* and created a nightly sensation singing "My Heart Belongs to Daddy."

In his first time out in a Broadway singing and dancing role, Walter Huston, age 54, not only gave the year's most applauded male performance in *Knickerbocker Holiday*, but also introduced a song, "September Song," that would go on to become a recognized classic. And who was its lyricist? Dramatist Maxwell Anderson, who had never before written the words to a popular song.

Two other long-lasting song hits, "I'll Be Seeing You" and "I Can Dream, Can't I?" were launched in *Right This Way*, one of the biggest flops of the year.

William Shakespeare, whose plays had long been considered boxoffice poison as musical-comedy source material, provided the inspiration for the year's most durable book show, *The Boys from Syracuse*.

An anything-for-a-laugh vaudeville explosion named *Hellzapoppin*, which received mostly negative reviews and, in one form or another, had been playing all over the country for years, turned out to be the biggest commercial hit not only of the year but of the decade.

Despite such surprises, there were many developments of the musical-comedy year that did go according to expected form. Rodgers and Hart had their third hit for producer Dwight Deere Wiman, *I Married an Angel* (the year's best-received score), and Cole Porter had his third hit for producer Vinton Freedley, *Leave It to Me!* Harold Rome and Charles Friedman, the men most responsible for putting *Pins and Needles* together, tried a sequel, *Sing Out the News*, which, predictably, suffered by comparison (though it was still the best of the year's three revues). Among performers, Victor Moore in *Leave It to Me!* and Jimmy Savo in *The Boys from Syracuse* won expected—and well-deserved—plaudits. And Imogene Coca was back again in her fourth Leonard Sillman revue, this one called *Who's Who*.

The number of 1938's new productions—both musical and nonmusical—was an even 100. Among comedies and dramas were Paul Vincent Carroll's *Shadow and Substance*, starring Sir Cedric Hardwicke; *On Borrowed Time* by Paul Osborn; Thornton Wilder's *Our Town*, the Pulitzer Prize winner for the 1937–1938 season; the WPA's Living Newspaper production of *One Third of a Nation*, by Arthur Arent; Clare Boothe's comedy, *Kiss the Boys Goodbye*; Maurice Evans' uncut version of *Hamlet*; and Raymond Massey in *Abe Lincoln in Illinois* by Robert E. Sherwood, which won the Pulitzer Prize for the season 1938–1939. Of the 11 musicals of the year, *Hellzapoppin* (which would eventually reach 1,404 performances), *I Married an Angel*, *Leave It to Me*, and *The Boys from Syracuse* all registered runs of over 200 performances.

The first four months of 1938 were dismal, both for the country at large and for the world at large. The year opened with a continued business recession resulting in almost six million people totally unemployed, and another five million partially unemployed. In Spain, Franco's bombing of Barcelona—which would continue for a year—began in mid-January. Two months later, after four years of often bloody preparation, Hitler's forces invaded Austria in a bloodless conquest. In April Édouard Daladier succeeded Léon Blum as Premier of France, and promptly repealed many of Blum's labor reforms. Japanese forces, taking advantage of their divided Chinese foe, smashed their way through the cities of Soochow, Amoy, Hankow, and Canton.

Nor could the musical theatre provide much relief. Apart from the "official" Broadway opening of *The Cradle Will Rock* early in January, the month could offer nothing better than *Right This Way*, which introduced Joe E. Lewis to the Broadway musical scene (it would not be a lasting friendship), and which had an Irving Kahal–Sammy Fain score that included "I'll Be Seeing You" and "I Can Dream, Can't I?" Nobody came and the show folded after two weeks.

February? Nothing. March? Almost nothing. On the first of the month, Leonard Sillman emerged with still another dewy-eyed show of fledgling talents. But instead of calling his New Faces revue *New Faces*, he called it *Who's Who*, a title preferred by his nominal producer, Elsa Maxwell. In return for the prestige of sponsoring the enterprise, society's most publicized party giver had assured Sillman that her moneyed friends would contribute substantially. They didn't. The Roosevelt Depres-

sion, y'know. Miss Maxwell, however, did make a contribution: $1,000 plus food for a cast that included, besides the faithful Imogene Coca (whose striptease in a polo coat had by now become a trademark), burlesque-trained Rags Ragland, German dancer Lotte Goslar, composer-singer June Sillman (the producer's sister), comic Mildred Todd (her takeoffs on Mrs. Roosevelt and Lynn Fontanne were especially appreciated), song writer–singer James Shelton, dancer Chet O'Brien (Marilyn Miller's husband), and Bowen Charleton "Sonny" Tufts, III. The revue was tailored for the social crowd it aimed to attract, and included a sketch, "Forgive Us Odets," about the upper classes plotting a revolt against labor, and a rather patronizing first act finale, "Dusky Debutantes," which had everyone in the cast in blackface.

The opening-night performance of *Who's Who* was a total distaster. Miss Maxwell had promised to bring along 375 of her most intimate—and paying—friends, but by curtain time they were nowhere to be seen. Critics were fuming and Sillman was frantic when shortly after nine Miss Maxwell and her entourage began traipsing down the aisles. "The curtain went up with half the audience still streaming in," Sillman has recalled. "They laughed, they screamed, but not at the show. They giggled at

their own priceless mots, spoken across the auditorium in hysterical soprano pitch or drunken basso with no regard for what was going on onstage. The last shrill members of Elsa's party were all seated by 10:30, just as the curtain came down on the first act." Then a third of the audience left in the middle of the second act to sail for Europe. The reviews were deadly and the show closed after three weeks. Sillman never did get his money for those 375 seats.

But the musical theatre perked up in May. May brought in *I Married an Angel*, a bright, witty, gossamer fantasy with songs by Rodgers and Hart and a book by Rodgers and Hart that had to do with a wealthy Budapest banker (Dennis King) who, disillusioned over his love affairs, vows that he will never marry anyone other than a real angel. So, "out of the everywhere into the here" flies Angel Brigitta (Vera Zorina, née Brigitta Hartwig) whom he marries and de-wings. Soon, however, the hero discovers that his wife's angelic honesty can get him into some embarrassing situations. It is only after a worldly friend (Vivienne Segal) teaches Brigitta the art of feminine deception that life really becomes heavenly for tenor and temptress. The production also marked the musical-comedy directorial debut of Joshua Logan who, because co-author

Talbot; Theatre Coll., NY Public Lib.
A scene from *Who's Who* with Bowen Charleton (Sonny Tufts), Michael Loring, Mildred Todd, Leona Sousa, and Peter Renwick.

Lorenz Hart would disappear for days, was also recruited to write most of the second act. (Actually, in 1933 *I Married an Angel* had been slated by M-G-M as a musical film written by Rodgers and Hart in collaboration with Moss Hart. When the company failed to do anything about it, Rodgers and Hart persuaded producer Dwight Deere Wiman to buy it for Broadway. Eventually, when M-G-M finally did decide to film it with Jeanette MacDonald and Nelson Eddy, the studio had to buy its original property back from Wiman.)

I Married an Angel was unanimously hailed by the critics, who indulged in such encomia as Brooks Atkinson's "musical comedy has met its masters and they have reared back and passed a 44th Street miracle," and John Anderson's "a winged wonderwork from the musical heavens of Rodgers and Hart." Apart from the freshly melodic songs (including "Spring Is Here" and "I Married an Angel"), what particularly delighted audiences were George Balanchine's first act honeymoon ballet and his second act parody of an entire Radio City Music Hall stage spectacle (the song was called "At the Roxy Music Hall," a reference to its late managing director, "Roxy" Rothafel). Here we found a chorus line of two (Vivienne Segal and Audrey Christie) simulating an entire battalion of well-drilled Rockettes, Miss Zorina rising from a sea of green cheesecloth to perform a "symbolic" dance with a headless dancer, and Walter Slezak as an underwater sea monster. To sing the praises of the Rockefeller pleasure dome was Miss Christie, who meticulously enumerated such wonders as the heartfelt dedication of the ushers, the colorful fountains, the plush seats, the sight and sound of the symphony orchestra, the naked statues, the "birds and roses" ballets, the super-duper organ, the changing lights, the movable stage, the whirling acrobats, the vastness of the balcony, the free drinking cups, the palatial size of the ladies' room—and the fact that everytime you go, it's the same old show.

The month of May ended—as did the 1937–1938 season—with *The Two Bouquets*, a brief stopover from London that used some thirty-two songs by some twenty uncredited Victorian composers. Critical admiration was about equal to critical detraction: those who liked it called it "impish," "charming" and "dainty"; those who didn't called it "arch," "coy" and "dull." Marcy Westcott and Alfred Drake and Patricia Morison and Winston O'Keefe played the two pairs of lovers.

Jerome Robinson; Theatre Coll., NY Public Lib.
Angel Vera Zorina and banker Dennis King begin their honeymoon in *I Married an Angel*.

With the recession just about over in June, the summer months provided a temporary breather from domestic and foreign problems. As if to show that all might just possibly be right with the world, Joe Louis knocked out Max Schmeling of Germany in the first round of their return heavyweight fight, "Wrong Way" Corrigan, supposedly heading for California, flew his nine-year-old, $600 plane to Dublin, and Howard Hughes set the round-the-world flight record of three days, nineteen hours, eight minutes, and ten seconds.

The 1938–1939 musical comedy season on Broadway began unpromisingly on September 21 with the premiere of *You Never Know*, based on the play *Candle-Light*, in which Gertrude Lawrence and Leslie Howard had appeared nine years before. The show marked the return of Cole Porter who had had a serious horseback-riding accident the previous autumn, but, unfortunately, whatever

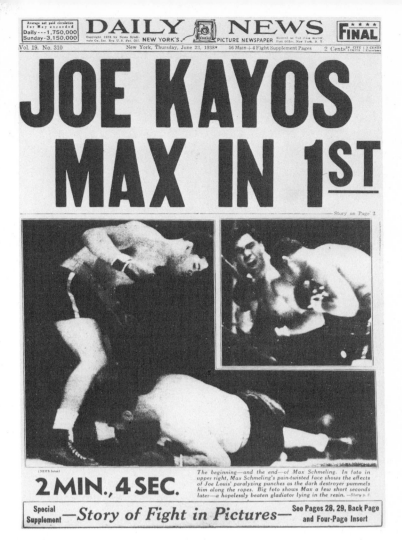

therapeutic value the writing assignment had was negated by the musical's reception. Most appraisers objected to the pallid story, which concerned itself with the romance between a butler masquerading as a nobleman and a maid masquerading as a titled lady. In addition to Porter's return, the enterprise also reunited Clifton Webb and Libby Holman for their first time together since *Three's a Crowd* and gave Lupe Velez her first opportunity to appear in a book musical (John Mason Brown commented that she was "so constantly wigwagging with her body that one tires of reading the message"). During the tryout tour, things looked so bleak that the Messrs. Shubert tried enlivening the occasion by securing the services of director George Abbott and by adding specialties by the dancing Hartmans and the dancing Preisser sisters. But the cause was hopeless.

Not so the score. Maintaining a high level of melody and wit, Porter's contributions included "At Long Last Love" (recalling the opening phrase of King Edward VIII's abdication speech two

years before), and "What Shall I Do?" the dilemma of a befuddled girl who loves not one but two ("But though I fairly itch to/ I don't know which to hitch to"). And in "From Alpha to Omega," Porter again indulged in the kind of "laundry list" song that, ever since "You're the Top," had become something of a trademark. Here he revealed the all-encompassing nature of love by cataloguing extremes, mostly either chronologically—"From love songs by Schumann to hits by Jerry Kern"—or geographically—"From Sarawak to Hackensack."

You Never Know existed for about two and a half months, when it was dispossessed at the Winter Garden to provide a home for a more profitable enterprise. The new tenant did not boast stars of the magnitude of Clifton Webb or Libby Holman or Lupe Velez, nor did it have a score by Cole Porter. Even on its own terms, Olsen and Johnson's *Hellzapoppin* was hard to define. But following its opening at the 46th Street Theatre, the night after *You Never Know*, it was apparent to the Shubert brothers that they had a potential gold mine. So

What Shubert and audiences got for their money were, among other attractions: pistol shots . . . an amply proportioned, deadpan lady fiddler . . . a magician whose tricks didn't work . . . a ticket seller hawking good seats to *I Married an Angel* . . . pistol shots . . . a man riding an eight-foot unicycle . . . a lady who spent almost the entire evening looking for Oscar (eventually Johnson invited her up on the stage. After he shuffled her off into the wings, a shot was heard and Johnson reemerged wiping blood from a sword) . . . eggs and bananas tossed into the audience . . . a trio of movie star impersonators . . . a gorilla dragging a girl out of a theatre box . . . a man rolling around on stage all evening trying to get out of a straitjacket . . . pistol shots . . . the simulated feeling of spiders on the neck and snakes on the ankles in a totally darkened theatre . . . "the world's only coloratura duo" . . . a man trying to deliver a plant to Mrs. Jones only to have it grow bigger every time he goes calling for her down the aisles (after the show was over he could be seen sitting on a branch of a tree in the lobby still mournfully crying for Mrs. Jones) . . . hula dancers . . . pistol shots . . . more pistol shots . . .

All this madcap foolery was preceded by a filmed introduction in the form of a newsreel, in which a Yiddish-accented Hitler, a Harlem-drawling Mussolini, and a gibberish-speaking FDR were all seen exhorting crowds in praise of *Hellzapoppin*. "It's the same old hooey we've been doing for twenty-five years," said Olsen at the time. "So why is it so successful? I think it's because when times are so troubled and everytime a person picks up a newspaper he feels like crying, people want good belly laughs more than ever."

DeMirjian
Clifton Webb, Rex O'Malley and Libby Holman in *You Never Know.*

they moved it to the larger, more prestigious Winter Garden, where it would remain over three years to succeed *Pins and Needles* as Broadway's longest-running musical.

Hellzapoppin was a rowdy, raucous free-for-all, a combination of vaudeville, revue, circus, chamber of horrors, and audience-participation show. It was, in fact, little different from the kind of mayhem in which John "Ole" Olsen and Harold "Chick" Johnson had stormed the barns ever since 1914. Its delayed Broadway invasion came about after Nils T. Granlund (better known as NTG), a nightclub impresario, had caught a performance in Philadelphia and had urged Lee Shubert to see it. Shubert was impressed with its possibilities. At the time, *Hellzapoppin* lasted only an hour. The producer made Olsen and Johnson an offer: add enough material to fill out a full evening's entertainment, and he'd book the show into one of his theatres. They did and he did.

DeMirjian; Theatre Coll., NY Public Lib.
The Radio Rogues (Sidney Chatton impersonating Edward G. Robinson, Jimmy Hollywood as George Arliss, and Eddie Bartell as Ed Wynn) surround Ole Olsen and Chic Johnson in—what else?—*Hellzapoppin*. The girls were named Sally Bond and Margie Young.

Another reason for the success of *Hellzapoppin* was Walter Winchell. Winchell was not only the drama critic for the *Daily Mirror*, but also the most influential syndicated columnist in the country. From his opening-night review—which began, "The slapstickiest, slaphappiest troupe of maniacs ever assembled on any stage is to be hilariously enjoyed" —he was unceasing in his plugs for *Hellzapoppin*, both in his column and in his radio broadcasts. Fact is, though, that while most drama appraisers were, in general, unhappy about the entertainment as a whole, they somehow managed to hand in notices that were calculated more to send patrons into the theatre than to keep them out. Brooks Atkinson, for example, had this to say: "Deciding that it might be a good idea to put on a show, Olsen and Johnson stood on a corner of the street and stopped every third man. Those were their actors. Taking an old broom they went up to the attic and swept out all the gags in sight. Those were their jokes . . . If you can imagine a demented vaudeville brawl without the Marx Brothers, *Hellzapoppin* is it, and a good part of it is loud, low and funny." (So of course on the theatre's marquee was emblazoned: " 'LOUD, LOW AND FUNNY' —Atkinson, *Times.*")

Richard Watts, Jr., even more of a nay-sayer, still admitted that "much of the madness was cheerful, hearty and enlivening." Some appraisers found its bang-bang pace too insistent; others that it was unable to maintain the initial pell-mell drive. John Mason Brown thought the first half-hour was "hilarious," but then felt that "suddenly it went dead and died a terrible death, a victim of its own energy." John Anderson was of similar mind: "It does everything to the audience but drag it up on the stage and spit in its eye . . . starts out to be hilariously insane at the top of its voice and firmly yells itself into a messy bore." But Richard Lockridge was in favor of it ("a good bit of pretty hysterical fun and a fair share of good vaudeville acts"), and though Burns Mantle gave it only "**," he

DeMirjian; Theatre Coll., NY Public Lib.
Shirley Wayne and girls from the *Hellzapoppin* chorus.

suggested it might be just the thing for those seeking an evening of old-time vaudeville. Joe Schoenfeld of *Variety* possibly retired the Clouded Crystal Ball Award by commenting that it was "entertaining, racy, fast and loud, but possibly not a $3.30 buy for very long." *Hellzapoppin* ended its run three years, two months and twenty-five days after its opening.

A revue of a far different nature was presented on Broadway the final week in September. *Sing Out the News* was the uptown sister of *Pins and Needles*. It was a $135,000 Max Gordon production (presented with George S. Kaufman and Moss Hart), it had settings by Jo Mielziner, it was housed in the elegant Music Box Theatre, and its cast included such popular performers as Hiram Sherman, Philip Loeb, Mary Jane Walsh, and Will Geer. But it kept itself morally uncorrupted by retaining *Pins and Needles* alumni Harold Rome for the songs and Charles Friedman as director. (Friedman, in fact, was originally to have written all the sketches, but Kaufman and Hart took over that department although they chose to receive no credit for the efforts.)

As in the previous revue, the tone of *Sing Out the News* was consistently antireactionary and strongly pro-FDR liberal (it took on war, Fascism, Nazism, Communism, business tycoons, Republicans, British foreign policy, and obstructionist congressmen). In the skit "I Married a Republican" (inspired by *I Married an Angel*), the GOP, desperately searching for a candidate to oppose Roosevelt, finds him when one of its leaders makes a wish and an angel (Hiram Sherman) floats down. Though at first he favors the New Deal line, he is persuaded to change his views and he becomes the candidate—at which point he loses his wings. In "Sing Ho for Private Enterprise," four moguls of industry on a Palm Beach beach fix their binoculars on the President fishing from the deck of a battleship, and blame everything, including a sudden downpour, on FDR and the New Deal. In a Hollywood sequence, the filming of *Marie Antoinette* is abruptly halted when Louis B. Mayer (Philip Loeb) discovers to his horror that it's all about a revolution. An Alpine scene shows Prime Minister Chamberlain trying to control a mountain-climbing party consisting of six would-be adversaries: France's Premier Édouard Daladier, Czech President Eduard Benes, Hitler, Stalin, Mussolini, and Hirohito. The first act finale, "Congressional Minstrels," finds the legislators and the President locking horns and telling the other to go to hell.

In some of its sequences, *Sing Out the News* strove for a deeper significance. "Peace and the Diplomat" was a ballet (staged by Charles Walters) in which the Goddess of Peace (Dorothy Fox), complete with olive branch and stuffed dove, is buffeted from diplomat to diplomat who maul her almost senseless. In "A Liberal Education," a father (Will Geer) is seen in Central Park on May Day with his son (Joey Faye). Being a good liberal, he cautions Junior to keep an open mind on all issues—only to have the boy jeered at by both the uppity maypole-dancing rich kids and a gang of tough radicals. When he tries to get both sides to become friends, he is arrested for disturbing the peace. The joyous hit of the show was the blockbusting Harlem block party led by Rex Ingram in celebration of the arrival of the new heir to the Jones family— "How could he be a dud/ Or a stick in the mud/ When he's Franklin D. Roosevelt Jones?"

Sing Out the News lasted no more than three months, possibly because of the stiff competition from the original model, *Pins and Needles*. The

reviews, however, ranged from enthusiastic (Atkinson, Brown, Whipple, Winchell) to generally favorable (Watts, Lockridge, Mantle), with only one daily critic, John Anderson, turning thumbs down. In fact, the entire production so impressed John Mason Brown that he wrote: "When in a mad and troubled world opinions on public matters can still be stated with the jubilant liberty with which they are stated in *Sing Out the News*, such freedom has in itself, alas, become news which merits being sung out with pride. It is with pride that I sing it out today."

Six days after the opening of *Sing Out the News*, the mad and troubled world listened with skepticism as Adolf Hitler gave assurance to Neville Chamberlain and Édouard Daladier, meeting in Munich, Germany, that he sought no further conquests than the Czechoslovakian territory known as the Sudetenland. With his demands met, the following day German troops crossed the Czech border, and four days later Czech President Benes resigned. Meanwhile, back in London, Prime Minister Chamberlain was assuring everyone that the Munich Pact would guarantee "peace in our time."

The depressing world situation, as country after country was being forced to give up its sovereignty and its freedom, was accompanied by a corollary belief in the United States as just about the last bastion of liberty left in the world. This renewed faith in America—either expressed or implied—was becoming an increasingly pertinent theme for the creators of musical comedy. It ran all through *I'd Rather Be Right, Pins and Needles,* and *Sing Out the News*. And it would be of paramount concern in *Knickerbocker Holiday*, which made its Broadway bow October 19.

Knickerbocker Holiday cost $60,000 to put on, and was neither a financial success nor, according to the daily reviewers, an unqualified artistic one. But the Maxwell Anderson–Kurt Weill musical did have the courage to attempt something unusual in the musical theatre: it expressed a philosophy about the most pressing issue of the day, the struggle between totalitarianism and democracy. To

Lucas-Pritchard; Theatre Coll., NY Public Lib.
The Harlem christening party in *Sing Out the News* with Lilyan Brown and Rex Ingram leading the celebrants in praise of "Franklin D. Roosevelt Jones." That's Hazel Scott just behind Ingram.

DEMOCRATS NOMINATE LEHMAN

BOX SCORES

New York
Journal AND **American**

AN AMERICAN PAPER FOR THE AMERICAN PEOPLE

7 RACE RESULTS
BASEBALL
★ ★ ★ ★ ★ ★
SPORTS COMPLETE

No. 18,557—DAILY   In Two Sections—Section One   FRIDAY, SEPTEMBER 30, 1938   THREE CENTS

CHAMBERLAIN, HITLER SIGN ANTI-WAR TREATY

Cubs Can Clinch   PIRATES

librettist Anderson, *Knickerbocker Holiday* offered the means of getting to the heart of the problem by returning to the settlement of New Amsterdam in the year 1647. His protagonist was Brom Broeck, the self-styled "First American," whose claim to the title rested on his conviction that only an American has "a really fantastic and inexcusable aversion to taking orders, coupled with a complete abhorrence for governmental corruption, and an utter incapacity for doing anything about it." How can you tell an American? Simple, he tells us, in song:

> It isn't that he's black or white
> It isn't that he works with tools
> It's only that it takes away his appetite
> To live by a book of rules.

Pitted against Brom as the symbol of authoritarianism is the newly arrived Dutch governor of the colony, Pieter Stuyvesant, firm in his belief that "a government is always a group of men organized to sell protection to the inhabitants of a limited area at a monopolistic price."

Anderson, naturally, was totally committed to the individualist. To him the essence of democracy was simply to be governed by amateurs. Yes, he seemed to be saying, I know that democracy is slow, corrupt and not very efficient, but with all its slowness, corruption and inefficiency, it is always to be preferred to an autocratic regime. According to the author, the ideal state was "the delicate balance between personal liberty and the minimum of authority which is necessary for the free growth of ideas in a tolerant society."

In *Knickerbocker Holiday,* the bumbling New Amsterdam Council is made to represent bumbling democracy. Included in its ranks are such men as Vanderbilt, Van Rensselaer, Van Cortlandt, and Roosevelt, all chosen "for their intolerance of corruption in which they have no share." When these subservient officials begin to chafe under Stuyvesant's iron-fisted control, the governor decided to embroil the settlers in a war against Connecticut ("To war, to war, to war!/ We don't know what we are fighting for . . ."). During an Indian uprising, a soldier is mistakenly thought to have been killed and he is carried onstage to the muffled cadence of the "Dirge for a Soldier" ("Roll, roll the drum for a soldier/ Grieve, grieve for the heart of dust . . ."). At the funeral, Brom delivers a brief eulogy: "The truth about a dead soldier is usually that he died young, in an unnecessary war, because of the ambition or stupidity of those in office. It was so in this case." At the end of the play, Stuyvesant is halted from putting down a rebellion lest posterity consider his actions too harsh. It also occurs to him, as he tells Brom, that he qualifies as an American since he too has never been able to take orders from anyone.

Reviewers, for the most part, admired the score and the production, but felt the philosophy—was Anderson really advocating anarchy?—both pedantic and confusing. There was also a problem about the star of the musical. Walter Huston was simply too attractive and charming to be accepted as anything more dangerous than a sardonic, mischievous scamp. Walter Huston a dictator? Not our Walter up there singing about his scars and hopping about on his wooden leg with all those cute little Dutch maidens. Not our Walter anxious to marry as soon as possible because, in the September of his years, he was fearful he didn't have time for the waiting

Walter Huston as Pieter Stuyvesant in *Knickerbocker Holiday*.

Pieter Stuyvesant (Walter Huston) kicks up his wooden leg and dances with the New Amsterdam maidens in *Knickerbocker Holiday*.

game. Richard Watts, Jr., speaking for the majority, even expressed sorrow that roguish Pieter Stuyvesant failed to end up winning the girl.

A more direct attitude toward dictators could be found in *Leave It to Me!* which opened early in November. Bella and Samuel Spewack adapted it from their play, *Clear All Wires*, and Cole Porter created the score.

The story of *Leave It to Me!* concerned a timid businessman, Alonzo P. Goodhue (Victor Moore), whose socially ambitious wife (Sophie Tucker) manages to get him appointed ambassador to the Soviet Union by making a large contribution to FDR's campaign. But "Stinky" Goodhue doesn't want to be an ambassador; all he wants is to go back to Topeka and pitch horseshoes. Aided by fast-talking newspaperman Buckley Joyce Thomas (William Gaxton), Goodhue does everything he can to get himself recalled. The first attempt occurs when he meets the German ambassador in Moscow. The Nazi goosesteps in briskly. His heels click. His right hand shoots out in the Nazi salute. His belly protrudes. Goodhue's pudgy face turns into a snarl. He juts out his jaw, knits his brows, looks at the inviting target with utter scorn, swings back his foot —and blackout. But kicking a Nazi in the stomach doesn't get Stinky recalled. The British ambassador conveys his government's position: "Britain views your deed with pride and alarm. It congratulates and condemns you." And from American Secretary of State Cordell Hull comes a message which, once decoded on a blackboard, spells out "SOCK HIM AGAIN."

A second attempt to get himself recalled results in Goodhue's shooting a counterrevolutionary and becoming the hero of a Red Square celebration. That's the first act finale, featuring a jigging Stalin and the singing of the very un–Cole Porterish Communist anthem, "The Internationale." Throughout the lengthy festivities, Mrs. Goodhue couldn't be happier. In a reference to the family of the ambassador to Great Britain, a post she had coveted for her husband, she beams: "I'll bet the Kennedy's are boiling."

But Stinky is beginning to like his job and is anxious to make a positive contribution to world peace. With Buck's help, he prepares the Goodhue Plan, in which he advocates sending French, German and Russian troops into each other's country so that the nationalities will be mixed and before long there will be a United States of Europe. That

does it. The mere idea of anyone advocating a one-worldish peace plan—no matter how simple-minded—is enough to send Goodhue on his way home to pitch horseshoes.

Once again, Victor Moore created a memorable portrayal of bungling innocence in a world of intrigue, and once again won the admiration of both critics and public. But the show-stopping highlight of *Leave It to Me!* occurred in an unmotivated scene on a Trans-Siberian Railway platform. It was there that Mary Martin, in her first Broadway role, sang "My Heart Belongs to Daddy"—and then proceeded to do an enticingly innocent striptease, egged on by a quartet of fur-wearing Russians (one of them was Gene Kelly, also in his first Broadway show). Wrote Sidney Whipple: "Miss Martin has the freshness and vitality of youth, but she also has poise and the gift of devilish humor, and I think she is a find."

The finding, of course, had been done some months before. At Miss Martin's audition, Cole Porter's first impression of her was that of "a dreary little girl who appeared to be the last word in scared dowdiness. My pianist played and she sang. I confess that such a moment is marked with five stars in my head; it was the finest audition I had ever heard. 'Dress her up!' I cried." The following morning, presumably dressed up, the singer showed up at the Imperial Theatre. "What I didn't know," she later recalled, "was that the show had been in rehearsal two and a half weeks and that June Knight

Vandamm; Theatre Coll., NY Public Lib.
On hand for the big Red Square parade in *Leave It to Me!* are Tamara, William Gaxton, Victor Moore, Walter Armin (as Stalin), Sophie Tucker, Eugene Sigaloff, and Alexander Asro.

Vandamm; Theatre Coll., NY Public Lib.
Mary Martin in *Leave It to Me!*

had left the part to marry a wealthy Texan. He didn't want her to do the song because he thought it was naughty. At the theatre, there was Billy Gaxton, with his hat down over his eyes walking around with his coat draped over his shoulders. Acting. They asked me to stand beside him and they said, 'Here are some words, say them.' And Billy, out of the corner of his mouth, said, 'Doesn't matter how you say 'em, just say 'em loud. Straight up to the balcony.' My first line was 'I'd like to renew my subscription.' So I looked up and yelled, 'I'D LIKE TO RENEW MY SUBSCRIPTION.' Then Sam Spewack came down the aisle and in the darkness I heard him saying, 'You start tomorrow. And never change the reading.' I didn't."

Leave It to Me!, after closing in July 1939, returned briefly in September. By that time, World War II had already begun and Stalin had allied himself with Hitler. Thus, for the tour, the role of the Russian dictator was eliminated, Goodhue's peace plan was drastically changed, and the program contained a note advising unwary playgoers that the musical was not intended as a satire on current events.

171

The final major musical-comedy debut of 1938 belonged to William Shakespeare. Adapting a musical from one of his plays had first occurred to Richard Rodgers earlier in the year. At the time he was on a train with his partner, Larry Hart, on the way to Atlantic City to work on the upcoming *I Married an Angel,* when he casually suggested the idea. Suddenly, all thoughts of *I Married an Angel* temporarily vanished while the writers began tossing possible plays back and forth. Since no one had ever tried treating Shakespeare to songs and dances before, they had a pretty unlimited field.

"One play occurred to us almost from the start, and for a very personal reason," Rodgers has recalled. "Larry had a younger brother named Teddy Hart who was a very clever comedian. He was short and dark and looked a lot like Larry. But the man he was always being mistaken for was another gifted clown, Jimmy Savo. 'What about doing *The Comedy of Errors*?' Larry piped excitedly. 'Teddy and Jimmy would be naturals for the twin Dromios.' It was an inspired idea and just as soon as *I Married an Angel* was out of the way, we went straight to work on the show that eventually became *The Boys from Syracuse.*"

Originally the idea was for Rodgers and Hart to collaborate on the book with producer-director George Abbott, but they willingly bowed out once they saw how perfectly Abbott had accomplished the task unaided. Nothing but the plot outline and bawdy spirit of the original remained except for the Seeress's single line, "The venom clamours of a jealous woman poisons more deadly than a mad dog's tooth"—a statement that always prompted Jimmy Savo to pop out of the wings and knowingly

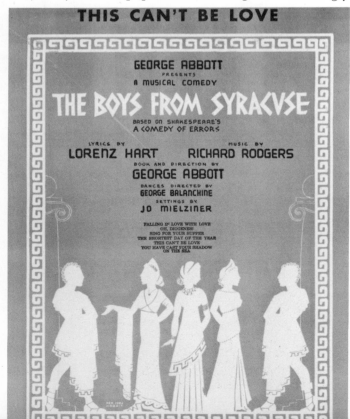

Richard Tucker; courtesy Lynn Farnol Group
Eddie Albert and Jimmy Savo in *The Boys from Syracuse.*

advise the audience, "Shakespeare!" In addition to twin Dromios Savo and Hart, the cast included twin Ephesuses Eddie Albert (Rudy Vallee had originally been sought for the role) and Ronald Graham, plus the attractive triad, Wynn Murray, Muriel Angelus and Marcy Westcott.

The November 23 Broadway opening of *The Boys from Syracuse* was greeted by a unanimous chorus of rave reviews, each critic outdoing the other in superlatives. Richard Watts, Jr., called it "the finest and most satisfying musical comedy that has reached New York in many a season of weary waiting." Brooks Atkinson felt that "nothing so gutsy has come along in a week. Nothing so original has come along for a longer period than that." Burns Mantle termed it "the liveliest and most colorful of recent bids for entertainment." Sidney Whipple, no equivocator he, hailed it as "the greatest musical comedy of its time." *Life* said it was "melodic entertainment at its best," and sister *Time* echoed, "Far and away the best musical in many a year." Such a reception should surely have insured a longer run than the respectable, though far from impressive, 235 performances that the show enjoyed.

But there has been no such limitation on the songs—lyrical, poetic moods such as "Falling in Love with Love" ("... is falling for make believe") and "You Have Cast Your Shadow on the Sea" and "The Shortest Day of the Year" ("... has the longest night of the year"), or rhythmically sassy items such as "This Can't Be Love" ("... because I feel so well") and the show-stopping trio, "Sing for Your Supper," gaily trilled by the Mlles. Murray, Angelus and Westcott. There were also the ingeniously comic pieces, particularly "What Can You Do with a Man?" a girl's plaint about a husband who reads Plato in bed while she's in her nicest negligee, and "He and She," which details the case histories of three couples: the first so accustomed to a multiplicity of affairs that they find no reason not to continue them after marriage; the second so fond of their children that they decide to get married; the third so virtuous that "when they died and went to heaven all the angels went to hell."

It would have been pleasanter to report that the year 1938 ended on the high musical note of *The Boys from Syracuse*. The unhappy final entry, *Great Lady*, arriving December 1, was a tasteless costume piece about the apparently insatiable amatory proclivities of Eliza Bowen, the lady who married both mansion owner Stephen Jumel and former Vice President Aaron Burr. The play even went in for such gimmicks as written commentaries that were flashed on a Telautograph screen preceding most of the scenes. One example of its graffiti humor: "Eliza is Now a Great Lady"—but with the "d" in "Lady" missing. Composer Frederick Loewe made his unfortunate Broadway debut with this one, which also provided temporary employment for such musical-comedy luminaries of the past as Norma Terris, Irene Bordoni and Helen Ford. The show closed after twenty performances.

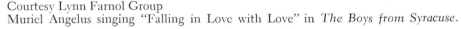

Courtesy Lynn Farnol Group
Muriel Angelus singing "Falling in Love with Love" in *The Boys from Syracuse*.

THE WEATHER

Today: Partly cloudy and warmer
Tomorrow: Fair, with moderate temperature
Temperatures Yesterday: Max., 67; Min., 61

Detailed Report on Page 30

NEW YORK
Herald Tribune

EXTR
LATE CITY EDIT

VOL. XCIX No. 33,892   Copyright, 1939, New York Tribune Inc.   FRIDAY, SEPTEMBER 1, 1939   THREE—CE New York City or

Hitler Starts Hostilities, Poland Is Invade
Danzig Annexed; Cities Bombed From Ai
Britain, France, U.S. Prepare to Meet Cris

S. S. America | **3 Million Begin Exodus** | **Britain** ... | ...

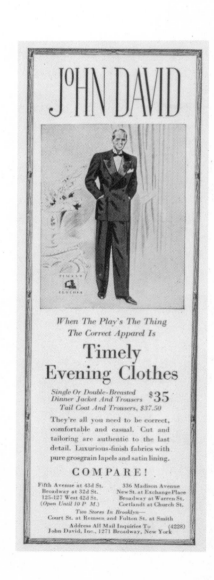

CHAPTER X

"... BETTER HAVE A LITTLE FUN ..."

On the first day of September 1939, after a decade of Depression and dust storms, wars in Ethiopia, China and Spain, bloodless coups in Austria, Czechoslovakia and Albania, the Earth, as inevitably as in a Greek tragedy, erupted in the most devastating conflagration of all times. With his blitzkrieg against Poland, Adolf Hitler set off a struggle that would eventually involve almost every country on the planet. All of the significant events of the year —the German takeover of Czechoslovakia in March, the fall of the Spanish government the same month, Japan's indiscriminate bombings of Chinese cities, Mussolini's annexation of Albania in April, Mussolini's and Hitler's rebuff to Roosevelt's peace plan, the ten-year German-Italian military assistance pact in May, the Nazi-Soviet nonaggression pact in August—all of these were part of one long discordant overture to the horrifying carnage that was soon to come.

Still, during most of 1939, the United States felt relatively safe. Roosevelt's frustrated pleas for a revision of the Neutrality Act had to wait until November for Congress to act—a full two months after the German invasion of Poland. In fact, the only foreign invasion that seemed to concern most Americans took place in June when Britain's King George VI and Queen Elizabeth joined Franklin and Eleanor for hot dogs at Hyde Park. In February, the Golden Gate Exposition opened in San Francisco, and in April President Roosevelt cut the ribbon at the New York World's Fair, "The World of Tomorrow," in a place called the Court of Peace. The same month the first public television program was beamed from the Empire State Building. In June, Pan American Airlines began regular transatlantic passenger service with the *Dixie Clipper* flying from Port Washington, New York, to Lisbon, Portugal, in 23 hours, 52 minutes. Even the racial indignity suffered by Marian Anderson when the DAR barred her from holding a concert at Washington's Constitution Hall became the catalyst for a thrillingly affirmative occasion when she sang before some 75,000 people from the steps of the Lincoln Memorial. In 1939, Americans could feel slightly smug about their economy, their relative racial harmony, their eased labor tensions, and, particularly, their distance from the problems of the Old World. And this mood was reflected in almost all the popular theatrical entertainments being offered along Broadway.

The sum total of all new productions in 1939 was the lowest of the decade. But of the 76 non-musical plays, audiences could enjoy such superior presentations as Shakespeare's *Henry VI, Part 1*, with Maurice Evans as Falstaff; Tallulah Bankhead in Lillian Hellman's *The Little Foxes*; Katharine Hepburn in *The Philadelphia Story* by Philip Barry; S. N. Behrman's *No Time for Comedy* starring Katharine Cornell and Laurence Olivier; Gertrude Lawrence in Samson Raphaelson's *Skylark*; the George S. Kaufman–Moss Hart comedy, *The Man who Came to Dinner*, with Monty Woolley; William Saroyan's Pulitzer Prize-winning *The Time of Your Life*; and the play that would become the longest-running Broadway attraction of all time, *Life with Father*, by Howard Lindsay and Russel Crouse.

Musicals, with 15 productions, accounted for

I'M SO WEARY OF IT ALL

JOHN C. WILSON
PRESENTS

BEATRICE LILLIE

in SET TO MUSIC

a new revue
with words and music by
NOEL COWARD

PRICE
75¢

I'M SO WEARY OF IT ALL
MAD ABOUT THE BOY
NEVER AGAIN
THE STATELY HOMES OF ENGLAND

CHAPPELL
& CO. INC.

roughly 20 percent of all theatrical entertainments, an unusually high figure. And except for some songs and sketches found in the seven revues offered during the year, the world of musical comedy was in happy isolation from the real world around it. Europe, for example, was represented by a dream trip to Louis XV's Versailles in *DuBarry Was a Lady* and a *Hellzapoppin* tour of *The Streets of Paris*. The only other musical journey abroad was to the Far East, a region rendered doubly inscrutable by rival Negro versions of Gilbert and Sullivan's *The Mikado*. Aspects of contemporary Americana were to be seen in two views of moviemaking (*Stars in Your Eyes* and *Yokel Boy*), in a tale about the problems of a summer theatre (*Very Warm for May*), and in a saga concerned with campus life at a football college (*Too Many Girls*).

Nineteen thirty-nine was an especially happy year for welcoming back some long-time favorites absent from the Broadway scene during the past three years—Ethel Merman and Jimmy Durante in *Stars in Your Eyes*, and later Ethel and Bert Lahr in *DuBarry Was a Lady*; Beatrice Lillie in *Set to Music*; Bobby Clark and Luella Gear in *The Streets of Paris*; Willie and Eugene Howard in *George White's Scandals*; and Bill Robinson in *The Hot Mikado*. Despite such stiff competition, Merman and Lahr emerged the year's shiniest stars and *DuBarry Was a Lady* the year's brightest show and biggest hit. (Others to go past the 200-per-

formance mark: *The Streets of Paris, Too Many Girls* and *Yokel Boy*.) Among song writers, Jerome Kern and Oscar Hammerstein, 2nd, probably made the most durable contributions, though their musical, *Very Warm for May*, was a flop. Of the five revues presented, the most favored was *The Streets of Paris*.

The final year of the decade could also take pride in the unusually large corps of talented performers either making their debuts or first winning prominence. Richard Haydn made a notable bow in *Set to Music* with, of all things, fish mimicry; Alfred Drake, Keenan Wynn and Gene Kelly attracted notice in *One for the Money*, and later in the season, Drake and Danny Kaye were featured in *The Straw Hat Revue*; Abbott and Costello and Carmen Miranda were enthusiastically welcomed in *The Streets of Paris*; Lena Horne was briefly seen in *Blackbirds*; Ann Miller began her career in *George White's Scandals*; Eddie Bracken personified Joe College and Desi Arnaz beat a mean conga drum in *Too Many Girls*; Phil Silvers made it out of burlesque into *Yokel Boy*, and Betty Grable made it in from the West Coast into *DuBarry Was a Lady*. The year also introduced a new producer to the musical field, Michael Todd, whose *Hot Mikado* competed for patrons with the Federal Theatre's *Swing Mikado*.

For *Set to Music*, the year's first musical entry in January, Noël Coward built a revue around the special talents of Beatrice Lillie. Actually, Coward did more rebuilding than building since seven of the numbers in the show were holdovers from a 1932 London offering known as *Words and Music*. Such as "Mad About the Boy," a four-part invention showing the effects of a dashing screen idol on a society woman ("On the silver screen/ He melts my foolish heart in every single scene"), a schoolgirl ("In my English prose/ I've done the tracing of his forehead and his nose"), a Cockney maid ("When I do the rooms/ I see 'is face in all the brushes and the brooms"), and a streetwalker ("Walking down the street/ His eyes look out at me from people that I meet"). Miss Lillie played the schoolgirl. Also from *Words and Music*: "Three White Feathers," which told the rags-to-royalty saga of poor little Bea, a pawnbroker's daughter, who feels out of her element on her way to being presented at court; and the finale, "The Party's Over," which captured so well the loneliness one feels once the guests have all gone and dawn begins to break.

To these *Words and Music* words and music were added "The Stately Homes of England," a putdown of British tradition originally in the operetta *Operette*, and two of Miss Lillie's best numbers, the blasé revelation, "I'm So Weary of It All," and the recollection of the gayest, maddest mahhhhhhvelous party, which she sang wearing a huge hat, dark sun glasses, a fisherman's shirt, several ropes of pearls, and a pair of slacks. (Coward's inspiration had been a wild Elsa Maxwell bash in the south of France for which both he and Miss Lillie had been expected to provide free entertainment.)

Well, it was all pretty chic and pretty chichi, with most critical observers crediting its pleasures more to Beatrice Lillie than to Noël Coward. (George Jean Nathan wrote: "With one dart of her eye she can spare a skit writer a dozen lines.") Richard Watts found Coward's work "tired, brittle, strangely lacking in vitality," though Brooks Atkinson's view was that "on the spur of the moment, it seems like the best show Noël Coward has written."

Equally posh—or trying to be—was Nancy Hamilton's *One for the Money*, which opened early in February. Scrupulously adhering to its title, the show was aimed squarely at, and staged specifically for, people with money. It was Park Avenue's answer to 7th Avenue's *Pins and Needles*, a proudly right-wing revue tailored for the International Ladies Garment Wearers as it celebrated the pleasures and minor frustrations of the socially registered. Among them were found some occasionally amusing observations on parlor-game addicts, modern art, bicycle riding (yes, bicycle riding), the complicated plots of Wagnerian operas, the art of jewelry smuggling, Eleanor Roosevelt (played by

The "Ordinary Family" of *One for the Money*: maid Brenda Forbes, father Philip Bourneuf, mother Nancy Hamilton, daughter Nell O'Day, and son Alfred Drake.

Miss Hamilton), torch songs, and Orson Welles (who, as depicted by Alfred Drake, knew Shakespeare backward at the age of two, forward at three, and personally at four). Indeed, the Depression seemed light years away when a revue could open on a scene in which a well-heeled family in formal attire sings "We think that right is right and wrong is left," and empathetically concludes:

> We're a very ordinary family,
> We are you—
> We are usually the ones who pay the piper just like you!
> We're the unremembered Pilgrims of this fair country,
> We're a very ordinary family!

The general consensus was that, while it was filled with intermittent pleasures, *One for the Money* was simply too much of a private joke. John Anderson called it "one of the sleekest and glossiest vacuums of the season, an intimate revue that is smartly, prettily and disastrously empty."

Five nights after the opening, there was another musical satire on Broadway, *Stars in Your Eyes*. Only it wasn't very satirical. Originally, it had been composer Arthur Schwartz's notion to do a musical comedy showing what might happen if, say, a left-wing writer were to become involved in the making of a typically elaborate Hollywood epic. So he got J. P. McEvoy to dream up a fable about the writer (played by Richard Carlson) changing a movie plot dealing with the Old Plantation South into one about the New Industrialized South ("The cornfields are so liberalized/ That even the scarecrows are unionized," went one of Dorothy Fields' original lyrics). For commercial value, they got Ethel Merman to play a temperamental movie star and Jimmy Durante a labor organizer. Under the title *Swing to the Left*, the musical was placed into production by Dwight Deere Wiman with Joshua Logan directing.

Then—trouble. Logan took issue with the social slant. That's fine for an intimate revue like *Pins and Needles*, he told Schwartz and McEvoy, but not for a fancy $4.40 Broadway show. Look what had happened to *Sing Out the News*. So they began altering scenes, scrapping songs, and chipping away at the story line. Merman was still the movie star and Carlson was still the writer, but Durante's labor organizer was turned into a studio troubleshooter, and the social commentary was all but eliminated.

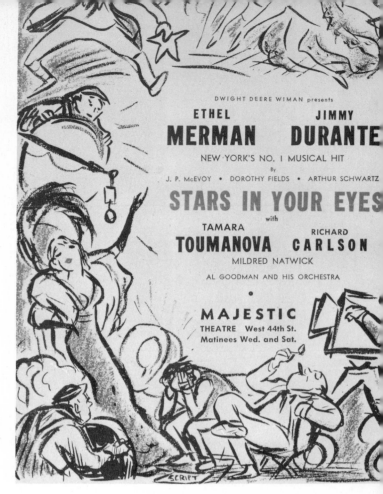

Drawing by Don Freeman

What was left when, as *Stars in Your Eyes*, the show came to New York was little more than another Merman-Durante vehicle, with a few extra dividends such as Mildred Natwick as a Dorothy Parker–type screen writer and the dancing of ballerina Tamara Toumanova. Few seemed to mind; everyone was having too good a time just enjoying the songs and antics of Ethel and Jimmy.

The score, the first Dorothy Fields–Arthur Schwartz collaboration, offered Miss Merman a whole range of properly Mermanesque songs—from the stridently unequivocating "This Is It!" (punctuated by the singer's series of "ohhhhhhhh" sounds as a male quartet did a reprise of the song) to the sassy "A Lady Needs a Change," and the choked-up threnody, "I'll Pay the Check." The nightly show-stopper turned out to be "It's All Yours," in which the two stars would go into convulsions trying to break each other up. But despite the appeal of the stellar twosome and the generally favorable reception, *Stars in Your Eyes* could twinkle no longer than 127 nights (and matinees).

The luckless entrepreneur, Lew Leslie, never wavered in his hopes of repeating the success of the *Blackbirds of 1928*. By the time he brought in his

Lucas-Pritchard; Theatre Coll., NY Public Lib.
Ethel Merman, chief star of Monotone Pictures Corp., filming a Southern epic in
Stars in Your Eyes.

new edition in February, his funds were so low that his wife, Belle Baker, had to hock her jewelry to raise enough cash to post the bond for the tryout theatre in Boston. But the sacrifice wasn't worth it; the show was a disaster, and remained only a little more than a week on Broadway. Though no admirer of the revue, Brooks Atkinson wrote, "A radiantly beautiful sepia girl, Lena Horne, sings 'Thursday' about a maid's day off and 'You're So Indifferent' in attractive style, and will be a winner when she gets proper direction." Most of the other observers thought so too.

The Negro revue or revue-type musical had just about run its course. Not one of the sixteen presented during the Thirties had been a success. Then along came *The Swing Mikado* on March 1, followed by *The Hot Mikado* on March 23.

The genesis of the duplicate black *Mikados* was one of those rare show-business phenomena that seem to be totally lacking in any sort of rationality. Seems that in Chicago the biggest hit the Federal Theatre there ever had was the all-Negro, jazzed up version of Gilbert and Sullivan's *The Mikado*, which played twenty-two weeks after its opening in September 1938. Producer Michael Todd had offered to buy the show and present it in New York but

he was told it wasn't for sale. The FTP had its own plans. It opened it in New York at a $1.10 top price, and audiences, spurred by the reviews, went to see the blackman's version of two Englishmen's lampoon of the Japanese ruling class. That didn't stop Todd. Since the original operetta was in public domain and not protected by the copyright law, there was nothing to prevent him from staging his own variation on the theme. Which he did, with Hassard Short directing, Nat Karson designing scenery and costumes, and Bill Robinson as the emperor aglow in a gold derby, gold suit, gold cane, and gold shoes. Todd scaled the tickets for his show up to $3.30, and decked it out with such spectacular effects as an erupting volcano and a waterfall with soap bubbles that towered forty feet high. Reviewers were somewhat divided as to the better show, the rougher, more spontaneous *Swing* or the slicker, gaudier *Hot*. But they all heartily approved of the idea.

At the boxoffice, though, despite the higher ticket price, the advantage seemed to be Todd's—even when, thirteen days after the Todd *Mikado* was unveiled, two producers were somehow able to get the Federal Theatre to let them take over the WPA *Mikado* and present it under *their* auspices.

179

WPA Federal Th. Photo; Theatre Coll., NY Public Lib.
Mabel Walker as Katisha and Edward Fraction as The Mikado strutting on down in *The Swing Mikado*.

Vandamm; Theatre Coll., NY Public Lib.
Bill Robinson was the rival *Hot Mikado*.

Where did they put it? Into the 44th Street Theatre, that's where, right across the street from the Todd-sponsored edition at the Broadhurst. (Todd got even by flying a flag on the side of the Sardi Building pointing to his show and completely obliterating the marquee of the 44th Street Theatre to anyone walking east on the block.) By that time, however, the Flushing Meadow World's Fair was beginning to distract pleasure-seekers from the accustomed Broadway showplaces. Todd got a bright idea. He sold the show to the Fair where it played four shows daily at a price scale of 40¢ to 99¢.

By this time the Federal Theatre was staggering from failures and abuse. But it was still not completely out. After a year and a half of preparation, it finally got around to opening its revue, *Sing for Your Supper*, on April 24. In spite of the problems besetting the beleaguered agency, the new show was far from innocent entertainment. It was, in fact, the only one of the year to deal in any way with the Nazi menace. The method here was choreographic: in "The Last Waltz," the Viennese dancing to "The Blue Danube" are joined by Adolf Hitler, who presently leads them in goosestepping to the "Horst Wessellied." The WPA even summoned up enough courage to strike back at its detractors by pointing proudly, in a song lyric of course, to the agency's many worthwhile projects—road building, school construction, reforestation,

etc.—all of which, it sarcastically noted, were accomplished by men "leaning on a shovel." There was also an exultant "Papa's Got a Job," with the cast breaking out with the good news just as papa's about to be evicted. Hector Troy and Robert Sour wrote the lyrics to Ned Lehac's music. Hector Troy? Actually, that was Harold "Heckie" Rome in disguise—a fact that may well have contributed to the number being compared with his "FDR Jones" in *Sing Out the News*.

The show's finale, however, was the true pulse-pounder of the evening. Called "The Ballad of Uncle Sam," it voiced the stirring belief that the strength of America lay in the diversity and divergence of its people. After lyricist John Latouche and composer Earl Robinson had changed the name to "Ballad for Americans," the piece became one of the most frequently performed morale-building wartime chorales.

But the critics didn't take kindly to *Sing for Your Supper* (the title song, incidentally, was completely unrelated to the Rodgers and Hart tune in *The Boys from Syracuse*). Congress didn't think much of the show either. By July 1939, when time came around for a renewal of the FTP's funds, the solons balked. And one of the reasons cited was *Sing for Your Supper*, whose length of preparation, alleged left-wing outlook, and lack of customers (it closed after about two months) all contributed to helping

WPA Federal Th. Photo; Theatre Coll., NY Public Lib.
The *Sing for Your Supper* first act finale "Papa's Got a Job," with Judy Goodrich about to tell Carl Chapin the good news.

Congress make up its mind to cut off funds from—and thereby kill—the entire project.

The hoped-for spillover of World's Fair tourists prompted Broadway producers once again to offer summertime productions. In mid-June, the Messrs. Shubert and the Messrs. Olsen and Johnson presented *The Streets of Paris*, with a cast headed by such top comedians as Bobby Clark, Bud Abbott and Lou Costello (their only Broadway appearance), and Luella Gear. The fact that Olsen and Johnson were credited as co-producers was the tip-off as to the kind of revue it was. For despite its title, *The Streets of Paris* was nothing more than a tonier version of *Hellzapoppin*.

Even the chorus girls in the opening scene, purporting to be their dressing room in Paris' Theatre Marigny, confess the fraudulence of the surroundings. But authenticity of locale counted for little in a revue that could offer Bobby Clark bellowing his way through the amorous saga of "Robert the Roué from Reading, Pa." ("And I usually play in the hay—Hey!"). Or Jean Sablon (he was the only authentic French headliner in it) crooning "Rendezvous Time in Paree," written by Al Dubin and Jimmy McHugh. Or the Hylton Sisters harmonizing "Three Little Maids in Paree" as a recurrent theme. Or the first act finale appearance of Carmen Miranda, the Brazilian Bombshell, in fruited headdress and six-inch heels, revealing the torrid delights to be found down "South American Way."

Bobby Clark's main sketch, "The Convict's Return," offered the comic in four roles—a doddering father, a faithful butler, an escaped convict, and the pursuing warden. At first the story proceeds relatively smoothly, then—with doors jamming and windows slamming—the pace gets wilder and wilder as Clark becomes increasingly frantic in his efforts to make costume changes fast enough to keep up with the action.

For a scene in a supposedly French rest home, Abbott and Costello threw in every burlesque trick they had ever known. Costello, mistaking the home for a hotel, becomes the victim of a series of side-splitting physical encounters. A swami asks him if he wants his palm read; when he agrees, the intruder whips out a paintbrush and smears red paint on his hand. After seeing another patient ask for and receive an apple dropped from above, Costello makes his request—and dozens of apples rain on his head. Still another patient comes in and his nurse orders Costello to pump him because he's a pump. As Lou dutifully pumps his arm, the man sprays water in his face. Toward the end, a nurse slips into his room, sees Costello in bed, exclaims, "Oh, what a beautiful bed of roses"—and douses him with water from a watering can.

Even within the framework of the low-comedy hijinks, the creators managed to find a spot for a musical roasting of Neville Chamberlain, whose Munich sellout of Czechoslovakia the previous September had made him the chief target of satirists. Performed as a new dance step, "Doin' the

Bud Abbott pulls the old shell game trick on Lou Costello in *The Streets of Paris*.

Richard Tucker; Theatre Coll., NY Public Lib.
"Doin' the Chamberlain" in *The Streets of Paris*.

Chamberlain" was sung by instructress Luella Gear, with the dancers led by Gower Champion and Jeanne Tyler, mostly crawling around and waving umbrellas. Described as "an English goosestep," the lyric offered such instructions as "First you squirm like a worm," "Be a wise side-stepper," and "Then appease just to please."

The Streets of Paris started out with a $3.30 top, but when business picked up the price of a ticket went to $4.40. In May of the following year, the revue was transferred to the World's Fair under Michael Todd's management, with Abbott and Costello co-starred with Gypsy Rose Lee.

July's single entry also did well. *Yokel Boy* was a Lew Brown show all the way, since he was producer, book writer, co-lyricist, and director. It had little in the way of plot—something about moviemaking in Lexington, Massachusetts—so it made sure little got in the way of the dances, singing, and comedy. It also marked the Broadway debut of a brash, breezy, 28-year-old clown named Phil Silvers. And it had one of the most confused and pretentious first act finales since Earl Carroll struck his mighty blow against Prohibition back in 1930.

The song, called "Uncle Sam's Lullaby," was a curiously tranquilizing panegyric to the strength of the United States and its ability to keep the enemy far from its shores. (The timing couldn't have been worse: the show opened just one week before Roosevelt's urgent plea to Congress for repeal of the arms embargo.) According to Richard Lockridge, the number "reports that Uncle Sam is busily trotting around soothing his nephews and nieces and assuring them that this land, which is your land and my land, will not become a war land. Then the curtains open and all the chorus men began to carry armloads of shells up runways, and large wheels, symbolizing large wheels, turn mightily. Then all the girls are dressed as soldiers and crawl up the sides of a pyramid, and airplanes float over them, and then, on my word, so do battleships. This symbolizes, I think, the downfall of displacement, the might of the United States, and the awareness of Lew Brown that these are desperate times which producers of musical comedies must face to the last chorus girl."

George White's Scandals was an August entry but the opening—on the 28th—was so close to September that it might be considered the first

183

Phil Silvers tries to lure Lois January to Hollywood in *Yokel Boy*. Buddy Ebsen, however, has his doubts.

attraction of the 1939 fall season. The revue was much the same mixture as before except that this edition kept up with the times by borrowing some of the now fashionable techniques of *Hellzapoppin*. It opened on a wild note with Willie and Eugene Howard as Sam Trylon and Max Perisphere welcoming all to "Scandals Day at the World's Fair," and kept up its brash and disheveled spirit throughout with the aid of such zanies as The Three Stooges and Ben Blue.

There were complaints about the offal barrel humor, best exemplified by the "Curb Your Dog" skit, which found Willie Howard as a French poodle "saluting" a German dachshund. In another scene, Willie played a professional picket whose lovemaking with his wife is interrupted by John L. Lewis (brother Eugene) because the lady refuses to sign up with the union. Marital problems were also the concern of a sketch in which Willie drops a quarter in a "Tell-u-vision" set to keep an eye on his wife's activities.

The Jack Yellen–Sammy Fain songs included "Are You Havin' Any Fun?" ("Better have a little fun/ You ain't gonna live forever"), an appropriate theme for the year, whose lyrics were printed on the wide-brimmed hats of the chorus girls so that audiences could sing along. Ella Logan sang songs both torchy ("Something I Dreamed Last Night") and tropical ("The Mexiconga"), the latter danced by 20-year-old Ann Miller. In a sentimental mood, the first act finale, "Tin Pan Alley," closed with a nostalgic tribute to an earlier *Scandals* composer, George Gershwin.

That's Ann Miller out in front, and Lois Andrews is the star on the far right.

Late in September, the Shuberts brought in *The Straw Hat Revue*, a straw hat revue co-producer Harry Kaufman had seen at Camp Tamiment, an adult camp in Bushkill, Pennsylvania. Max Liebman, who had put it all together, featured Imogene Coca in a variety of numbers, the most hilarious being "Soused American Way," in which she did an impression of Carmen Miranda in *The Streets of Paris* (a concurrently running Shubert offering, which, naturally, they were not above plugging).

Jerome Robinson; Theatre Coll., NY Public Lib.
Danny Kaye and Imogene Coca in the operetta spoof, "The Grand Chandelier" in *The Straw Hat Revue*.

Young talent was also served—and even better—by *Too Many Girls*, which arrived at the Imperial Theatre on October 18. Rodgers and Hart, who had worked so well with the kids of *Babes in Arms*, now concerned themselves with an equally crew-cut crew, the undergraduates of Pottawatomie College, Stop Gap, New Mexico (an institution so backward it was described as "one of those colleges that plays football on Friday"). There, as befits a musical-comedy campus, the students have their minds only on football (the traditional rival is Texas Gentile), romance (virginal coeds are identified by their yellow beanies), and, of course, singing and dancing. With George Abbott presiding as producer-director, a script by George Marion, Jr., and dances by Robert Alton, the show treated audiences to an evening that was "gay, tuneful and attractively acted" (Watts), "lively and good looking" (Lockridge), "bright, fresh and youthful" (Anderson), "light, sprightly and colorful" (Abel Green, *Variety*), "invariably cheerful and bright" (Whipple), and "fresh, humorous and exhilarating" (Atkinson).

It was all fun of a pretty casual nature (costing only $8,000 to bring in), and the press was divided between pleasure and pain at its informality (Robert Coleman wrote: "At a $2.20 top, we would be inclined to recommend it, but at $3.30 we honestly cannot"). Highlights included a funny, if not too original operetta burlesque (in a Shubert show, that almost amounted to heresy), and there was praise for both singer Alfred Drake and a graceful, slim 26-year-old comic who did a patter song about "Anatole of Paris," a woman-hating hat designer. Richard Watts welcomed him with: "Danny Kaye seems to be what I hope will not sound too patronizing to call a comedian of promise."

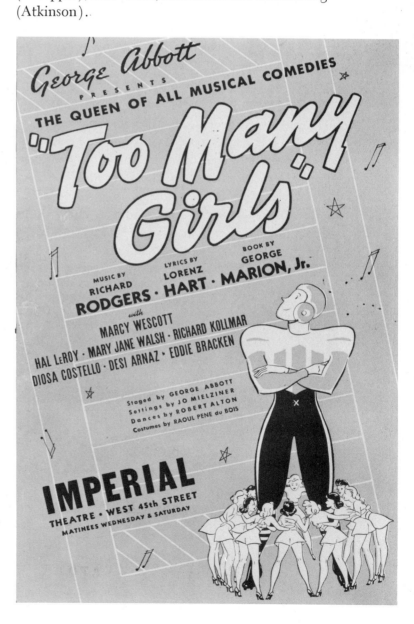

Vandamm; Theatre Coll., NY Public Lib.
Marcy Westcott, Richard Kollmar, Mary Jane Walsh, and Eddie Bracken sing "I Like
to Recognize the Tune" in *Too Many Girls*.

While the story of *Too Many Girls* counted for little (even George Abbott called it "contrived and artificial"), it did provide a sturdy enough framework for the energetic carryings-on by its talented young cast, including Richard Kollmar, Hal LeRoy, Desi Arnaz, and Eddie Bracken as All-American football heroes who are paid to enroll at the college to serve as bodyguards for heiress Marcy Westcott. Mary Jane Walsh, Diosa Costello and Leila Ernst completed the four paired-off couples, and conspicuous in the chorus was a towering towhead named Van Johnson.

While most of the songs bore some relationship to college life and football, there was always room for an unmotivated show-stopper. When someone tossed out a line about not wanting to return to New York, it was tossed out simply to cue the song, "Give It Back to the Indians," a genial catalogue of such unbearable aspects of life in the big city as the carnival atmosphere along Broadway, the additional tax on cigarettes, the murderous traffic conditions, radical soapbox speeches, the sagging stock market, the crowds at the Radio City Music Hall, open street excavations, the lack of support

for cultural endeavors, the success of *Tobacco Road*, The Bronx, Long Island smoke, New Jersey's glue pots, South Brooklyn's somnolence, and ended with:

> Swing bands give you heebie-jeebies,
> Dewey's put an end to sin,
> Men wear clothes like Lucius Beebe's—
> Give it back to the Innnnnnn-dians!

Those irritating swing bands were also the subject of a song all their own, "I Like to Recognize the Tune," in which Rodgers and Hart let loose some of their personal feelings about melodic distortions. The score's two most popular ballads were both concerned—albeit vaguely—with the educational process: "I Didn't Know What Time It Was," which shows how wisdom comes when one is in love, and "Love Never Went to College," in which Love is personified and made both illiterate and all-powerful. The proximity of the college campus to the Mexican border provided the excuse for the big dance routines to spotlight Puerto Rican Costello and Cuban Desi Arnaz (and his conga drum) in such torrid turns as "All Dressed Up Spic

186

and Spanish" and "She Could Shake the Maracas." The biggest laugh of the evening came when Eddie Bracken, looking for girl friend Leila Ernst, discovers not only her symbolic beanie in the muzzle of a cannon, but also her stockings, panties and bra. The show lasted the season to become the third longest running musical of the year.

Back in 1933, producer Max Gordon had told composer Jerome Kern, "I'll produce anything you write and I don't want to hear it in advance. Now, how about your next show? Is it mine?" Yes, it was —six years later.

Jerome Kern returned to Broadway from Hollywood with a musical called *Very Warm for May*, and there were reasons to believe that the occasion would find an equally warm reception in November. Max Gordon producing. Kern writing again with Oscar Hammerstein. Vincente Minnelli directing. And a theme, like other recent successes, with its accent on youth: a group of college kids who spend their summer at an avant-garde barn theatre and turn it into a success. But unlike *Babes in Arms*, to which it was distantly related, *Very Warm for May* turned out to be burdened by a plot that was heavy-handed and confusing. Yet, even so, there were winning performances by rising young players such as Grace McDonald (a *Babes in Arms* alumna), Frances Mercer, Hiram Sherman, Richard Quine, and dancers Don Loper and Maxine Barrat, as well as by more seasoned troupers Jack Whiting, Eve

As usual, Vincente Minnelli's name is misspelled.

Note that cover was designed before Phil Regan was replaced by Ronald Graham.

Arden, and Donald Brian (Broadway's original Prince Danilio in *The Merry Widow*).

Jerome Kern's cheeriest welcome mat was typed out by Sidney Whipple, who hailed the composer for "a set of melodies that are as far above the spine-shattering, footle-tootle of Tin Pan Alley as a Strauss waltz is above 'Waltz Me Around Again, Willie.'" Whipple also proved himself something of a seer when he wrote, "The most charming song is 'All the Things You Are' and I have no hesitation in predicting that it will take the country by storm." Most of the other reviewers also singled out the song for special praise.

Very Warm for May—despite its hit song, its lovely score, and its bright performances—lasted less than two months on Broadway. It was the final work Jerome Kern would create for the theatre.

An even greater November disaster, Erik Charell's *Swingin' the Dream*, also ended a career: it was the final stage production at the Center Theatre. This time, Mr. Charell, the *White Horse Inn*–keeper, offered a musical version of Shakespeare's *A Midsummer Night's Dream*, but the treatment fell far short of *The Boys from Syracuse*, the previous Shakespearean transformation. Set in New Orleans in 1890, *Swingin' the Dream* involved the governor of Louisiana, a group of simpleminded artisans including Louis Armstrong as Bully Bottom and Jackie "Moms" Mabley as Quince, and some jitterbugging and Lindy-hopping fairies led by Juan Hernandez's Oberon, Maxine Sullivan's Titania, and Butterfly McQueen's Puck. At a $2.20 top, they even threw in Benny Goodman and his Sextette. The title of the most popular of the Eddie De Lange–Jimmy Van Heusen songs, "Darn that Dream," proved an unintentional capsule review of the entire proceedings. The *Dream* stopped swinging after only two weeks.

On December 6, the final musical of both the year and the decade arrived on Broadway. It was *DuBarry Was a Lady*, one of the entertainment triumphs of the 1930s.

Nothing new or novel about *DuBarry*. Just a big, splashy, slickly put together show, featuring two of the stage's most outstanding musical-comedy performers, Ethel Merman (in a role originally conceived for Mae West) and Bert Lahr, and songs by one of its most renowned composers, Cole Porter. All the ingredients were there for a high-spirited, dazzling carnival, and they were assembled and put into shape by expert hands.

The tale concerned itself with the fortunes of a nightclub washroom attendant, Louie Blore (Bert Lahr), who has won $75,000 in the Irish Sweepstakes. Louie now hopes that his newly achieved affluence will also win him May Daley (Ethel Mer-

man), the Club Petite's stellar attraction, but her heart has already been lost to newspaper columnist Alex Bartin (Ronald Graham) who is, for the moment, inconveniently married. Louie's attempt to foil their romance by giving Alex a Mickey Finn only results in his mistakenly taking it himself. In a dream sequence at Le Petit Trianon, Louie has become Louis XV of France and May is DuBarry, his "mistress in name only." The king, we find, is a very concerned monarch. Among his plans to bring back prosperity to France is to build a bridge across the Seine lengthwise, and he demonstrates his democratic spirit by telling a curtseying young lady to "skip the dip." But still Louis cannot get anywhere with DuBarry, and he splutters in frustration. DuBarry tries to calm him down:

> DuBarry: Now please, Sire.
> King: Sire! Sire! I'm a hell of a sire. I haven't got any dam.
> DuBarry: No? You've only got every damn dam in the court.

In the dream, as in real life, there is the problem of another lover, also played by Ronald Graham. The king is about to clap him in jail for his revolutionary songs, but DuBarry wins his pardon by granting Louis his long-delayed visit to her chamber that night. However, the king's son, the dauphin (Benny Baker), foils the assignation by shooting his

Richard Tucker
King Louis XV (Bert Lahr) is frustrated in his attempt to spend the night with DuBarry (Ethel Merman) in *DuBarry Was a Lady*.

Bert Lahr and Ethel Merman vow their eternal "Friendship" in *DuBarry Was a Lady*.

The frequently hilarious monkeyshines of the story were perfectly matched by Cole Porter's contributions. In "When Love Beckoned," the naively romantic Ethel Merman described her "terrific surprise" when she discovered love among the gin mills of New York's 52nd Street. In "It Ain't Etiquette," Bert Lahr was given a tune to allow him to mock refinement by citing such rules of behavior as:

If you thought you were gypped at the Fair last year
And that Grover is just all wet
Don't suggest what he can do with the Perisphere
It ain't chic, it ain't smart, it ain't etiquette.

The production numbers at the nightclub celebrated burlesque shows in "Come on In," and the multiple amorous adventures that happened when "Katie Went to Haiti" ("For Katie knew her Haiti/ And prac-ti-cal-ly alllllllllllll Haiti knew Katie!"). Toward the end of the evening, May and Louie vowed their eternal "Friendship" in such mock hillbilly sentiments as "If you're ever down a well, ring my bell," and "If you ever lose your teeth when you're out to dine, borrow mine."

In the dream flashback, Porter used the dainty musical form of the minuet as contrast to the *double entendre* lyric of "But in the Morning, No"—including references to doing the crawl and the breast stroke (as in swimming), selling a seat (as on the stock exchange), anteing up (as in poker), and double entry (as in bookkeeping). Since the court of Louis XV was only a dream, anachronisms hardly mattered. In "Give Him the Oo-La-La," a dash of French flirtation was coupled with a political prediction:

If Mr. Roosevelt desires to rule-la-la
Until the year 1944
He'd better teach Eleanor how to oo-la-la
And he'll be elected once more.

It was also during the dream sequence that the show's hit ballad, "Do I Love You?" was first sung, and that 23-year-old Betty Grable (appearing on Broadway for the first time) and Charles Walters did "Well, Did You Evah?" a collection of examples of the unflappable way smart society receives bad news.

DuBarry Was a Lady ended the decade of the Thirties with a bawdy, gaudy, glittering look at mid-18th-century France that made it seem not too far removed from modern Broadway. It was all reas-

father in the seat of his satin britches with a bow and arrow. Stretched prone on a table, Louis complains to DuBarry when she visits him: "I can't go through life looking like a weather vane." To which DuBarry offers soothing consolation: "Don't let it worry you. If they never get it out, you'll still be doing something for France. You can hang a flag on it on Bastille Day."

Back at the Club Petite after awakening from his dream, Louie Blore selflessly offers Alex $10,000 to get a divorce so that he can marry May Daley. But when he also finds that he must pay $25,000 in taxes, Louie sadly realizes that it's back to the washroom for him.

Lucas & Monroe; Theatre Coll., NY Public Lib.
Ethel Merman belting out "Katie Went to Haiti" in *DuBarry Was a Lady*.

suringly familiar territory to audiences confused and upset by events beyond.

As the world itself was irretrievably sinking into the savagery and squalor of World War II, the musical productions being displayed at the close of 1939—*Pins and Needles, Hellzapoppin, The Streets of Paris, Yokel Boy, Too Many Girls, Very Warm for May, DuBarry Was a Lady*—offered theatregoers a good deal of boisterous fun, a measure of social commentary, some lavish spectacle, three or four brilliant clowns, many talented, youthful performers, and a worthy number of distinctively original songs. In the decades to come the themes would become more and more dependent upon pretested literary and dramatic works as the medium itself would continue to seek new ways to say it with music. But the foundations that the future would build upon were laid during a turbulent ten years in which the American Musical Theatre not only roused the tired businessman from his torpor, but woke up to its own unlimited potential for growth both in form and in content.

CASTS AND CREDITS OF BROADWAY MUSICALS OF THE THIRTIES

The list of musicals contains all 175 productions shown in New York between January 1, 1930, and December 31, 1939. Only the more recognized forms of musical theatre are included—musical comedy, musical play, operetta, revue, and opera when presented for a regular run. The list does not include one-man or one-woman shows, vaudeville, foreign productions, revivals, or plays with music.

All billings are, as closely as possible, the same as those used for each production when it played in New York. The wording of the credits, however, has been unified, and recognition has been given to those who, for one reason or another, failed to receive any in the official billing. Changes in individuals' names, cast replacements, literary and theatrical derivations, and other pertinent data have also been included. Musical numbers include only the best known songs from each score.

1930

January 14.

Edgar Selwyn presents
BOBBY CLARK & PAUL McCULLOUGH in

"STRIKE UP THE BAND"

Book by Morrie Ryskind, based on book by George S. Kaufman
Lyrics by Ira Gershwin
Music by George Gershwin
Directed by Alexander Leftwich Dances by George Hale
Settings by Raymond Sovey Costumes by Charles LeMaire
Music director, Hilding Anderson

with

Blanche Ring Jerry Goff Doris Carson Dudley Clements
Gordon Smith Margaret Schilling Red Nichols Orchestra
(incl. Benny Goodman, Gene Krupa, Glenn Miller, Jimmy Dorsey,
Jack Teagarden)

Musical Numbers
"I Mean to Say"—Smith, Carson
"A Typical Self-Made American"—Clements, Goff
"Soon"—Goff, Schilling
"If I Became the President"—Ring, Clark
"Hangin' Around with You"—Smith, Carson
"Strike Up the Band!"—Goff, company; Nichols Orch.
"Mademoiselle in New Rochelle"—Clark, McCullough
"I've Got a Crush on You" (originally in *Treasure Girl*)—
  Carson, Smith

(Note: Original version of *Strike Up the Band*, with book by George
S. Kaufman, opened at Broadway Theatre, Long Branch, N. J., Aug.
29, 1927. It closed after two weeks at the Shubert Theatre,
Philadelphia. The cast included Lew Hearn, Jimmie Savo, Edna
May Oliver, Roger Pryor, Vivian Hart, Morton Downey.)

Times Square Theatre *191 performances*

1930

February 11.   Charles B. Dillingham presents
FRED STONE in

"RIPPLES"

Book by William Anthony McGuire
Lyrics by Irving Caesar & Graham John
Music by Oscar Levant & Albert Sirmay
Directed by William Anthony McGuire   Dances by William Holbrook,
    Mary Read
Settings by Joseph Urban   Costumes by Charles LeMaire
Music director, Gus Salzer

with

DOROTHY STONE
Paula Stone   Mrs. Fred Stone   Eddie Foy, Jr.
Andrew Tombes   Kathryn Hereford   Charles Collins
Janet Martin

Musical Numbers
"Is It Love?" (Caesar-Levant)—Collins, D. Stone
"There's Nothing Wrong with a Kiss" (Caesar, John-Levant)—Foy, P. Stone
"I'm a Little Bit Fonder of You" (Caesar; originally in *Mercenary
    Mary*, London; added during run)—Tombes, Martin

New Amsterdam Theatre   *55 performances*

February 11.   Ruth Selwyn's

"NINE-FIFTEEN REVUE"

Sketches by Ring Lardner, Paul Gerard Smith, Eddie Cantor, Anita
Loos, John Emerson, Geoffrey Kerr, H. W. Hanemann, Robert Ruskin,
A. Dorian Otvos, Ruth Wilcox
Lyrics by Paul James (James P. Warburg), Ira Gershwin, Edward
Eliscu, Ted Koehler, Philip Broughton
Music by Kay Swift, George Gershwin, Manning Sherwin, Rudolf Friml,
Ned Lehac, Ralph Rainger, Roger Wolfe Kahn, Vincent Youmans, Harold
Arlen, Victor Herbert, Will Johnstone
Directed by Alexander Leftwich (uncredited)   Dances by Busby
Berkeley, Leon Leonidoff
Settings by Clark Robinson   Costumes by Kiviette
Music director, Don Voorhees

with

Ruth Etting   Harry McNaughton   Fred Keating
Joe & Pete Michon   Paul Kelly   Charles Lawrence
Helen Gray   Frances Shelley   Lynn Dore   Mary Murray
Gracella & Theodore   Oscar Ragland   Nan Blackstone
Margaret Merle

Musical Numbers
"Up Among the Chimney Pots" (James-Swift)—Etting
"Toddlin' Along" (Gershwin-Gershwin)—Blackstone
"World of Dreams" (Eliscu-Herbert)—Merle; danced by Gracella &
     Theodore
"Get Happy" (Koehler-Arlen)—Etting

George M. Cohan Theatre   *7 performances*

1930

February 18.   Florenz Ziegfeld presents
ED WYNN in

"SIMPLE SIMON"

Book by Ed Wynn & Guy Bolton
Lyrics by Lorenz Hart
Music by Richard Rodgers
Directed by Zeke Colvan   Dances by Seymour Felix
Settings by Joseph Urban   Costumes by John Harkrider
Music director, Oscar Bradley

with

Ruth Etting   Harriet Hoctor   Will Ahearn
Bobbe Arnst   Alan Edwards   Doree Leslie
Lennox Pawle   Hugh Cameron   Douglas Stanbury
(Note: Miss Etting replaced Lee Morse during tryout.)

Musical Numbers
"Don't Tell Your Folks"—Ahearn, Arnst
"I Still Believe in You"—Etting
"Send for Me"—Leslie, Edwards
"I Can Do Wonders with You"—Leslie, Edwards
"Ten Cents a Dance"—Etting
"Love Me or Leave Me" (Gus Kahn–Walter Donaldson; added in April)
    —Etting
(Note: "Dancing on the Ceiling," sung by Leslie, cut during tryout.)

Ziegfeld Theatre   *135 performances*

Return Engagement: March 9, 1931
Presented by Ed Wynn
Miss Etting succeeded by Wini Shaw, Mr. Ahearn by David Breen, Miss
Arnst by Laine Blaire, Mr. Edwards by Jack Squires, Miss Leslie by
Margaret Breen

Majestic Theatre   *16 performances*

1930

February 25.   Lew Leslie's

"INTERNATIONAL REVUE"

Sketches by Nat Dorfman, Lew Leslie
Lyrics by Dorothy Fields
Music by Jimmy McHugh
Directed by Lew Leslie & Edward Clark Lilley   Dances by Busby
Berkeley, Harry Crosley, Chester Hale
Settings by Anthony Street   Costumes by Dolly Tree
Music director, Harry Levant

with

GERTRUDE LAWRENCE   HARRY RICHMAN
Jack Pearl   Florence Moore   Moss & Fontana
Anton Dolin   Harry Jans & Harold Whalen   Bernice & Emily
Esther Muir   Livia Marracci   Radaelli   Robert Hobbs
Viola Dobos
ARGENTINITA
(Note: Dave Apollon in cast during tryout. Argentinita and Miss
Moore out of cast after one week. In May, Miss Lawrence succeeded
by Frances Williams.)

Musical Numbers
"On the Sunny Side of the Street"—Richman
"Exactly Like You"—Lawrence, Richman
"The Margineers"—Pearl
"Keys to Your Heart"—Hobbs; danced by Moss & Fontana
"Cinderella Brown"—Lawrence

Majestic Theatre   *95 performances*

March 3.   George White presents

"FLYING HIGH"

Book by John McGowan, B. G. DeSylva & Lew Brown
Lyrics by B. G. DeSylva & Lew Brown
Music by Ray Henderson
Directed by George White & Edward Clark Lilley   Dances by Bobby
    Connolly
Settings by Joseph Urban   Costumes by Charles LeMaire
Music director, Al Goodman

with

BERT LAHR
OSCAR SHAW
Grace Brinkley   Kate Smith   Russ Brown   Pearl Osgood
Dorothy Hall   Gale Quadruplets   Gus Schilling   (chorus)
(Note: Mr. Shaw replaced Jack [John] Barker during tryout.)

Musical Numbers
"I'll Know Him"—Brinkley
"Wasn't It Beautiful While It Lasted?"—Brinkley, Shaw
"Thank Your Father"—Shaw, Brinkley
"Good for You—Bad for Me"—Brown, Osgood
"Red Hot Chicago"—Smith, Gale Quadruplets
"Without Love"—Brinkley, Shaw; reprised by Smith
"Mrs. Krause's Blue-Eyed Baby Boy"—Lahr

Apollo Theatre   *357 performances*

1930

April 7.   William B. Friedlander presents

"JONICA"

Book by Moss Hart (credited without permission), from unproduced
play, *Have a Good Time, Jonica*, by Dorothy Heyward
Lyrics by William Moll
Music by Joseph Meyer
Directed by William Friedlander   Dances by Pal'mere Brandeaux
Settings by William Hawley
Music director, Carl C. Gray

with

Joyce Barbour	Earle S. Dewey	Nell Roy	Harry T. Shannon
June O'Dea	Jerry Norris	Bert Matthews	Irene Swor

Musical Numbers
"Tie Your Cares to a Melody"—Norris, Barbour, Matthews
"I Want Someone" (William B. Friedlander)—Roy, Norris
"If You Were the Apple"—Norris, Roy

Craig Theatre   *40 performances*

1930

April 14.

Messrs. Shubert present

"THREE LITTLE GIRLS"

Book by Marie Armstrong Hecht & Gertrude Purcell, from German
operetta, *Three Poor Little Girls*, by Herman Feiner & Bruno
Hardt-Warden
Lyrics by Harry B. Smith
Music by Walter Kollo
Directed by J. J. Shubert
Settings by Watson Barratt   Costumes by Ernest Schrapps
Music director, Louis Kroll
(Note: Frank Smithson credited as director during tryout.)

with

Natalie Hall   Bettina Hall   Charles Hedley
Raymond Walburn   Stephen Mills   Lorraine Weimar
Harry Puck   Martha Lorber   George Dobbs
Thelma Goodwin   Margaret Adams

Musical Numbers
"Love's Happy Dream"—N. Hall, Hedley
"Letter Song"—Hedley
"Dream On"—N. Hall, B. Hall

Shubert Theatre   *104 performances*

June 4.   The Theatre Guild, Inc., presents

"THE GARRICK GAIETIES"

Sketches by Carroll Carroll, Leo Poldine (Leopoldine Damrosch) &
Gretchen Damrosch Finletter, Benjamin M. Kaye, Newman Levy, Sterling
Holloway & Louis Simon, Sally Humason, Landon Herrick
Lyrics by Edward Eliscu, Henry Myers, Johnny Mercer, Ira Gershwin,
E. Y. Harburg, Thomas McKnight, Newman Levy, Paul James (James P.
Warburg), Ronald Jeans, Allen Boretz, Joshua Titzell, Marc Blitzstein
Music by Richard Myers, Charles Schwab, Willard Robison, Everett
Miller, Vernon Duke, Kay Swift, Marc Blitzstein, Ned Lehac, Peter
Nolan, Harold Goldman
Directed by Philip Loeb   Dances by Olin Howland
Settings by Kate Drain Lawson   Costumes by Miss Lawson, Louis
Simon, Henri Peine du Bois
Music director, Tom Jones

with

Albert Carroll   Edith Meiser   Philip Loeb
Sterling Holloway   Nan Blackstone   Ruth Chorpenning
Hildegarde Halliday   Roger Stearns   James Norris
Otto Hulett   Cynthia Rogers   Imogene Coca
Velma Vavra   Donald Stewart   Ray Heatherton   Ted Fetter
William Tannen
(Note: In Sept., Lee Strasberg [stage manager] added to cast.)

Musical Numbers
"Lazy Levee Loungers" (Robison)—Blackstone
"I Am Only Human After All" (Harburg, Gershwin-Duke)—Norris, Vavra,
    Loeb, Coca, Blackstone, Holloway
"Johnny Wanamaker" (James-Swift)—Stewart, Norris, Heatherton,
    Fetter
"Out of Breath" (Mercer-Miller)—Holloway, Rogers
"Put It Away Till Spring" (Titzell-Nolan)—Tannen, Coca

Guild Theatre   158 *performances*

Return Engagement: Oct. 16, 1930

Albert Carroll   Doris Vinton   Philip Loeb
Sterling Holloway   Katherine Carrington   Ruth Chorpenning
Neal Caldwell   Roger Stearns   James Norris   Otto Hulett
Edgar Stehli   Imogene Coca   Neile Goodelle
Donald Stewart   William Holbrook   Donald Burr
Rosalind Russell

Added Musical Numbers

"The Butcher, the Baker, the Candle-Stick Maker" (Kaye-Mana-Zucca)
    —Burr
"The Three Musketeers" (Lorenz Hart–Richard Rodgers; originally
    in 1925 *Garrick Gaieties*)—Loeb, Holloway, Caldwell
"Rose of Arizona" (Hart-Rodgers; originally in 1926 *Garrick Gaieties*)
    —Chorpenning, Carrington, Norris, Vinton, Holloway, Russell,
    Hulett, Carroll, Burr, Caldwell, Stehli, Stearns, Holbrook

Guild Theatre   *12 performances*

June 6.   Cleon Throckmorton presents

"CHANGE YOUR LUCK"

Book by Garland Howard
Lyrics & music by J. C. Johnson
Directed by Cleon Throckmorton   Dances by Lawrence Deas & Speedy
Smith
Settings by Cleon Throckmorton
Music director, Stanley Bennett

with

Hamtree Harrington   Alberta Hunter   Leigh Whipper
Speedy Smith   Garland Howard   Sam Cross   Sammy Van
Cora La Redd   Alberta Perkins   Neeka Shaw
Sterling Grant   4 Hot Poppers   Sisters of Mercy

Musical Numbers
"Walk Together, Children"—Cross
"Mr. Mammy Man"—Shaw, Howard
"Change Your Luck"—Harrington, Hunter
"St. Louis Blues" (W. C. Handy)—4 Hot Poppers

George M. Cohan Theatre   17 performances

June 10.   Messrs. Shubert present

"ARTISTS AND MODELS" (Paris-Riviera Edition)

Book & lyrics uncredited; from English musical, *Dear Love*, by Dion
Titheradge, Lauri Wylie, Herbert Clayton, Haydn Wood, Joseph Tunbridge,
& Jack Waller
Music by Harold Stern & Ernie Golden
Directed by Frank Smithson   Dances by Pal'mere Brandeaux
Settings by Watson Barratt   Costumes by Ernest Schrapps
Music director, Max Meth

with

Aileen Stanley   George Hassell   Vera Pearce   Phil Baker
Miss Florence
Havana Cubanola Rhumba Band   Harry Welsh   Mary Adams
Dolores DeMonde   Naomi Johnson   Halfred Young
Rath Brothers   Stanley Harrison   Wesley Pierce & Hazel Harris
Kay McKay
(Note: In July, Phil Baker & Aileen Stanley received star billing
along with Shaw & Lee who were added to cast.)

Musical Numbers
"My Real Ideal" (Sammy Lerner–Burton Lane)—Adams, DeMonde
"Jimmy and Me"—Stanley
"Two Perfect Lovers" (Lerner-Lane)—Adams, Young

(Note: *Artists and Models* known as *Dear Love* during tryout. Original
production first presented at the Palace Theatre, London, Nov. 14,
1929. It ran 132 performances, with a cast including Tom Burke,
Vera Pearce, Claude Hulbert, Sydney Howard.)

Majestic Theatre   *55 performances*

June 23.

James M. Graf, with Paul M. Trebitsch, presents

"MYSTERY MOON"

Book by Fred Herendeen
Lyrics & music by Monte Carlo & Alma Sanders
Directed by Victor Morley   Dances by Bunny Weldon
Settings by Theatrical Art Studios   Costumes by Brooks
Music director, Ernie Valle   Orchestrations, Hilding Anderson,
Maurice DePackh, Hans Spialek, Joe Weiss

with

Frances Shelley	Kitty Kelly	Charles Lawrence	Juliana
Nat Nazarro, Jr.	Jane Taylor	Arthur Campbell	
Pauline Dee			

Musical Numbers
"It's All OK"—Taylor, Campbell
"Mystery Moon"—Dee, Campbell, Taylor
"Why Couldn't We Incorporate?"—Kelly, Lawrence

Royale Theatre   *1 performance*

1930

July 1.   **"EARL CARROLL VANITIES"** (8th Edition)

Sketches by Eddie Welch, Eugene Conrad
Lyrics by Ted Koehler, E. Y. Harburg
Music by Harold Arlen, Jay Gorney
Directed by Earl Carroll & Priestley Morrison   Dances by LeRoy Prinz
Settings by Hugh Willoughby   Costumes by Charles LeMaire, Vincente Minnelli
Music director, Ray Kavanaugh   Orchestrations, Domenico Savino

with

Herb Williams	Jimmie Savo	Jack Benny	Patsy Kelly
Dorothy Britton	Collette Sisters	John Hale	Irene Ahlberg
Betty Veronica	Harry Stockwell	Frank & Harry Condos	
Thelma White	Faith Bacon		

Musical Numbers
"One Love" (Koehler-Arlen)—Hale; fan dance by Bacon
"Hittin' the Bottle" (Koehler-Arlen)—Veronica
"The March of Time" (Koehler-Arlen)—Stockwell, Hale
"I Came to Life" (Harburg-Gorney)—Hale, Stockwell
"Out of a Clear Blue Sky" (Koehler-Arlen)—Collette Sisters

New Amsterdam Theatre   *215 performances*

July 8.   The Satirists, Inc., present

"WHO CARES?"

Sketches by Edward Clark Lilley, Bertrand Robinson, Kenneth Webb,
John Cantwell
Lyrics by Harry Clark
Music by Percy Wenrich
Directed by George Vivian & Edward Clark Lilley   Dances by William
    Holbrook
Settings by Cirker & Robbins
Music director, Irving Schloss

with

Peggy O'Neill	Florenz Ames	William Holbrook	
Robert Pitkin	John Cherry	Margaret Dale	Ralph Riggs
Templeton Brothers	Olive Olsen	Don Lanning	
Marjorie Seltzer	Arthur Hartley		

Musical Numbers
"Who Cares?"—Chorus
"Believe It or Not"—Seltzer, Hartley
"Make My Bed Down in Dixieland"—Lanning

46th Street Theatre   *32 performances*

August 21.   Max Rudnick presents

"HOT RHYTHM"

Sketches by Will Morrissey, Ballard Macdonald, Edward Hurley, Johnny
Lee Long, Dewey "Pigmeat" Markham
Lyrics by Don Heywood
Music by Porter Grainger
Directed by Will Morrissey   Dances by Nat Cash, Eddie Rector, Midge
Miller
Settings by Wertheim Studios   Costumes by Reine Costumes
Music director, Maurice Coffin

with

Mae Barnes	Al Vigel	Eddie Rector
Dewey "Pigmeat" Markham	Johnny Lee Long	Ravella Hughes
Madeline Belt	Johnnie Hudgins	Inez Seeley	Edith Wilson
Hilda Perlino	Arthur Bryson	

Musical Numbers
"Say the Word that Will Make You Mine"—Barnes
"Loving You the Way I Do" (Jack Scholl–Eubie Blake, Eddie
     De Lange)—Hughes, Vigel, Belt, Bryson
"Hot Rhythm"—Barnes

Times Square Theatre   73 performances

September 2.   Dwight Deere Wiman & William A. Brady, Jr., with Tom Weatherly, present

"THE SECOND LITTLE SHOW"

Sketches by Norman Clark, Marc Connelly, William Miles, Donald
Blackwell, James Coghlan, Bert Hanlon
Lyrics mostly by Howard Dietz
Music mostly by Arthur Schwartz
Directed by Mr. Wiman & Monty Woolley   Dances by Dave Gould
Settings by Jo Mielziner   Costumes by Raymond Sovey, Helene Pons
Music director, Gus Salzer
(Note: Mr. Brady withdrew as co-producer during run.)

with

AL TRAHAN   YUKONA CAMERON   RUTH TESTER
JAY C. FLIPPEN
Gloria Grafton   Tashamira   Joey Ray   Ned Wever
Helen Gray   Davey Jones   Arline Judge (chorus)
Fay Brady (chorus)
(Note: Marion Harris added to cast during run.)

Musical Numbers
"You're the Sunrise"—Grafton, Ray; danced by Gray
"What a Case I've Got on You"—Gray, Jones
"Lucky Seven"—Ray
"Sing Something Simple" (Herman Hupfeld)—Tester, with Judge, Brady

Royale Theatre   *63 performances*

1930

September 17.   Arthur Hammerstein presents

"LUANA"

Book by Howard Emmett Rogers, from play, *Bird of Paradise,* by
Richard Walton Tully
Lyrics by J. Keirn Brennan
Music by Rudolf Friml
Directed by Howard Emmett Rogers   Dances by Earl Lindsey
Settings by Cirker & Robbins   Costumes by Charles LeMaire
Music director, Ivan Rudisill   Orchestrations, Joseph Meyer

with

Ruth Altman   Robert Chisholm   Lillian Bond
Marguerita Silva   Joseph Macaulay   Harry Jans & Harold Whelan
Doris Carson   Donald Novis   Sally Rand (chorus)

Musical Numbers
"Luana"—Novis
"Aloha"—Altman
"My Bird of Paradise"—Macaulay, Altman
"A Son of the Sun"—Chisholm

Hammerstein's Theatre   *21 performances*

1930

September 20.   Messrs. Shubert present

"NINA ROSA"

Book by Otto Harbach
Lyrics by Irving Caesar
Music by Sigmund Romberg
Directed by J. J. Shubert & J. C. Huffman
Settings by Watson Barratt   Costumes by Orry Kelly
Music director, Max Meth   Orchestrations, Hans Spialek

with

GUY ROBERTSON   ETHELIND TERRY
ARMIDA   LEONARD CEELEY
Cortez & Peggy   Don Barclay   Marion Marchante
Yo-Hay-Tong   Jack Sheehan   Kalil-Ogly
Stanley Jessup   Clay Clement   Victor Casmore   Frank Horn
George Kirk   Zachary Caully

Musical Numbers
"Nina Rosa"—Robertson, Horn, Kirk, Caully
"Your Smiles, Your Tears"—Terry, Robertson
"Serenade of Love"—Ceeley, Terry, Armida
"My First Love, My Last Love" (Harbach, Caesar-Romberg)—Terry,
    Robertson

Majestic Theatre   *137 performances*

1930

September 23.   Morris Green & Lewis E. Gensler present
JOE COOK in

"FINE AND DANDY"

Book by Donald Ogden Stewart; additional scenes by Joe Cook
Lyrics by Paul James (James P. Warburg)
Music by Kay Swift
Directed by Morris Green & Frank McCoy   Dances by Dave Gould,
Tom Nip, Eugene Van Grona, Merriel Abbott
Settings by Henry Dreyfuss   Costumes by Charles LeMaire
Music director, Gene Salzer   Orchestrations, Hans Spialek

with

| Nell O'Day | Dave Chasen | Eleanor Powell | Alice Boulden |
| John Ehrle | David Morris | Joe Wagstaff | Dora Maugham |

Musical Numbers
"Fine and Dandy"—Cook, Boulden; reprised by O'Day
"Can This Be Love?"—Boulden
"Let's Go Eat Worms in the Garden"—Boulden, Wagstaff
"Jig Hop"—Powell

Erlanger's Theatre   *255 performances*

1930

October 7.

Marty Forkins presents

"BROWN BUDDIES"

Book by Carl Rickman
Lyrics mostly by Millard Thomas
Music mostly by Joe Jordan
Directed by Ralph Rose   Dances by Addison Carey, Charles Davis
Settings by Theodore Kahn, Edward Sundquist   Costumes by Brooks, Inc., Ida Bell
Music director, Charles L. Cooke   Orchestrations, Messrs. Cooke & Jordan

with

BILL ROBINSON   ADELAIDE HALL
Ada Brown   Alma Smith   Shelton Brooks   Pike Davis
William Fountaine

Musical Numbers
"Happy" (Bob Joffe–Nat Reed)—Robinson, Hall
"Brown Buddies"—Robinson
"When a Black Man's Blue"—Brown
"Dancin' 'Way Your Sin" (J. C. Johnson)—Brown

Liberty Theatre   *113 performances*

October 13.   Bobby Connolly & Arthur Swanstrom present

"PRINCESS CHARMING"

Book by Jack Donahue, from Hungarian operetta by Ferencz Martos, &
English version by Arthur Wimperis & Lauri Wylie
Lyrics by Arthur Swanstrom
Music by Albert Sirmay & Arthur Schwartz
Directed by Bobby Connolly & Edward Clark Lilley   Dances by
Albertina Rasch
Settings by Joseph Urban   Costumes by Charles LeMaire
Music director, Alfred Goodman

with

EVELYN HERBERT   ROBERT HALLIDAY
GEORGE GROSSMITH   JEANNE AUBERT
VICTOR MOORE
Douglass Dumbrille   Howard St. John   Paul Huber
Duke McHale   Roy Gordon   Dorothea James
Portia Grafton

Musical Numbers
"Palace of Dreams"—Herbert
"Trailing a Shooting Star"—Herbert, Halliday
"I Love Love" (Walter O'Keefe–Robert Dolan)—Aubert
"You"—Herbert, Halliday
"I'll Never Leave You"—Herbert, Halliday

(Note: The first English-language version was presented at the
Palace Theatre, London, Oct. 21, 1926. It ran 362 performances.
The cast included Bernard Clifton, W. H. Berry, Alice Delysia, George
Grossmith, Winnie Melville, John Clarke.)

Imperial Theatre   *56 performances*

1930

October 14.   Alex A. Aarons & Vinton Freedley present

"GIRL CRAZY"

Book by Guy Bolton & John McGowan
Lyrics by Ira Gershwin
Music by George Gershwin
Directed by Alexander Leftwich   Dances by George Hale
Settings by Donald Oenslager   Costumes by Kiviette
Music director, Earl Busby   Orchestrations, Russell Bennett

with

Willie Howard   Allen Kearns   Ginger Rogers   William Kent
Ethel Merman   Antonio & Renée DeMarco   The Foursome
Eunice Healey   Lew Parker   Roger Edens (pianist)
Red Nichols Orchestra (incl. Benny Goodman, Gene Krupa, Glenn Miller,
Jimmy Dorsey, Jack Teagarden)

Musical Numbers
"Bidin' My Time"—The Foursome
"Could You Use Me?"—Rogers, Kearns
"Embraceable You"—Rogers, Kearns
"Sam and Delilah"—Merman
"I Got Rhythm"—Merman
"But Not for Me"—Rogers, Howard
"Treat Me Rough"—Kearns
"Boy! What Love Has Done to Me!"—Merman

Alvin Theatre   *272 performances*

October 15   Max Gordon presents
CLIFTON WEBB
FRED ALLEN   LIBBY HOLMAN   in

"THREE'S A CROWD"

Compiled by Howard Dietz
Sketches by Howard Dietz, Groucho Marx & Arthur Sheekman, William
Miles & Donald Blackwell, Laurence Schwab, Fred Allen, Corey Ford
Lyrics mostly by Howard Dietz
Music mostly by Arthur Schwartz
Directed by Hassard Short   Dances by Albertina Rasch
Settings by Albert R. Johnson   Costumes by Kiviette
Music director, Nicholas Kempner

with

Tamara Geva   Earl Oxford   Portland Hoffa   Margaret Lee
Amy Revere   Marybeth Conoly   The California Collegians
(incl. Fred MacMurray)

Musical Numbers
"Something to Remember You By"—Holman (to MacMurray)
"Talkative Toes" (Dietz-Vernon Duke)—Geva
"Out in the Open Air" (Dietz–Burton Lane)—Webb, Lee
"All the King's Horses" (Dietz, Edward Brandt–Alec Wilder)—Lee
"Body and Soul" (Edward Heyman, Robert Sour–Johnny Green)—Holman;
     danced by Webb, Geva
"The Moment I Saw You"—Webb, Revere
"Yaller" (Richard Myers–Charles Schwab)—Holman
"Right at the Start of It"—Webb, Allen, Holman

Selwyn Theatre   *271 performances*

October 22. Lew Leslie's

"BLACKBIRDS" (1930 Edition)

Sketches by Flournoy Miller
Lyrics by Andy Razaf
Music by Eubie Blake
Directed by Lew Leslie   Dances by Al Richards
Settings by Ward & Harvey   Costumes by Vincente Minnelli
Music director, Eubie Blake   Orchestrations, Ken Macomber
Vocal arrangements, J. Rosamond Johnson

with

ETHEL WATERS   BUCK & BUBBLES
FLOURNOY MILLER   BERRY BROTHERS
Jazzlips Richardson   Mantan Moreland   Jimmy Baskette
Cecil Mack Choir   Al Richards   Minto Cato   Neeka Shaw
Broadway Jones

Musical Numbers
"Memories of You"—Cato
"You're Lucky to Me"—Shaw, Bubbles; reprised by Waters
"That Lindy Hop"—chorus
"My Handy Man Ain't Handy No More"—Waters
"Baby Mine"—Waters, Mack Choir

Royale Theatre   *26 performances*

November 5.   Lew Fields & Lyle D. Andrews present

"THE VANDERBILT REVUE"

Sketches by Kenyon Nicholson, Ellis Jones, Sig Herzig, Edwin
Gilbert & Arthur Burns, James Coghlan
Lyrics mostly by Dorothy Fields
Music mostly by Jimmy McHugh
Directed by Lew Fields & Theodore Hammerstein   Dances by John
E. Lonergan, Jack Haskell
Settings by Ward & Harvey   Costumes by Robert Stevenson
Music director, Gus Salzer

with

Lulu McConnell   Joe Penner   Evelyn Hoey   Richard Lane
Olga Markoff   Franker Woods   Jacques Fray & Mario Braggiotti
Francesca Braggiotti   Teddy Walters   Tonia Ingre
Charles Barnes   Dorothy Dixon   Jean Carpenter
Dalsky's Russian Choir   Gus Schilling
(Note: Madge Evans was in cast during tryout.)

Musical Numbers
"Button Up Your Heart"—Hoey, Barnes
"Blue Again"—Hoey
"What's My Man Gonna Be Like?" (Cole Porter)—Hoey
"I Give Myself Away" (Edward Eliscu–Jacques Fray)—Barnes, Hoey

Vanderbilt Theatre   *13 performances*

November 7.   G. W. McGregor presents

"THE WELL OF ROMANCE"

Book & lyrics by Preston Sturges
Music by H. Maurice Jacquet
Directed by J. H. Benrimo   Dances by Leon Leonidoff, Florence Rogge
Settings by Gates & Morange
Music director, H. Maurice Jacquet

with

NORMA TERRIS   HOWARD MARSH
Max Figman   Lina Abarbanell   Louis Sorin   Laine Blaire
Tommy Monroe

Musical Numbers
"The Well of Romance"—Blaire, Monroe
"Be Oh So Careful, Ann"—Abarbanell
"Dream of Dreams"—Terris, Marsh

Craig Theatre   *8 performances*

November 15.   Messrs. Shubert present
CHARLES (CHIC) SALE in

"HELLO, PARIS"

Book by Edgar Smith, from novel, *They Had to See Paris*, by
Homer Croy
Lyrics by Charles O. Locke & Frank Bannister
Music by Russell Tarbox & Maury Rubens
Directed by Ben Holmes   Dances by Pal'mere Brandeaux
Settings by Watson Barratt
Music director, Tom Jones
(Note: During tryout, lyrics credited to Mr. Locke & Ned Washington,
music to Mr. Tarbox & Michael Cleary, dances to George Cunningham.)

with

POLLY WALKER

Jack Good	Nat C. Haines	Stella Mayhew	Georgia Hayes
Mary Adams	Marie Starner	Charles Columbus	
Maurice LePue	Louis LaGranna	J. Clifford Rice	
Ethel Wilson	Claire Hooper	Olga Markoff	
Riva Reyes	Don Morrell		

AMERIQUE & NEVILLE
LOIS DEPPE & HIS JUBILEE SINGERS
(Note: During tryout, Miss Walker replaced Eileen Dougall, Mr.
Columbus replaced Glen Dale. In Dec., Miss Walker
succeeded by Miss Adams, Miss Adams by Dorothy Dare.)

Musical Numbers
"I Stumbled Over You" (Henry Dagand–Rubens)—Walker, Columbus
"Deep Paradise"—Deppe, Jubilee Singers
"Got to Have Hips Now"—Mayhew

Shubert Theatre   *33 performances*

1930

November 17.

Billy Rose presents

JAMES BARTON   FANNIE BRICE   GEORGE JESSEL
in

"SWEET AND LOW"

Sketches by David Freedman
Lyrics by Billy Rose, Edward Eliscu, Mort Dixon, Ira Gershwin, Malcolm McComb, Allen Boretz, Ballard Macdonald, Charlotte Kent
Music by Harry Archer, Will Irwin, Harry Warren, Ned Lehac, Vivian Ellis, Spoliansky, Dana Suesse, Duke Ellington, Louis Alter, Phil Charig & Joseph Meyer
Directed by Alexander Leftwich   Dances by Danny Dare, Busby Berkeley
Settings by Jo Mielziner   Costumes by James Reynolds
Music director, Bill Daly

with

BORRAH MINEVITCH   MOSS & FONTANA
Hannah Williams   Paula Trueman   Arthur Treacher
Hal Thompson   Jerry Norris   Roger Pryor Dodge
Bubber Miley (cornet)
(Note: Moss & Fontana and Mr. Treacher out of cast in Dec.; Mr. Minevitch out in Jan. 1931. Eugene Van Grona added in Jan.
In Feb., Hannah Williams succeeded by Dorothy Williams; in March, Dorothy Williams by Audrey Christie.)

Musical Numbers
"Cheerful Little Earful" (Gershwin, Rose-Warren)—Williams, Norris
"Would You Like to Take a Walk?" (Dixon, Rose-Warren)—Williams, Thompson
"East St. Louis Toodle-oo" (Ellington)—Dodge, Miley
"Overnight" (Kent, Rose-Alter)—Brice
"Sweet So and So" (Gershwin-Charig, Meyer)—Williams, Norris

(Note: *Sweet and Low* was a revised version of *Corned Beef and Roses*, which opened in Philadelphia, Oct. 27, 1930. Mr. Barton then replaced Hal Skelly, and Moss & Fontana and Mr. Minevitch were added. Though most of the songs were the same in both versions, the original included "Gimme a Watch and Chain" [George M. Cohan], sung by Mr. Skelly & company, "Sky City" [Lorenz Hart–Richard Rodgers], sung by Alfredo Chigi, and "You Can't Stop Me from Loving You" [Mann Holiner–Alberta Nichols], sung by Miss Williams & Mr. Skelly. *Crazy Quilt*, a third version of the same basic revue, may be found under date of May 19, 1931.)

46th Street Theatre   *184 performances*

1930

November 18.   Florenz Ziegfeld presents
MARILYN MILLER
FRED—THE ASTAIRES—ADELE   in

"SMILES"

Book by William Anthony McGuire
Lyrics by Clifford Grey, Harold Adamson; additional lyrics by Ring
Lardner
Music by Vincent Youmans
Directed by William Anthony McGuire   Dances by Ned Wayburn
Settings by Joseph Urban   Costumes by John Harkrider
Music director, Frank Tours

with

TOM HOWARD   EDDIE FOY, JR.   PAUL GREGORY
Larry Adler   Clare Dodd   Georgia Caine   Edward Raquello
Kathryn Hereford   Adrian Rosley   Bob Hope (chorus)
Virginia Bruce (chorus)
(Note: Harriette Lake [Ann Sothern] in cast during tryout.)

Musical Numbers
"Time on My Hands" (Adamson, Mack Gordon–Youmans)—Miller,
    Gregory (Miss Miller's refrain, "What Can I Say?" lyric
    by Lardner)
"Be Good to Me" (Lardner-Youmans)—Astaires
"If I Were You, Love" (Lardner-Youmans)—Astaires
"I'm Glad I Waited" (Grey, Adamson-Youmans)—Miller, F. Astaire
"You're Driving Me Crazy" (Walter Donaldson; added Dec.)—
    A. Astaire, Foy

Ziegfeld Theatre   *63 performances*

1930

December 8. E. Ray Goetz presents

"THE NEW YORKERS"

Book by Herbert Fields, from story by Peter Arno
Lyrics & Music by Cole Porter
Directed by E. Ray Goetz & Monty Woolley   Dances by George Hale
Settings by Dale Stetson   Costumes by Peter Arno, Charles LeMaire
Music director, Al Goodman   Orchestrations, Hans Spialek

with

FRANCES WILLIAMS   CHARLES KING
HOPE WILLIAMS   ANN PENNINGTON
RICHARD CARLE   MARIE CAHILL
FRED WARING PENNSYLVANIANS (incl. Stuart Churchill,
James "Poley" McClintock, Charles Henderson)
LOU CLAYTON, EDDIE JACKSON & JIMMY DURANTE
Oscar Ragland   Barrie Oliver   Kathryn Crawford
Paul Huber   Ralph Glover   Tammany Young
Iris Adrian (chorus)

Musical Numbers
"Where Have You Been?"—King, H. Williams
"I'm Getting Myself Ready for You"—F. Williams, Oliver,
      Pennington, King
"Love for Sale"—Crawford, Three Girl Friends
"The Great Indoors"—F. Williams
"Wood" (Durante)—Clayton, Jackson & Durante
"Take Me Back to Manhattan"—F. Williams
"Let's Fly Away"—King, H. Williams
"I Happen to Like New York" (added Jan. 1931)—Ragland

Broadway (formerly Colony) Theatre   *168 performances*

December 22. Arthur Hammerstein presents
W. C. FIELDS in

"BALLYHOO"

Book & lyrics by Harry Ruskin & Leighton K. Brill; additional
Lyrics by Oscar Hammerstein, 2nd
Music by Louis Alter
Directed by Reginald Hammerstein   Dances by Earl Lindsey
Settings by Cirker & Robbins   Costumes by Charles LeMaire
Music director, Oscar Bradley

with

Grace Hayes	Janet Reade	Chaz Chase	Max Hoffman, Jr.
Jack Colby	Don Tomkins	Jeanie Lang	Floria Vestoff
Andy Rice, Jr.	Ted Black's Band		

Musical Numbers
"No Wonder I'm Blue" (Hammerstein-Alter)—Hayes
"That Tired Feeling"—Reade, Rice
"I'm One of God's Children" (Hammerstein, Ruskin-Alter)—
    Hayes, Black Band

(Note: In Jan. 1931, Mr. Hammerstein no longer credited as
producer; musical then became cooperative venture.)

Hammerstein's Theatre   *68 performances*

1930

December 30.   Messrs. Shubert present

"MEET MY SISTER"

Book by Harry Wagstaff Gribble, from German operetta, *Meine
Schwester und Ich,* by Blum (based on French play by Berr & Verneuil)
Lyrics & music by Ralph Benatzky
Directed by William Mollison   Dances by John Pierce
Settings by Watson Barratt
Music director, Irving Schloss

with

BETTINA HALL
Walter Slezak   George Grossmith   Harry Welsh
Olive Olsen   Kay McKay   Boyd Davis

(Note: In Jan., 1931, Mr. Grossmith succeeded by David Hutcheson;
in May, Miss Olsen by Peggy O'Neill.)

Musical Numbers
"Always in My Heart"—Hall
"Radziwill"—Hall, Slezak
"She Is My Ideal"—Slezak

(Note: *Meine Schwester und Ich* first presented in Berlin, March 29, 1930.)

Shubert Theatre   *167 performances*

January 19.   Jack Yellen & Lou Holtz present

"YOU SAID IT"

Book by Jack Yellen & Sid Silvers
Lyrics by Jack Yellen
Music by Harold Arlen
Directed by John Harwood   Dances by Danny Dare
Settings by Donald Oenslager   Costumes by Kiviette
Music director, Louis Gress   Orchestrations, Howard Jackson
Special music effects, Fred Waring   Vocal arrangements, Charles Henderson

with

LOU HOLTZ
MARY LAWLOR   STANLEY SMITH
Lyda Roberti
Hughie Clarke   Peggy Bernier   George Haggarty
Benny Baker   3 Slate Brothers
(Note: In May, Miss Lawlor succeeded by June O'Dea.)

Musical Numbers
"You Said It"—Lawlor, Smith
"Learn to Croon"—Smith
"Sweet and Hot"—Bernier, Clarke, Roberti

46th Street Theatre   *192 performances*

1931

February 10.   Laurence Schwab & Frank Mandel present

"AMERICA'S SWEETHEART"

Book by Herbert Fields
Lyrics by Lorenz Hart
Music by Richard Rodgers
Directed by Monty Woolley   Dances by Bobby Connolly
Settings by Donald Oenslager   Costumes by Charles LeMaire
Music director, Alfred Goodman   Orchestrations, Russell Bennett

with

Jack Whiting   Gus Shy   Jeanne Aubert   John Sheehan
Inez Courtney   Harriette Lake (Ann Sothern)   Dorothy Dare
Vera Marsh   Virginia Bruce   Hilda, Louise & Maxine Forman
Lee Dixon (chorus)   Jack Donohue (chorus)
(Note: In April, Mr. Shy succeeded by Bobby Jarvis; in June, Mr.
Whiting by Max Hoffman, Jr.)

Musical Numbers
"I've Got Five Dollars"—Lake, Whiting
"Sweet Geraldine"—Forman sisters
"There's So Much More"—Aubert, Shy
"We'll Be the Same"—Lake, Whiting
"How About It?"—Courtney, Whiting
"Innocent Chorus Girls of Yesterday"—chorus
"A Lady Must Live"—Aubert

Broadhurst Theatre   *135 performances*

1931

February 18. Morris Green & Lewis E. Gensler present
TED HEALY in

"THE GANG'S ALL HERE"

Book by Russel Crouse, with Oscar Hammerstein, 2nd, & Morrie
Ryskind
Lyrics by Owen Murphy & Robert A. Simon
Music by Lewis E. Gensler
Directed by Oscar Hammerstein, 2nd (uncredited) & Frank McCoy
Dances by Dave Gould, Tilly Losch
Settings by Henry Dreyfuss   Costumes by Russell Patterson
Music director, Gene Salzer   Orchestrations, Hans Spialek

with

Tom Howard   Gina Malo   Zelma O'Neal   Shaw & Lee
Ruth Tester   Hal LeRoy   Gomez & Winona   Jack McCauley
Jack Barker   John Gallaudet
(Note: During tryout, Miss Malo replaced Ruby Keeler Jolson;
Mr. Howard replaced Dallas Welford. In March, Miss
Malo succeeded by Caryl Bergman.)

Musical Numbers
"Baby Wanna Go Bye-Bye"—O'Neal, Gallaudet
"Adorable Julie"—Healy, Malo
"By Special Permission of the Copyright Owners, I Love You"
    —Tester, McCauley

Imperial Theatre   *23 performances*

February 23.   Walter Greenough presents

"THE VENETIAN GLASS NEPHEW"

Book by Ruth Hale, from novel by Elinor Wylie
Lyrics & music by Eugene Bonner
Directed by Walter Greenough
Settings by Edgar Bohlman & Sointu Syrjala   Costumes by Brooks
Music director, Leon Barzin

with

George Houston	Mary Silveira	Louis Yaeckel
Dodd Mehan	Raymond Huntley	Edgar Stehli
Gage Clarke	Lee Burgess	

Musical Numbers
None listed individually.

Vanderbilt Theatre   *8 performances*

March 17.

Morris Gest & Messrs. Shubert present
AL JOLSON in

"THE WONDER BAR"

Book by Irving Caesar & Aben Kandel, from German musical, *Wunderbar*,
by Geza Herczeg & Karl Farkas
Lyrics by Irving Caesar
Music by Robert Katscher
Directed by William Mollison   Dances by Albertina Rasch, John Pierce
Settings by Watson Barratt   Costumes by Charles LeMaire
Music director, Louis Silver

with

Trini   Rex O'Malley   Patsy Kelly   Wanda Lyon
Vernon Steele   Arthur Treacher   Doris Groday
Carol Chilton & Maceo Thomas   Al Segal
Signorina Medea Columbara

Musical Numbers
"Good Evening, Friends"—Jolson
"Oh, Donna Clara" (Beda, Caesar–J. Petersburski)—Jolson
"Elizabeth"—Kelly

(Note: First English-language version adapted by Rowland Leigh and
presented at the Savoy Theatre, London, Dec. 5, 1930. It ran for
210 performances. The cast included Carl Brisson, Dorothy Dickson,
& Elsie Randolph.)

Nora Bayes Theatre   *86 performances*

May 4.

Blackbirds Productions, Inc. (Lew Leslie) presents
ETHEL WATERS in

"RHAPSODY IN BLACK"

Lyrics mostly by Mann Holiner
Music mostly by Alberta Nichols
Directed by Lew Leslie
Music director, Pike Davis

with

VALAIDA   CECIL MACK CHOIR   BERRY BROTHERS
Al Moore   Eddie Rector   Blue McAllister   Avis Andrews
Eloise Uggams   Robert Ecton   Geneva Washington

Musical Numbers
"Till the Real Thing Comes Along"—Waters; reprised by Berry Bros.
"What's Keeping My Prince Charming?"—Waters, McAllister
"Rhapsody in Blue" (George Gershwin)—Mack Choir, Valaida, Berry
"Eli Eli" (traditional, in Hebrew)—Andrews, Uggams, Mack Choir
"I'm Feelin' Blue" (Dorothy Fields–Jimmy McHugh; cut from
    International Revue)—Waters, Valaida, Moore
"March of the Toys" (Victor Herbert; originally in *Babes in Toyland*)
    —Valaida, Rector
"St. Louis Blues" (W. C. Handy)—Mack Choir, Ecton, Washington
"You Can't Stop Me from Loving You" (originally in *Corned Beef and
    Roses*; added during run)—Waters, McAllister

Sam H. Harris Theatre   *80 performances*

1931

May 19   FANNIE BRICE   PHIL BAKER   TED HEALY   in
Billy Rose's

"CRAZY QUILT"

Sketches by David Freedman; additional dialogue by Herman Timberg
Lyrics by Billy Rose, Mort Dixon, Bud Green, Ira Gershwin, Lorenz
Hart, James Dyrenforth, Ned Wever
Music by Harry Warren, Richard Rodgers, Rowland Wilson, Manning
Sherwin, Carroll Gibbons
Directed by Billy Rose   Dances by Sammy Lee
Costumes by Fannie Brice   Lighting by Clark Robinson
Music director, Charles Drury

with

GOMEZ & WINONA   LEW BRICE   ETHEL NORRIS
Tamara   Vale & Stewart   Tom Monroe   Rodger Davis
Marion Bonnell

Musical Numbers
"I Found a Million Dollar Baby (in a Five and Ten Cent Store)"
    (Dixon, Rose-Warren)—Healy, Baker, F. Brice, L. Brice
"Would You Like to Take a Walk?" (Dixon, Rose-Warren; originally in
    Sweet and Low)—Norris, Monroe
"Rest Room Rose" (Hart-Rodgers; added in June)—Brice

(Note: *Crazy Quilt* was a revised version of *Sweet and Low*.)

44th Street Theatre   **79 performances**

1931

June 1.

Dwight Deere Wiman, with Tom Weatherly, presents
BEATRICE LILLIE   ERNEST TRUEX   in

"THE THIRD LITTLE SHOW"

Sketches by Noël Coward, S. J. Perelman, Harry Wall, Peter Spencer, Edward Eliscu, Marc Connelly
Lyrics by Max & Nat Lief, Harold Adamson, Earle Crooker, Edward Eliscu, Grace Henry, Noël Coward, Herman Hupfeld
Music by Michael Cleary, Burton Lane, Noël Coward, Henry Sullivan, Ned Lehac, Morris Hamilton, Herman Hupfeld, William (Morgan) Lewis
Directed by Alexander Leftwich   Dances by Dave Gould
Settings by Jo Mielziner   Costumes by Raymond Sovey
Music director, Max Meth   Orchestrations, Howard Jackson

with

Constance Carpenter	Carl Randall	Edward Arnold
Jerry Norris	Walter O'Keefe	Gertrude McDonald
Sandra Gale	William Griffith	Dorothy Fitzgibbon

Musical Numbers
"Say the Word" (Adamson-Lane)—Fitzgibbon, Norris
"Mad Dogs and Englishmen" (Coward; originally in *Words and Music*)
    —Lillie
"You Forgot Your Gloves" (Eliscu-Lehac)—Carpenter, Norris
"When Yuba Plays the Rumba on His Tuba" (Hupfeld)—O'Keefe
"There Are Fairies at the Bottom of My Garden" (Rose Fyleman–Liza
    Lehmann)—Lillie
(Note: "Any Little Fish" [Coward; originally in *Cochran's 1931
Revue*], sung by Mr. Truex, cut during tryout.)

Music Box Theatre   *136 performances*

1931

June 3.

Max Gordon presents
FRED & ADELE ASTAIRE
FRANK MORGAN
HELEN BRODERICK
TILLY LOSCH in

"THE BAND WAGON"

Sketches by George S. Kaufman & Howard Dietz
Lyrics by Howard Dietz
Music by Arthur Schwartz
Directed by Hassard Short   Dances by Albertina Rasch
Settings by Albert R. Johnson   Costumes by Kiviette, Constance Ripley
Music director, Al Goodman   Orchestrations, Russell Bennett

with

Philip Loeb	John Barker	Roberta Robinson
Francis Pierlot	Jay Wilson	Peter Chambers

Musical Numbers
"Sweet Music"—F. & A. Astaire
"High and Low" (originally in *Here Comes the Bride*, London)—
    Robinson, Barker
"Hoops"—F. & A. Astaire
"Confession"—chorus
"New Sun in the Sky"—F. Astaire
"Miserable with You"—A. Astaire, Morgan
"I Love Louisa"—F. & A. Astaire, company
"Dancing in the Dark"—Barker; danced by Losch
"Where Can He Be?"—Broderick
"The Beggar Waltz"—danced by Losch, F. Astaire
"Nanette"—Morgan, Loeb, Pierlot, Barker
"White Heat"—F. & A. Astaire

New Amsterdam Theatre   *260 performances*

1931

July 1.   Florenz Ziegfeld presents

"ZIEGFELD FOLLIES" 1931

Sketches by Mark Hellinger, J. P. Murray, Gene Buck
Lyrics by Gene Buck, Joseph McCarthy, Charles Farrell, Mack Gordon
J. P. Murray, Barry Trivers, E. Y. Harburg, Jack Norworth, Noël Coward
Music by Harry Revel, Ben Oakland, Dave Stamper, Dimitri Tiomkin,
Noël Coward, Nora Bayes, James Monaco, Chick Endor, Walter
Donaldson, Jay Gorney
Directed by Gene Buck & Edward Clark Lilley   Dances by Bobby
Connolly, Albertina Rasch
Settings by Joseph Urban   Costumes by John Harkrider
Music director, Oscar Bradley   Orchestrations, Maurice DePackh,
Will Vodery, Howard Jackson

with

Harry Richman   Helen Morgan   Ruth Etting   Jack Pearl
Hal LeRoy   Mitzi Mayfair   Albert Carroll   Collette Sisters
Reri   Cliff Hall   Gladys Glad   Frank & Milt Britton & Gang
Pearl Osgood   Ford Buck & John Bubbles   Arthur Campbell
Dorothy Dell   Earl Oxford   Faith Bacon   Edith Borden
(Note: Reri out of cast by Aug.)

Musical Numbers
"Half Caste Woman" (Coward; originally in *Cochran's 1931 Revue,*
        London)—Morgan
"Shine on Harvest Moon" (Norworth-Bayes; originally in *Follies
        of 1908*)—Etting, Oxford
"You Made Me Love You" (McCarthy-Monaco)—Richman
"Cigarettes, Cigars" (Cordon-Revel)—Etting
"Do the New York" (Murray, Trivers-Oakland)—Richman
"Help Yourself to Happiness" (Gordon, Richman-Revel)—Richman

Ziegfeld Theatre   *165 performances*

July 21.

Heywood Broun, with Milton Raison, presents

"SHOOT THE WORKS!"

Sketches by Nunnally Johnson, Heywood Broun, H. I. Phillips, Peter Arno, E. B. White, Sig Herzig, Milton Lazarus, Dorothy Parker
Lyrics by Nat & Max Lief, Dorothy Fields, E. Y. Harburg, Leo Robin, Ira Gershwin, Irving Berlin
Music by Michael Cleary, Jimmy McHugh, Ann Ronell, Robert Stolz, Jay Gorney, Vernon Duke, Irving Berlin, Phil Charig, Joseph Meyer
Directed by Ted Hammerstein   Dances by Johnny Boyle
Settings by Henry Dreyfuss   Costumes by Charles LeMaire, Kiviette
Music director, Harry Archer   Orchestrations, Frank Barry, King Ross

with

Heywood Broun	George Murphy	William O'Neal
Jack Hazzard	Johnny Boyle	Imogene Coca	Frances Dewey
Al Gold	Bobby Gillette	Lee Brody	Julie Johnson
Taylor Gordon	Frances Nevins		

Musical Numbers
"How's Your Uncle?" (Fields-McHugh)—Gold, Dewey
"Muchacha" (Harburg-Gorney, Duke)—Nevins
"Begging for Love" (Berlin)—Murphy, Johnson

George M. Cohan Theatre   *87 performances*

August 27. "EARL CARROLL VANITIES" (9th Edition)

Sketches by Ralph Spence, Eddie Welch
Lyrics mostly by Harold Adamson
Music mostly by Burton Lane
Directed by Earl Carroll & Edgar MacGregor   Dances by George Hale,
Gluck Sandor
Settings by Vincente Minnelli, Hugh Willoughby   Costumes by Mr.
Minnelli, Charles LeMaire
Music director, Ray Kavanaugh   Orchestrations, Domenico Savino

with

WILL MAHONEY   LILLIAN ROTH
WILLIAM DEMAREST
Frank Mitchell & Jack Durant   Milton Watson   Lucille Page
Woods Miller   Slate Brothers   Olive Olsen   Helen Lynd
Dan Carthe   Beryl Wallace   Irene Ahlberg
(Note: During run, Miss Roth succeeded by Lillian Dawson.)

Musical Numbers
"Have a Heart"—Roth, Miller
"Heigh Ho, the Gang's All Here"—chorus
"Good Night, Sweetheart" (Jimmy Campbell, Reg Connelly–Ray Noble)
     —Watson, Miller; danced by Ahlberg, Wallace
"Bolero" (Maurice Ravel)—chorus
"Tonight or Never" (Ray Klages, Jack Meskill–Vincent Rose)—
     Roth, Watson

Earl Carroll Theatre; 44th Street Theatre (March 1932)
                                        278 performances

1931

September 8.   Laurence Schwab & Frank Mandel present

"FREE FOR ALL"

Book by Oscar Hammerstein, 2nd, & Mr. Schwab
Lyrics by Oscar Hammerstein, 2nd
Music by Richard A. Whiting
Directed by Mr. Hammerstein   Dances by Bobby Connolly
Settings by Donald Oenslager   Costumes by Kiviette
Music director, John McManus (Benny Goodman's Band, incl. Glenn Miller)

with

JACK HALEY

Peter Higgins	Vera Marsh	Lillian Bond	Jeanette Loff
Edward Emery	Don Tomkins	Dorothy Knapp	Tamara
Seth Arnold	David Hutcheson	Grace Johnston	
Thelma Tipson			

Musical Numbers
"I Love Him, the Rat"—Marsh, Hutcheson
"Not that I Care"—Marsh, Haley; reprised by Tamara, Higgins
"When Your Boy Becomes a Man"—Johnston

Manhattan (formerly Hammerstein's) Theatre   *15 performances*

1931

September 10.   Harry Thomashevsky presents
                         BORES THOMASHEVSKY in

"THE SINGING RABBI"

Book by Bores & Harry Thomashevsky
Lyrics by L. Wolfe Gilbert
Music by J. Rumshinsky
Directed by William E. Morris   Dances by Florenz Ames
Settings by Orestes Raineri
Music director, Harry Lubin

with

REGINA ZUCKERBERG
Florenz Ames   Sam Ash   Philip Ryder   Flora LeBreton

Musical Numbers
"Sholom Aleichem"—Thomashevsky
"Hear O Israel"—Ash
"A Vision of the Future"—Thomashevsky

Selwyn Theatre   *4 performances*

1931

September 15.   Forbes Randolph presents

"FAST AND FURIOUS"

Sketches by Forbes Randolph, John Wells
Lyrics mostly by Mack Gordon
Music mostly by Harry Revel
Directed by Howard Smith   Dances by Al Richards,
Jack Donohue
Settings by Cirker & Robbins   Costumes by Eaves, Schneider & Blythe
Music director, Joe Jordan

with

Tim Moore   Dusty Fletcher   Juano Hernandez
Jackie (Moms) Mabley   Neeka Shaw   Etta Moten
Ruby Elzy   Ruby Greene   Lois Deppe   Edna Guy

Musical Numbers
"Walking on Air"—Shaw
"So Lonesome" (J. Rosamond Johnson–Joe Jordan)—Greene, Elzy
"Where's My Happy Ending?" (Gordon, Harold Adamson–Revel)—
    Elzy

New Yorker Theatre   *7 performances*

September 14.   **"GEORGE WHITE'S SCANDALS"** (11th Edition)

Sketches by George White, Lew Brown, Irving Caesar, Harry Conn
Lyrics by Lew Brown
Music by Ray Henderson
Directed by Mr. White
Settings by Joseph Urban   Costumes by Charles LeMaire
Music director, Al Goodman   Orchestrations, Howard Jackson

with

RUDY VALLEE   ETHEL MERMAN
WILLIE & EUGENE HOWARD   EVERETT MARSHALL
RAY BOLGER   GALE QUADRUPLETS
Ethel Barrymore Colt   Loomis Sisters   Barbara Blair
Peggy Moseley   Ross McLean   Jane Alden   Joan Abbott
Dorothy & Harry Dixon   Alice Faye (chorus)

Musical Numbers
"Life Is Just a Bowl of Cherries"—Merman
"The Thrill Is Gone"—Marshall, with Vallee, McLean; danced by
     Dixons
"This Is the Missus"—Vallee, with Moseley
"Ladies and Gentlemen, That's Love"—Merman
"That's Why Darkies Were Born"—Marshall
"My Song"—Vallee, Merman

Apollo Theatre   *202 performances*

1931

September 29.   Harrison Hall presents

"NIKKI"

Book by James Monk Saunders, from his short stories, *Nikki and Her War Birds*, novel, *A Single Lady*, film, *The Last Flight*
Lyrics by James Dyrenforth
Music by Philip Charig
Directed by William B. Friedlander   Dances by Pal'mere Brandeaux
Settings by P. Dodd Ackerman, Karle O. Amend
Music director, Jules Lenzberg   Orchestrations, Louis Katzman

with

FAY WRAY
Douglass Montgomery   Archie Leach (Cary Grant)
Nathaniel Wagner   Louis Jean Heydt   Rudolfo Badaloni
Bobbie Tremaine   John Brooke   Frank Chapman
Adele Dixon (chorus)

Musical Numbers
"Taking Off"—Montgomery, Wagner, Brooke, Leach
"On Account of I Love You"—Wray, Montgomery, Wagner, Leach
"Wonder Why"—Wray

Longacre Theatre   **39 performances**

October 13.   Messrs. Shubert present

"EVERYBODY'S WELCOME"

Book by Lambert Carroll, from play, *Up Pops the Devil*, by Frances
Goodrich & Albert Hackett
Lyrics mostly by Irving Kahal
Music mostly by Sammy Fain
Directed by William Mollison   Dances by William Holbrook, Albertina
Rasch
Settings by Watson Barratt   Costumes by Ernest Schrapps, Alison
McLennan Hunter
Music director, Tom Jones
(Note: During tryout, book credited to Harold Atteridge.)

with

FRANCES WILLIAMS
OSCAR SHAW   ANN PENNINGTON
HARRIETTE LAKE (ANN SOTHERN)   JACK SHEEHAN
CECIL LEAN   JIMMY & TOMMY DORSEY ORCHESTRA
(Note: During tryout, Mr. Sheehan replaced Harry Ritz, Mr. Lean
replaced Al Ritz, & part played by Jimmy Ritz eliminated. In
Feb. 1932, Mr. Lean succeeded by Victor Morley.)

Musical Numbers
"All Wrapped Up in You" (Mack Gordon–Harry Revel)—Shaw, Lake
"As Time Goes By" (Herman Hupfeld)—Williams
"Even as You and I"—Shaw, Lake
"Is Rhythm Necessary?"—Williams, Pennington

Shubert Theatre   *139 performances*

1931

October 15.   Max Gordon presents

"THE CAT AND THE FIDDLE"

Book & lyrics by Otto Harbach
Music by Jerome Kern
Directed by José Ruben   Dances by Albertina Rasch
Settings by Henry Dreyfuss   Costumes by Constance Ripley, Kiviette
Music director, Victor Baravalle   Orchestrations, R. Russell Bennett

with

Georges Metaxa	Bettina Hall	Odette Myrtil
Eddie Foy, Jr.	José Ruben	Lawrence Grossmith
Doris Carson	George Meader	Flora LeBreton
Lucette Valsy	Peter Chambers	

(Note: In July 1932, Mr. Foy succeeded by Bobby Jarvis; Mr. Grossmith by Arthur Treacher. In Aug., Mr. Metaxa by Michael Bartlett.)

Musical Numbers
"The Night Was Made for Love"—Meader
"I Watch the Love Parade"—Meader, LeBreton
"Try to Forget"—Hall, Foy, Carson
"Poor Pierrot"—Valsy, Chambers
"She Didn't Say 'Yes' "—Hall
"A New Love Is Old"—Metaxa
"One Moment Alone"—Hall, Metaxa

Globe Theatre   *395 performances*

October 27. Laurence Schwab & Frank Mandel present

"EAST WIND"

Book by Oscar Hammerstein, 2nd, & Frank Mandel
Lyrics by Oscar Hammerstein, 2nd
Music by Sigmund Romberg
Directed by Mr. Hammerstein   Dances by Bobby Connolly
Settings by Donald Oenslager   Costumes by Charles LeMaire
Music director, Oscar Bradley   Orchestrations, Hans Spialek

with

J. Harold Murray   Charlotte Lansing   Joe Penner
Vera Marsh   William Williams   Greek Evans   Ahi
Dennie Moore   Bobby Dolan (piano)

Musical Numbers
"East Wind"—Murray
"Are You Love?"—Lansing, Williams, Murray
"You Are My Woman"—Murray
"I'd Be a Fool"—Lansing

Manhattan Theatre   *23 performances*

1931

November 2.   Ed Wynn presents Himself in

"THE LAUGH PARADE"

Sketches by Ed Wynn, Ed Preble
Lyrics by Mort Dixon & Joe Young
Music by Harry Warren
Directed by Mr. Wynn   Dances by Albertina Rasch
Settings & costumes by Weld   Lighting by Clark Robinson
Music director, John McManus   Orchestrations, Russell Bennett,
Hans Spialek
(Note: Dances credited to Sammy Lee during tryout.)

with

Jeanne Aubert	Lawrence Gray	Bartlett Simmons
Eunice Healey	Jack Powell	Ed Cheney

Musical Numbers
"Ooh! That Kiss"—Aubert, Gray
"The Torch Song"—Simmons
"You're My Everything"—Aubert, Gray

Imperial Theatre   **231 performances**

November 3.

Peter Arno presents
BOBBY CLARK & PAUL McCULLOUGH in

"HERE GOES THE BRIDE"

Book by Peter Arno, additional dialogue by Roger Pryor
Lyrics by Edward Heyman
Music by John W. Green; additional music by Henry Myers
Directed by Edward Clark Lilley   Dances by Russell Markert
Settings by Mr. Arno   Costumes by Kiviette
Music director, Adolph Deutsch   Orchestrations, Conrad Salinger

with

Grace Brinkley   Paul Frawley   Dorothy Dare
Victoria (Vicki) Cummings   Eric Blore   Dudley Clements
Frances Langford   Coletta Ryan   Philip Lord
John Gallaudet

Musical Numbers
"My Sweetheart 'Tis of Thee"—Brinkley, Frawley
"One Second of Sex"—Cummings, Gallaudet
"Hello, My Lover, Goodbye"—Langford

46th Street Theatre   *7 performances*

December 25.

Moveing Day Co., Inc., presents
FLOURNOY MILLER & AUBREY LYLES in

"SUGAR HILL"

Book by Charles Tazewell
Lyrics by Jo Trent
Music by James P. Johnson
Director uncredited
Settings by Theodore Kahn   Costumes by Mahieu
Music director uncredited

with

Broadway Jones	Carrie Huff	Edna Moten	Juanita Stinette
Tressa Mitchell	Chappy Chapelle	Teddy Woods	
Ina Duncan			

Musical Numbers
"Hot Harlem"—Jones
"Fooling Around with Love"—Moten, Woods
"Hanging Around Yo' Dore"—Moten, Jones

Forrest Theatre   *11 performances*

December 26.   Sam H. Harris presents

"OF THEE I SING"

Book by George S. Kaufman & Morrie Ryskind
Lyrics by Ira Gershwin
Music by George Gershwin
Directed by George S. Kaufman   Dances by George Hale
Settings by Jo Mielziner   Costumes by Charles LeMaire
Music director, Charles Previn   Orchestrations, Russell Bennett,
William Daly

with

WILLIAM GAXTON   LOIS MORAN   VICTOR MOORE
Grace Brinkley   June O'Dea   Dudley Clements
Edward H. Robins   Florenz Ames   George Murphy
George E. Mack   Ralph Riggs   Sam Mann   Harold Moffatt

Musical Numbers
"Wintergreen for President"—chorus
"Love Is Sweeping the Country"—Murphy, O'Dea
"Of Thee I Sing (Baby)"—Gaxton, Moran
"Who Cares?"—Gaxton, Moran
"Hello, Good Morning"—Murphy, O'Dea
"The Illegitimate Daughter"—Ames
"Because, Because"—Brinkley, Murphy

Music Box Theatre; 46th Street Theatre (Oct. 1932)
441 performances

Return Engagement: May 15, 1933
Miss Moran succeeded by Harriette Lake (Ann Sothern), Miss Brinkley
by Betty Allen.

Imperial Theatre   *32 performances*

January 18.   Messrs. Shubert present
                QUEENIE SMITH in

"A LITTLE RACKETEER"

Book by Harry Clarke, from German play by F. Kalbfuss & R. Wilde
Lyrics by Edward Eliscu
Music by Haskell Brown
Directed by William Caryl   Dances by Albertina Rasch, Jack Donohue
Settings by Watson Barratt   Costumes by Ernest Schrapps, Alison
McLellan Hunter
Music director, Maury Rubens
(Note: During tryout, music first credited to Henry Sullivan, then
to Dimitri Tiomkin & Louis Alter. Edward Royce originally credited
as director.)

with

WILLIAM KENT   BARBARA NEWBERRY
JOHN GARRICK   CARL RANDALL
Hamtree Harrington   Lorraine Weimar   Tommy & Betty Wonder
Jeanette Bradley   George Marshall   Colleen Ward
Princess Yo Hay Tong   Khalil Oglou Mazini
GRACE HAYES
(Note: During tryout, Miss Hayes replaced Ruth Shields, Mr. Garrick
replaced John Price Jones, Mr. Randall replaced Wesley Pierce.)

Musical Numbers
"Blow, Gabriel"—Hayes
"Mr. Moon" (Lee Warner–Lupin Fein–Moe Jaffe)—Garrick, Hayes
"You and I Could Be Just Like That"—Smith, Garrick

44th Street Theatre   *48 performances*

January 28.   Vincent Youmans presents

"THROUGH THE YEARS"

Book by Brian Hooker, from play, *Smilin' Through*, by Allen Langdon
Martin
Lyrics by Edward Heyman
Music by Vincent Youmans
Directed by Edgar MacGregor   Dances by Jack Haskell, Max Scheck
Settings by Ward & Harvey   Costumes by John Booth
Music director, William Daly

with

Natalie Hall   Michael Bartlett   Charles Winninger
Reginald Owen   Nick Long, Jr.   Martha Mason
Gregory Gaye

Musical Numbers
"Kathleen Mine"—Bartlett, Hall
"Kinda Like You"—Mason, Long
"Through the Years"—Hall
"You're Everywhere"—Hall, Bartlett
"Drums in My Heart"—Gaye

Manhattan Theatre   *20 performances*

1932

February 17.   Sam H. Harris presents
MARY BOLAND   J. HAROLD MURRAY   in

"FACE THE MUSIC"

Book by Moss Hart
Lyrics & music by Irving Berlin
Directed by Hassard Short & George S. Kaufman   Dances by
Albertina Rasch
Settings by Albert Johnson   Costumes by Kiviette, Weld
Music director, Frank Tours   Orchestrations, Russell Bennett,
Mr. Tours, Maurice DePackh

with

Andrew Tombes   Hugh O'Connell   Katherine Carrington
Joseph Macaulay   Margaret Lee   Jack Good
Blue & White Marimba Band   Jean Sergent   Clyde Fillmore
Edward Gargan   David Burns   Oscar Polk
(Note: In May, Mr. Murray succeeded by John Garrick.)

Musical Numbers
"Let's Have Another Cup o' Coffee"—Murray, Carrington
"On a Roof in Manhattan"—Murray, Carrington
"My Rhinestone Girl"—Macaulay
"Soft Lights and Sweet Music"—Murray, Carrington
"I Say It's Spinach"—Murray, Carrington
"Manhattan Madness"—Murray

New Amsterdam Theatre   *165 performances*

Return Engagement: Jan. 31, 1933
Mr. Garrick succeeded by John Barker, Miss Carrington by Nancy
McCord, Mr. Tombes by Robert Emmett Keane, Mr. O'Connell by
Charles Lawrence.

44th Street Theatre   *32 performances*

1932

March 3. Messrs. Shubert present

"MARCHING BY"

Book by Harry B. Smith & Harry Clarke, from German operetta, *Hotel Stadt-Lemberg*, by Ernst Neubach
Lyrics by Harry B. Smith; additional lyrics by Mack Gordon
Music by Jean Gilbert; additional music by Harry Revel
Directed by J. C. Huffman   Dances by Allan K. Foster
Settings by Watson Barratt   Costumes by Ernest Schrapps
Music director, George Hirst

with

GUY ROBERTSON   SOLLY WARD
LEONARD CEELEY   DESIRÉE TABOR
ETHEL NORRIS
Donald Burr   Hugh Miller   Victor Casmore
Kathleen Edwardes   Arthur Geary   Philip Lord
(Note: Miss Tabor replaced Mady Christians during tryout.)

Musical Numbers
"All's Fair in Love and War"—Ceeley, chorus
"I've Gotta Keep My Eye on You" (Gordon-Revel)—Norris, Burr
"I Love You, My Darling" (Edward Eliscu–George Hirst, Gilbert)—
    Tabor, Robertson
"Forward March into My Arms"—Norris, Burr

(Note: *Marching By* known as *Arms and the Maid* at beginning of tryout.)

46th Street Theatre   *12 performances*

1932

March 8.   Florenz Ziegfeld presents

"HOT-CHA!"

Book by Lew Brown, Ray Henderson, Mark Hellinger, based on story,
An Old Spanish Custom, by H. S. Kraft
Lyrics by Lew Brown
Music by Ray Henderson
Directed by Edgar MacGregor & Edward Clark Lilley   Dances by
Bobby Connolly
Settings by Joseph Urban   Costumes by Charles LeMaire
Music director, Al Goodman   Orchestrations, Russell Bennett

with

BERT LAHR   LUPE VELEZ
Marjorie White   Lynne Overman
June Knight   June MacCloy   Velez & Yolanda
Antonio & Renée DeMarco   Tito Coral   Revva Reyes
Robert Gleckler   Roy Sedley   Jack Holland   Eleanor Powell
Miriam Battista   Marjorie Logan   Jules Epailly
Hernandez Brothers   Rose Louise (Gypsy Rose Lee) (chorus)
Iris Adrian (chorus)
BUDDY ROGERS
(Note: Mr. Rogers succeeded by Art Jarrett in May.)

Musical Numbers
"You Can Make My Life a Bed of Roses"—Knight, Rogers
"Conchita"—Velez
"It's Great to Be Alive"—Knight
"I Make Up for That in Other Ways"—Lahr
"There I Go Dreaming Again"—Knight
"There's Nothing the Matter with Me"—White; danced by Powell

Ziegfeld Theatre   *119 performances*

1932

April 4. Max Rudnick & Ben Bernard present

"BLACKBERRIES OF 1932"

Sketches by Lee Posner & Eddie Green
Lyrics & music by Donald Heywood & Tom Peluso
Directed by Mr. Bernard   Dances by Sidney Sprague, Lew Crawford
Settings by Myer Kanin
Music director, Sam Wooding

with

Tim Moore   Eddie Green   Mantan Moreland
Dewey "Pigmeat" Markham   Jackie (Moms) Mabley
Georgette Harvey   Johnny Lee Long

Musical Numbers
"Blackberries" (Heywood)
"Brown Sugar" (Heywood)
"Love Me More, Love Me Less" (Bernard-Peluso)

Liberty Theatre   *24 performances*

1932

May 16.

Hyman Adler presents

"THERE YOU ARE"

Book by Carl Bartfeld
Lyrics by William Heagney & Tom Connell
Music by William Heagney

Directed by Horace Sinclair	Dances by Vaughn Godfrey
Settings by Carlo Studios	Costumes by Eaves, Bertha Beres
Music director, Fred Hoff	Orchestrations, Irving Schloss, Roy Webb

with

ILSE MARVENGA

Hyman Adler	Roy Cropper	Joseph Lertora	Berta Donn
Adrian Rosley	Peggy O'Connor	Robert Capron	

Musical Numbers
"Lover's Holiday"—Marvenga
"Wings of the Morning"—Cropper
"Legend of the Mission Bells"—Adler

George M. Cohan Theatre   *8 performances*

May 26.   Walter Campbell & Jesse Wank present

"YEAH MAN"

Sketches by Leigh Whipper, Billy Mills
Lyrics & music by Al Wilson, Charles Weinberg, Ken Macomber
Directed by Walter Campbell   Dances by Marcus Slayter
Music director, Billy Butler   Orchestrations, Charles Cooke,
Lorenzo Caldwell, Mr. Butler

with

Mantan Moreland	Billy Mills	Leigh Whipper
Marcus Slayter	Eddie Rector	Melodee Four
Rose Henderson	Lily Yuen	

Musical Numbers
"That's Religion" (Porter Grainger)—Mills
"Dancin' Fool"—Yuen
"Gotta Get de Boat Loaded"—chorus

Park Lane Theatre   *4 performances*

June 6.

Forrest C. Haring & John H. Del Bondio present
FRANK MORGAN in

"HEY NONNY NONNY!"

Sketches by Frank Sullivan, Florence Calkins, E. B. White, Ogden
Nash, Richy Craig, Jr., Harry Ruskin
Lyrics mostly by Max & Nathaniel Lief
Music mostly by Michael H. Cleary
Directed by Alexander Leftwich   Dances by Dave Gould
Settings by Raymond Sovey, Jo Mielziner   Costumes by Helene Pons,
Mme. Berthe
Music director, Sherry Magee

with

Richy Craig, Jr.   Ann Seymour
Dorothy McNulty (Penny Singleton)   Jack McCauley
Joan Carter-Waddell   Jerry Norris   Frances Maddux
Ernest Sharpe   Ralph Sanford

Musical Numbers
"Hey Nonny Nonny" (Ogden Nash–Will Irwin)—principals
"On My Nude Ranch with You"—McNulty, McCauley
"Wouldn't That Be Wonderful?" (Herman Hupfeld)—McNulty, Norris

Shubert Theatre   *32 performances*

August 30.   Messrs. Shubert (uncredited) present
FRED & DOROTHY STONE in

"SMILING FACES"

Book by Harry Clarke
Lyrics by Mack Gordon
Music by Harry Revel
Directed by R. H. Burnside   Dances by Merriel Abbott
Settings by Watson Barratt   Costumes by Ernest Schrapps
Music director uncredited
(Note: During tryout, dances credited to Jack Donohue & Albertina
Rasch; direction to Zeke Colvan.)

with

Roy Royston   Charles Collins   Doris Patston
Hope Emerson   Eddie Garvie
(Note: During tryout, Dorothy Stone replaced Paula Stone, Mr.
Collins replaced Billy Taylor.)

Musical Numbers
"There Will Be a Girl"—D. Stone, Collins
"Quick Henry the Flit"—Royston
"I Stumbled Over You and Fell in Love"—Patston, Royston

Shubert Theatre   *33 performances*

1932

September 6. Norman Anthony, Lewis Gensler, Bobby Connolly, Russell Patterson
present

"BALLYHOO OF 1932"

Sketches by Norman Anthony; additional dialogue by Sig Herzig
Lyrics by E. Y. Harburg
Music by Lewis Gensler
Directed by the Producers & Gus Shy   Dances by Bobby Connolly
Settings and costumes by Russell Patterson
Music director, Max Meth   Orchestrations, Hans Spialek

with

WILLIE & EUGENE HOWARD
JEANNE AUBERT
Lulu McConnell
Bob Hope   Vera Marshe
Hugh Cameron   Gloria Gilbert   Tom Harty
Donald Stewart   Ralph Sanford   Dorissa Nelova
Paul & Grace Hartman   Nina Mae McKinney   Sunny O'Dea

Musical Numbers
"Falling Off the Wagon"—Harty, Marshe
"Thrill Me"—Aubert, Stewart
"How Do You Do It?"—Stewart
"Ballyhujah"—Howard, chorus
"Riddle Me This"—Stewart; danced by Gilbert, O'Dea

44th Street Theatre   *95 performances*

September 15.   Max Gordon presents
CLIFTON WEBB
CHARLES BUTTERWORTH
TAMARA GEVA   PATSY KELLY   in
The Howard Dietz Revue

"FLYING COLORS"

Sketches by Howard Dietz; additional dialogue by Charles Sherman,
George S. Kaufman, Corey Ford
Lyrics by Howard Dietz
Music by Arthur Schwartz
Directed by Mr. Dietz   Dances by Albertina Rasch
Settings & lighting by Norman Bel Geddes   Costumes by Constance
Ripley
Music director, Al Goodman   Orchestrations, Russell Bennett, Hans
Spialek, Edward Powell, Arthur Schutt   Vocal arrangements, Andre
Kostelanetz, Bobby Dolan
(Note: Miss Rasch replaced Agnes de Mille and Warren Leonard during tryout.)

with

Philip Loeb   Vilma & Buddy Ebsen   Larry Adler
Imogene Coca   Jean Sargent   Monette Moore   Jay Wilson
George Kirk

Musical Numbers
"Two-Faced Woman"—Geva
"A Rainy Day"—Webb
"Mother Told Me So"—chorus
"A Shine on Your Shoes"—Ebsens, Moore, Adler
"Alone Together"—Sargent; danced by Webb, Geva
"Louisiana Hayride"—company
"Fatal Fascination"—Butterworth, Kelly
"Meine Kleine Akrobat"—Webb
"Smokin' Reefers"—Sargent

Imperial Theatre   188 *performances*

1932

September 27. "EARL CARROLL VANITIES" (10th Edition)

Sketches by Jack McGowan, additional dialogue by Eugene Conrad
Lyrics by Edward Heyman, Ted Koehler, Haven Gillespie, Charles
Tobias, Sidney Clare
Music by Richard Myers, Harold Arlen, Henry Tobias, André Renaud,
Peter Tinturin
Directed by Earl Carroll & Edgar MacGregor   Dances by Ned McGurn,
Gluck Sandor
Settings & costumes by Vincente Minnelli
Music director, Ray Kavanaugh   Orchestrations, Edward Powell

with

Will Fyffe   André Randall   Edwin Styles   Milton Berle
Helen Broderick   Harriet Hoctor   Helen Jackson Girls
Lillian Shade   Josephine Huston   Max Wall   Beryl Wallace
Marcelle Edwards   Keith Clark   André Renaud   John Hale
Brice Hutchins (Robert Cummings)
(Note: Mr. Fyffe out of cast in Oct.)

Musical Numbers
"My Darling" (Heyman-Myers)—Hale, Huston
"Along Came Love" (Gillespie, C. Tobias–H. Tobias)—Huston
"I Gotta Right to Sing the Blues" (Koehler-Arlen)—Shade

Broadway Theatre   *87 performances*

October 5.

Lee Shubert presents

"NEW AMERICANA"

Sketches by J. P. McEvoy
Lyrics by E. Y. Harburg, Johnny Mercer
Music by Richard Myers, Harold Arlen, Burton Lane, Jay Gorney,
Vernon Duke, Henry Souvaine
Directed by Harold Johnsrud   Dances by John Boyle, Charles Weidman
Settings by Albert R. Johnson   Costumes by Constance Ripley
Music director, Jay Gorney   Orchestrations, Conrad Salinger

with

George Givot   Albert Carroll   Don Barclay   Gordon Smith
Rex Weber   Ralph Locke   Francetta Malloy
Peggy Cartwright   Lloyd Nolan   Georgie Tapps
Charles Weidman Dancers (incl. José Limon, Letitia Ide)
Doris Humphrey Group   Lillian Fitzgerald   Alfred Rode
Tzigane Orch.   Sue Hastings Marionettes   The Musketeers
(Note: Phil Baker added to cast in Nov. & received featured billing.)

Musical Numbers
"Whistling for a Kiss" (Mercer, Harburg-Myers)—Fitzgerald, Weber
"Satan's Li'l Lamb" (Mercer, Harburg-Arlen)—Malloy, Musketeers;
    danced by Humphrey, Limon, Weidman
"You're Not Pretty but You're Mine" (Harburg-Lane)—Cartwright, Smith
"Would'ja for a Big Red Apple?" (Mercer-Souvaine)—Cartwright, Smith
"Brother, Can You Spare a Dime?" (Harburg-Gorney)—Weber
"Let Me Match My Private Life with Yours" (Harburg-Duke)—Carroll

Shubert Theatre   77 *performances*

1932

October 28.   Tillie Leblang (uncredited) presents

"TELL HER THE TRUTH"

Book & lyrics by R. P. Weston & Bert Lee, from novel, *Nothing but the Truth*, by Frederick Isham, & play based on novel by James Montgomery
Music by Joseph Tunbridge & Jack Waller
Directed by Morris Green & Henry Thomas
Settings by Teichner Studios   Costumes by Jay-Thorpe
Music director, Gene Salzer

with

John Sheehan, Jr.	Lillian Emerson	Andrew Tombes
Thelma White	Hobart Cavanaugh	William Frawley
Margaret Dumont	Lou Parker	Louise Kirtland
Raymond Walburn	Edith Davis	

Musical Numbers
"Sing, Brothers!"—Frawley, company
"Happy the Day"—Emerson, Sheehan
"Horrortorio!"—Sheehan, Tombes, Walburn, Frawley, Cavanaugh

(Note: A previous musical version of the same story, *Yes, Yes, Yvette*, by Mr. Montgomery, William Cary Duncan, Irving Caesar, & Phil Charig, was presented at the Sam H. Harris Theatre, Oct. 3, 1927. It ran for 40 performances, with the cast including Charles Winninger, Jeanette MacDonald, & Jack Whiting. *Tell Her the Truth* was first presented at the Saville Theatre, London, June 14, 1932. It ran for 234 performances. The cast included Bobby Howes, Wylie Watson, & Peter Haddon.)

Cort Theatre   *11 performances*

November 8.   Peggy Fears & A. C. Blumenthal (uncredited) present

"MUSIC IN THE AIR"

Book & lyrics by Oscar Hammerstein, 2nd
Music by Jerome Kern
Directed by Messrs. Kern & Hammerstein
Settings by Joseph Urban   Costumes by John Harkrider, Howard Shoup
Music director, Victor Baravalle   Orchestrations, Russell Bennett

with

REINALD WERRENRATH   NATALIE HALL
TULLIO CARMINATI   KATHERINE CARRINGTON
AL SHEAN   WALTER SLEZAK
Nicholas Joy   Ivy Scott   Marjorie Main   Dorothy Johnson
Prince Alexis Obolensky   Harry Mestayer   Desha
Vivian Vance (chorus)
(Note: In March 1933, Miss Carrington succeeded by Ann Barrie; in
July, Mr. Carminati by Donald Brian, Miss Hall by Desirée Tabor.)

Musical Numbers
"I've Told Ev'ry Little Star"—Slezak; reprised by Carrington
"There's a Hill Beyond a Hill"—chorus
"And Love Was Born"—Werrenrath
"I'm Alone"—Hall
"I Am So Eager"—Carminati, Hall
"One More Dance"—Carminati
"When the Spring Is in the Air"—Carrington
"In Egern on the Tegern See"—Scott
"The Song Is You"—Carminati; reprised by Hall, Carminati
"We Belong Together"—Slezak, Carrington, Werrenrath, company

Alvin Theatre; 44th Street Theatre (March 1933)

342 performances

1932

November 22.   Morris Green & Tillie Leblang (uncredited) present
GRACE MOORE in

"THE DUBARRY"

Book by Rowland Leigh & Desmond Carter, from Viennese operetta, *Die DuBarry* by Paul Knepler, J. M. Willeminsky & Hans Cremer (based on *Gräfin DuBarry* by F. Zell & Richard Genée)
Lyrics by Rowland Leigh
Music by Karl Millöcker, arranged by Theo Mackeben
Directed by Morris Green & Rowland Leigh   Dances by Dorothea Burke
Settings & costumes by Vincente Minnelli
Music director, Gustave Salzer

with

William Hain	Pert Kelton	Robinson Newbold	Percy Waram
Max Figman	Nana Bryant	Marion Green	Helen Raymond

Consuelo Flowerton (chorus)
(Note: Mr. Hain replaced Howard Marsh during tryout. Mr. Newbold succeeded by Andrew Tombes in Jan. 1933.)

Musical Numbers
"If I Am Dreaming"—Hain
"I Give My Heart"—Moore
"The DuBarry"—Moore, chorus

(Note: *Gräfin DuBarry* was first presented at the Theatre an der Wien, Vienna, Oct. 31, 1879; *Die DuBarry* at the Admiralspalast, Berlin, 1931. The English-language version was first presented at His Majesty's Theatre, London, April 14, 1932. It ran for 397 performances. The cast included Anny Ahlers, Heddle Nash, & Mimi Crawford.)

George M. Cohan Theatre   *87 performances*

1932

November 22.   "GEORGE WHITE'S MUSIC HALL VARIETIES"

Sketches by Billy K. Wells, George White
Lyrics by Irving Caesar, Herb Magidson, Herman Hupfeld, Ted Koehler
Music by Carmen Lombardo, Sammy Stept, Harold Arlen, Herman Hupfeld
Directed by George White   Dances by Russell Markert
Settings by Daziens   Costumes by Charles LeMaire, Kiviette
Music director, Al Goodman   Orchestrations, Maurice DePackh

with

HARRY RICHMAN   LILY DAMITA   BERT LAHR
ELEANOR POWELL
Vivian Fay   Loomis Sisters   Betty Kean   Hilda Knight
Helen Arnold
(Note: Miss Damita out of cast in Dec.; Willie & Eugene Howard
and Tom Patricola added Jan. 1933.)

Musical Numbers
"So I Married the Girl" (Magidson-Stept)—Richman, Damita
"I Love a Parade" (Koehler-Arlen; originally in *Rhythmania*)
     —Richman
"Cabin in the Cotton" (Caesar-Arlen)—Lahr
"Let's Put Out the Lights and Go to Sleep" (Hupfeld)—Richman,
     Damita, Lahr

Casino (formerly Earl Carroll) Theatre   *72 performances*

November 26.   Laurence Schwab & B. G. DeSylva present

"TAKE A CHANCE"

Book by B. G. DeSylva & Laurence Schwab, additional dialogue by Sid
Silvers
Lyrics by B. G. DeSylva
Music by Richard A. Whiting, Herb Brown Nacio (Nacio Herb Brown),
Additional music by Vincent Youmans
Directed by Edgar MacGregor   Dances by Bobby Connolly
Settings by Cleon Throckmorton   Costumes by Kiviette, Charles
LeMaire
Music director, Max Meth   Orchestrations, Stephen Jones, Edward
Powell, Russell Bennett, William Daly   Miss Merman's vocal
arrangements by Roger Edens

with

JACK HALEY   ETHEL MERMAN   JACK WHITING
Sid Silvers   June Knight   Mitzi Mayfair
Robert Gleckler   Oscar Ragland
(Note: During tryout, after story greatly revised, Mr. Haley
replaced Eddie Foy, Jr., Mr. Whiting replaced Lou Holtz, Miss
Mayfair replaced Doris Groday. In June 1933, Messrs. Haley &
Silvers succeeded by Ole Olsen & Chick Johnson, Miss Knight by
Barbara Newberry, Miss Mayfair by Miss Groday.)

Musical Numbers
"Should I Be Sweet?" (DeSylva-Youmans)—Knight
"Turn Out the Lights" (DeSylva-Whiting, Nacio)—Silvers, Haley,
     Whiting, Knight
"Oh, How I Long to Belong to You" (DeSylva-Youmans)—Knight,
   Whiting
"Rise 'n' Shine" (DeSylva-Youmans)—Merman
"You're an Old Smoothie" (DeSylva-Whiting, Nacio)—Haley, Merman
"Eadie Was a Lady" (DeSylva, Roger Edens–Whiting)—Merman

(Note: *Take a Chance* originally tried out under title *Humpty
Dumpty.*)

Apollo Theatre   243 performances

November 29.   Dwight Deere Wiman & Tom Weatherly present
FRED ASTAIRE in

"GAY DIVORCE"

Book by Dwight Taylor, adapted by Kenneth Webb & Samuel Hoffenstein
from unproduced play by J. Hartley Manners
Lyrics & music by Cole Porter
Directed by Howard Lindsay   Dances by Carl Randall, Barbara
Newberry
Settings by Jo Mielziner   Costumes by Raymond Sovey
Music director, Gene Salzer   Orchestrations, Hans Spialek, Russell
Bennett

with

CLAIRE LUCE   LUELLA GEAR
G. P. Huntley, Jr.   Betty Starbuck   Erik Rhodes   Eric Blore
Roland Bottomley
(Note: In May 1933, Miss Luce succeeded by Dorothy Stone; in
June, Mr. Astaire by Joseph Santley.)

Musical Numbers
"After You"—Astaire
"I Still Love the Red, White and Blue"—Gear
"Night and Day"—Astaire, Luce
"How's Your Romance?"—Rhodes
"I've Got You on My Mind"—Astaire, Luce
"Mister and Missus Fitch"—Gear

Ethel Barrymore Theatre; Shubert Theatre (Jan. 1933)
                                        248 performances

1932

December 7. Courtney Burr presents
BEATRICE LILLIE   BOBBY CLARK & PAUL McCULLOUGH
in

"WALK A LITTLE FASTER"

Sketches by S. J. Perelman, Robert McGunigle
Lyrics by E. Y. Harburg
Music by Vernon Duke
Directed by Monty Woolley   Dances by Albertina Rasch
Settings by Boris Aronson   Costumes by Kiviette
Music director, Nick Kempner   Orchestrations, Russell Bennett,
Conrad Salinger

with

John Hundley   Donald Burr   Evelyn Hoey
Dave & Dorothy Fitzgibbon   Jerry Norris
Dorothy McNulty (Penny Singleton)   Sue Hicks
Edgar Fairchild & Robert Lindholm (duo-pianos)

Musical Numbers
"That's Life"—Clark & McCullough
"April in Paris"—Hoey
"Where Have We Met Before?"—Hundley, Hicks
"A Penny for Your Thoughts"—Norris, McNulty
"So Nonchalant"—Hoey
"Speaking of Love"—Burr; danced by Fitzgibbons

St. James (formerly Erlanger's) Theatre   *119 performances*

December 26.   Mawin Productions, Inc., presents

"SHUFFLE ALONG OF 1933"

Book by Flournoy E. Miller
Lyrics & music by Noble Sissle & Eubie Blake
Directed by Walter Brooks   Dances by Davis & Carey
Settings by Carl Amend   Costumes by Robert Stevenson
Music director, Mr. Blake   Orchestrations, Will Vodery

with

FLOURNOY MILLER   NOBLE SISSLE
Mantan Moreland   George McClennon   Edith Wilson
Taps Miller   4 Flash Devils   Lavada Carter

Musical Numbers
"Sing and Dance Your Troubles Away"—Carter
"Bandana Ways"—Wilson, 4 Flash Devils
"Dustin' Around"—McClennon

Mansfield Theatre   *17 performances*

1933

January 20.   Alex A. Aarons & Vinton Freedley present

"PARDON MY ENGLISH"

Book by Herbert Fields
Lyrics by Ira Gershwin
Music by George Gershwin
Directed by John McGowan, Vinton Freedley   Dances by George Hale
Settings by John Wenger   Costumes by Robert Stevenson
Music director, Earl Busby   Orchestrations, Russell Bennett,
William Daly, Adolph Deutsch

with

JACK PEARL
Lyda Roberti
Carl Randall   Barbara Newberry   George Givot
Josephine Huston   Gerald Oliver Smith   Eleanor Shaler
Cliff Hall   Harry T. Shannon
(Note: Mr. Givot replaced Jack Buchanan during tryout.)

Musical Numbers
"Lorelei"—Randall, Newberry
"Isn't It a Pity?"—Givot, Huston
"My Cousin in Milwaukee"—Roberti
"Where You Go I Go"—Roberti, Pearl

Majestic Theatre   *46 performances*

February 14.   George White's

"MELODY"

Book by Edward Childs Carpenter
Lyrics by Irving Caesar
Music by Sigmund Romberg
Directed by George White   Dances by Bobby Connolly
Settings by Joseph Urban   Costumes by Charles LeMaire
Music director, Al Goodman

with

Evelyn Herbert	Everett Marshall	Walter Woolf
Jeanne Aubert	Hal Skelly	George Houston
Ina Ray (Hutton)	Vivian Fay	Louise Kirtland
Victor Morley	Mildred Parisette	Milton Douglas
Venita Varden	Consuelo Flowerton	
Rose Louise (Gypsy Rose Lee) (chorus)		Barry Hyams (chorus)

Musical Numbers
"Melody"—Herbert
"You Are the Song"—Herbert, Marshall
"Give Me a Roll on the Drum"—Herbert
"Tonight May Never Come Again"—Herbert, Woolf

Casino (formerly Earl Carroll) Theatre   *79 performances*

1933

March 4.   Lew Brown & Ray Henderson & Waxey Gordon (uncredited) present
LUPE VELEZ   JIMMY DURANTE   HOPE WILLIAMS
in

"STRIKE ME PINK"

Sketches by Lew Brown & Ray Henderson; additional dialogue by Mack
Gordon, Jack McGowan
Lyrics by Lew Brown
Music by Ray Henderson
Directed by Messrs. Brown, Henderson, McGowan   Dances by Seymour
Felix
Settings by Henry Dreyfuss   Costumes by Kiviette, Charles LeMaire
Music director, Al Goodman

with

HAL LEROY   ROY ATWELL   EDDIE GARR
Ruth Harrison & Alex Fisher   Johnny Downs   Gracie Barrie
Milton Watson   Dorothy Dare   Carolyn Nolte
Will Vodery Singers
GEORGE DEWEY WASHINGTON
(Note: Original tryout cast included Art Jarrett, Mr. Washington,
Mr. Downs, Melissa Mason, Pearl Osgood, Nan Blackstone, Eddie
Conrad, Vicki Cummings. Smith & Dale joined company in Washington.)

Musical Numbers
"Strike Me Pink"—Downs, Dare; danced by LeRoy
"It's Great to Be Alive" (originally in *Hot-Cha!*)—Barrie
"Home to Harlem"—Washington, Vodery Singers
"Let's Call It a Day"—Nolte, Watson
"Restless"—Nolte
"Hollywood, Park Avenue and Broadway"—Velez, Williams, Durante

(Note: During tryout, musical known as *Forward March.*)

Majestic Theatre   *105 performances*

273

April 8.

Allan K. Foster presents
GERTRUDE "BABY" COX in

"HUMMIN' SAM"

Book by Eileen Nutter, from play, *In Old Kentucky,* by Charles T. Dazey
Lyrics & music by Alexander Hill
Director uncredited   Dances by Carey & Davis
Costumes by Brooks
Music director, Jimmie Davis   Orchestrations, Arthur Knowlton

with

EDITH WILSON
Jones & Allen   Madeline Belt   Speedy Smith
Cecil Rivers & Flo Brown   3 Miller Brothers   Louise Lovelle
Robert Underwood

Musical Numbers
"Pinching Myself"—Cox, Belt
"Jubilee"—chorus
"I'll Be True but I'll Be Blue"—3 Sepia Songbirds

New Yorker Theatre   *1 performance*

1933

April 13.

John Krimsky & Gifford Cochran present

"THE THREEPENNY OPERA"

Book & lyrics by Gifford Cochran & Jerrold Krimsky, from German
musical, *Die Dreigroschenoper*, by Bertolt Brecht (based on *The
Beggar's Opera*, by John Gay)
Music by Kurt Weill
Directed by Francesco von Mendelssohn
Settings by Cleon Throckmorton, from designs by Caspar Neher
Music director, Macklin Marrow   Orchestrations, Mr. Weill

with

Robert Chisholm	Rex Weber	Steffi Duna	Rex Evans
Josephine Huston	Evelyn Beresford	George Heller	
Harry Belaver	Herbert Rudley	Burgess Meredith	
Marjorie Dille			

Musical Numbers
"Legend of Mackie Messer"—Heller
"Pirate Jenny"—Duna
"Soldier Song"—Chisholm, Weber
"Love Duet"—Duna, Chisholm
"Lucy's Song"—Huston
"Ballad of the Easy Life"—Chisholm
"Jealousy Duet"—Huston, Duna
"Song of the Aimlessness of Life"—Weber

(Note: *Die Dreigroschenoper* was first presented at the
Schiffbaurdamm Theatre, Berlin, August 28, 1928, with Lotte Lenya in the cast.
A second English-language adaptation, by Marc Blitzstein, opened at the Theatre
de Lys, New York, March 10, 1954. It ran for 95 performances. Reopening
Sept. 20, 1955, it ran for 2,611.)

Empire Theatre   *12 performances*

June 1.

Frank Fay presents
FRANK FAY   BARBARA STANWYCK   in

"TATTLE TALES"

Sketches by Frank Fay & Nick Copeland
Lyrics by George Waggoner, Leo Robin, Edward Eliscu, William Walsh,
Frank Fay, Willard Robison
Music by Edward Ward, Ralph Rainger, Willard Robison, Howard
Jackson, Eddie Blenbryer
Directed by Frank Fay   Dances by John Lonergan, Danny Dare, LeRoy
Prinz
Settings by Martin   Costumes by Elizabeth Zook
Music director, Arnold Johnson   Orchestrations, Howard Jackson,
Edward Ward

with

Nick Copeland	William Hargrave	Ray Mayer
Dorothy Dell	Edyth Evans	Don Cumming
Lillian Reynolds	Mary Barnett	Les Crane

Musical Numbers
"I'll Take an Option on You" (Robin-Rainger)—Fay
"Hang Up Your Hat on Broadway" (Waggoner-Ward)—Fay, company
"Sing American Tunes" (Fay, Walsh-Ward)—Dell, Barnett, Clark

(Note: *Tattle Tales* was first presented on Dec. 29, 1932, at the
Belasco Theatre, Los Angeles. In addition to Mr. Fay, the cast
included Janet Reade, Guy Robertson, Paal & Leif Rocky, Betty Grable,
Charles Kaley.)

Broadhurst Theatre   *28 performances*

July 5.   Harry Meyer presents

"SHADY LADY"

Book by Estelle Morando, revised by Irving Caesar (uncredited)
Lyrics by Bud Green, Stanley Adams
Music by Sammy Stept, Jesse Greer

Directed by Theodore Hammerstein	Dances by Jack Donohue
Settings by Tom Adrian Cracroft	Costumes by Brooks, Billi
Livingston	
Music director, Max Hoffmann, Sr.	Orchestrations, Charles Cooke,
Henry Redfield	

with

HELEN KANE	LESTER ALLEN	CHARLES PURCELL
Helen Raymond	Max Hoffman, Jr.	Louise Kirtland
Audrey Christie	Jack Donohue	

Musical Numbers
"I'll Betcha that I'll Getcha" (Adams-Greer)—Kane, Allen
"Swingy Little Thingy" (Green-Stept)—Hoffman, Christie,
    Allen
"Hiya, Sucker" (Adams-Greer)—Raymond

Shubert Theatre   *30 performances*

1933

September 12.　　Earl Carroll presents

"MURDER AT THE VANITIES"

Book by Earl Carroll & Rufus King; additional dialogue by Eugene Conrad
Lyrics by Ned Washington, Paul Francis Webster, Edward Heyman, Herman Hupfeld
Music by Victor Young, John Jacob Loeb, Herman Hupfeld, Johnny Green, Richard Myers
Directed by Mr. Carroll & Burk Symon　　　　Dances by Chester Hale, Ned McGurn
Settings by Max Teuber　　Costumes by Brymer
Music director, Ray Kavanaugh　　Orchestrations, Edward Powell, Hans Spialek

with

James Rennie	Bela Lugosi	Olga Baclanova	Billy House
Jean Adair	Lisa Gilbert	Naomi Ray	Pauline Moore
Woods Miller	Paul Gerrits	Una Vallon	Beryl Wallace
Gay Orlova	Hope Carol		

(Note: In Oct., Miss Adair succeeded by Minnie Dupree; in Nov., Mr. Lugosi by William Balfour; in Jan. 1934, Miss Baclanova by Louise Kirtland, Mr. Rennie by Lew Eckles.)

Musical Numbers
"Sweet Madness" (Washington-Young)
"Virgins Wrapped in Cellophane" (Webster-Loeb)
"Weep No More, My Baby" (Heyman-Green)—Vallon, House
"Savage Serenade" (Hupfeld)—Vallon

New Amsterdam Theatre　　　*207 performances*

September 25.   Messrs. Shubert (uncredited) present
JOE COOK in

"HOLD YOUR HORSES"

Book by Russel Crouse & Corey Ford, from their play written with
Charles Beahan; additional dialogue by Joe Cook
Lyrics mostly by Owen Murphy, Robert A. Simon
Music mostly by Russell Bennett
Directed by R. H. Burnside & John Shubert   Dances by Robert Alton,
Harriet Hoctor
Settings & costumes by Russell Patterson
Music director, Gene Salzer   Orchestrations, Russell Bennett

with

HARRIET HOCTOR

Tom Patricola	Ona Munson	Rex Weber	Inez Courtney
Dave Chasen	Stanley Smith	Frances Upton	Jack Powell

Musical Numbers
"Hold Your Horses"—Cook, Munson
"If I Love Again" (J. P. Murray–Ben Oakland)—Weber
"High Shoes"—Courtney, Patricola

Winter Garden   *88 performances*

1933

September 30.   Sam H. Harris presents
MARILYN MILLER   CLIFTON WEBB
HELEN BRODERICK   in

"AS THOUSANDS CHEER"

Sketches by Moss Hart
Lyrics & music by Irving Berlin
Directed by Hassard Short   Dances by Charles Weidman
Settings by Albert Johnson   Costumes by Irene Sharaff, Varady
Music director, Frank Tours   Orchestrations, Adolph Deutsch, Mr.
Tours, Helmy Kresa

with

ETHEL WATERS
Leslie Adams   Hal Forde   Jerome Cowan   Harry Stockwell
Thomas Hamilton   Hamtree Harrington   Peggy Cornell
Katherine Litz   Letitia Ide   José Limon
(Note: In July 1934, Mr. Webb succeeded by Charles Collins, Miss
Miller by Dorothy Stone.)

Musical Numbers
"How's Chances?"—Webb, Miller
"Heat Wave"—Waters; danced by Ide, Limon
"Lonely Heart"—Stockwell; danced by Ide, Limon
"Easter Parade"—Miller, Webb, company
"Suppertime"—Waters
"Harlem on My Mind"—Waters
"Not for All the Rice in China"—Miller, Webb

Music Box Theatre   **400** *performances*

October 14.

Dwight Deere Wiman, with the Westport County Playhouse, presents

PEGGY WOOD HELEN FORD GEORGE MEADER

in

"CHAMPAGNE, SEC"

Book by Alan Child (Lawrence Langner), from Viennese operetta, *Die Fledermaus*, by Karl Haffner & Richard Genée (based on French play, *Le Réveillon*, by Henri Meilhac & Ludovic Halevy, from German story, *Das Gafängnis*, by Julius Benedix)
Lyrics by Robert A. Simon
Music by Johann Strauss, Jr.
Directed by Monty Woolley
Settings by Jo Mielziner Costumes by Brooks
Music director, Rudolph Thomas

with

Joseph Macaulay	John E. Hazzard	John Barclay
George Trabert	Kitty Carlisle	Olive Jones
William McCarthy	Eleanor Tennis	Paul Haakon

Musical Numbers
None listed individually.

(Note: *Die Fledermaus* was first presented at the Theatre-an-der-Wien, Vienna, April 5, 1874. In addition to *Champagne, Sec*, it has been seen in New York in the following adaptations: *The Merry Countess*, by Gladys Unger & Arthur Anderson, at the Casino Theatre, Aug. 20, 1912 [135 performances]; *A Wonderful Night*, by Fanny Todd Mitchell, with Archie Leach [Cary Grant] in the cast, at the Majestic Theatre, Oct. 31, 1929 [125 performances]; *Rosalinda*, by Gottfried Reinhardt, John Meehan, Jr., & Paul Kerby, at the 44th Street Theatre, Oct. 28, 1942 [521 performances]. In 1950, *Fledermaus*, by Garson Kanin & Howard Dietz, was added to the repertory of the Metropolitan Opera.)

Morosco Theatre; Shubert Theatre (Nov.); 44th Street Theatre (Dec.) 113 performances

October 21.　　Sam H. Harris presents

"LET 'EM EAT CAKE"

Book by George S. Kaufman & Morrie Ryskind
Lyrics by Ira Gershwin
Music by George Gershwin
Directed by George S. Kaufman　　　Dances by Eugene Van Grona, Ned
McGurn
Settings by Albert R. Johnson　　　Costumes by Kiviette, John Booth
Music director, William Daly　　　Orchestrations, Edward Powell

with

WILLIAM GAXTON　　　LOIS MORAN　　　VICTOR MOORE
Dudley Clements　　　Philip Loeb　　　Edward H. Robins
Florenz Ames　　　Ralph Riggs　　　George E. Mack
Harold Moffatt　　　Grace Worth　　　Consuelo Flowerton

Musical Numbers
"Wintergreen for President" (originally in *Of Thee I Sing*)—chorus
"Union Square"—chorus
"Down with Ev'rything that's Up"—Loeb
"Mine"—Gaxton, Moran
"On and On and On"—Gaxton, Moran, company
"Let 'Em Eat Cake"—Gaxton, company
"Blue, Blue, Blue"—chorus
"No Comprenez, No Capish"—chorus

(Note: *Let 'Em Eat Cake* was a sequel to *Of Thee I Sing*.)

Imperial Theatre　　　*90 performances*

1933

November 18.   Max Gordon presents

"ROBERTA"

Book & lyrics by Otto Harbach, from novel, *Gowns by Roberta*,
by Alice Duer Miller
Music by Jerome Kern
Directed by Hassard Short (uncredited)   Dances by José Limon,
John Lonergan (uncredited)
Settings by Clark Robinson   Costumes by Kiviette
Music director, Victor Baravalle   Orchestrations, R. Russell Bennett

with

Lyda Roberti   Bob Hope   Fay Templeton   Tamara
George Murphy   Sydney Greenstreet   Raymond Middleton
Helen Gray   William Hain   Roberta Beatty   Nayan Pearce
California Collegians (incl. Fred MacMurray)
(Note: In June 1934, Mr. Murphy succeeded by Bobby Jarvis; in July,
Mr. Hope by Marty May, Miss Roberti by Odette Myrtil.)

Musical Numbers
"Let's Begin"—Murphy; reprised by Middleton, Hope, Tamara
"You're Devastating"—Hope; reprised by Tamara
"Yesterdays"—Templeton
"Something Had to Happen"—Roberti, Hope, Middleton
"The Touch of Your Hand"—Tamara, Hain
"I'll Be Hard to Handle" (Bernard Dougall–Kern)—Roberti
"Smoke Gets in Your Eyes"—Tamara

(Note: Musical titled *Gowns by Roberta* at beginning of tryout.)

New Amsterdam Theatre   *295 performances*

December 2.

Sepia Guild Players, Inc., present
Lew Leslie's

"BLACKBIRDS" (1933-1934 Edition)

Sketches by Nat Dorfman, Mann Holiner, Lew Leslie
Lyrics by Mann Holiner, Ned Washington, Joe Young
Music by Alberta Nichols, Victor Young
Directed by Lew Leslie   Dances by Al Richards
Settings by Mabel A. Buell   Costumes by Charles LeMaire
Music director, Ken Macomber   Orchestrations, Mr. Macomber, Ferde
Grofé, Will Vodery, Joe Jordan

with

BILL ROBINSON
John Mason   Edith Wilson   Eddie Hunter
Worthy & Thompson   Kathryn Perry   Speedy Smith
Slappy Wallace   Brady Jackson   Blue McAllister
James Boxwill   Gretchen Branch   Phil Scott   Eloise Uggams
Toni Ellis   Martha Thomas   Cecil Mack Choir
Pike Davis's Orchestra

Musical Numbers
"I Just Couldn't Take It, Baby" (Holiner-Nichols)—Branch, Scott,
     Perry, Uggams
"Your Mother's Son-in-Law" (Holiner-Nichols)—Mason, Wilson, Ellis,
     Thomas
"A Hundred Years from Today" (Young, Washington-Young)—Perry

Apollo Theatre   *25 performances*

January 4.

Mrs. Florenz Ziegfeld (Billie Burke) & Messrs. Shubert (uncredited) present

"ZIEGFELD FOLLIES"

Sketches by H. I. Phillips, Fred Allen, Harry Turgend, David Freedman
Lyrics by E. Y. Harburg, Ballard Macdonald, Billy Rose, Billy Hill, Edward Heyman
Music by Vernon Duke, Samuel Pokrass, Joseph Meyer, Richard Myers, Dana Suesse, Peter DeRose, Basil Adlam, Billy Hill, James F. Hanley
Directed by Bobby Connolly, Edward Clark Lilley, John Murray Anderson   Dances by Robert Alton
Settings by Watson Barratt, Albert Johnson   Costumes by Kiviette, Russell Patterson, Raoul Pène du Bois, Charles LeMaire
Music director, John McManus

with

FANNIE BRICE
WILLIE & EUGENE HOWARD   EVERETT MARSHALL
JANE FROMAN   VILMA & BUDDY EBSEN
PATRICIA BOWMAN   DON ROSS
Oliver Wakefield   Cherry & June Preisser   Vivian Janis
Eve Arden   Betzi Beaton   Victor Morley
Brice Hutchins (Robert Cummings)   Judith Barron
Ina Ray (Hutton)   Jacques Cartier
(Note: Georges Metaxa in cast during tryout.)

Musical Numbers
"Water Under the Bridge" (Harburg-Duke)—Marshall
"I Like the Likes of You" (Harburg-Duke)—Barron, Hutchins; danced by Ebsens
"Suddenly" (Harburg-Duke)—Froman, Marshall
"Countess Dubinsky" (Macdonald, Rose-Meyer)—Brice
"To the Beat of the Heart" (Harburg-Pokrass)—Marshall; danced by Cartier
"What Is There to Say?" (Harburg-Duke)—Froman, Marshall
"The Last Roundup" (Hill)—Ross; reprised by Howards
"Wagon Wheels" (Hill-DeRose)—Marshall
"Rose of Washington Square" (Macdonald-Hanley; originally in *Ziegfeld Midnight Frolic*, 1919)—Brice
"The House Is Haunted" (Rose-Adam)—Froman
"You Oughta Be in Pictures" (Heyman-Suesse; added during run)—Froman

Winter Garden   *182 performances*

1934

January 30.   Harry Cort & Charles Abramson present

"ALL THE KING'S HORSES"

Book & lyrics by Frederick Herendeen, from play, *Carlo Rocco*, by Lawrence
Clarke & Max Giersberg
Music by Edward A. Horan
Directed by José Ruben   Dances by Theodor Adolphus
Settings by Ward & Harvey   Costumes by John Booth, Jr.
Music director, Oscar Bradley   Orchestrations, Russell Bennett,
Hans Spialek

with

GUY ROBERTSON   NANCY McCORD
ANDREW TOMBES   BETTY STARBUCK
Doris Patston   Frank Greene   Jack Edwards   Russell Hicks
(Note: In March, Mr. Tombes succeeded by Bernard Granville; in
April, Mr. Granville by Billy House.)

Musical Numbers
"Evening Star"—McCord
"I Found a Song"—Robertson, McCord, Tombes
"I've Gone Nuts Over You"—Tombes, Starbuck

Shubert Theatre; Imperial Theatre (March)   120 *performances*

February 20.   Harry Moses presents

"4 SAINTS IN 3 ACTS"

Words by Gertrude Stein
Music by Virgil Thomson
Scenario by Maurice Grosser
Directed by John Houseman   Dances by Frederick Ashton
Settings & costumes by Florine Stettheimer & Kate Drain Lawson
Lighting by Feder
Music director, Alexander Smallens   Choral director, Eva Jessye

with

Edward Mathews   Beatrice Robinson-Wayne   Bruce Howard
Altona Hines   Abner Dorsey

Musical Numbers
None listed separately.

44th Street Theatre; Empire Theatre (April)   *48 performances*

1934

March 15.   Charles B. Dillingham presents
Leonard Sillman's

"NEW FACES"

Sketches by Viola Brothers Shore, Nancy Hamilton, Newman Levy,
John Goodwin, William Griffith, Mindret Lord, Beth Wendall
Lyrics by Nancy Hamilton, June Sillman, Everett Marcy,
Viola Brothers Shore, J. J. Robbins, E. Y. Harburg, Robert Sour,
Harold Goodman, James Shelton, Haven Johnson
Music by Martha Caples, Warburton Guilbert, James Shelton, Haven
Johnson, Sandro Corona, George Grande, Donald Honrath, Morgan Lewis,
Cliff Allen, George Hickman, Charles Schwab, Walter Feldkamp
Directed by Leonard Sillman   Supervised by Elsie Janis
Settings & costumes by Sergei Soudeikine
Music director, Gene Salzer   Orchestrations, Hans Spialek

with

Leonard Sillman   Imogene Coca   Nancy Hamilton
Louise (Teddy) Lynch   Hildegarde Halliday
Dorothy Kennedy-Fox   Frances Dewey   Billie Haywood
Cliff Allen   Charles Walters   James Shelton   Roger Stearns
O. Z. Whitehead   Henry Fonda   Edith Sheridan
Mildred Todd   Allen Handley   Gordon Orme   Melvin Parks
Dolores Hart   Helen O'Hara   Gus Schirmer

Musical Numbers
"Lamplight" (Shelton)—Shelton, with Fonda, Coca
"My Last Affair" (Johnson)—Haywood
"The Gutter Song" (Shelton)—Shelton
"You're My Relaxation" (Sour-Schwab)—Dewey, Orme, Halliday, Handley
" 'Cause You Won't Play House" (Harburg-Lewis)—Coca, Walters

(Note: *New Faces* was a revised version of *Low and Behold,*
first presented at the Pasadena Playhouse, May 16, 1933. The
cast included Marguerite Namara, Paal & Leif Rocky, Billy
Griffith, Leonard Sillman, June Sillman, Betzi Beaton, Teddy
Hart, Kay Thompson, Lois January, Charles [Chuck] Walters,
Tyrone Power, Jr., Eunice Quedens [Eve Arden].)

Fulton Theatre   *149 performances*

1934

June 7.   Patrick A. Leonard presents

"CAVIAR"

Book by Leo Randole
Lyrics by Edward Heyman
Music by Harden Church
Directed by Clifford Brooke   Dances by John Lonergan
Settings & costumes by Steele Savage
Music director, Ivan Rudisill   Orchestrations, Hans Spialek

with

Nanette Guilford	George Houston	Alice Dudley	Jack Cole
Dudley Clements	Tesore Mio	Walter Armin	
Hugh Cameron	Billie Leonard	Don Connolly	

Musical Numbers
"You're One in a Million"—Leonard, Connolly
"Dream Kingdom"—Guilford
"Silver Sails"—Houston

Forrest Theatre   *20 performances*

June 25.   Dmitri Ostrov presents

"GYPSY BLONDE"

Book by Kenneth Johns, from *The Bohemian Girl* by Alfred Bunn
(based on ballet, *The Gypsy*, by Jules Henri Vernoy de St Georges)
Lyrics by Frank Gabrielson
Music by Michael Balfe
Directed by Dmitri Ostrov   Dances by Vaughn Godfrey
Settings by Karl Amend   Costumes by Eaves
Music director, Fred Hoff

with

GEORGE TRABERT   ISABEL HENDERSON
JOHN DUNSMURE   BELLE DIDJAH
Helene Arden   John Hendricks   Evelyn Wyckoff (chorus)

Musical Numbers
"I Dreamt that I Dwelt in Marble Halls"—Henderson
"The Heart Bow'd Down"—Hendricks
"I'm a Gypsy Blonde"—Henderson

(Note: *The Bohemian Girl* was first presented at the Drury Lane
Theatre, London, Nov. 27, 1843.)

Lyric Theatre   *24 performances*

August 23.

White Horse Tavern Productions, Inc., presents

"KEEP MOVING"

Sketches by Newman Levy, Jack Scholl, George Rosener
Lyrics by Jack Scholl
Music by Max Rich
Directed by Mr. Rosener   Dances by Harry Losee
Settings by Clark Robinson   Costumes by Robert Stevenson
Music director, Dell Lampe

with

TOM HOWARD

Joan Abbott	Woods Miller	Billy Taylor	Nayan Pearce
Dan Carthay	Clyde Hager	Harriet Hutchins	
William Redford	Ernest Lambert	Kay Picture	
Singer Midgets			

Musical Numbers
"Hot-Cha Chiquita"—Abbott
"Now Is the Time"—Pearce, Carthay
"Keep Moving"—company

Forrest Theatre   *20 performances*

August 27.   Messrs. Shubert present

"LIFE BEGINS AT 8:40"

Sketches by David Freedman, H. I. Phillips, Alan Baxter, Henry Clapp
Smith, Ira Gershwin & E. Y. Harburg, Frank Gabrielson
Lyrics by Ira Gershwin & E. Y. Harburg
Music by Harold Arlen
Directed by John Murray Anderson & Philip Loeb   Dances by Robert
Alton, Charles Weidman
Settings by Albert Johnson   Costumes by Kiviette, James Reynolds,
Raoul Pène du Bois. Billi Livingston, Wynn, Pauline Lawrence,
Irene Scharoff
Music director, Al Goodman   Orchestrations, Hans Spialek

with

BERT LAHR   RAY BOLGER   LUELLA GEAR
FRANCES WILLIAMS
Brian Donlevy   Earl Oxford   Dixie Dunbar
Robert Wildhack   Bartlett Simmons   Ofelia & Pimento
Esther Junger   James MacColl   Josephine Huston
Walter Dare Wahl   Emmett Oldfield   Adrienne Matzenauer
(Note: Mr. Oxford succeeded by John [Jack] McCauley, Feb. 1935.)

Musical Numbers
"Spring Fever"—Williams
"Shoein' the Mare"—Matzenauer; danced by Junger, Ofelia & Pimento
"Things"—Lahr
"You're a Builder-Upper"—Bolger, Dunbar
"Fun to Be Fooled"—Williams; danced by Junger
"What Can You Say in a Love Song?"—Huston, Simmons
"Let's Take a Walk Around the Block"—Oxford, Dunbar
"Quartet Erotica"—MacColl, Donlevy, Bolger, Lahr
"I Couldn't Hold My Man"—Gear

Winter Garden   *237 performances*

August 28.

R. A. Reppil (Arthur Lipper, Jr.) presents

"SALUTA"

Book by Will Morrissey, revised by Eugene Conrad & Maurice Marks
Lyrics by Will Morrissey & Milton Berle
Music by Frank D'Armond
Directed by Edwin Saulpaugh   Dances by Boots McKenna
Settings by Hugh Willoughby   Costumes by John Booth, Jr.
Music director, John McManus

with

Milton Berle
Thelma White   Ann Barrie   Milton Watson
Edward J. Lambert   Chaz Chase   Dudley Clements
William Hargrave   The Maxcellas
Felicia Sorel & Demetrios Vilan

Musical Numbers
"Just Say the Word" (Berle-D'Armond)—Watson
"Chill in the Air" (Morrissey-D'Armond)—White
"The Great Dictator and Me"—Berle

Imperial Theatre   *39 performances*

September 22.   Max Gordon presents

"THE GREAT WALTZ"

Book by Moss Hart, from Viennese operetta, *Waltzes from Vienna*,
by A. M. Willner, Heinz Reichert & Ernst Marischka, & English version
by Caswell Garth
Lyrics by Desmond Carter
Music by Johann Strauss, Sr., & Johann Strauss, Jr.
Directed & lighted by Hassard Short   Dances by Albertina Rasch
Settings by Albert Johnson   Costumes by Doris Zinkeisen, Irene
Sharaff
Music director, Frank Tours   Orchestrations, Erich Wolfgang
Korngold, Julius Bittner, G. A. Clutsam, Herbert Griffith, Frank Tours

with

Marion Claire	Marie Burke	Guy Robertson
H. Reeves-Smith	Ernest Cossart	Dennis Noble
Alexandra Danilova	Jessie Busley	Solly Ward
Robert Fischer	Meg Mundy (chorus)	

Musical Numbers
"Love Will Find You"—Claire, Robertson
"For We Love You Still"—Burke
"While You Love Me"—Claire, Robertson
"Danube So Blue"—Claire, company

(Note: *Waltzes from Vienna* was first presented in Vienna in 1930.
The original English-language version was first presented at the
Alhambra Theatre, London, Aug. 17, 1931. It ran 607 performances.
The cast included Marie Burke, Esmond Knight, Dennis Noble, &
Davy Bernaby.)

Center Theatre   298 *performances*

Return Engagement: August 5, 1935
Miss Claire succeeded by Lee Whitney.

Center Theatre   49 *performances*

October 23.

Arch Selwyn & Harold B. Franklin, with Charles B. Cochran, present
YVONNE PRINTEMPS in

"CONVERSATION PIECE"

Book, lyrics & music by Noël Coward
Directed by Mr. Coward
Settings & costumes by G. E. Calthrop
Music director, Victor Baravalle   Orchestrations, Charles Prentice

with

Pierre Fresnay
Irene Browne   Athole Stewart   Carl Harbord   Sylvia Leslie
Moya Nugent   Betty Shale   Maidie Andrews
George Sanders   Sidney Grammer   Antony Brian
Pat Worsley

Musical Numbers
"I'll Follow My Secret Heart"—Printemps
"Regency Rakes"—Sanders, Grammer, Brian, Worsley
"Charming, Charming"—Printemps, Andrews, Leslie, Nugent
"Dear Little Soldiers"—Printemps, Andrews, Leslie, Nugent
"There's Always Something Fishy About the French"—Leslie,
    Nugent
"English Lesson"—Printemps
"Nevermore"—Printemps

(Note: *Conversation Piece* was first presented at His Majesty's
Theatre, London, Feb. 16, 1934. It ran for 177 performances. The
New York company is much the same, except that Mr. Fresnay replaced
Mr. Coward [as he had also done in London].)

44th Street Theatre   *55 performances*

1934

Jack McGowan & Ray Henderson present

"SAY WHEN"

Book by Jack McGowan
Lyrics by Ted Koehler
Music by Ray Henderson
Directed by Bertram Harrison   Dances by Russell Markert
Settings by Clark Robinson   Costumes by Charles LeMaire
Music director, Max Meth   Orchestrations, Conrad Salinger, Russell
Bennett

with

HARRY RICHMAN
BOB HOPE   LINDA WATKINS   TAYLOR HOLMES
Cora Witherspoon   Dennie Moore
Lillian Emerson   Nick Long, Jr.   Charles Collins
Prince Michael Romanoff

Musical Numbers
"When Love Comes Swinging Along"—Richman, Emerson
"It Must Have Been the Night"—Collins, Long, Emerson
"Say When"—Richman
"Put Your Heart in a Song"—Richman
"Don't Tell Me It's Bad"—Watkins, Hope

Imperial Theatre   *76 performances*

1934

November 21.
Vinton Freedley presents
WILLIAM GAXTON   ETHEL MERMAN   VICTOR MOORE
in

"ANYTHING GOES"

Book by Guy Bolton & P. G. Wodehouse, revised by Howard Lindsay &
Russel Crouse
Lyrics & music by Cole Porter
Directed by Howard Lindsay   Dances by Robert Alton
Settings by Donald Oenslager   Costumes by Jenkins
Music director, Earl Busby   Orchestrations, Russell Bennett,
Hans Spialek

with

BETTINA HALL
Helen Raymond   Vera Dunn   Houston Richards
Leslie Barrie   Vivian Vance   George E. Mack
The Foursome   Paul Everton
(Note: In Sept., 1935, Miss Merman succeeded by Benay Venuta;
in Oct., Miss Hall by Irene Delroy.)

Musical Numbers
"I Get a Kick Out of You"—Merman, Gaxton
"All Through the Night"—Hall, Gaxton
"You're the Top"—Merman, Gaxton
"Anything Goes"—Merman, The Foursome
"Blow, Gabriel, Blow"—Merman
"Be Like the Bluebird"—More
"The Gypsy in Me"—Hall

Alvin Theatre   *420 performances*

November 26.   Perry-Wood Co. presents

"AFRICANA"

Book, lyrics & music by Donald Heywood
Additional lyrics by Abe Tuvim
Directed by Peter Morell
Settings by Anthony Continer
Music director, Mr. Heywood   Orchestrations, Philip Ellis, Fredda
Feranda   Choral director, Philomena Perry

with

Jack Carr	Howard Gould	Walter Richardson	Nita Gale
Joseph Byrd	Gretchen Branch	Hesla Tamanya	
King Yafouba	Prince Soyonga		

Musical Numbers
"Yamboo"
"Stop Beating Those Drums"
"No Peace in My Soul"

Venice (formerly Jolson) Theatre   *3 performances*

November 28. Arch Selwyn & Harold B. Franklin present

"REVENGE WITH MUSIC"

Book & lyrics by Howard Dietz, from Spanish novel, *El Sombrero de Tres Picos*, by Pedro de Alarcon (based on folk tale)
Music by Arthur Schwartz
Directed by Komisarjevsky & Worthington Miner, also Howard Dietz (uncredited), Marc Connelly (uncredited)   Dances by Michael Mordkin
Settings by Albert R. Johnson   Costumes by Constance Ripley
Music director, Victor Baravalle   Orchestrations, Russell Bennett

with

CHARLES WINNINGER   LIBBY HOLMAN
GEORGES METAXA
Ilka Chase   Rex O'Malley

Joseph Macaulay   Ivy Scott   Detmar Poppen   Margaret Lee
George Kirk   Marcus Blechman (chorus)   André Charise (chorus)
(Note: Mr. Kirk replaced Alan Marshal during tryout. In Jan 1935,
Miss Chase succeeded by Ara Gerald; in Feb., Mr. O'Malley by David
Morris; in April, Mr. Winninger by William Kent.)

Musical Numbers
"When You Love Only One"—Holman
"Never Marry a Dancer"—Lee
"If There Is Someone Lovelier than You"—Metaxa
"That Fellow Manuelo"—Macaulay
"Maria"—Metaxa, Holman
"You and the Night and the Music"—Metaxa, Holman
"Wand'rin' Heart"—Holman

New Amsterdam Theatre   *158 performances*

December 13.   Lew Brown's

"CALLING ALL STARS"

Sketches by Lew Brown, A. Dorian Otvos, Alan Baxter
Lyrics by Lew Brown
Music by Harry Akst
Directed by Mr. Brown & Thomas Mitchell   Dances by Sara Mildred
Strauss, Maurice Kusell
Settings by Nat Karson   Costumes by Billi Livingston
Lighting by Feder
Music director, Al Goodman   Orchestrations, Hans Spialek, Conrad
Salinger
(Note: Harold Winston credited as co-director during tryout.)

with

LOU HOLTZ   PHIL BAKER   EVERETT MARSHALL
GERTRUDE NIESEN   MITZI MAYFAIR
JACK WHITING   PATRICIA BOWMAN   PATSY FLICK
Judy Canova   Martha Raye   Al Bernie
Harry (Bottle) McNaughton   Ella Logan
Edgar Fairchild & Robert Lindholm (duo-pianos)

Musical Numbers
"I'd Like to Dunk You in My Coffee"—Whiting, Mayfair
"If It's Love"—Whiting, Logan, Raye, Canova
"I Don't Want to Be President"—Whiting, Mayfair
"Straw Hat in the Rain"—Marshall
"Stepping Out of the Picture"—Niesen

Hollywood Theatre   *36 performances*

1934

December 25.   William A. Brady & Marilyn Miller (uncredited) present
Leonard Sillman's

"FOOLS RUSH IN"

Sketches by Norman Zeno, Viola Brothers Shore, Richard Whorf
Lyrics by Norman Zeno, June Sillman
Music by Will Irwin, Richard Lewine
Directed by Leonard Sillman   Dances by Chester O'Brien, Edwin
Strawbridge, Arthur Bradley
Settings & costumes by Russell Patterson
Music director, Max Meth   Orchestrations, Conrad Salinger, Hans
Spialek, Russell Bennett

with

IMOGENE COCA   RICHARD WHORF
BETZI BEATON   BILLY MILTON
Dorothy Kennedy-Fox   Cyrena Smith   Karl Swenson
Miriam Battista   Vandy Cape   Charles Walter
Mildred Todd   Peggy Hovenden   Billie Heywood
Roger Stearns   Edward Potter   Cliff Allen   Elinor Flynn
O. Z. Whitehead   Teddy Lynch   Janet Fox   Olga Vernon
Robert Burton
LEONARD SILLMAN

Musical Numbers
"Love, Come Take Me" (Zeno-Irwin)—Vernon
"Rhythm in My Hair" (Zeno-Irwin)—Lynch, Vernon, Heywood,
     Kennedy-Fox, Walter
"Wicked, Unwholesome, Expensive" (Zeno-Irwin)—Smith & Stearns,
     Todd & Burton, Hovenden & Milton
"Let's Hold Hands" (Sillman-Lewine)—Flynn, Milton

The Playhouse   *14 performances*

December 27.   Eddie Dowling presents

"THUMBS UP!"

Sketches by H. I. Phillips, Alan Baxter, Ronald Jeans, Ballard
Macdonald, Charles Sherman
Lyrics by Ballard Macdonald, Earle Crooker, John Murray Anderson,
Irving Caesar, Jean Herbert, Karl Stark, Vernon Duke, James F. Hanley
Music by James F. Hanley, Henry Sullivan, Gerald Marks, Vernon Duke
Directed by John Murray Anderson & Edward Clark Lilley   Dances
by Robert Alton
Settings by Ted Weidhass   Costumes by James Reynolds, Raoul Pène
du Bois, Thomas Becker, James Morcom
Music director, Gene Salzer   Orchestrations, Hans Spialek, Conrad
Salinger, David Raksin

with

BOBBY CLARK & PAUL McCULLOUGH		HAL LEROY
J. HAROLD MURRAY	EDDIE GARR	RAY DOOLEY
PICKENS SISTERS	PAUL DRAPER	ROSE KING
SHEILA BARRETT	EUNICE HEALEY	JACK COLE
ALICE DUDLEY	MARGARET ADAMS	AL SEXTON
HUGH CAMERON	BARNETT PARKER	
IRENE McBRIDE		

Billie Worth (chorus)   John Fearnley (chorus)
EDDIE DOWLING
(Note: Mr. Garr out of cast in Feb. 1935. In Jan., Mr. Murray
succeeded by George Houston; in March, Mr. LeRoy by Duke McHale.)

Musical Numbers
"Zing! Went the Strings of My Heart!" (Hanley)—LeRoy, Healey
"Lily Belle May June" (Crooker-Sullivan)—Dooley, LeRoy
"Eileen Avourneen" (Anderson-Sullivan)—Murray
"Autumn in New York" (Duke)—Murray

St. James Theatre   *156 performances*

1934

December 27.   Russell Janney presents

"THE O'FLYNN"

Book & lyrics by Brian Hooker & Mr. Janney, from play by Justin
Huntly McCarthy
Music by Franklin Hauser
Directed by Robert Milton   Dances by Louis Chalif
Settings & costumes by James Reynolds
Music director, Giuseppe Bamboschek

with

George Houston	Lucy Monroe	Walter Munroe
William Balfour	Colin Campbell	Will Philbrick
Frank Fenton	H. Cooper-Cliffe	

Musical Numbers
"Child of Erin" (Janney-Hauser)
"Lovely Lady" (Janney-Hauser)
"Song of My Heart" (Hooker-Hauser)

Broadway Theatre   *11 performances*

December 29.   Messrs. Shubert present

"MUSIC HATH CHARMS"

Book & lyrics by Rowland Leigh, George Rosener, John Shubert
Music by Rudolf Friml
Directed by George Rosener   Dances by Alex Yakovleff
Settings by Watson Barratt   Costumes by Ernest Schrapps
Music director, Al Goodman

with

NATALIE HALL   ROBERT HALLIDAY
ANDREW TOMBES   PAUL HAAKON   BILLY REY
CONSTANCE CARPENTER
Harry Mestayer   Gracie Worth   Cyril Chadwick
Robert Lee Allen   Nina Whitney   Truman Gaige
John Clarke   Elizabeth Crandell

Musical Numbers
"Maria"—Halliday
"Sweet Fool"—Carpenter, Tombes
"It's You I Want to Love Tonight"—Hall
"My Heart is Yours"—Halliday, Hall

(Note: Under the title *Annina,* musical toured major cities during
winter of 1934. Maria Jeritza & Allan Jones were in the cast.)

Majestic Theatre   *29 performances*

1935

May 20.   The Theatre Guild presents

"PARADE"

Sketches by Paul Peters, George Sklar, Frank Gabrielson,
David Lesan, Kyle Crichton, Michael Blankfort, Alan Baxter,
Harold Johnsrud, Turner Bullock
Lyrics by Paul Peters, George Sklar, Kyle Crichton
Music by Jerome Moross
Directed by Philip Loeb   Dances by Robert Alton
Settings by Lee Simonson   Costumes by Constance Ripley, Irene
Sharaff, Billi Livingston
Music director, Max Meth   Orchestrations, Conrad Salinger, Russell
Bennett, David Raksin, Mr. Moross

with

JIMMY SAVO
Charles D. Brown   Vera Marsh   Earl Oxford   Esther Junger
Eve Arden   Ralph Riggs   Jean Travers   Dorothy Fox
Charles Walters   Leon Janney   Evelyn Dall   Avis Andrews
Melton Moore   Ezra Stone   Edgar Allen   David Lesan
David Lawrence

Musical Numbers
"Life Could Be So Beautiful"—chorus
"You Ain't So Hot"—Andrews
"Fear in My Heart"—Oxford, Travers

Guild Theatre   *40 performances*

June 4. **"EARL CARROLL SKETCH BOOK"** (2nd Edition)

Sketches by Eugene Conrad, Charles Sherman, Royal Foster
Lyrics & music mostly by Murray Mencher, Charles Newman & Charles Tobias
Directed by Earl Carroll & Edward Clark Lilley   Dances by Boots McKenna
Settings by Clark Robinson   Costumes by Samuel Lang, John Booth, Billi Livingston, Wynn, Bob Stevenson, Giles Borbridge
Music director, Ray Kavanaugh   Orchestrations, Robert Russell Bennett, Donald J. Walker, David Raksin

with

KEN MURRAY
Peter Higgins   Jane Moore & Billy Revel   Sibyl Bowan
Arrens & Broderick   The Hudson Wonders   Sassafras
Lillian Carmen   Bert Lynn   Duffin & Draper   Sunnie O'Dea
Billy Rayes   Beryl Wallace

Musical Numbers
"Let's Swing It"—Carmen
"At Last" (Charles Tobias, Sam Lewis–Henry Tobias)—O'Dea, Higgins
"Let the Man who Makes the Gun" (Ray Egan–Gerald Marks)—Carmen

Winter Garden; Majestic Theatre (Sept.)   *207 performances*

August 23.

Harold Berg presents

"SMILE AT ME"

Sketches & lyrics by Edward J. Lambert
Music by Gerald Dolin
Directed by Frank Merlin   Dances by Paul Florenz
Settings by Karl Amend   Costumes by Dorothy Van Winkle
Music Director, Mr. Dolin

with

Jack Osterman	Edward J. Lambert	Eddie Bruce
Ruth Edell	Hal Thompson	Avis Andrews
Dorothy Morrison	Jesse Wolk	Gene Fontaine

Musical Numbers
"Smile at Me"—Thompson, Fontaine
"Tired of the South"—Andrews
"There's a Broadway Up in Heaven"—Osterman, company

Fulton Theatre   *27 performances*

September 19.   Messrs. Shubert present
                BEATRICE LILLIE
                            ETHEL WATERS   in

"AT HOME ABROAD"

A Vincente Minnelli Production
Sketches by Howard Dietz, Marc Connelly, Dion Titheradge, Raymond
Knight, Reginald Gardiner
Lyrics by Howard Dietz
Music by Arthur Schwartz
Directed by Vincente Minnelli & Thomas Mitchell   Dances by Gene
Snyder, Harry Losee
Settings & costumes by Vincente Minnelli
Music director, Al Goodman   Orchestrations, Russell Bennett, David
Raksin, Hans Spialek, Donald Walker, Phil Walsh

with

HERB WILLIAMS   ELEANOR POWELL
REGINALD GARDINER   PAUL HAAKON
EDDIE FOY, JR.   VERA ALLEN
Nina Whitney   James MacColl   Woods Miller
The Continentals   6 Spirits of Rhythm   Sue Hastings Marionettes
(Note: Mr. Foy out of cast in Oct. In Nov., Mr. MacColl succeeded
by Jack McCauley; in Jan. 1936, Miss Powell by Mitzi Mayfair.)

Musical Numbers
"That's Not Cricket"—Powell
"Hottentot Potentate"—Waters
"Paree"—Lillie
"Farewell, My Lovely"—Miller; danced by Haakon, Whitney
"The Lady with the Tap"—Powell
"Thief in the Night"—Waters
"O Leo"—Lillie, Williams, company
"Love Is a Dancing Thing"—Miller; danced by Haakon, Whitney
"What a Wonderful World"—Powell, Miller, Marionettes
"Loadin' Time"—Waters, 6 Spirits
"Get Yourself a Geisha"—Lillie
"Got a Bran' New Suit"—Waters, Powell

Winter Garden; Majestic Theatre (Jan. 1936)   *198 performances*

October 10.   The Theatre Guild presents

"PORGY AND BESS"

Book by DuBose Heyward, from play, *Porgy*, by Dorothy & DuBose
Heyward, and novel, *Porgy*, by DuBose Heyward
Lyrics by DuBose Heyward & Ira Gershwin
Music by George Gershwin
Directed by Rouben Mamoulian
Settings by Sergei Soudeikine   Costumes by Theatre Guild Workroom
Music director, Alexander Smallens   Orchestrations, George Gershwin
Choral director, Eva Jessye

with

Todd Duncan   Anne Brown   Warren Coleman
Ford Buck & John Bubbles   Edward Matthews   Ruby Elzy
Abbie Mitchell   Georgette Harvey   Helen Dowdy
J. Rosamond Johnson   Musa Williams (chorus)

Musical Numbers
"Summertime" (Heyward-Gershwin)—Mitchell
"A Woman Is a Sometime Thing" (Heyward-Gershwin)—Matthews, chorus
"Gone, Gone, Gone" (Heyward-Gershwin)—chorus
"My Man's Gone Now" (Heyward-Gershwin)—Elzy, chorus
"It Takes a Long Pull to Get There" (Heyward-Gershwin)—Matthews,
    chorus
"I Got Plenty o' Nuttin'" (Heyward, Gershwin-Gershwin)—Duncan
"Bess, You Is My Woman Now" (Heyward, Gershwin-Gershwin)—Duncan,
    Brown
"Oh, I Can't Sit Down" (Gershwin-Gershwin)—Band, chorus
"It Ain't Necessarily So" (Gershwin-Gershwin)—Bubbles
"What You Want wid Bess?" (Heyward, Gershwin-Gershwin)—Brown,
    Coleman
"I Loves You, Porgy" (Heyward, Gershwin-Gershwin)—Brown, Duncan
"A Red-Headed Woman" (Gershwin-Gershwin)—Coleman, chorus
"There's a Boat dat's Leavin' Soon for New York" (Gershwin-Gershwin)—
    Bubbles
"Oh, Bess, Oh Where's My Bess?" (Gershwin-Gershwin)—Duncan
"I'm on My Way" (Heyward-Gershwin)—Duncan, chorus

Alvin Theatre   *124 performances*

October 12.   Sam H. Harris & Max Gordon present
                MARY BOLAND in

                "JUBILEE"

                Book by Moss Hart
                Lyrics & music Cole Porter
                Directed by Hassard Short & Monty Woolley   Dances by Albertina
                Rasch
                Settings by Jo Mielziner   Costumes by Irene Sharaff, Connie DePinna
                Music director, Frank Tours   Orchestrations, Russell Bennett

                               with

                June Knight   Melville Cooper
                Derek Williams   May Boley   Charles Walters
                Margaret Adams   Mark Plant   Richie Ling   Dorothy Fox
                Olive Reeves-Smith   Jackie Kelk   Montgomery Clift
                Leo Chalzell   Ted Fetter   Wyn Cahoon (chorus)
                Adele Jurgens (chorus)
                (Note: Miss Boland succeeded by Laura Hope Crews in Feb. 1936.)

                Musical Numbers
                "Why Shouldn't I?"—Adams
                "The Kling-Kling Bird on the Divi-Divi Tree"—Williams
                "When Love Comes Your Way"—Williams, Adams
                "Begin the Beguine"—Knight; danced with Walters
                "A Picture of Me Without You"—Knight, Walters
                "Me and Marie"—Cooper, Boland
                "Just One of Those Things"—Knight, Walters

                Imperial Theatre   *169 performances*

1935

November 3.   Greenwich Musical Guild presents

"PROVINCETOWN FOLLIES"

Sketches by Frederick Herendeen, Gwynn Langdon, Barrie Oliver,
George K. Arthur
Lyrics mostly by Frederick Herendeen
Music mostly by Dave Stamper
Directed by Lee Morrison   Dances by Mary Read

with

Barrie Oliver	Beatrice Kay	Phyllis Austen	Billy Green
Marie Alverez	Eileen Graves	Cyril Smith	Wood Hawkins

Musical Numbers
"New Words for an Old Love Song"
"Poor Porgy" (Herendeen–Sylvan Green)
"Red Sails in the Sunset" (James Kennedy–Hugh Williams)—Austen

Provincetown Playhouse   *63 performances*

1935

November 16.   Billy Rose's

"JUMBO"

Book by Ben Hecht & Charles MacArthur
Lyrics by Lorenz Hart
Music by Richard Rodgers
Directed by John Murray Anderson & George Abbott   Dances by
Allan K. Foster
Settings by Albert Johnson   Costumes by Raoul Pène du Bois
Music director, Adolph Deutsch   Orchestrations, Mr. Deutsch,
Murray Cutter, Joseph Nussbaum, Hans Spialek, Conrad Salinger

with

JIMMY DURANTE   PAUL WHITEMAN & HIS ORCHESTRA
Donald Novis   Gloria Grafton   A. P. Kaye   A. Robins
Poodles Hanneford   Bob Lawrence   Arthur Sinclair
George Watts   "Big Rosie"
Lipman Duckatt (Larry Douglas) (chorus)
(Note: Blanche Ring in cast during Oct. previews.)

Musical Numbers
"Over and Over Again"—Lawrence, chorus
"The Circus Is on Parade"—chorus
"The Most Beautiful Girl in the World"—Novis, Grafton
"My Romance"—Novis, Grafton
"Little Girl Blue"—Grafton
(Note: "There's a Small Hotel" cut during previews.)

Hippodrome   *233 performances*

1935

December 5.   Laurence Schwab presents

"MAY WINE"

Book by Frank Mandel, from story, *The Happy Alienist,* by Wallace
Smith & Erich Von Stroheim
Lyrics by Oscar Hammerstein, 2nd
Music by Sigmund Romberg
Directed by José Ruben
Settings by Raymond Sovey   Costumes by Kay Morrison
Music director, Robert Dolan   Orchestrations, Don Walker

with

Walter Woolf King	Nancy McCord	Walter Slezak
Robert C. Fischer	Leo G. Carroll	Vera Van Roy Gordon
Robert Sloane	Maury Tuckerman	Earle MacVeigh
Jack Cole Alice Dudley		

Musical Numbers
"Dance, My Darlings"—McCord
"I Built a Dream One Day"—Slezak, King, Fischer
"Somebody Ought to Be Told"—Van
"Something New Is in My Heart"—McCord; dance by Cole &
     Dudley
"Just Once Around the Clock"—Van, King, Carroll

St. James Theatre   *213 performances*

December 25.   "GEORGE WHITE'S SCANDALS," (12th Edition)

Sketches by George White, Billy K. Wells, Howard Shiebler, A. Dorian Otvos
Lyrics by Jack Yellen
Music by Ray Henderson
Directed by George White   Dances by Russell Markert
Settings by Russell Patterson, Walter Jagemann   Costumes by Charles LeMaire
Music director, Tom Jones   Orchestrations, Russell Bennett, Conrad Salinger

with

RUDY VALLEE   BERT LAHR
WILLIE & EUGENE HOWARD   GRACIE BARRIE
CLIFF EDWARDS   JANE COOPER
Hal Forde   Estelle Jayne   Sam, Ted & Ray   Peggy Moseley
Lois Eckhart   Harold Willard   Apollo Quartet
(Note: Lyda Roberti & Sheila Barrett in cast during tryout. Mr.
Vallee out of cast in March 1936. Willie & Eugene Howard, & Helen
Morgan featured for tour.)

Musical Numbers
"Life Begins at Sweet Sixteen"—Barrie
"Cigarette"—Willard, Eckhart
"I'm the Fellow who Loves You"—Vallee, Barrie, Lahr, W. Howard,
        Eckhart, Moseley
"Pied Piper of Harlem"—Vallee
"May I Have My Gloves?"—Vallee, Moseley
"I've Got to Get Hot"—Barrie

New Amsterdam Theatre   *110 performances*

1936

January 22.   Society of Illustrators & Tom Weatherly present

"THE ILLUSTRATORS' SHOW"

Sketches by Harry Evans, Max Liebman, Hi Alexander, Frank Gabrielson,
David Lesan, Kenneth Webb, Donald Blackwell, Napier Moore, Otto
Soglow
Lyrics mostly by Frank Loesser
Music mostly by Irving Actman
Directed by Tom Weatherly   Dances by Carl Randall
Settings by Arne Lundborg   Costumes by Carl Sidney
Music director, Gene Salzer

with

HELEN LYND   EARL OXFORD   NIELA GOODELLE
GOMEZ & WINONA
Otto Soglow   O. Z. Whitehead   Elizabeth Houston
Don Harden

Musical Numbers
"If You Don't Love Me"—Goodelle, Oxford
"Bang—the Bell Rang"
"A Waltz Was Born in Vienna" (Earle Crooker–Frederick Loewe)—
    Goodelle, Oxford; danced by Gomez & Winona

48th Street Theatre   *5 performances*

315

1936

January 30.

Mrs. Florenz Ziegfeld (Billie Burke) & Messrs. Shubert (uncredited) present

"ZIEGFELD FOLLIES" (1936 Edition)

Sketches by David Freedman
Lyrics by Ira Gershwin
Music by Vernon Duke
Directed by John Murray Anderson & Edward Clark Lilley   Dances by
Robert Alton, George Balanchine
Settings & costumes by Vincente Minnelli
Music director, John McManus   Orchestrations, Hans Spialek, Conrad
Salinger, Russell Bennett, Don Walker

with

FANNIE BRICE
BOB HOPE   GERTRUDE NIESEN   HUGH O'CONNELL
HARRIET HOCTOR   EVE ARDEN   JUDY CANOVA
CHERRY & JUNE PREISSER   JOHN HOYSRADT
Nicholas Brothers   Duke McHale   Rodney McLennan
Stan Kavanaugh   Ben Yost Varsity 8   George Church
JOSEPHINE BAKER

Musical Numbers
"He Hasn't a Thing Except Me"—Brice
"Island in the West Indies"—Niesen; danced by Baker
"Words Without Music"—Niesen; danced by Hoctor
"Maharanee"—Baker, McLennan
"That Moment of Moments"—Niesen, McLennan; danced by Hoctor
"I Can't Get Started"—Hope, Arden
"Modernistic Moe"—Brice

Winter Garden   *115 performances*

Return Engagement: Sept. 14, 1936
FANNIE BRICE   BOBBY CLARK
Alex Harrison & Ruth Fisher   Cherry & June Preisser
Stan Kavanaugh   Gypsy Rose Lee   Cass Daley
Hugh Cameron   Ben Yost Varsity 8
JANE PICKENS

Added Musical Numbers
"Midnight Blue" (Edgar Leslie–Joseph Burke)—Pickens
"You Don't Love Right" (Tot Seymour–Vee Lawnhurst)—Daley

Winter Garden   *112 performances*

1936

April 11. Dwight Deere Wiman presents

"ON YOUR TOES"

Book by Richard Rodgers, Lorenz Hart & George Abbott
Lyrics by Lorenz Hart
Music by Richard Rodgers
Directed by Worthington Miner, George Abbott (uncredited)   Dances
by George Balanchine
Settings by Jo Mielziner   Costumes by Irene Sharaff
Music director, Gene Salzer   Orchestrations, Hans Spialek

with

RAY BOLGER   LUELLA GEAR   TAMARA GEVA
DORIS CARSON   MONTY WOOLLEY
David Morris   Robert Sidney   Demetrios Vilan
Earle MacVeigh   George Church
Edgar Fairchild & Adam Carroll (duo-pianos)

Musical Numbers
"It's Got to Be Love"—Carson, Bolger
"Too Good for the Average Man"—Gear, Woolley
"There's a Small Hotel"—Carson, Bolger
"The Heart Is Quicker than the Eye"—Gear, Bolger
"Quiet Night"—MacVeigh
"Glad to Be Unhappy"—Carson, Morris
"On Your Toes"—Carson, Bolger, Morris
"Slaughter on Tenth Avenue"—danced by Bolger, Geva, Church

Imperial Theatre; Majestic Theatre (Dec.)   **315 performances**

1936

May 19. Leonard Sillman's

"NEW FACES OF 1936"

Sketches by Mindret Lord, Everett Marcy, Edwin Gilbert, Edwin
Meiss, Irvin Graham, Leonard Sillman, Homer Fickett, Joseph Alger,
Mort Lewis
Lyrics by Edwin Gilbert, Bickley Reichner, June Sillman, Everett
Marcy, Edward Heyman, Jean Sothern, Lawrence Harris
Music by Alex Fogarty, Irvin Graham, Forman Bown, Joseph Meyer,
Muriel Pollack, Bud Harris
Directed by Mr. Sillman & Anton Bundsmann   Dances by Ned McGurn
Settings & costumes by Stewart Chaney   Lighting by Feder
Music director, Ray Kavanaugh   Orchestrations, Hans Spialek,
David Raksin

with

Imogene Coca   Jack Smart   Helen Craig   Marion Pearce
Karl Swenson   Billie Haywood   Cliff Allen   Robert Bard
Tom Rutherford   Jack & June Blair   Marsha Norman
Gerry Probst   Nancy Noland   Ralph Blane   George Byron
Rose Dexter   Van Johnson   Winnie Johnson
Gloria Rondell   Melvin Parks   Kathryn Mayfield
Marion Martin   Stretch Johnson   Bobby Johnson
(Note: In Aug., Charles Kemper added to cast & featured with Miss
Coca; in Oct., the Duncan Sisters added & starred.)

Musical Numbers
"You Better Go Now" (Reichner-Graham)—Noland, Rutherford
"It's High Time I Got the Low-Down on You" (Heyman-Meyer)—
    Dexter, W. Johnson, S. Johnson, B. Johnson
"Your Face Is So Familiar" (Gilbert-Fogarty)—Blane

Vanderbilt Theatre   *193 performances*

1936

October 1.

Laurence Rivers, Inc. (Rowland Stebbins) presents
WILLIAM GAXTON   KITTY CARLISLE   in
Erik Charell's

"WHITE HORSE INN"

Book by David Freedman, from German operetta, *Im Weissen Rössl*,
By Hans Müller, Erik Charell, Robert Gilbert (based on farce by
Oskar Blumenthal & G. Kandelburg), & English version by Harry Graham
Lyrics by Irving Caesar
Music mostly by Ralph Benatzky
Directed by Erik Charell   Dances by Max Rivers
Settings by Ernst Stern   Costumes by Irene Sharaff
Music director, Victor Baravalle   Orchestrations, Hans Spialek

with

ROBERT HALLIDAY
Billy House   Carol Stone   Buster West   Frederick Graham
Melissa Mason   Oscar Ragland   Arnold Korff
Alfred Drake (chorus)
(Note: Miss Stone succeeded by Ann Barrie in Feb. 1937.)

Musical Numbers
"I Cannot Live Without Your Love"—Gaxton, Carlisle
"White Horse Inn"—Carlisle, Halliday
"Blue Eyes" (Caesar–Robert Stolz)—Halliday, Stone
"White Sails" (Caesar–Vivian Ellis)—Halliday, Stone
"Leave It to Katarina" (Caesar–Jara Benes)—Carlisle
"In a Little Swiss Chalet" (Norman Zeno–Will Irwin)—West, Mason

(Note: *Im Weissen Rössl* was first presented at the Grosses
Schauspielhaus, Berlin, Nov. 8, 1930. The first English-language
version was presented at the Coliseum, London, April 8, 1931. It
ran 651 performances. The cast included Clifford Mollison, Lea
Seidl, George Gee, & Bruce Carfax.)

Center Theatre   *223 performances*

October 29.   Vinton Freedley presents

J
  I   N
    M   A
      M   M
        Y   R
          D E
          M U
        L   R
      E   A
   H   N
 T   T
E   E

BOB HOPE in

"RED HOT AND BLUE!"

Book by Howard Lindsay & Russel Crouse
Lyrics & music by Cole Porter
Directed by Howard Lindsay   Dances by George Hale
Settings by Donald Oenslager   Costumes by Constance Ripley
Music director, Frank Tours   Orchestrations, Russell Bennett

with

Polly Walters   Paul & Grace Hartman   Forrest Orr
Dorothy Vernon   Thurston Crane   Lew Parker
Vivian Vance   Houston Richards

Musical Numbers
"Ours"—Vernon, Crane
"Down in the Depths (on the Ninetieth Floor)"—Merman
"You've Got Something"—Hope, Merman
"It's De-Lovely"—Merman, Hope
"A Little Skipper from Heaven Above"—Durante
"Ridin' High"—Merman
"The Ozarks Are Calling Me Home" (added)—Merman
"Red, Hot and Blue"—Merman
"You're a Bad Influence on Me"—Merman

(Note: The crossed billing came about because neither star was willing to accept second—or right side—place.)

Alvin Theatre   *183 performances*

1936

November 2.   Jack Kirkland & Sam H. Grisman present

"FORBIDDEN MELODY"

Book & lyrics by Otto Harbach
Music by Sigmund Romberg
Directed by Macklin Megley & José Ruben
Settings by Sergei Soudeikine   Costumes by Ten Eyck
Music director, Robert Dolan   Orchestrations, Donald Walker

with

CARL BRISSON   RUBY MERCER   RUTH WESTON
JOSEPH GREENWALD   JACK SHEEHAN
Leo Chalzel   June Havoc   Arthur Vinton   Lillion Clark
Daniel Harris

Musical Numbers
"Lady in the Window"—Clark, Harris
"You Are All I've Wanted"—Brisson
"No Use Pretending"—Mercer, Brisson

New Amsterdam Theatre   *32 performances*

November 19.   The Group Theatre presents

"JOHNNY JOHNSON"

Play & lyrics by Paul Green
Music by Kurt Weill
Directed by Lee Strasberg
Settings by Donald Oenslager   Costumes by Paul DuPont
Music director, Lehman Engel   Orchestrations, Mr. Weill

with

Russell Collins   Albert Von Dekker   Lee J. Cobb   Art Smith
Gerrit (Tony) Kraber   Robert Lewis   Sanford Meisner
Paula Miller   Joseph Pevney   Roman Bohnen   Will Lee
Elia Kazan   Luther Adler   Jules (John) Garfield
Morris Carnovsky   Phoebe Brand   Grover Burgess
Susanna Senior

Musical Numbers
"Aggie's Song"—Senior
"Johnny's Song"—Collins
"O Heart of Love"—Brand
"On the Rio Grande"—Kraber
"Song of the Guns"—chorus
"Mon Ami, My Friend"—Miller
"Psychiatry Song"—Carnovsky

44th Street Theatre   *68 performances*

1936

November 24. John C. Wilson presents
GERTRUDE LAWRENCE   NOËL COWARD   in

"TONIGHT AT 8:30"

Plays, lyrics & music by Noël Coward
Directed by Mr. Coward
Settings by G. E. Calthrop
Music director, John McManus

with

Joyce Carey   Alan Webb   Moya Nugent
Edward Underdown

Musical Numbers
From *Red Peppers*
"Has Anybody Seen Our Ship?"—Lawrence, Coward
"Men About Town"—Lawrence, Coward
From *Shadow Play*
"Play, Orchestra, Play!"—Coward, Lawrence
"You Were There"—Lawrence, Coward
From *Family Album*
"Here's a Toast"—Coward, Lawrence, cast
"Hearts and Flowers"—Lawrence, Coward

(Note: *Tonight at* 8:30 was comprised of nine one-act plays,
each evening offering a set of three, one of which was always a
musical. The first bill was originally presented at the Phoenix
Theatre, London, Jan. 9, 1936, with Miss Lawrence & Mr. Coward. The
productions, in various combinations of plays, ran 157 performances.)

National Theatre   *118 performances*

1936

December 19. Earl Dancer & J. H. Levy present

"BLACK RHYTHM"

Book, lyrics & music by Donald Heywood
Directed by Earl Dancer & Donald Heywood
Music director, Donald Heywood

with

Avon Long   Jeni LeGon   Joe Byrd   Speedy Wilson
Maude Russell   Walter Richardson   Babe Matthews
Geneva Washington   Wen Talbott Choir   Savoy Lindy Hoppers

Musical Numbers
"Bow Down, Sinners"—Richardson
"Black Rhythm"—Washington, Long
"Here 'Tis"—LeGon

Comedy Theatre   *6 performances*

1936

December 25.

Messrs. Shubert present
BEATRICE LILLIE   BERT LAHR   in
Vincente Minnelli's

"THE SHOW IS ON"

Sketches by David Freedman, Moss Hart
Lyrics by Howard Dietz, Ted Fetter, Lorenz Hart, E. Y. Harburg,
Norman Zeno, Ira Gershwin, Stanley Adams, Herman Hupfeld
Music by Arthur Schwartz, Hoagy Carmichael, Vernon Duke, Richard
Rodgers, Harold Arlen, Will Irwin, Herman Hupfeld, George Gershwin
Directed by Vincente Minnelli & Edward Clark Lilley   Dances by
Robert Alton
Settings & costumes by Vincente Minnelli
Music director, Gordon Jenkins   Orchestrations, Mr. Jenkins

with

REGINALD GARDINER   MITZI MAYFAIR
PAUL HAAKON   GRACIE BARRIE
CHARLES WALTERS   VERA ALLEN
Robert Shafer   Jack McCauley   Evelyn Thawl
Ralph Riggs   Roy Campbell's Continentals
(Note: Gil Lamb in cast during tryout.)

Musical Numbers
"Now" (Fetter-Duke)—Barrie, Shafer; danced by Haakon, Thawl
"Rhythm" (Hart-Rodgers)—Lillie, with Gardiner
"Song of the Woodman" (Haburg-Arlen)—Lahr
"Casanova" (Fetter-Duke)—Barrie; danced by Haakon
"Long as You've Got Your Health" (Harburg, Zeno-Irwin)—Barrie;
     danced by Mayfair, Walters
"Buy Yourself a Balloon" (Hupfeld)—Lillie
"By Strauss" (Gershwin-Gershwin)—Barrie, Shafer; danced by Mayfair
"Little Old Lady" (Adams-Carmichael)—Mayfair, Walters

Winter Garden   *237 performances*

Return Engagement: Sept. 18, 1937
Cast headed by Willie & Eugene Howard, Rose King & Chic York,
Terry Lawlor, Jack Good, Jack McCauley, Demetrios Vilan,
Roy Cropper.

Winter Garden   *17 performances*

January 23.   John & Jerrold Krimsky present

"NAUGHTY-NAUGHT ('00)"

Book by John Van Antwerp (Jerrold Krimsky)
Lyrics by Ted Fetter
Music by Richard Lewine
Directed by Morgan Lewis
Settings by Eugene Dunkel   Costumes by Eaves
Music director, Howard Johnson

with

| Bartlett Robinson | Eleanor Phelps | Leslie Litomy |
| Alexander Clark | Barbara Hunter | Harry Meehan |

Musical Numbers
"Naughty-Naught"—chorus
"Love Makes the World Go Round"—Phelps, Robinson
"Zim Zam Zee"—Hunter, chorus

American Music Hall   *173 performances*

1937

February 4.

Messrs. Shubert present

DENNIS KING HELEN GLEASON ERNEST TRUEX

in

"FREDERIKA"

Book & lyrics by Edward Eliscu, from German operetta, *Friederike*,
by Ludwig Hezer & Fritz Löhner, & English version, *Frederica*,
by Adrian Ross & Harry Pepper
Music by Franz Lehár
Directed by Hassard Short Dances by Chester Hale
Settings by Watson Barratt Costumes by William Weaver
Music director, Hilding Anderson Orchestrations, William Challis

with

George Trabert Arthur Vinton Doris Patston Edith King
Edith Gresham Charles Columbus Todd Bolender (chorus)

Musical Numbers
"Rising Star"—King, Trabert
"One"—Gleason
"Why Did You Kiss My Heart Awake?"—Gleason

(Note: *Friederike* was first presented at the Metropol Theatre, Berlin,
Oct. 4, 1928, with the cast headed by Richard Tauber and Kathe Dorsch.
The first English-language version, *Frederica*, was presented at the
Palace Theatre, London, Sept. 9, 1930. The cast included Joseph
Hislop and Lea Seidl.)

Imperial Theatre *95 performances*

1937

April 14.   Dwight Deere Wiman presents

"BABES IN ARMS"

Book by Richard Rodgers & Lorenz Hart
Lyrics by Lorenz Hart
Music by Richard Rodgers
Directed by Robert Sinclair   Dances by George Balanchine
Settings by Raymond Sovey   Costumes by Helene Pons
Music director, Gene Salzer   Orchestrations, Hans Spialek

with

MITZI GREEN
RAY HEATHERTON   DUKE McHALE
WYNN MURRAY   HAROLD & FAYARD NICHOLAS
Rolly Pickert   Grace McDonald   Ray McDonald
Alfred Drake   Aljan de Loville   George E. Mack
Ethel Intropidi   George Watts   Aileen Poe   Alex Courtney
Clifton Darling   James Gillis   Robert Rounseville
Dan Dailey (chorus)   Bronson Dudley (chorus)
Edgar Fairchild & Adam Carroll (duo-pianos)
(Note: Miss Green succeeded by Evelyn Wyckoff for tour.)

Musical Numbers
"Where or When"—Green, Heatherton
"Babes in Arms"—Green, Heatherton, Drake, chorus
"I Wish I Were in Love Again"—G. McDonald, Pickert
"Way Out West"—Murray, Courtney, Darling, Gillis, Rounseville
"My Funny Valentine"—Green
"Johnny One Note"—Murray; danced by Green, McHale
"Imagine"—Murray, Courtney, Darling, Gillis, Rounseville
"All at Once"—Green, Heatherton
"The Lady Is a Tramp"—Green

Shubert Theatre; Majestic Theatre (Oct.)   *289 performances*

1937

Charles H. Abramson presents

"ORCHIDS PREFERRED"

Book & lyrics by Frederick Herendeen
Music by Dave Stamper
Directed by Alex Leftwich   Dances by Robert Sanford
Settings by Frederick Fox   Costumes by Jenkins
Music director, Louis Gress   Orchestrations, Paul Sprosty

with

Eddie Foy, Jr.	Benay Venuta	Jack Whitredge
Vicki Cummings	Hilda Knight	Frances Thress
Men of Gotham	Leslie Austin	Walton & Joanne
John Donaldson	Cela Krebs	

(Note: Miss Krebs replaced Ethel Barrymore Colt during tryout.)

Musical Numbers
"I'm Leaving the Bad Girls for Good"—Foy
"Boy, Girl, Moon"—Cummings, Donaldson
"What Are You Going to Do About Love?"—Venuta

Imperial Theatre   *7 performances*

May 18.

Albert Bannister & J. Edmund Byrne present
DOROTHY STONE   CHARLES COLLINS   ROSCO ATES
in

"SEA LEGS"

Book & lyrics by Arthur Swanstrom, from play, *The Cat Came Back*,
by Lawrence E. Johnson, Beula King & Avery Hopwood
Music by Michael H. Cleary
Directed by Bertram Harrison   Dances by Johnny Mattison
Settings by Mabel Buell   Costumes by Brooks, Jay-Thorpe
Music director, Frank Cork   Orchestrations, Joseph Jordan

with

Rosie Moran   Mary Sargent   Kathryn Mayfield
Charles King   Deedee   Ben Yost's Catalina Eight
Patricia Knight

Musical Numbers
"The Opposite Sex"—King, Deedee, Right, Catalina 8
"Ten O'Clock Town"—Collins, Stone, Catalina 8
"Touched in the Head"—Collins, Stone

Mansfield Theatre   *15 performances*

1937

June 16. **"THE CRADLE WILL ROCK"**

Book, lyrics & music by Marc Blitzstein
Directed by Orson Welles
Lighting by Feder
Piano, Mr. Blitzstein

with

Howard DaSilva	Will Geer	John Adair	Hiram Sherman
Peggy Coudray	Olive Stanton	Blanche Collins	
Frank Marvel	John Hoysradt	Dulce Fox	
George Fairchild	Marian Rudley	Edward Fuller	
Bert Weston	Hansford Wilson	Marc Blitzstein	

Musical Numbers
"Croon-Spoon"—Sherman, Fox
"The Freedom of the Press"—Geer, Weston
"Honolulu"—Sherman, Fox, Weston, Geer
"The Rich"—Fuller, Hoysradt
"Art for Art's Sake"—Fuller, Hoysradt
"Nickel Under the Foot"—Stanton
"The Cradle Will Rock"—DaSilva
"Joe Worker"—Collins

(Note: *The Cradle Will Rock* was originally to have been presented by the WPA Federal Theatre Project [John Houseman, producer], but government sponsorship was withdrawn following the June 15, 1937, dress rehearsal.)

Venice Theatre   *19 performances*

Special Engagement: Dec. 5, 1937
Presented by the Mercury Theatre

Mercury (formerly Comedy) Theatre   *Sunday evenings only*

First Regular Run: Jan. 3, 1938
Presented by Sam H. Grisman, with The Mercury Theatre

Windsor Theatre; Mercury Theatre (Feb. 28)   *108 performances*

July 22.   WPA Variety Theatre (Frank Merlin, producer) presents

"SWING IT"

Book by Cecil Mack
Lyrics by Cecil Mack & Milton Reddie
Music by Eubie Blake
Directed by Cecil Mack & Jack Mason   Dances by Benny Johnson,
Miriam Schiller
Settings by Walter Walden   Costumes by Alexander Jones
Music director, Lorenzo Caldwell   Orchestrations, Mr. Caldwell

with

Genora English	James Mordecai	George Booker
Frances Everett	Marion Brantley	Olena Williams
Edward Frye	James Boxwell	

Musical Numbers
"Shine" (Lew Brown, Mack–Ford Dabney)—chorus
"By the Sweat of Your Brow"—Boxwell
"Huggin' and Muggin' "—English, Mordecai

Adelphi Theatre   *60 performances*

September 2. The Center Theatre (John Kenneth Hyatt, director) presents

"VIRGINIA"

Book by Laurence Stallings, Owen Davis
Lyrics by Laurence Stallings & Albert Stillman
Music by Arthur Schwartz
Directed by Leon Leonidoff & Edward Clark Lilley   Dances by
Florence Rogge
Settings by Lee Simonson   Costumes by Irene Sharaff
Music director, John McManus   Orchestrations, Hans Spialek, Phil
Wall, Will Vodery
(Note: During run, book rewritten & restaged by Harry Wagstaff
Gribble.)

with

Anne Booth   Nigel Bruce   Gene Lockhart   Mona Barrie
Ronald Graham   Bertha Belmore   Dennis Hoey
Ford L. Buck & John W. Bubbles   Patricia Bowman
Avis Andrews   Gordon Richards   Lansing Hatfield
Valia Valentinoff   Billy Redfield (chorus)   Nora Kaye (chorus)

Musical Numbers
"An Old Flame Never Dies"—Booth
"Send One Angel Down"—Andrews
"If You Were Someone Else" (Stillman-Schwartz)—Graham
"Goodbye, Jonah" (Stillman-Schwartz)—Buck & Bubbles
"My Heart Is Dancing" (Stillman-Schwartz)—Booth; danced by Bowman
"You and I Know"—Booth, Graham
"I'll Be Sittin' in de Lap of the Lord" (Stillman-Schwartz)—
     Andrews, Buck & Bubbles

Center Theatre   *60 performances*

October 1.   WPA Federal Theatre presents

"A HERO IS BORN"

Book by Theresa Helburn, from story by Andrew Lang
Lyrics by Agnes Morgan
Music by A. Lehman Engel
Directed by Agnes Morgan
Settings by Tom Adrian Cracroft   Costumes by Alexander Jones
Music director, Alexander Saron   Orchestrations, Mr. Saron

with

Margaret Wycherley   Frederic Tozere   Edward Forbes
Marjorie Brown   Helen Morrow   John Furman
Drue Leyton   Ben Starkie   William Phelps

Musical Numbers
"Woe Is Me"—Brown, Morrow
"Fiddle Dee Dee"—Wycherley, Tozere
"A Love-Lorn Maid"—Forbes

Adelphi Theatre   *50 performances*

October 9.   John & Jerrold Krimsky present

"THE FIREMAN'S FLAME"

Book by John Van Antwerp (Jerrold Krimsky)
Lyrics by Ted Fetter
Music by Richard Lewine
Directed by Morgan Lewis
Settings by Eugene Dunkel   Costumes by Kermit Love
Music director, Al Evans   Orchestrations, Ben Ludlow

with

Ben Cutler   Cynthia Rogers   Philip Bourneuf
Alan Handley   Rose Lieder   Isham Keith   Grace Coppin
Harry Meehan

Musical Numbers
"Doin' the Waltz"—Coppin
"Do My Eyes Deceive Me?"—Rogers, Cutler
"It's a Lovely Night on the Hudson River"—Cutler, Rogers

American Music Hall   *204 performances*

November 2. Sam H. Harris presents
GEORGE M. COHAN in

"I'D RATHER BE RIGHT"

Book by George S. Kaufman & Moss Hart
Lyrics by Lorenz Hart
Music by Richard Rodgers
Directed by George S. Kaufman Dances by Charles Weidman,
Ned McGurn
Settings by Donald Oenslager Costumes by Irene Sharaff, John
Hambleton
Music director, Harry Levant Orchestrations, Hans Spialek

with

Taylor Holmes	Joy Hodges	Joseph Macaulay
Austin Marshall	Florenz Ames	Marion Green
Bijou Fernandez	Irene McBride	Mary Jane Walsh
Georgie Tapps	Margaret Sande	Marie Nash (chorus)

Musical Numbers
"Have You Met Miss Jones?"—Marshall, Hodges
"Take and Take and Take"—Walsh; danced by McBride
"A Little Bit of Constitutional Fun"—Walsh, chorus
"Sweet Sixty-Five"—Hodges, Marshall; danced by Tapps
"We're Going to Balance the Budget"—Cohan, chorus
"I'd Rather Be Right"—Hodges, Marshall, Walsh, Cohan
"Off the Record"—Cohan

Alvin Theatre; Music Box Theatre (May 1938)

290 performances

1937

November 27.   Labor Stage, Inc., presents

"PINS AND NEEDLES"

Sketches by Charles Friedman, Arthur Arent, David Gregory, Emanuel
Eisenberg, Marc Blitzstein
Lyrics & music by Harold J. Rome
Directed by Charles Friedman   Dances by Benjamin Zemach, Gluck
Sandor
Settings by Sointu Syrjala
Pianos, Baldwin Bergersen & Harold J. Rome
(Note: By May 1938, Robert H. Gordon credited for direction, Adele
Jerome for dances. By April 1939, dances credited to Felicia
Sorel. By Nov., all sketches credited to Joseph Schrank.)

with

ILGWU PLAYERS
Millie Weitz   Ruth Rubinstein   Al Levy   Lynne Jaffee
Nettie Harary   Hy Goldstein   Paul Seymour   Enzo Grassi
Al Eben   Murray Modick
(Note: Original company toured from March to Dec. 1938, &
temporarily replaced by second company in New York. Cast included
Irwin Corey & Berni Gould. Harry Clark joined original company
for tour & return.)

Musical Numbers
"Sing Me a Song with Social Significance"—chorus
"Sunday in the Park"—company
"Nobody Makes a Pass at Me"—Weitz
"Chain Store Daisy"—Rubinstein
"One Big Union for Two"—chorus
"Four Little Angels of Peace"—Goldstein, Eben, Modick, Seymour
"Doin' the Reactionary"—Harary, Levy
"I've Got the Nerve to Be in Love" (added April 1939)—Ruth
    Elbaum, Levy
"The Red Mikado" (added April 1939)—company
"Mene Mene Tekel" (added July 1939)—Dorothy Harrison
"The Harmony Boys" (added Oct. 1939)—Eben, Gould, Clark
"It's Better with a Union Man" (added Nov. 1939)—Clark
"We Sing America" (added Nov. 1939)—company

(Note: In April 1939, title changed to *Pins and Needles 1939*;
in Sept., to *Pins and Needles 1940*; in Nov., to *New Pins and
Needles*.)

**Labor Stage (formerly Princess Theatre); Windsor Theatre
(June 1939)   1,108 performances**

December 1. Messrs. Shubert present
ED WYNN in

"HOORAY FOR WHAT!"

Book by Howard Lindsay & Russel Crouse, from idea by E. Y. Harburg
Lyrics by E. Y. Harburg
Music by Harold Arlen
Directed by Howard Lindsay Dances by Robert Alton, Agnes de Mille
Settings by Vincente Minnelli Costumes by Raoul Pène du Bois
Music director, Robert Emmett Dolan Orchestrations, Don Walker
Vocal arrangements, Kay Thompson, Hugh Martin
(Note: During tryout, Miss de Mille received credit for all dances.)

with

PAUL HAAKON
JUNE CLYDE VIVIAN VANCE
JACK WHITING
The Briants Sue Hastings Marionettes Al Gordon's Dogs
5 Reillys Leo Chalzel Robert Shafer Ruthanna Boris
Detmar Poppen Hugh Martin Ralph Blane Harold Cook
John Smedberg Meg Mundy (chorus)
(Note: During tryout, Miss Clyde replaced Hannah Williams, Miss
Vance replaced Kay Thompson. In March 1938, Miss Clyde succeeded
by Dorothy Stone, Mr. Whiting by Charles Collins.)

Musical Numbers
"God's Country"—Whiting, Reillys
"I've Gone Romantic on You"—Whiting, Clyde
"Moanin' in the Mornin'"—Vance
"Down with Love"—Whiting, Clyde, Vance
"In the Shade of the New Apple Tree"—Whiting, Clyde, with Blane,
  Martin, Cook, Smedberg
(Note: "Buds Won't Bud," sung by Hannah Williams, cut during
tryout.)

Winter Garden *200 performances*

December 22.   Messrs. Shubert present
JACK BUCHANAN
EVELYN LAYE   ADELE DIXON   in

"BETWEEN THE DEVIL"

Book & lyrics by Howard Dietz
Music by Arthur Schwartz
Directed by Hassard Short, Edward Duryea Dowling, Fred DeCordoba
(uncredited) & John Hayden   Dances by Robert Alton
Settings by Albert Johnson   Costumes by Kiviette
Music director, Don Voorhees
(Note: Mr. Hayden replaced Edward Clark Lilley during tryout.)

with

CHARLES WALTERS   VILMA EBSEN
WILLIAM KENDALL
The Debonairs   The Tune Twisters   Noel Cravat
Eric Brotherson (chorus)
(Note: Mr. Kendall replaced Leo G. Carroll during tryout.)

Musical Numbers
"I See Your Face Before Me"—Laye; reprised by Dixon, Buchanan
"Triplets"—Tune Twisters
"You Have Everything"—Walters, Ebsen
"By Myself"—Buchanan
"I'm Against Rhythm"—Walters, Ebsen

Imperial Theatre   *93 performances*

December 25.   Messrs. Shubert present
KITTY CARLISLE   MICHAEL BARTLETT   in

"THREE WALTZES"

Book by Clare Kummer & Rowland Leigh, from Viennese operetta, *Drei Walzer*, by Paul Knepler & Armin Robinson
Lyrics by Clare Kummer
Music by Johann Strauss, Sr., Johann Strauss, Jr., Oscar Straus
Directed by Hassard Short   Dances by Chester Hale
Settings by Watson Barratt   Costumes by Connie DePinna
Music director, Harold Levey   Orchestrations, Conrad Salinger,
Hilding Anderson, Don Walker

with

GLENN ANDERS   ANN ANDREWS
Rosie Moran
John Barker   Victor Morley   Marguerita Sylva
Marion Pierce   Charlie Arnt   Ruth MacDonald (Ruth Hammond)
Ivy Scott   Louis Sorin   Harry Mestayer
Jayne Manners (chorus)
(Note: During tryout, Miss Carlisle replaced Margaret Bannerman.
In March 1938, Miss Pierce succeeded by Miss Manners.)

Musical Numbers
"Springtime in the Air" (Kummer-Strauss, Sr.)—Bartlett
"To Love Is to Live" (Kummer, Strauss, Jr.)—Carlisle, Bartlett
"Our Last Valse" (Kummer-Straus)—Carlisle, Bartlett

(Note: *Drei Walzer* was first presented in Zurich, Oct. 5, 1935.)

Majestic Theatre   *122 performances*

1938

January 4.   Alice Alexander presents

"RIGHT THIS WAY"

Book by Marianne Brown Waters, Parke Levy, Allan Lipscott
Lyrics by Marianne Brown Waters, Irving Kahal
Music by Bradford Greene, Sammy Fain
Directed by Bertrand Robinson   Dances by Marjery Fielding
Settings by Nat Karson   Costumes by Miles White
Music director, Max Meth   Orchestrations, Hans Spialek, Maurice
DePackh, Claude Austin

with

GUY ROBERTSON   TAMARA   JOE E. LEWIS
BLANCHE RING   LEONA POWERS   THELMA WHITE
Jack Williams   April   Henry Arthur

Musical Numbers
"I Can Dream, Can't I?" (Kahal-Fain)—Tamara
"Tip Your Hat" (Waters-Greene)—Ring
"I'll Be Seeing You" (Kahal-Fain)—Tamara

46th Street Theatre   *15 performances*

1938

March 1.

Elsa Maxwell presents
Leonard Sillman's

"WHO'S WHO"

Sketches by Everett Marcy, Leonard Sillman
Lyrics by June Sillman, Neville Fleeson, James Shelton
Music by Baldwin Bergersen, Irvin Graham, James Shelton, Lew Kessler,
Paul McGrane
Directed by Leonard Sillman
Settings by Mercedes   Costumes by Billi Livingston
Music director, Earl Busby   Orchestrations, Richard DuPage

with

Imogene Coca	Rags Ragland	Lotte Goslar
Michael Loring	June Sillman	James Shelton
Mildred Todd	Jack & June Blair	Leone Sousa
Edna Russell	Joseph Beale	Johnnie Tunsill
Chet & Mort O'Brien	Bowen Charleton (Sonny Tufts)	

Musical Numbers
"Rinka Tinka Man" (Sillman-Kessler)—Russell, Tunsill
"Sunday Morning in June" (Fleeson-McGrane)—Blairs
"I Dance Alone" (Shelton)—Shelton
"Train Time" (Sillman-Bergersen)—Sillman, Loring

Hudson Theatre   *23 performances*

May 11.

Dwight Deere Wiman presents
DENNIS KING   VERA ZORINA
VIVIENNE SEGAL   WALTER SLEZAK   in

"I MARRIED AN ANGEL"

Book by Richard Rodgers & Lorenz Hart, from Hungarian play by Janos Vaszary
Lyrics by Lorenz Hart
Music by Richard Rodgers
Directed by Joshua Logan   Dances by George Balanchine
Settings by Jo Mielziner   Costumes by John Hambleton
Music director, Gene Salzer   Orchestrations, Hans Spialek

with

AUDREY CHRISTIE   CHARLES WALTERS
Morton L. Stevens   Charles Laskey   Casper Reardon (harpist)
(Note: During tour, Miss Zorina succeeded by Karen Van Ryn,
Miss Christie by Bobbe Arnst, Mr. Walters by Dan Dailey.)

Musical Numbers
"Did You Ever Get Stung?"—King, Segal, Walters
"I Married an Angel"—King
"I'll Tell the Man in the Street"—Segal, Slezak
"How to Win Friends and Influence People"—Christie, Walters
"Spring Is Here"—King, Segal
"A Twinkle in Your Eye"—Segal
"At the Roxy Music Hall"—Christie, company

Shubert Theatre   338 *performances*

1938

May 31.

Marc Connelly with Bela Blau, presents

"THE TWO BOUQUETS"

Book & lyrics by Eleanor & Herbert Farjeon
Music by uncredited Victorian composers
Directed by Mr. Connelly   Dances by Leslie French, Felicia Sorel
Settings by Robert Barnhart   Costumes by Raoul Pène du Bois
Music director, Macklin Marrow

with

Leo G. Carroll	Viola Roache	Leslie French
Gabrielle Brune	Robert Chisholm	Marcy Westcott
Winston O'Keefe	Patricia Morison	Alfred Drake
Enid Markey	Joan Wetmore	Jane Archer
John Tyers (chorus)	Robert Rounseville (chorus)	

Musical Numbers
"Bashful Lover" (Farjeon–C. Moulton)—Drake
"Sweet Blossoms" (Farjeon–M. Pinsuti)—Morison, Westcott
"Toddy's the Drink for Me" (Farjeon-traditional)—Chisholm

(Note: *The Two Bouquets* first presented at the Ambassador's Theatre, London, Aug. 13, 1936. It ran for 301 performances.)

Windsor Theatre   *55 performances*

September 21. Messrs. Shubert, with John Shubert, present
CLIFTON WEBB
LUPE VELEZ   LIBBY HOLMAN
PAUL & GRACE HARTMAN   in

"YOU NEVER KNOW"

Book by Rowland Leigh, from Viennese musical comedy, *Bei Kerzenlicht,* by Karl Farkas & Robert Katscher (based on play by Siegfried Geyer)
Lyrics & music mostly by Cole Porter
Directed by Rowland Leigh   Dances by Robert Alton
Settings by Albert Johnson, Watson Barratt   Costumes by Jenkins, Wilma, Veronica, Brooks, Charles LeMaire
Music director, John McManus   Orchestrations, Hans Spialek

with

TOBY WING
Charles Kemper   The Debonairs   Don Harden
Roger Stearns   Truman Gaige   Jean Morehead
REX O'MALLEY
JUNE PREISSER

Musical Numbers
"By Candlelight" (Leigh-Katscher)—Webb, O'Malley; reprised by Webb, Velez
"Maria"—Webb; danced with Morehead
"You Never Know"—Holman
"What Is That Tune?"—Holman
"For No Rhyme or Reason"—Wing, Kemper, Debonairs; danced by Hartmans
"From Alpha to Omega"—Webb, Velez
"What Shall I Do?"—Velez
"At Long Last Love"—Webb
"No" (Dana Suesse)—Holman, Webb

(Note: *Bei Kerzenlicht* first presented at the Deutsche Volkstheatre, Vienna, April 30, 1937.)

Winter Garden   78 *performances*

September 22.   Olsen & Johnson present

"HELLZAPOPPIN"

Sketches by Ole Olsen & Chic Johnson; additional dialogue by Tom
McKnight
Lyrics mostly by Charles Tobias
Music mostly by Sammy Fain
Directed by Edward Duryea Dowling
Costumes by Veronica & Mahieu
Music director, Harold Stern   Vocal arrangements, Phil Ellis

with

OLE OLSEN & CHIC JOHNSON
DEWEY BARTO & GEORGE MANN
THE RADIO ROGUES   HAL SHERMAN
RAY KINNEY & ALOHA MAIDS
WALTER NILSSON   THE CHARIOTEERS
BETTYMAE & BEVERLY CRANE   THEO HARDEEN
The Starlings   Reed, Dean & Reed   Shirley Wayne
Whitey's Steppers
(Note: In June 1940, Messrs. Olsen & Johnson succeeded by Happy
Felton & J. C. Flippen.)

Musical Numbers
"Fuddle Dee Duddle"—Bonnie & Mel Reed; danced by Cranes
"Abe Lincoln" (Alfred Hayes–Earl Robinson)—Charioteers
"It's Time to Say 'Aloha' "—Starlings, Cranes
"Boomps-a-Daisy" (Annette Mills; added during run)—chorus

(Note: By June 1941, title changed to *The New Hellzapoppin*.)

46th Street Theatre; Winter Garden (Nov.)   *1,404 performances*

September 24. Max Gordon, with George S. Kaufman & Moss Hart, presents

"SING OUT THE NEWS"

Sketches by George S. Kaufman & Moss Hart (uncredited)
Lyrics & music by Harold J. Rome
Diected by Charles Friedman   Dances by Ned McGurn, Dave Gould,
Charles Walters
Settings by Jo Mielziner   Costumes by John Hambleton
Music director, Max Meth   Orchestrations, Hans Spialek

with

PHILIP LOEB   HIRAM SHERMAN   MARY JANE WALSH
WILL GEER   DOROTHY FOX
Rex Ingram   Michael Loring   Ginger Manners
Leslie Litomy   Joey Faye   Christina Lind   Benjamin Wailes
June Allyson (chorus)   Hazel Scott (chorus)
Richard Huey (chorus)

Musical Numbers
"How Long Can Love Keep Laughing?"—Loring, Lind
"Plaza 6-9423"—Sherman
"My Heart Is Unemployed"—Walsh, Loring
"Yip-Ahoy"—Loeb
"F.D.R. Jones"—Ingram

Music Box Theatre   *105 performances*

1938

October 19.

The Playwrights Co. presents
WALTER HUSTON   in

"KNICKERBOCKER HOLIDAY"

Book & lyrics by Maxwell Anderson
Music by Kurt Weill
Directed by Joshua Logan   Dances by Carl Randall, Edwin Denby
Settings by Jo Mielziner   Costumes by Frank Bevan
Music director, Maurice d'Abravanel   Orchestrations, Mr. Weill

with

Jeanne Madden   Ray Middleton   Richard Kollmar
Mark Smith   Clarence Nordstrom   Howard Freeman
Francis Pierlot   George Watts   Robert Rounseville (chorus)

Musical Numbers
"It Never Was You"—Kollmar, Madden
"How Can You Tell an American?"—Kollmar, Middleton
"September Song"—Huston
"There's Nowhere to Go but Up"—Kollmar, Nordstrom, chorus
"The Scars"—Huston

Ethel Barrymore Theatre   *168 performances*

1938

Otober 29. John & Jerrold Krimsky present

"THE GIRL FROM WYOMING"

Book by J. Van Ostend Van Antwerp (Jerrold Krimsky)
Lyrics by Ted Fetter
Music by Richard Lewine
Directed by Robert Ross   Dances by John Pierce
Settings by Eugene Dunkel   Costumes by Peggy Clark
Music director, Al Evans   Orchestrations, Ben Ludlow

with

Philip Huston   June Walker   George Petrie   Anne Hunter
Tony Kraber   James Russo   Jackie Susann (chorus)

Musical Numbers
"Boston in the Spring"—Huston
"The Dying Cowboy"—Petrie, Kraber
"Stay East, Young Man"—Huston

American Music Hall   *86 performances*

1938

November 9.
Vinton Freedley presents
WILLIAM GAXTON   VICTOR MOORE   in

"LEAVE IT TO ME!"

Book by Bella & Samuel Spewack, from their play, *Clear All Wires*
Lyrics & music by Cole Porter
Directed by Mr. Spewack   Dances by Robert Alton
Settings by Albert Johnson   Costumes by Raoul Pène du Bois
Music director, Max Meth   Orchestrations, Donald J. Walker

with

SOPHIE TUCKER   TAMARA
Mary Martin   Edward H. Robins   Alexander Asro
George Tobias   Walter Armin   Joseph Kallini   Gene Kelly
April   Kay Picture   George E. Mack   Adele Jergens (chorus)
(Note: By Feb 1939, Miss Martin received feature billing.)

Musical Numbers
"Get Out of Town"—Tamara
"Most Gentlemen Don't Like Love"—Tucker
"From Now On"—Gaxton, Tamara
"I Want to Go Home"—Moore
"My Heart Belongs to Daddy"—Martin
"Tomorrow"—Tucker, chorus
"Far, Far Away"—Gaxton, Tamara

Imperial Theatre   *291 performances*

Return Engagement: Sept. 4, 1939
Miss Martin succeeded by Mildred Fenton

Imperial Theatre   *16 performances*

November 23.   George Abbott presents

"THE BOYS FROM SYRACUSE"

Book by George Abbott, from play, *The Comedy of Errors*, by William Shakespeare
Lyrics by Lorenz Hart
Music by Richard Rodgers

Directed by Mr. Abbott	Dances by Robert Alton
Settings by Jo Mielziner	Costumes by Irene Sharaff
Music director, Harry Levant	Orchestrations, Hans Spialek

with

Jimmy Savo	Wynn Murray	Eddie Albert
Muriel Angelus	Teddy Hart	Marcy Westcott
Ronald Graham	Betty Bruce	
Bob Lawrence	Heidi Vosseler	George Church
Robert Sidney	Burl Ives	Dolores Anderson

(Note: In May 1939, Mr. Albert succeeded by Mr. Graham, Mr. Graham by Mr. Lawrence.)

Musical Numbers
"Dear Old Syracuse"—Savo, Albert
"What Can You Do With a Man?—Murray, Hart
"Falling in Love with Love"—Angelus
"The Shortest Day of the Year"—Graham, Anderson; danced by
    Bruce, Vosseler, Church
"This Can't Be Love"—Westcott, Albert
"He and She"—Murray, Savo
"You Have Cast Your Shadow on the Sea"—Westcott, Albert
"Sing for Your Supper"—Angelus, Westcott, Murray; danced by Bruce
"Oh, Diogenes"—Murray; danced by Church, Bruce

Alvin Theatre   *235 performances*

1938

December 1.   Dwight Deere Wiman & J. H. Del Bondio present

"GREAT LADY"

Book by Earle Crooker & Lowell Brentano
Lyrics by Earle Crooker
Music by Frederick Loewe
Directed by Bretaigne Windust   Dances by William Dollar
Settings by Albert Johnson   Costumes by Lucinda Ballard, Scott
Wilson
Music director, John Fredhoven   Orchestrations, Hans Spialek

with

NORMA TERRIS   TULLIO CARMINATI
IRENE BORDONI   HELEN FORD
JOSEPH MACAULAY   SHEPPERD STRUDWICK
Annabelle Lyon   Leda Anchutina   André Eglevsky
Robert Shanley   Dorothy Kirsten   Walter Cassel
Alicia Alonzo (chorus)   Nora Kaye (chorus)
Jerome Robbins (chorus)   Paul Godkin (chorus)

Musical Numbers
"I Have Room in My Heart"—Terris, Strudwick
"May I Suggest Romance?"—Bordoni
"There Had to Be the Waltz"—Terris, Strudwick

Majestic Theatre   *20 performances*

1939

January 18. John C. Wilson presents
BEATRICE LILLIE in

"SET TO MUSIC"

Sketches, lyrics & music by Noël Coward
Directed by Mr. Coward
Settings & costumes by G. E. Calthrop
Music director, John McManus   Orchestrations, Hans Spialek

with

Richard Haydn   Penelope Dudley Ward   Maidie Andrews
Hugh French   Eva Ortega   Angus Menzies   Kenneth Carten
Antony Pelissier   Gladys Henson   Moya Nugent
Laura Duncan

Musical Numbers
"Mad About the Boy"*—Ward, Henson, Duncan, Lillie
"The Stately Homes of England" (originally in *Operette*)—French,
    Menzies, Carten, Pelissier
"I'm So Weary Of It All"—Lillie
"Children of the Ritz"*—Ortega
"Never Again"—Ortega, French
"Three White Feathers"*—Lillie
"I've Been to a Marvelous Party"—Lillie
"The Party's Over Now"*—Ward, French

* Originally in *Words and Music*

(Note: *Set to Music* was an American version of *Words and Music*,
first presented at the Adelphi Theatre, London, Sept. 16, 1932.
It ran 164 performances. The cast included Ivy St. Helier, John
Mills, Edward Underdown, Romney Brent, Steffi Duna, Joyce Barbour,
Graham Payn, Moya Nugent, Norah Howard.)

Music Box Theatre   *129 performances*

1939

February 4. Gertrude Macy & Stanley Gilkey, with Robert F. Cutler, present

"ONE FOR THE MONEY"

Sketches & lyrics by Nancy Hamilton
Music by Morgan Lewis
Directed by John Murray Anderson & Edward Clark Lilley   Dances by
Robert Alton
Settings & costumes by Raoul Pène du Bois
Music director, Ray Kavanaugh   Orchestrations, Hans Spialek

with

Brenda Forbes   Nancy Hamilton   Ruth Matteson
Grace McDonald   Frances Comstock   Philip Bourneuf
Alfred Drake   Nell O'Day   Gene Kelly   Robert Smith
Don Loper & Maxine Barrat   Nadine Gae   Keenan Wynn
George Lloyd   William Archibald
(Note: During summer theatre run in Sept. 1938, cast headed by
Rose Hobart, Alan Hewitt, Isham Keith, Patti Pickens. Hugh Martin
& Joe Moon played duo-pianos.)

Musical Numbers
"Rhapsody"—Drake, Matteson; danced by Loper & Barrat,
    McDonald & Kelly, Gae & Archibald
"Teeter Totter Tessie"—McDonald, Kelly, company
"I Only Know"—Drake, Comstock
"I Hate Spring" (Hamilton-Caples; added during run)—Forbes

Booth Theatre   *132 performances*

1939

February 9. Dwight Deere Wiman presents
ETHEL MERMAN   JIMMY DURANTE   in

"STARS IN YOUR EYES"

Book by J. P. McEvoy
Lyrics by Dorothy Fields
Music by Arthur Schwartz
Directed by Joshua Logan   Dances by Carl Randall
Settings by Jo Mielziner   Costumes by John Hambleton
Music director, Al Goodman   Orchestrations, Hans Spialek, Donald
J. Walker, Al Goodman

with

TAMARA TOUMANOVA   RICHARD CARLSON
Mildred Natwick
Robert Ross   Ted Gary   Dan Dailey, Jr.   Roger Stearns
Clinton Sundberg   Mary Wickes   Robert Shanley
Edward Kane   Davis Cunningham   Nancy Wiman
Walter Cassel   David Morris   Alicia Alonzo (chorus)
Nora Kaye (chorus)   Maria Karniloff (chorus)
Jerome Robbins (chorus)   Paul Godkin (chorus)

Musical Numbers
"This Is It"—Merman, with Cassel, Shanley, Kane, Cunningham
"All the Time"—Carlson, Toumanova
"A Lady Needs a Change"—Merman
"Terribly Attractive"—Durante, Natwick
"Just a Little Bit More"—Merman; reprised by Carlson
"I'll Pay the Check"—Merman
"It's All Yours"—Merman, Durante

Majestic Theatre   *127 performances*

February 11.   Lew Leslie's

"BLACKBIRDS OF 1939"

Sketches by Lew Leslie
Lyrics by Johnny Mercer, Mitchell Parish, Dorothy Sachs, Irving
Taylor
Music by George Gershwin, Sammy Fain, Louis Haber, Vic Mizzy,
Rube Bloom
Directed by Lew Leslie   Dances by Eugene Van Grona
Settings by Mabel Buell   Costumes by Frances Feist
Music director, uncredited   Orchestrations, Ferde Grofé,
Ken Macomber   Vocal arrangements, J. Rosamond Johnson

with

Lena Horne   Hamtree Harrington   Dewey "Pigmeat" Markham
Tim Moore   Bobby Evans   Taps Miller   Kate Hall
Sammy Fain

Musical Numbers
"Rhapsody in Blue" (Gershwin)—chorus
"Thursday" (Sachs-Haber)—Horne
"Father Divine" (Sachs-Haber)—Markham
"You're So Indifferent" (Parish-Fain)—Horne

Hudson Theatre   9 performances

1939

March 1.   Chicago Federal Theatre presents

"THE SWING MIKADO"

Book & lyrics by William S. Gilbert
Music by Arthur Sullivan
Directed by Harry Minturn   Dances by Sammy Dyer, Hazel Davis
Settings by Clive Rickabaugh   Costumes by John Pratt
Music director, Edward Wurtzebach   Orchestrations, Charles Levy

with

Edward Fraction	Maurice Cooper	Herman Greene
William Franklin	Gladys Boucree	Mabel Walker

Musical Numbers
Same as original operetta.

(Note: *The Swing Mikado* was first presented at the Great Northern Theatre, Chicago, in Sept. 1938. It ran for 22 weeks. On May 1, 1939, following its Federal Theatre–sponsored run, it was presented at the 44th Street Theatre by the Marolin Corp. [Bernhard Ulrich & Melvin Ericson]. The original *Mikado* was first presented at the Savoy Theatre, London, March 14, 1885.)

New Yorker Theatre; 44th Street Theatre (May)
86 performances

March 23. Michael Todd presents

"THE HOT MIKADO"

Book & lyrics by William S. Gilbert
Music by Arthur Sullivan
Directed by Hassard Short   Dances by Truly McGee
Settings & costumes by Nat Karson
Music director, William Parson   Orchestrations, Charles L. Cooke

with

BILL ROBINSON
Robert Parrish   Eddie Green   Gwendolyn Reyde
Rose Brown   Rosetta LeNoire   Maurice Ellis

Musical Numbers
Same as original operetta.

(Note: After its run on Broadway, *The Hot Mikado* was presented at
the Hall of Music, New York World's Fair. The original *Mikado*
was first presented at the Savoy Theatre, London, March 14, 1885.)

Broadhurst Theatre   *85 performances*

1939

April 24.   WPA Federal Theatre presents

"SING FOR YOUR SUPPER"

Sketches by David Lesan, Turner Bullock, Charlotte Kent, Jack Murray
Lyrics by John Latouche, Robert Sour, Hector Troy (Harold Rome)
Music by Lee Wainer, Ned Lehac, Earl Robinson
Directed by Harold Hecht, H. Gordon Graham & Robert H. Gordon
Dances by Ned McGurn, Anna Sokolow
Settings by Herbert Andrews   Costumes by Mary Merrill
Music director, Fred Hott   Orchestrations, Walter Paul

with

Gordon Clarke	Peggy Coudray	Paula Laurence
Coby Ruskin	Genora English	Bowen (Sonny) Tufts
James Mordecai	Carl Chapin	Hansford Wilson
Bidda Blakely	Edward Fuller	Virginia Bolen

Musical Numbers
"Imagine My Finding You Here" (Sour-Lehac)—Tufts
"Papa's Got a Job" (Troy, Sour-Lehac)—company
"Ballad of Uncle Sam" ("Ballad for Americans") (Latouche-Robinson)
     —Clarke, chorus

Adelphi Theatre   *60 performances*

June 19.

Messrs. Shubert, with Olsen & Johnson, present
BOBBY CLARK
LUELLA GEAR   BUD ABBOTT & LOU COSTELLO
CARMEN MIRANDA   in

"THE STREETS OF PARIS"

Sketches by Charles Sherman, Tom McKnight, S. Jay Kaufman, Edward
Duryea Dowling, James Laver, Lee Brody, Frank Eyton
Lyrics by Al Dubin
Music by Jimmy McHugh
Directed by Edward Duryea Dowling   Dances by Robert Alton
Settings by Lawrence L. Goldwasser   Costumes by Irene Sharaff
Music director, John McManus   Orchestrations, Hans Spialek
Vocal arrangements, Hugh Martin

with

JEAN SABLON
Della Lind   "Think a Drink" Hoffman   Yvonne Bouvier
Gloria Gilbert   Jo & Jeanne Readinger
Gower Champion & Jeanne Tyler   Margaret Irving
John (Jack) McCauley   Hylton Sisters   Ward & Van
Billy Branch   Ramon Vinay   Ben Dova   Hugh Martin

Musical Numbers
"Danger in the Dark"—Lind, Vinay; danced by Readingers
"Three Little Maids"—Hyltons
"Is It Possible?"—Clark, Lind
"Doin' the Chamberlain"—Gear; danced by Gower & Jeanne, chorus
"Rendezvous Time in Paree"—Sablon, Bouvier
"South American Way"—Miranda, Vinay, Hyltons, Lind; danced by
    Readingers, Gower & Jeanne
"Robert the Roué"—Clark

Broadhurst Theatre   *274 performances*

1939

July 6.   Lew Brown presents

"YOKEL BOY"

Book by Lew Brown
Lyrics by Lew Brown & Charles Tobias
Music by Sam H. Stept
Directed by Mr. Brown   Dances by Gene Snyder
Settings by Walter Jagemann   Costumes by Frances Feist
Music director, Al Goodman
(Note: Gordon Wiles credited as director during tryout.)

with

BUDDY EBSEN   JUDY CANOVA
DIXIE DUNBAR   PHIL SILVERS   JACKIE HELLER
LOIS JANUARY
Ralph Riggs   Mark Plant   Lew Hearn   Ralph Holmes
Charles Althoff
(Note: Mr. Hearn replaced Jack Pearl during tryout. Mr. Heller
out of cast and part eliminated in Aug.)

Musical Numbers
"A Boy Named Lem"—Canova, Heller, Dunbar
"Comes Love"—Canova; danced by Dunbar
"Uncle Sam's Lullaby"—Plant, company
"Beer Barrel Polka" (Brown–Jaromir Vejvoda; added in Aug.)—chorus

Majestic Theatre   *208 performances*

August 28.   **"GEORGE WHITE'S SCANDALS"** (1939 Edition)

Sketches by Matt Brooks, Eddie Davis, George White
Lyrics by Jack Yellen; additional lyrics by Herb Magidson
Music by Sammy Fain
Directed by George White & William K. Wells
Settings by Albert Johnson   Costumes by Charles LeMaire
Music director, Charles Drury

with

WILLIE & EUGENE HOWARD   THE THREE STOOGES
BEN BLUE   ELLA LOGAN   ANN MILLER
RAYMOND MIDDLETON
Billy Rayes   Ross Wyse, Jr. & June Mann   Kim Loo Sisters
Jack Williams   Collette Lyons   Craig Mathues
Knight Sisters   Betty Allen   Lois Andrews   Harold Whalen
Harry Stockwell   Fred Manatt
Victor Arden & Phil Wall (duo-pianos)
(Note: Mr. Middleton out of cast in Sept.)

Musical Numbers
"Are You Havin' Any Fun?"—Logan, Loo Sisters, Stooges
"The Mexiconga"—Logan, Loo Sisters; danced by Miller
"Goodnight, My Beautiful"—Stockwell; danced by Knight Sisters
"Something I Dreamed Last Night"—Logan

Alvin Theatre   *120 performances*

1939

September 29.   The Straw Hat Company (Harry Kaufman & Messrs. Shubert) presents

"THE STRAW HAT REVUE"

Sketches by Max Liebman
Lyrics & music by Sylvia Fine & James Shelton
Directed by Max Liebman   Dances by Jerome Andrews
Settings by Edward Gilbert
Music director, Edward A. Hunt

with

IMOGENE COCA
DANNY KAYE   JAMES SHELTON   ALFRED DRAKE
Lee Brody   Robert Burton   Ruthanna Boris   Dorothy Bird
Leon Barte   Meta Mata & Otto Hari   Jerome Andrews
Albia Kavan   Jerome Robbins   Bronson Dudley

Musical Numbers
"Four Young People" (Shelton)—Drake, Bird, Andrews, Kavan
"Anatole of Paris" (Fine)—Kaye
"Our Town" (Shelton)—Shelton, company

Ambassador Theatre   *75 performances*

October 18. George Abbott presents

"TOO MANY GIRLS"

Book by George Marion, Jr.
Lyrics by Lorenz Hart
Music by Richard Rodgers
Directed by George Abbott   Dances by Robert Alton
Settings by Jo Mielziner   Costumes by Raoul Pène du Bois
Music director, Harry Levant   Orchestrations, Hans Spialek
Vocal arrangements, Hugh Martin

with

MARCY WESTCOTT
HAL LEROY   MARY JANE WALSH
RICHARD KOLLMAR   DIOSA COSTELLO   DESI ARNAZ
EDDIE BRACKEN
Leila Ernst   Clyde Fillmore   Hans Robert   James MacColl
Ivy Scott   Byron Shores   Van Johnson   Mildred Law
(Note: Mr. Kollmar succeeded by Mr. Johnson in April 1940.)

Musical Numbers
"Love Never Went to College"—Westcott, Kollmar
"All Dressed Up (Spic and Spanish)"—Costello, chorus
"I Like to Recognize the Tune"—Bracken, Westcott, Walsh, Kollmar,
    LeRoy
"She Could Shake the Maracas"—Costello, Arnaz
"I Didn't Know What Time It Was"—Westcott, Kollmar
"Give It Back to the Indians"—Walsh; danced by LeRoy

Imperial Theatre   *249 performances*

November 17.   Max Gordon presents

"VERY WARM FOR MAY"

Book & lyrics by Oscar Hammerstein, 2nd
Music by Jerome Kern
Directed by Vincente Minnelli & Oscar Hammerstein, 2nd, Hassard
Short (uncredited)   Dances by Albertina Rasch, Harry Losee
Settings and costumes by Vincente Minnelli
Music director, Robert Emmett Dolan   Orchestrations, Russell Bennett

with

Jack Whiting   Eve Arden   Hiram Sherman
Grace McDonald   Frances Mercer   Donald Brian
Richard Quine   Don Loper & Maxine Barrat   Hollace Shaw
Ray Mayer   Evelyn Thawl
Matty Malneck Orchestra (incl. Milton DeLugg)   Avon Long
Robert Shackleton   Max Showalter   Vera Ellen
Helena Bliss   June Allyson   Billie Worth   Kay Picture
Ralph Stuart
(Note: Mr. Whiting succeeded by Guy Robertson in Jan. 1940.)

Musical Numbers
"In Other Words, Seventeen"—McDonald, Brian; reprised by Arden
"All the Things You Are"—Sherman, Mercer, Shaw, Stuart
"Heaven in My Arms"—Whiting, Mercer, Shaw
"That Lucky Fellow"—Shackleton; reprised (as "That Lucky Lady")
    by McDonald
"In the Heart of the Dark"—Shaw
"All in Fun"—Mercer, Whiting

Alvin Theatre   *59 performances*

1939

November 29.   . Erik Charell, with Jean Rodney, presents

"SWINGIN' THE DREAM"

Book by Gilbert Seldes & Erik Charell, from play, *A Midsummer Night's Dream*, by William Shakespeare
Lyrics by Eddie De Lange
Music by Jimmy Van Heusen
Directed by Mr. Charell & Philip Loeb   Dances by Agnes de Mille, Herbert White
Settings by Herbert Andrews, Walter Jagemann   Costumes by Mr. Andrews
Music director, Don Voorhees   Orchestrations, Phil Wall, Harb Quigley, Fletcher Henderson   Vocal arrangements, Lyn Murray

with

BENNY GOODMAN   LOUIS ARMSTRONG
MAXINE SULLIVAN

Eleanor Lynn   Boyd Crawford   Dorothy McGuire
Thomas Coley   Joseph Holland   George LeSoir   Ruth Ford
Butterfly McQueen   Juan Hernandez   Oscar Polk
Nicodemus   Jackie ("Moms") Mabley   Troy Brown
Gerald de la Fontaine   Bill Bailey   Deep River Boys
Dorothy, Etta & Vivian Dandridge   Rhythmettes
Muriel Rahn (chorus)   Warren Coleman (chorus)
Benny Goodman Sextette (Lionel Hampton, Fletcher Henderson, Charles Christian, Aruthur Bernstein, Nick Fatool)
Bud Freeman Summa Cum Laude (Max Kaminsky, Peewee Russell, Eddie Condon, Brad Gowan, Dave Bowman, Sidney Catlett)

Musical Numbers
"Peace, Brother"—Deep River Boys; reprised by Armstrong,
     Nicodemus, Brown, Mabley, Fontaine, Polk
"Swingin' a Dream"—Dandridge Sisters; reprised by Sullivan,
     Deep River Boys
"Darn That Dream"—Sullivan, Armstrong, Bailey, Dandridge
     Sisters, Rhythmettes, Deep River Boys

Center Theatre   *13 performances*

December 6.

B. G. DeSylva presents
BERT LAHR   ETHEL MERMAN   in

"DUBARRY WAS A LADY"

Book by Herbert Fields & B. G. DeSylva
Lyrics & music by Cole Porter
Directed by Edgar MacGregor   Dances by Robert Alton
Settings & costumes by Raoul Pène du Bois
Music director, Gene Salzer   Orchestrations, Hans Spialek

with

BETTY GRABLE   BENNY BAKER
Ronald Graham   Charles Walters   Kay Sutton
Hugh Cameron   Roy Ross, Audrey Palmer & Jack Stanton
Geraldine Spreckels   Harold Cromer   Walter Armin
Janis Carter   Betty Allen   Johnny Barnes
Adele Jergens (chorus)
(Note: During tryout, Mabel Todd role eliminated; Mr. Graham
replaced Phil Regan. In June 1940, Miss Grable succeeded by
Ruth Bond. In July, Mr. Walters by Jack Stanton; in Sept., by
David Shelley. In Aug., Miss Merman succeeded by Betty Allen;
in Oct., by Gypsy Rose Lee; in Nov., by Frances Williams.)

Musical Numbers
"When Love Beckoned (in Fifty-Second Street)"—Merman
"But in the Morning, No!"—Merman, Lahr
"Do I Love You?"—Graham, Merman
"Give Him the Oo-La-La"—Merman
"Well, Did You Evah?"—Grable, Walters
"It Was Written in the Stars"—Graham
"Katie Went to Haiti"—Merman
"Friendship"—Merman, Lahr

46th Street Theatre; Royale Theatre (Oct. 1940)
408 performances

LONDON PRODUCTIONS OF BROADWAY MUSICALS OF THE THIRTIES

1931

July 7. *Nina Rosa*
Geoffrey Gwyther, Ethelind Terry (succeeded by Helen Gilliland), Freddie Forbes, Robert Chisholm.
Lyceum Theatre; 111 performances.

1932

March 4. *The Cat and the Fiddle*
Francis Lederer, Peggy Wood, Alice Delysia, Henri Leoni, Morton Selten, Martin Walker, Muriel Barron.
Palace Theatre; 219 performances.

1933

Feb. 24. *The One Girl (Smiles)*
Roy Royston, Robert Naylor, Lupino Lane, Guy Middleton, Louise Browne, Pearl Osgood.
Hippodrome; 42 performances.

May 19. *Music in the Air*
Arthur Margetson, Mary Ellis, Eve Lister, Bruce Carfax, Horace Hodges, Lance Fairfax.
His Majesty's Theatre; 275 performances.

Nov. 2. *Gay Divorce*
Fred Astaire, Claire Luce, Eric Blore, Erik Rhodes, Olive Blakeney, Claud Allister, Fred Hearne.
Palace Theatre; 180 performances.

1935

Feb. 21. *Stop Press* (based on *As Thousands Cheer*)
Dorothy Dickson, Phyllis Monkman, Edwin Styles, Robert Helpmann.
Adelphi Theatre; 148 performances.

June 14. *Anything Goes*
Jack Whiting, Sydney Howard, Jeanne Aubert, Adele Dixon, Betty Kean, Peter Haddon.
Palace Theatre; 261 performances.

Dec. 6. *A Royal Exchange (All the King's Horses)*
Ramon Novarro, Doris Kenyon, Eddie Foy, Jr., Doris Carson.
His Majesty's Theatre

1937

Feb. 5. *On Your Toes*
Jack Whiting, Gina Malo, Olive Blakeney, Vera Zorina, Eddie Pola, Vernon Kelso, Jack Donohue, Hyacinth (Hy) Hazell.
Palace Theatre; 123 performances.

1942

Oct. 22. *DuBarry Was a Lady*
Frances Day, Bud Flanagan, Bruce Trent, Arthur Riscoe, Jackie Hunter, Inga Andersen.
His Majesty's Theatre; 178 performances.

1945

March 1. *Three Waltzes*
Evelyn Laye, Esmond Knight, Charles Goldner, Bruce Winston.
Prince's Theatre; 189 performances.

1963

Nov. 7. *The Boys from Syracuse*
Sonny Farrar, Denis Quilley, Bob Monkhouse, Ronnie Corbett, Maggie Fitzgibbon, Lynn Kennington, Paula Hendrix, Pat Turner.
Theatre Royal, Drury Lane; 100 performances.

FILM VERSIONS OF BROADWAY MUSICALS OF THE THIRTIES

(Note: Asterisk indicates repetition of stage role in film. Date refers to film's release.)

1931

Dec. 13.   *Flying High*
Bert Lahr*, Charlotte Greenwood, Pat O'Brien, Charles Winninger, Kathryn Crawford, Hedda Hopper.
M-G-M. Directed by Charles F. Reisner.

1932

March 27.   *Girl Crazy*
Bert Wheeler, Robert Woolsey, Eddie Quillan, Dixie Lee.
Radio. Directed by William A. Seiter.

1933

Nov. 25.   *Take a Chance*
James Dunn, Charles "Buddy" Rogers, Cliff Edwards, June Knight*, Lillian Roth.
Paramount. Directed by Laurence Schwab & Monte Brice.

1934

Feb. 14.   *The Cat and the Fiddle*
Ramon Novarro, Jeanette MacDonald, Frank Morgan, Vivienne Segal, Charles Butterworth, Jean Hersholt, Joseph Cawthorn.
M-G-M. Directed by William K. Howard.

Feb. 17.   *Wonder Bar*
Al Jolson*, Dolores Del Rio, Dick Powell, Kay Francis, Ricardo Cortez, Guy Kibbee, Louise Fazenda, Hugh Herbert, Ruth Donnelly.
Warner Bros. Directed by Lloyd Bacon & Busby Berkeley.

May 18.   *Murder at the Vanities*
Carl Brisson, Victor McLaglen, Kitty Carlisle, Jack Oakie, Gail Patrick, Dorothy Stickney, Duke Ellington Orchestra, Ann Sheridan, Toby Wing.
Paramount. Directed by Mitchell Leisen.

Oct. 3.   *The Gay Divorcée*
Fred Astaire*, Ginger Rogers, Alice Brady, Edward Everett Horton, Erik Rhodes*, Eric Blore*, Betty Grable.
RKO-Radio. Directed by Mark Sandrich.

Dec. 14.   *Music in the Air*
Gloria Swanson, John Boles, Douglass Montgomery, Al Shean*, Reginald Owen, Joseph Cawthorn.
Fox. Directed by Joe May.

1935

Feb. 12.   *Roberta*
Irene Dunne, Fred Astaire, Ginger Rogers, Randolph Scott, Victor Varconi, Helen Westley.
RKO-Radio. Directed by William A. Seiter.

Feb. 13.   *All the King's Horses*
Carl Brisson, Mary Ellis, Edward Everett Horton, Eugene Pallette.
Paramount. Directed by Frank Tuttle.

June 21.   *Princess Charming*
Evelyn Laye, Henry Wilcoxin, Yvonne Arnaud.
Gaumont-British. Directed by Maurice Elvey.

1936

Feb. 6.   *Anything Goes*
Bing Crosby, Ethel Merman*, Charles Ruggles, Ida Lupino, Grace Bradley, Arthur Treacher.
Paramount. Directed by Lewis Milestone.

1938

Nov. 4.   *The Great Waltz*
Fernand Gravet, Luise Rainer, Miliza Korjus, Hugh Herbert, Lionel Atwill.
M-G-M. Directed by Julien Duvivier.

1939

Jan. 13.   *Trois Valses (Three Waltzes)*
Yvonne Printemps, Pierre Fresnay, Henri Guisol.
Vedis Films. Directed by Ludwig Berger.

Sept. 19.   *Babes in Arms*
Judy Garland, Mickey Rooney, Charles Winninger, Guy Kibbee, June Preisser, Margaret Hamilton.
M-G-M. Directed by Busby Berkeley.

Oct. 24.   *On Your Toes*
Eddie Albert, Vera Zorina, Alan Hale, James Gleason, Frank McHugh.
Warner Bros. Directed by Ray Enright.

1940

July 15.   *The Boys from Syracuse*
Joe Penner, Martha Raye, Allan Jones, Rosemary Lane, Irene Hervey.
RKO-Radio. Directed by A. Edward Sutherland.

Sept. 17.   *Strike Up the Band*
Judy Garland, Mickey Rooney, Paul Whiteman Orchestra, June Preisser, William Tracy.
M-G-M. Directed by Busby Berkeley.

Oct. 4.   *Too Many Girls*
Lucille Ball, Richard Carlson, Ann Miller, Eddie Bracken*, Hal LeRoy*, Desi Arnaz*, Frances Langford, Van Johnson*.
*RKO-Radio. Directed by George Abbott.**

1941

Dec. 19.   *Hellzapoppin*
Ole Olsen* & Chic Johnson*, Martha Raye, Mischa Auer, Robert Paige, Jane Frazee, Hugh Herbert.
Universal. Directed by Henry C. Potter.

1942

March 23.   *Yokel Boy*
Joan Davis, Albert Dekker, Eddie Foy, Jr., Alan Mowbray.
Republic. Directed by Joseph Santley.

May 21.   *I Married an Angel*
Jeanette MacDonald, Nelson Eddy, Edward Everett Horton, Binnie Barnes, Reginald Owen.
M-G-M. Directed by W. S. Van Dyke, 2nd.

1943

May 5.   *DuBarry Was a Lady*
Lucille Ball, Gene Kelly, Red Skelton, Virginia O'Brien, Rags Ragland, Tommy Dorsey Orchestra.
M-G-M. Directed by Roy Del Ruth.

Aug. 3.   *Girl Crazy (2nd film version)*
Judy Garland, Mickey Rooney, June Allyson, Nancy Walker, Gil Stratton, Rags Ragland, Guy Kibbee, Tommy Dorsey Orchestra.
M-G-M. Directed by Norman Taurog.

1944

Jan. 19.   *Broadway Rhythm (Very Warm for May)*
George Murphy, Ginny Simms, Charles Winninger, Gloria DeHaven, Nancy Walker, Ben Blue, Lena Horne, Eddie "Rochester" Anderson.
M-G-M. Directed by Roy Del Ruth.

Feb. 29.   *Knickerbocker Holiday*
Nelson Eddy, Charles Coburn, Constance Dowling, Shelley Winters.
United Artists. Directed by Harry Brown.

1949

July 8.   *Red, Hot and Blue!*
Betty Hutton, Victor Mature, June Havoc, William Demarest, Frank Loesser, Raymond Walburn.
Paramount. Directed by John Farrow.

1952

May 29. *Lovely to Look At (Roberta) (2nd film version)*
Kathryn Grayson, Howard Keel, Red Skelton, Ann Miller, Marge & Gower Champion, Zsa Zsa Gabor, Kurt Kasznar.
M-G-M. Directed by Mervyn LeRoy.

1956

Jan. 23. *Anything Goes (2nd film version)*
Bing Crosby, Jeanmaire, Donald O'Connor, Mitzi Gaynor, Phil Harris.
Paramount. Directed by Robert Lewis.

1962

Dec. 5. *Jumbo*
Jimmy Durante*, Doris Day, Martha Raye, Stephen Boyd, Dean Jagger.
M-G-M. Directed by Charles Walters & Busby Berkeley.

1965

Dec. 6. *When the Boys Meet the Girls (Girl Crazy) (3rd film version)*
Harve Presnell, Connie Francis, Herman's Hermits, Liberace, Louis Armstrong.
M-G-M. Directed by Alvin Ganzer.

Bibliography

LIBRETTOS & LYRICS (alphabetically by title)

Conversation Piece by Noël Coward (incl. in *Play Parade* Vol. 2, Heinemann, London, 1950)

Cradle Will Rock, The by Marc Blitzstein (Random House, 1938)

Fireman's Flame, The by John Van Antwerp, Ted Fetter (Samuel French paperback, 1938)

4 Saints in 3 Acts by Gertrude Stein (incl. in *Selected Operas & Plays of Gertrude Stein*, U. of Pittsburgh Press, 1970)

I'd Rather Be Right by George S. Kaufman, Moss Hart, Lorenz Hart (Random House, 1937)

Johnny Johnson by Paul Green (incl. in *Five Plays of the South*, Hill & Wang paperback, 1963)

Knickerbocker Holiday by Maxwell Anderson (Anderson House, 1938)

Let 'Em Eat Cake by George S. Kaufman, Morrie Ryskind, Ira Gershwin (Knopf, 1933)

Naughty-Naught by John Van Antwerp, Ted Fetter (Samuel French paperback, 1941)

Of Thee I Sing by George S. Kaufman, Morrie Ryskind, Ira Gershwin (Knopf, 1932; Samuel French paperback, 1935)

One for the Money by Nancy Hamilton (incl. in *Three to One*, Samuel French paperback, 1952)

Threepenny Opera, The by Bert Brecht, translated by Eric Bentley (incl. in *The Modern Theatre*, Vol. 1, Doubleday Anchor paperback, 1955)

Tonight at 8:30 by Noël Coward (incl. in *Play Parade* Vol. 3, Heinemann, London, 1954)

White Horse Inn by Erik Charell, Harry Graham (Samuel French paperback, London, 1957)

COMPLETE VOCAL SCORES (alphabetically by title)

Anything Goes by Cole Porter (Harms, Inc., 1934)

Babes in Arms by Lorenz Hart, Richard Rodgers (Chappell, 1937)

Boys from Syracuse, The by Lorenz Hart, Richard Rodgers (Chappell, 1938)

Cat and the Fiddle, The by Otto Harbach, Jerome Kern (T. B. Harms, 1931)

Conversation Piece by Noël Coward (Chappell, 1934)

Fireman's Flame, The by Ted Fetter, Richard Lewine (Chappell, 1937)

4 Saints in 3 Acts by Gertrude Stein, Virgil Thomson (Beekman, 1934)

Frederika by Edward Eliscu, Franz Lehár (Chappell, 1937)

Girl Crazy by Ira Gershwin, George Gershwin (New World, 1930)

Great Waltz, The by Desmond Carter, Johann Strauss (Chappell, 1934)

Johnny Johnson by Paul Green, Kurt Weill (Samuel French, 1940)

Knickerbocker Holiday by Maxwell Anderson, Kurt Weill (DeSylva, Brown & Henderson, 1938)

Melody by Irving Caesar, Sigmund Romberg (Harms, Inc., 1933)
Music in the Air by Oscar Hammerstein, 2nd, Jerome Kern (T. B. Harms, 1932)
Naughty-Naught by Ted Fetter, Richard Lewine (Chappell, 1937)
Nina Rosa by Irving Caesar, Sigmund Romberg (Harms, Inc., 1930)
Of Thee I Sing by Ira Gershwin, George Gershwin (New World, 1931)
Porgy and Bess by DuBose Heyward, Ira Gershwin, George Gershwin (Gershwin, 1935)
Red, Hot and Blue! by Cole Porter (Chappell, 1936)
Roberta by Otto Harbach, Jerome Kern (T. B. Harms, 1933)
Strike Up the Band by Ira Gershwin, George Gershwin (New World, 1930)

COLLECTIONS OF SONGS (alphabetically by composer)

The Noël Coward Song Book (Simon & Schuster, 1953)
The George & Ira Gershwin Song Book (Simon & Schuster, 1960)
The Jerome Kern Song Book (Simon & Schuster, 1955)
The Cole Porter Song Book (Simon & Schuster, 1959)
The Rodgers & Hart Song Book (Simon & Schuster, 1951)

COLLECTIONS OF LYRICS (alphabetically by lyricist)

Coward, Noël: *The Lyrics of Noël Coward* (Doubleday, 1965)
Gershwin, Ira: *Lyrics on Several Occasions* (Knopf, 1959)
Hammerstein, Oscar, 2nd: *Lyrics* (Simon & Schuster, 1949)
Porter, Cole: *103 Lyrics of Cole Porter* (Random House, 1954)

BIOGRAPHIES & AUTOBIOGRAPHIES (alphabetically by subject)

Abbott, George
    Mister Abbott by George Abbott (Random House, 1963)
Anderson, John Murray
    Out Without My Rubbers by John Murray Anderson & Hugh Abercrombie Anderson (Library Publishers, 1954)
Arlen, Harold
    Harold Arlen: Happy with the Blues by Edward Jablonski (Doubleday, 1961)
Astaire, Fred
    Steps in Time by Fred Astaire (Harper, 1959)
Brice, Fanny
    The Fabulous Fanny by Norman Katkov (Knopf, 1953)
Cohan, George M.
    George M. Cohan: Prince of the American Theater by Ward Morehouse (Lippincott, 1943)
Coward, Noël
    A Talent to Amuse by Sheridan Morley (Doubleday, 1970)
de Mille, Agnes
    Dance to the Piper by Agnes de Mille (Little, Brown, 1952)
Duke, Vernon
    Passport to Paris by Vernon Duke (Little, Brown, 1955)

Durante, Jimmy
  Schnozzola by Gene Fowler (Viking, 1951)
Gershwin, George & Ira
  The Gershwin Years by Edward Jablonski & Lawrence D. Stewart (Double-day, 1958)
Gordon, Max
  Max Gordon Presents by Max Gordon & Lewis Funke (Geis, 1963)
Hammerstein, Oscar, 2nd
  The Rodgers and Hammerstein Story by Stanley Green (John Day, 1963)
Horne, Lena
  Lena by Lena Horne & Richard Schickel (Doubleday, 1965)
Lahr, Bert
  Notes on a Cowardly Lion by John Lahr (Knopf, 1969)
Langner, Lawrence
  The Magic Curtain by Lawrence Langner (Dutton, 1951)
Lawrence, Gertrude
  A Star Danced by Gertrude Lawrence (Doubleday, 1945)
Lee, Gypsy Rose
  Gypsy by Gypsy Rose Lee (Harper, 1957)
Maney, Richard
  Fanfare by Richard Maney (Harper, 1957)
Merman, Ethel
  Who Could Ask for Anything More? by Ethel Merman & Pete Martin (Doubleday, 1955)
Moore, Grace
  You're Only Human Once by Grace Moore (Doubleday, 1944)
Porter, Cole
  Cole Porter: The Life that Late He Led by George Eells (Putnam, 1967)
Richman, Harry
  A Hell of a Life by Harry Richman & Richard Gehman (Duell, Sloane & Pearce, 1966)
Rodgers, Richard
  The Rodgers & Hammerstein Story by Stanley Green (John Day, 1963)
Romberg, Sigmund
  Deep in My Heart by Elliott Arnold (Duell, Sloane & Pearce, 1949)
Rose, Billy
  Billy Rose: Manhattan Primitive by Earl Conrad (World, 1968)
Shubert, Lee & J. J.
  The Brothers Shubert by Jerry Stagg (Random House, 1968)
Sillman, Leonard
  Here Lies Leonard Sillman by Leonard Sillman (Citadel, 1959)
Stone, Fred
  Rolling Stone by Fred Stone (Whittlesey House, 1945)
Straus, Oscar
  Prince of Vienna by Bernard Grun (Putnam, 1957)
Vallee, Rudy
  My Time Is Your Time by Rudy Vallee & Gil McKean (Obolensky, 1962)

THEATRE HISTORY & CRITICISM (alphabetically by author)

Atkinson, Brooks: *Broadway* (Macmillan, 1970)
Baral, Robert: *Revue* (Fleet, 1962)

Brown, John Mason: *Broadway in Review* (Norton, 1940)

———: *Two on the Aisle* (Norton, 1938)

Downer, Alan S.: *American Drama and Its Critics* (Gemeni paperback, 1965)

Engel, Lehman: *The American Musical Theatre* (CBS Legacy, 1967)

Green, Abel, & Laurie, Joe, Jr.: *Show Biz* (Holt, 1951)

Green, Stanley: *The World of Musical Comedy* (Barnes, 1968)

Lewine, Richard, & Simon, Alfred: *Encyclopedia of Theatre Music* (Random House, 1961)

Lewis, Emory: *Stages* (Prentice-Hall, 1969)

Mander, Raymond, & Mitchenson, Joe: *Musical Comedy* (Davies, London, 1969)

Mantle, Burns: *The Best Plays* (annual volumes) (Dodd, Mead)

Morris, Lloyd: *Curtain Time* (Random House, 1953)

Nathan, George Jean: *Encyclopaedia of the Theatre* (Knopf, 1940)

———: *The Entertainment of a Nation* (Knopf, 1942)

Parks, Melvin: *Musicals of the 1930s* (Museum City of New York)

Rush, David Alan: *History & Evaluation of the ILGWU Labor Stage & Its Production of "Pins and Needles"* (U. of Iowa thesis)

Smith, Cecil: *Musical Comedy in America* (Theatre Arts, 1950)

Taubman, Howard: *The Making of the American Theatre* (Coward-McCann, 1967)

NATIONAL & WORLD HISTORY (alphabetically by author)

Allen, Frederick Lewis: *Since Yesterday* (Harper, 1940; Bantam paperback, 1965)

Bendiner, Robert: *Just Around the Corner* (Harper, 1967)

Boardman, Fon W., Jr.: *The Thirties* (Walck, 1967)

Bowen, Ezra (editor): *This Fabulous Century—Vol. 4 (1930–1940)* (Time-Life, 1970)

Congdon, Don (editor): *The '30's—A Time to Remember* (Simon & Schuster, 1962)

Dille, John (editor): *Time Capsules 1932, 1933, 1939* (Time-Life, 1967, 1968)

Ellis, Edward Robb: *A Nation in Torment* (Coward-McCann, 1970)

Laver, James: *Between the Wars* (Vista, London, 1961)

Leighton, Isabel (editor): *The Aspirin Age* (Simon & Schuster, 1949; Clarion paperback, 1968)

Mattfeld, Julius: *Variety Music Cavalcade* (Prentice-Hall, 1962)

Morison, Samuel Eliot: *The Oxford History of the American People* (Oxford, 1965)

Phillips, Cabell: *From the Crash to the Blitz* (Macmillan, 1969)

Stillman, Edmund: *The American Heritage History of the 20s and 30s* (American Heritage, 1970)

Terkel, Studs (editor): *Hard Times* (Pantheon, 1970)

Discography {alphabetically by title}

Anything Goes (Porter; 1934)
    Columbia ML 4751. Mary Martin.
    Epic FLS 15100. Original 1962 cast.
    JJC 3004. Ethel Merman.

As Thousands Cheer (Berlin; 1933)
    Monmouth-Evergreen 6811. Annette Sanders, Steve Clayton.

At Home Abroad (Dietz-Schwartz; 1935)
    JJC 3003. Beatrice Lillie.
    Monmouth-Evergreen 6604/5. Dussault, Morrow, Kenyon, David.

Babes in Arms (Hart-Rodgers; 1937)
    Columbia OS 2570. Mary Martin.

Band Wagon, The (Dietz-Schwartz; 1931)
    Columbia ML 4751. Mary Martin.
    M-G-M E 3051. 1953 film soundtrack.
    Monmouth-Evergreen 6604/5. Dussault, Morrow, Kenyon, David.
    RCA International 1037. Fred & Adele Astaire.

Between the Devil (Dietz-Schwartz; 1937)
    Monmouth-Evergreen 6604/5. Dussault, Morrow, Kenyon, David.

Boys from Syracuse, The (Hart-Rodgers; 1938)
    Capitol STAO 1933. Original 1963 cast.
    Columbia OS 2580. Jack Cassidy, Portia Nelson.

Cat and the Fiddle, The (Harbach-Kern; 1931)
    Epic LN 3569. Doreen Hume, Denis Quilley.

Conversation Piece (Coward; 1934)
    Columbia SL 163. Lily Pons, Noël Coward, Richard Burton.

Cradle Will Rock, The (Blitzstein; 1937)
    American Legacy 1001. Original cast.
    M-G-M SE 4289-2. Original 1964 cast.

Face the Music (Berlin; 1932)
    Monmouth-Evergreen 6811. Annette Sanders, Steve Clayton.

Flying Colors (Dietz-Schwartz; 1932)
    Monmouth-Evergreen 6604/5. Dussault, Morrow, Kenyon, David.

4 Saints in 3 Acts (Stein-Thomson; 1934)
    RCA Victor LM 2756. Original cast.

Girl Crazy (Gershwin-Gershwin; 1930)
    Columbia OS 2560. Mary Martin.

Great Waltz, The (Strauss, Jr. & Sr.; 1934)
    Capitol SVAS 2426. Original 1965 cast.

Johnny Johnson (Green-Weill; 1936)
    Heliodor 25024. Burgess Meredith, Lotte Lenya, Evelyn Lear.

Jumbo (Hart-Rodgers; 1935)
    Columbia OS 2260. 1962 film soundtrack.

Life Begins at 8:40 (Gershwin, Harburg-Arlen; 1934)
    Crewe 1345. David Burns, Estelle Parsons, Blossom Dearie.

Music in the Air (Hammerstein-Kern; 1932)
    RCA Victor LK 1025. Jane Pickens.

Of Thee I Sing (Gershwin-Gershwin; 1931)
    Capitol S 350. Original 1952 cast.

On Your Toes (Hart-Rodgers; 1936)
    Columbia OS 2599. Jack Cassidy, Portia Nelson.
    Decca 9015. Original 1954 cast.

Pins and Needles (Rome; 1937)
    Columbia OS 2210. Barbra Streisand, Harold Rome.

Porgy and Bess (Heyward, Gershwin-Gershwin; 1935)
    Columbia OS 2016. 1959 film soundtrack.
    Decca 79024. Original 1942 cast.
    Odyssey 32 36 0018. Lawrence Winters, Camilla Williams.
    RCA Camden 500. Lawrence Tibbett, Helen Jepson.
    RCA Victor LSC 2679. William Warfield, Leontyne Price.

Red, Hot and Blue! (Porter; 1936)
    JJC 3004. Ethel Merman.

Revenge with Music (Dietz-Schwartz; 1934)
    Monmouth-Evergreen 6604/5. Dussault, Morrow, David.

Roberta (Harbach-Kern; 1933)
    Columbia OS 2530. Jack Cassidy, Joan Roberts.
    Decca 8007. Alfred Drake, Kitty Carlisle.
    M-G-M E 3230. 1952 film soundtrack.

Set to Music (Coward; 1939)
    JJC 3003. Beatrice Lillie.

Stars in Your Eyes (Fields-Schwartz; 1939)
    JJC 3004. Ethel Merman.

Take a Chance (DeSylva-Youmans; 1932)
    Monmouth-Evergreen 6401/2. Ellie & Bob Quint, Millie Slavin.

Threepenny Opera, The (Weill; 1933)
    Columbia 02S 201. Lotte Lenya (in German).
    M-G-M S 3121. Original 1954 cast.

Three's a Crowd (Dietz-Schwartz; 1930)
    Monmouth-Evergreen 6604/5. Nancy Dussault, Neal Kenyon.

Through the Years (Heyman-Youmans; 1932)
    Monmouth-Evergreen 6401/2. Bob Quint, Millie Slavin, Nolan Van Way.

Tonight at 8:30 (Coward; 1936)
Parlophone 10506. Gertrude Lawrence, Noël Coward.

Very·Warm for May (Hammerstein-Kern; 1939)
Monmouth-Evergreen 6808. Susan Watson, Reid Shelton, Danny Carroll.

White Horse Inn (Benatzky-Stolz; 1936)
Angel S 35815. Andy Cole, Mary Thomas.

Note: Many obscure show tunes of the 1930s may be heard on the following Ben Bagley albums: *Cole Porter Revisited* (Crewe 1340); *Rodgers & Hart Revisited* (Crewe 1341); *Vernon Duke Revisited* (Crewe 1342); *Rodgers & Hart Revisited Vol. 2* (Crewe 1343); *Harold Arlen Revisited* (Crewe 1345); *Arthur Schwartz Revisited* (Crewe 1350).

Index

All titles of musicals are in italics; all titles of songs and sketches are enclosed in quotation marks. Page numbers in italics refer to listings found under "Casts and Credits" section.

Wilde, Elizabeth, 130
Williams, Frances, 20, 38, 54, 101
Williams, Herb, 113
Williams, Hope, 38, 77, 80
Wiman, Dwight Deere, 45, 89, 142, 159, 162, 178
Winchell, Walter, 24, 30, 104, 122, 130, 165, 167
"Window Dresser Goes to Bed, The," 101
Windsor Theatre, 145, 154
Winninger, Charles, 108
Winter Garden, 82, 96, 138, 163, 164
"Wintergreen for President," 57, 76
"Without Love," 24
Wodehouse, P. G., 105
Wonder Bar, The, 44, 229
Wonderful Night, A, 20
Woof Woof, 20
Woollcott, Alexander, 72
Woolley, Monte, 74, 127, 128
Works Progress Administration (WPA), 143, 146

"Would You Like to Take a Walk?" 36
Wray, Fay, 54
Wynn, Ed, 23, 41, 56, 140, 154-155
Wynn, Keenan, 176

Yeah Man, 65, 256
Yellen, Jack, 43, 123, 184
"Yesterdays," 93
Yokel Boy, 176, 183, *361*
"You Ain't So Hot," 111
"You and the Night and the Music," 107-108
"You Can't Stop Me from Loving You," 36
"You Have Cast Your Shadow on the Sea," 173
"You Made Me Love You," 49
You Never Know, 162-163, *345*
You Said It, 43, 225
"You Were There," 135

"You're a Builder-Upper," 101
"You're Devastating," 93
"You're Driving Me Crazy," 38
"You're Everywhere," 64
"You're Lucky to Me," 35
"You're My Everything," 56
"You're the Top," 107
"You're So Indifferent," 179
Youmans, Vincent, 23, 38, 64, 72, 73

Zeno, Norman, 136
Ziegfeld, Florenz, 23, 38, 52, 64, 65
Ziegfeld Follies (1931), 49, 234
Ziegfeld Follies (1934), 95, 96-98, 285
Ziegfeld Follies (1936), 128-129, *316*
Ziegfeld Theatre, 22
"Zing! Went the Strings of My Heart!" 109
Zorina, Vera, 159, 161, 162